The time is long past when easy generalizations can be made about "hunter-gatherers," "African foragers," or "the Kalahari Bushmen" or "Pygmies." During the past three decades there has been a wave of important ethnographic studies of African foraging populations by ethnographers from Europe, Australia, North America, and Japan. African historical and archaeological research have further enriched our understanding of hunter-gatherers. This volume provides case-studies and comparative essays by some of the leading specialists in the field. The contributors document the range of variation in economic life, settlement patterns, social institutions, gender relations, and religious beliefs, and debate the implications of the cultural diversity present in hunter-gatherer societies. The book is an important documentary source, which includes chapters representing most of the theoretical orientations common in anthropology today, as well as a stimulating introduction to and analysis of current thinking about African foraging populations.

Cultural diversity among twentieth-century foragers

Cultural diversity among twentieth-century foragers

An African perspective

edited by

Susan Kent

Anthropology Program, Old Dominion University,
Norfolk, VA

Published by the Press Syndicate of the University of Cambridge
The Pitt Building, Trumpington Street, Cambridge CB2 1RP
40 West 20th Street, New York, NY 10011–4211, USA
10 Stamford Road, Oakleigh, Melbourne 3166, Australia

First published 1996

Printed in Great Britain at the University Press, Cambridge

A catalogue record for this book is available from the British Library

Library of Congress cataloguing in publication data

Cultural diversity among twentieth-century foragers/edited by Susan Kent.
    p.   cm.
ISBN 0 521 48237 2 (hc)
1. Hunting and gathering societies.
2. Pluralism (Social sciences).
3. Subculture.   I. Kent, Susan, 1952– .
GN388.C85   1996   95–17648
306.3′64–dc20   CIP

ISBN 0 521 48237 2 hardback

CE

This book is dedicated to:
The people of Kutse, Botswana, and to
twentieth-century foragers everywhere

Contents

Illustrations

Contributors

DR ALAN BARNARD Department of Social Anthropology, University of Edinburgh

DR RODERIC BLACKBURN Kinderhook, NY

DR MATHIAS GUENTHER Department of Sociology/Anthropology, Wilfred Laurier University, Waterloo, Ontario

DR BARRY HEWLETT Department of Anthropology, Washington State University

DR MITSUO ICHIKAWA Center for African Area Studies, Kyoto University

DR SUSAN KENT Anthropology Program, Old Dominion University, Norfolk, VA

DR GEORGE SILBERBAUER Department of Anthropology/Sociology, Monash University

DR HELGA VIERICH Department of Anthropology, University of Alberta

DR NURIT BIRD-DAVID Department of Anthropology, Tel Aviv University

DR NICK BLURTON JONES Graduate School, Moore Hall, University of California

DR KRISTEN HAWKES Department of Anthropology, University of Utah

DR ROBERT HITCHCOCK Department of Anthropology, University of Nebraska

DR DAOU V. JOIRIS Institut de Sociologie, Université Libre de Bruxelles

DR JAMES O'CONNELL Department of Anthropology, University of Utah

DR HIDEAKI TERASHIMA Faculty of Humanities, Kobe Gakuin University

DR THOMAS WIDLOK Department of Anthropology, London School of Economics

1 Cultural diversity among African foragers: causes and implications

Susan Kent

While understanding diversity has been a hallmark of anthropological inquiries since the inception of the discipline, hunter-gatherer (or forager) studies tend to stress similarities. Some cross-cultural studies focus on a single aspect which all foragers by definition share: subsistence strategies that emphasize wild plants and animals. Thus, cultural differences in the areas of language, religion, social organization, hunting, politics, mobility, and history tend to be ignored. An example of how diversity can be masked by a fallacious uniformity is the common practice of grouping Northwest Coast hunter-gatherer-fisher Indians in the same category as hunter-gatherer Basarwa (Bushman or San; e.g., Cosmides and Tooby 1992:217). Though they have similar food procurement strategies (an emphasis on the use of wild plants and animals), these two groups differ in almost every other way possible – from the environment they occupy to their stratification, hierarchies, and gender relations, as well as the organization of their economics.

Several seminal books have unintentionally supported the mistaken view that all hunter-gatherer societies are quite similar. Both *Man the hunter* (Lee and DeVore 1968) and *Woman the gatherer* (Dahlberg 1981) represented state-of-the-art thinking on foragers at the time of their publication. However, both these books and those that followed implied a more or less intrinsic similarity between hunter-gatherers because of their reliance on wild plants and animals. In a later book on hunter-gatherers, Leacock and Lee (1982:6; emphasis added) wrote, "The contributors to this volume share an interest in discovering the *commonalities* among gatherer-hunters . . ." Today "commonalities" of hunter-gatherers have been stressed by researchers to the point of being misleading; they actually mask the very diversity anthropology seeks to discover and understand.

After a long period of recognizing broad economic similarities (i.e., hunting and gathering as a major orientation), researchers such as Binford (1980, 1987) began to explore gross categories of hunter-gatherers. Binford labeled two types based on different mobility

1

patterns: collectors and foragers (1980). The former primarily occupy a base camp and gather locally available wild resources to bring back to camp (examples are Northwest Coast Indians, some Okiek groups, and Inuit). Foragers are defined as groups who move their camps to the resources (examples include the Basarwa, Pygmies, and Hadza). Many societies practice both strategies, although usually one or the other dominates. Binford (1982) also distinguished semi-sedentary and sedentary hunter-gatherers from nomadic hunter-gatherers. He attributed differences to variations in their environments in terms of the abundance and distribution of wild plants and animals. Other anthropologists grappling with extinct groups with no modern analog have separated hunter-gatherers by sociopolitical organization, differentiating between complex and non-complex societies (Price and Brown 1985). Woodburn (1982) proposed classifying hunter-gatherer societies by their economic system: those with immediate-return economies and demand sharing (also usually highly, strongly, or assertively egalitarian), and those with delay-returned economies, surpluses, and storage (usually more strongly or completely *non*-egalitarian). Other anthropologists have proposed additional classification schemes for types of hunter-gatherers, with varying degrees of success (see Testart 1982, 1987).

Only by first acknowledging and clarifying diversity in the culture and behavior of foragers can we identify similarities, which may then become valuable for formulating models of modern and past hunter-gatherers. However, if diversity is ignored, researchers may indiscriminately attribute group-specific cultural traits to all foragers. Such inaccurate generalizations would invalidate any resultant conclusions. *Cultural diversity among twentieth-century foragers: an African perspective* is devoted to elucidating and understanding the many differences between and within hunter-gatherer societies. Some of its authors examine differences between particular foraging societies, such as various groups of Basarwa (Silberbauer, Guenther, Barnard and Widlok, Vierich and Hitchcock), Pygmies (Hewlett, Joiris, Ichikawa and Terashima), and Okiek (Blackburn). Other authors, such as Blurton Jones *et al.*, focus on differences between ethnically unrelated foragers – the Hadza of East Africa and the Ju/'hoansi Basarwa of Ngamiland.

Genesis of the book

My interest in compiling a book on hunter-gatherer diversity developed out of other anthropologists' reactions to my work with G/wi, G//ana, and Kũa Basarwa from Kutse, a recently sedentary community located in the Kalahari Desert of Botswana. Kutse residents tend to follow social patterns dissimilar from those of the Ju/'hoansi (or !Kung) Basarwa studied by Lee (1979) or Marshall (1976). Descriptions of customs or behavior which differ from the Ju/'hoansi often evoke criticism since they are generally considered the archetypical Bushmen or Basarwa. These criticisms arise from the mistaken belief that *all* Basarwa practice *hxaro*, rely on mongongo nuts, have namesakes, are degraded agro-pastoralists, speak similar languages, share a common history of contact and interaction with non-Basarwa groups, or exhibit other similar features (e.g., see Wilmsen 1983, 1989; Wilmsen and Denbow 1990).

The following chapters attest to the cultural and behavioral diversity among Basarwa groups. For instance, Barnard and Widlok point out in chapter 4 that minimally 22 percent of adult male Nharo Basarwa hunt at least once a year or more. This figure contrasts with the G/wi, G//ana, and Kūa Basarwa described in chapters 2 and 6. At Kutse (chapter 6), 100 percent of the adult males hunt at least once a year and most hunt much more, as often as every day or two. The same is not the case for those Kūa living in the Eastern Kweneng District discussed in chapter 5 by Vierich and Hitchcock.

In many cases, outsiders, including anthropologists, are generally unaware of the differences between groups. Consequently, researchers lump them together as "Bushmen" or Basarwa, as if there were one typical group that such a designation appropriately describes. If this assumption of a "typical" group were valid, how should it be defined? Are the Nharo or the Ju/'hoansi (!Kung) in the 1990s, who are not full-time foragers, the "typical" group (Draper and Kranichfeld 1990; Lee 1992b; Barnard and Widlok, chapter 4, this volume)? Or are the full-time hunter-gatherers at Kutse in the 1990s, or the full-time Ju/'hoansi hunter-gatherers of the 1950s and 1960s "typical" (chapter 6, this volume; Lee 1979)? Or should we consider part-time Kūa foragers of the Eastern Kalahari during the 1970s and 1980s as the "typical" Basarwa (Vierich and Hitchcock, chapter 5, this volume)? While it may be simpler to over-generalize and portray all Basarwa as a single entity, it is neither accurate nor helpful in understanding foragers.

Several years ago, discussions with scholars such as Barry Hewlett, who works with very different African hunter-gatherers than the Basarwa (see chapter 9), indicated that misconceptions of a homogeneous hunter-gatherer society extended far beyond the Basarwa. As Hewlett predicted, researchers later generalized from one group of Pygmies not only to all Pygmy groups, but to all tropical-forest foragers (e.g., Bailey *et al.* 1989; Headland and Bailey 1991; however, see rebuttals by Bahuchet, McKey, and de Garine 1991; Brosius 1991; Dwyer and Minnegal 1991; Endicott and Bellwood 1991; Laden 1992; Stearman 1991). Through such examples, it becomes apparent that researchers who work with foragers either are themselves uninformed of the diversity among Basarwa, Pygmies, and other hunter-gatherers, or have unintentionally conveyed a picture of homogeneity within and between specific groups. How many heated arguments and disagreements in forager studies are fueled by ignorance of the diversity among and between specific groups? How much important information is missed because of the assumption that each group must be the same?

I hope this volume will accomplish several aims: (1) that it will demonstrate that there is an enormous amount of diversity among forager groups often thought to be more or less homogeneous (e.g., among the Basarwa, Pygmies, Okiek, or between general hunter-gatherer groups, such as the Hadza and Basarwa); (2) that it will demonstrate that one learns much more about similarities between groups by first studying differences than by concentrating primarily on similarities; and (3) that it will confirm that it is more productive to view hunter-gatherers from a variety of perspectives, instead of a single personal theoretical orientation.

To accomplish its aims, *Cultural diversity among twentieth-century foragers* delineates differences between and within groups that traditionally have been categorized together. To account for the diversity, the following chapters present interpretations based on solid, reliable ethnographic data (also see Harpending 1991; Lee and Guenther 1991, 1993). Thus, most chapters detail the diversity present in whichever facet of culture is under examination, which I suggest is essential to determine the causes and meanings of this diversity. This is *not* a call to return to the Boasian school of providing detailed descriptive information devoid of theory and interpretation. It is instead a call to avoid the current trend in anthropological inquiry where data are ignored if they do not fit one's theoretical predictions (Kent 1992).

On one point the authors are united: anthropologists cannot discuss diversity without also discussing similarity. These are not necessarily mutually exclusive categories. It is no longer appropriate, and indeed it may be misleading, to concentrate on either the shared similarities *or* the differences between groups. This point is made again and again in each chapter and its recognition demands a methodological change in how we interpret data. The authors demonstrate, in addition, that it is necessary to discuss how behavior – such as settlement or mobility patterns, plant exploitation, sharing, and hunting skill – is tied to culture, be it economic, sociopolitical, religious and or of ethos, or cultural transmission.

The book's geographical focus is on Africa, where diversity among foraging groups is so extensive as to allow a comprehensive discussion of the topic. In addition, some of the most heated debates concerning classification, comparative studies, and cross-cultural studies of hunter-gatherers center on African foragers.

Diverse approaches to diversity

As editor, I have deliberately invited people with different theoretical perspectives to contribute to the book in order to look at foragers from a variety of angles. Most of the current major theoretical orientations for studying foragers are represented here. Thus, not only is this book about diversity, but it also represents diversity itself, from the societies described to the environments they inhabit, to the theoretical orientations of the authors who describe them. As Barnard and Widlok have noted (chapter 4, this volume), the book, then, is not just about cultural diversity among African foragers, but is a textbook on methodological diversity in anthropological approaches and thought. Such a blending of ideas and theoretical orientations is, I believe, the direction anthropology needs to take if we are to gain greater knowledge and understanding about human culture and behavior.

There is important common ground between the authors in spite of their different perspectives. For example, all have conducted long-term fieldwork with the groups they discuss (from three to twenty years of periodic collection of data). In addition, most authors are conversant, through either fieldwork or familiarization with the literature, with more than one group within the larger categories of Basarwa, Pygmy, or Okiek. It is interesting to note that each author independently questions, if not rejects, strictly ecological interpretations or interpretations based on political economy, even though this was never an explicit part of the project. Their data, extensive personal experience, and interpretations simply fit within more culturally oriented views of these populations. Even those societies most intimately involved with non-foragers are considered to represent autonomous ethnic groups who differ in recognizable ways from their non-foraging neighbors (e.g., Blackburn, chapter 8, and Hewlett, chapter 9).

The Basarwa of Southern Africa and the Pygmies of Central Africa have been more studied by anthropologists than any other African foraging groups; they are therefore better represented here than are the Hadza or Okiek. In each section, complementary facets of cultural diversity are examined. For example, Basarwa hunting variation is discussed in chapter 6, and Pygmy gathering and wild plant diversity are discussed in chapter 11. These two chapters provide interesting contrasts and similarities on the subject of diversity in wild resource acquisition and use, both because the authors have different theoretical orientations and because the two groups themselves vary. Another example is George Silberbauer's description of the world view, ethos, and other symbolic, non-materialist facets of G/wi culture (chapter 2), which complements but contrasts with Daou Joiris' description of the ritual and religious beliefs of Baka and Aka Pygmies (chapter 10).

The book is organized according to broad cultural categories, beginning with the Basarwa and moving north to the Hadza and Okiek, then west to the Pygmies. Chapters are linked through the authors' commitment to documenting and explaining diversity. This is accomplished by references to the authors' previous research from a retrospective, philosophical perspective (e.g., Silberbauer, chapter 2), or by presenting new, unpublished data (e.g., Guenther, chapter 3; Barnard and Widlok, chapter 4; Kent, chapter 6; Blurton Jones, Hawkes, and O'Connell, chapter 7; Blackburn, chapter 8; Joiris, chapter 10; Ichikawa and Terashima, chapter 11). It is also accomplished through examinations of diversity from specific theoretical perspectives (e.g., Blurton Jones *et al.*, chapter 7), through reinterpretations or new views of previously collected data (e.g., Barnard and Widlok, chapter 4; Vierich and Hitchcock, chapter 5; Hewlett, chapter 9), or through descriptive analyses embedded in particular theoretical orientations (e.g., Kent, chapter 6; Blackburn, chapter 8; Ichikawa and Terashima, chapter 11). Scholars with ecological, environmental, and evolutionary perspectives emphasize certain aspects of culture and society, while symbolic and structuralist anthropologists emphasize others. Diversity as both subject and method is a strength of this book.

Causes of intra-cultural diversity

Foragers as a group may not be any more diverse than farmers or other broad economic categories, since the degree of diversity displayed between different farming communities can equal or surpass that between forager groups (e.g., the differences between Pande farmers and Yangere farmers in the Central African Republic are no less than the differences between Aka and Baka Pygmies; Barry Hewlett 1993: personal communication). However, diversity, as noted by the authors, exists on an intra-cultural level as well.

What causes this level of cultural diversity? It is not coincidental that a constant in all chapters concerns the fluid (Joiris, chapter 11), shifting (Vierich and Hitchcock, chapter 5), opportunistic (Silberbauer, chapter

2; Barnard and Widlok, chapter 4), and flexible (Guenther, chapter 3; Ichikawa and Terashima, chapter 11) social and political organization and general lifestyle of modern foragers. This constant supersedes uniformity or diversity in the environments inhabited by each group. As noted by Bird-David (chapter 12), some anthropologists claim that within-group diversity is the most distinctive characteristic hunter-gatherer societies have in common! This section attempts to address, from one theoretical perspective, the question of why so much diversity exists within specific forager societies in order to raise some interesting points that readers can keep in mind while studying the chapters that follow.

I have suggested elsewhere that cognitive flexibility may be one of the most important traits that emerged in anatomically modern humans during the Upper Paleolithic (Kent 1989b). It is based on an emphasis on learned behavior in contrast to instinctual behavior, and on cultural transmission in contrast to genetic transmission. The consequence of dependence on learned behavior and cultural transmission is a freedom from the constraints of rigid behavior forced by instinctual thinking and acting. Such flexibility may account for the initial success of hominids in general and of *Homo sapiens sapiens* in particular (see Tooby and Cosmides 1992:112). The ability to innovate and change their behavior allowed hominids to thrive in radically different habitats and to defend themselves from a variety of stronger predators (i.e., natural selection was positive for learned behavior at the expense of instinctual behavior). Foley (1988:212–13, 215) is correct when he states that earlier hominids appear to have been more habitat-specific and possessed a less flexible pattern of behavior. Only with the appearance of anatomically modern humans was there technological variability, innovation, and flexibility (Foley 1988:213, 215).[1]

Cognitive flexibility increased in non-human primates, through hominids, as the genus and later the species evolved, and is most highly developed in modern humans.[2] Nonetheless, the existence of this pan-

---

[1] However, the archaeological record with which I am familiar does not support Foley's contention that forager culture and behavior as we know it (and as described in the following chapters) developed only in tandem with the emergence of farming. While Upper Paleolithic complex hunter-gatherers may have been quite different from the band-level highly egalitarian societies discussed in this book, with the exception of the Okiek analyzed in chapter 8, the band-level forager model is applicable to, for example, prehistoric Paleo-Indians and early Archaic populations, who occupied North America long before the appearance of the first farmers.

[2] New ideas are often merely the reshuffling of old ideas. After a period of embracing the concept of cultural evolution and borrowing terminology from biology (the hey-day of Sahlins, Service, Steward, and hunter-gatherer studies), anti-evolutionary thought in all subdisciplines of anthropology became popular (e.g., as noted by Binford 1983 and

hominid, if not general pan-hominoid, trait does not mean that modern human foragers are an appropriate analog for pre-modern, pre-*sapiens* hominids, as Foley (1988) convincingly demonstrates.[3]

The term "cognitive flexibility" (i.e., freedom from instincts) applies to the physical design of the brain and its thought processes (see Tooby and Cosmides 1992 for a contrasting view of this concept). *Cognitive* flexibility enables, but does not produce, within-group *cultural* flexibility. Cultural flexibility itself varies according to cultural context.[4] Cognitive flexibility can also result in cultural rigidity, which is common in most complex societies (as in the presence of ranking or gender inequality). Cultural rigidity, however, in no way implies that the culture itself is static, but only that there is a rigidity or conformity in thought and behavior. This rigidity or conformity is institutionalized through stratification and hierarchies, and other types of institutionalized segmentation, which reduces the cultural and behavioral options open to the majority of individuals in a society, e.g., strictly prescribed gender roles and rigid divisions of labor by sex, age, or status. Cultural flexibility, on the other hand, can be found in many of the forager societies discussed in the following chapters, as in the fluidity between men's and women's activities (also see Kent 1993a, 1995a).

I have discussed elsewhere the presence of underlying universal principles which structure culture (Kent 1984, 1987, 1990a, 1991a). These principles are a product of the anatomically modern human brain and its internal design, though their manifestations are different in different societies and the result is visible in cross-cultural variability.

Without this frame or structure which emanates from a brain that has the same species-wide internal configuration, however, "social and mental life in every culture would be so different as to be unrecognizable as *human* life" (Cosmides and Tooby 1992:207; original emphasis). It

---

Hallpike 1986, among others). Discounting accusations of functionalism (used as a derogatory term to imply theories that are tautological and non-explanations or, at best, "just so" stories), there recently has been a resurgence of evolutionary biological perspectives in anthropology (as one example, see Blurton Jones *et al.*, chapter 7, this volume).

[3] If nothing else, the substantial increase in cranial capacity from the various australopithecines to anatomically modern humans precludes the use of modern human behavioral analogs for pre-modern human behavior, particularly since much of the brain's expansion occurred in the frontal lobe. For example, Middle Paleolithic foragers appear to have been quite different from Upper Paleolithic and later foragers (Gamble 1992).

[4] This view allows us to dismiss criticisms that label cultural explanations of phenomena as "non-explanations" and underlying cognitive principles that structure culture as "mentalist non-explanations." Both are legitimate explanations; they are simply at different levels. Both are necessary for a complete understanding of any one phenomenon. To focus on one or the other is valid as long as either explanation is viewed as partial without the other.

thus makes all types of cultures known today recognizable as culture, but it does not generate the specifics of culture, such as social exchange or, more relevant to this discussion, cultural flexibility.

Thus, cognitive flexibility, a basic property defining anatomically modern humans, encourages diversity, which has enabled humans to cope with changing environments and social, political, and other cultural situations. From cognitive flexibility as the basic blueprint of the mind emerged cultural flexibility. This cultural flexibility, a feature of highly egalitarian hunter-gatherer culture, allowed foraging to persist as a subsistence strategy into the late twentieth century. This fact makes foraging one of the most successful endeavors ever adopted by humans, if longevity is a criterion of success (the popular figure is that an estimated 99 percent of all of human existence has been spent as hunter-gatherers; Lee and DeVore 1968:3; also see Barkow *et al.* 1992:5). So, although all modern humans have *cognitive* flexibility, which is genetically transmitted, only highly egalitarian foragers also have *cultural* flexibility, which is socially transmitted.

Cognitive evolution, which allows flexibility, depends on physical evolution predicated upon genetic inheritance, natural selection, and reproductive success. However, the flexibility of a society's culture depends on cultural reproduction, not on physical or sexual reproduction (and this differs from Blurton Jones *et al.*, chapter 7; but also see Hewlett, chapter 9, this volume; Boyd and Richerson 1985:7–10; Hewlett and Cavalli-Sforza 1986; Durham 1991).

Cultural evolution in action

Depending on a number of variables, such as random chance (i.e., history), internal–external transformations (i.e., innovation or diffusion of new traits), and change (environmental or cultural), culture can evolve or, in other words, change through time. Such change can be seen, for example, in the sedentarization of the Basarwa. Cultural evolution here stems from the fact that sedentary lifestyles require cultural unity and within-group conformity in order to be viable, regardless of why a society became sedentary in the first place. Sedentary societies have to discourage individual variability and its consequences, or they cannot remain aggregated or sedentary. Instead they would revert to a nomadic, band-level existence capable of accommodating such cultural flexibility. Sedentary Kutse (G/wi, G//ana, and Kũa) residents occupying a recently established sedentary Kalahari community provide an interesting case study of evolution in action (most residents have been sedentary 15–25 years).

According to my perspective, individuals are born neither aggressive or passive, nor egalitarian or non-egalitarian (i.e., hierarchical or non-hierarchical). These traits are culturally determined and there is a continuum in the importance accorded them in different societies. What is culturally inherent in traditional Basarwa society, but is not physically inherent, therefore, is an emphasis on passivity (at least in thought, if not in behavior) and on egalitarianism. The Okiek place somewhat less emphasis on these traits and other groups place even less or actually promote the opposite. This can be seen cross-culturally as a continuum between highly egalitarian societies and highly *non*-egalitarian societies.

Nomadic Basarwa society has been characterized as acephalous, lacking social or political stratification or hierarchies (Lee 1979; Silberbauer 1981a). As long as Basarwa were nomadic, the lack of formal leadership was viable. The only leaders were not leaders in the usual sense of the term. No one was more important than anyone else: the ideas of skillful individuals were more valued than others only in a situation related to their skill. At most, these leaders can be viewed as situational, transitory, and informal. The term "advisors" is perhaps a more appropriate descriptive one, since the status and power of these individuals are the same as everyone else's, at least among Central Kalahari Basarwa (though not necessarily among the Ju/'hoansi; Lorna Marshall 1994: personal communication).

When a dispersed nomadic mobility pattern is abandoned, the absence of a formal leader becomes a serious liability, threatening the stability of a newly aggregated sedentary community, such as Kutse. A traditional method of resolving disputes without the presence of an arbitrator – i.e., mobility – is not feasible in a sedentary context. Thus far, resolution of conflict in the sedentary community has not been possible without much physical violence (Kent 1989b). The current flux being experienced by Kutse (resulting in numerous injuries of varying severity and one murder committed by the 30–35-year-old victim's biological brother) will not continue. Eventually, Kutse will either disband as a community or a leader will emerge who possesses status that gives him/her the political power to implement decisions and to arbitrate disputes.

It is fascinating to observe that among Basarwa who have been sedentary for centuries, in contrast to Kutse where they have been sedentary for only one or two decades, formal political leadership is emerging. The new leader often arises by an ephemeral, situationally specific advisor being elevated in status and influence. The individual's traditionally temporary status is now maintained on a continual basis in these established sedentary communities. Trance dancers at Ghanzi, consistent with their traditional role of restoring harmony to a community, are emerging as Nharo community leaders (Guenther 1975, 1976; also see Hitchcock and Holm 1985). Also interesting, as a contrast, is the source of violence reported for the less egalitarian Okiek (Blackburn, chapter 8). The Okiek dispute ownership of resources and co-residence (Blackburn 1993: personal communication), while Kutse discord revolves around concepts relevant to a highly egalitarian society, such as questions about whether people are sharing enough. At Kutse, disputes over sharing often erupt among families who traditionally would not have shared because they do not belong to the same sharing network. These families probably would not have resided next to one another for more than a month or two at a time, but today they are continuously located near each other in the sedentary, aggregated Kutse community (Kent 1995b).

An evolution or change in the culture of groups of Basarwa is occurring to allow for the stability of sedentary aggregations. Those sedentary communities that are successful are slightly more stratified (compared to other more mobile groups), in that they have leaders, though not necessarily the same kind of leaders as are found elsewhere. In other words, they have evolved a position of leadership that has slightly modified their culture by introducing a degree of political stratification. This stratification has prevented their cultural extinction without their having to forsake sedentism.

In the Kutse case, there is conflict in the form of discord and physical violence because a strongly egalitarian, acephalous society cannot also be sedentary and aggregated. There are, on the other hand, benefits for a slightly less egalitarian sedentary aggregation with a nominal leader, which would reduce strife (i.e., a leadership position, however it may be expressed). Such leaders have the social and political status to achieve social cohesion and unanimity. This is why there are few or no highly egalitarian year-round sedentary aggregated societies. I predict that, at the same time as the emergence of leaders, informal or formal rules will eventually develop which will discourage the cultural flexibility common in the more highly egalitarian societies. All of this will reduce a society's cultural heterogeneity. The Kutse example illustrates cultural evolution in action.

The question remains, however: can the physical evolution model – natural selection and descent through modification – be applied to cultural evolution? I suggest not. Physical evolution is much more rigid and deterministic than is cultural evolution. As Durham states (1991:458): "it is people, not 'nature,' who do most of the selecting in cultural evolution and it is communication, not reproduction, that is the principal mechanism of transmission."[5] In cultural evolution individuals or groups select those traits they deem valuable and reject others (Durham 1991:197). Traits may be ignored at first and later adopted, or adopted and then rejected (there is the potential for rejecting traits that does not occur in physical evolution). Thus, while we might be able to see the above example of sedentarization at Kutse as cultural evolution, it is not productive to view it from the perspective of Darwinian jargon and concepts.

Using terminology appropriate in physical evolutionary writing to describe cultural/social evolutionary behavior has resulted in the fallacious notion that people in social interactions (i.e., those based on learning within a cultural milieu) react in as rigid or preprogrammed a manner as they do in physical interactions (i.e., those based on genetic inheritance within a physical environment). It also presupposes a cross-cultural homogeneity in cause and response. For example, this supposition underlies some anthropologists' view of the sharing of meat or other items as always economically and/or reproductively motivated with its roots ultimately in issues of physical evolution – fitness and reproduction (e.g., Hill 1983; Hawkes 1991).

How does this relate to cultural diversity? Guenther (chapter 3) proposes that diversity at the level of individual societies (the focus of this book), and the cultural flexibility that permits diversity, are more pronounced among many foragers, particularly highly egalitarian band-level ones, than among many farmers or pastoralists. Even the less strongly egalitarian Okiek are depicted as having wide variability within and between groups (Blackburn, chapter 8), although they stand out from the others in this volume for reasons discussed below. I believe the causes of diversity described here result from two important factors which characterize most highly egalitarian foragers: (1) their mobility;

---

[5] I disagree with Boyd and Richerson (1985:4), who write that "the parallels [between genetic and cultural inheritance systems] are profound enough that there is no need to invent a completely new conceptual and mathematical apparatus to deal with culture" (also see 1985:30–1). In my opinion these processes are far too dissimilar to use the same terminology and interpretations. Substantial differences between physical and cultural evolution exist (as also noted by Boyd and Richerson, 1985:7): what is the advantage of using the same terms for different processes? New terms need not be added to burden us with more jargon as there are terms already well entrenched in anthropological writing (e.g., innovation, diffusion). I am not arguing against cultural evolution (a criticism levied by Tooby and Cosmides, 1992:82–3 against Gould, 1977a,b,c), I am only arguing against the use of terminology that is pertinent for physical evolution – reproductive success, fitness maximization, selection – for cultural evolution. Using the same terminology for physical and cultural evolution results in misleading deterministic views of culture and behavior and masks the differences, which partially stem from the more rigid transfer of genetic material and the more variable transfer of cultural material (e.g., Hewlett, chapter 9; Ichikawa and Terashima, chapter 11, this volume).

and, most importantly, (2) their cultural flexibility. These lead to institutionalized within-group cultural diversity (what Guenther calls "social-structural flexibility of culture and behavior," chapter 3, and what Barnard [1993:33] calls "a foraging *mode of thought*"; original emphasis). This view explains why some strongly egalitarian nomadic part-time hunters/farmers culturally resemble highly egalitarian foragers in more respects than they do less egalitarian sedentary, aggregated farmers (and why sedentary, aggregated, non-egalitarian foragers such as Northwest Coast Indians culturally resemble sedentary aggregated farmers more than they do nomadic dispersed highly egalitarian Basarwa foragers). In other words, the economic strategy employed has been spuriously correlated with the degree of flexibility. The concept of egalitarianism goes far beyond an ideology in these societies. Numerous societies have an ideal of egalitarianism, even some of the most stratified, hierarchical societies, such as many Western ones, where morally and legally "all people are created equal." However, such ideas are often superficial or represent goals to be attained rather than reality. In contrast, highly egalitarian band-level societies institutionalize equality. Egalitarianism permeates every facet of their culture and behavior; one example is the practice of demand sharing (Peterson 1993; Kent 1993a). In these societies, relationships established and maintained through sharing (among other behaviors) are legitimized by a strongly egalitarian ethos.

Mobility and the band-level configuration of culture (Guenther, chapter 3), emphasizing individual autonomy and extreme egalitarianism in all facets of culture, are, I suggest, the causal agents or facilitators of high levels of cultural flexibility within a society.[6] There is, however, a continuum of cultural flexibility upon which all societies can be comparatively situated.

How is cultural flexibility and the resultant diversity maintained in those societies in which it is a characteristic? There is a combination of traits that are more fundamental to the foraging groups described in this book than their somewhat similar resource procurement. This amalgam of traits includes a relatively loose attachment to the group, partly as the result of their mobility pattern; an individual autonomy regardless of gender, and in some cases regardless of age; and a set of beliefs and

[6] Barnard (1993:33) writes that the Basarwa are foragers in many ways – "kin classification, sharing, and reciprocity can be seen as social 'foraging', for relatives and for relationships of exchange." Guenther (1979a and chapter 3) states that Basarwa religious ideology is an example of "foraging" for ideas. Barnard (1993:33) also notes that "Even the Khoekhoe word *saan* or *san*, so popular as an ethnic label for 'Bushmen', means simply 'foragers' – with all the negative as well as the positive connotations 'foraging' conjures."

values that are fluid and non-dogmatic. The entire assemblage of traits is the key to how strongly egalitarian foragers readily adapt, adopt, and alter their ways depending on changing circumstances. Lack of a centralized authority also contributes to diversity, coupled with a cultural transmission of traits that is mostly informal and individual, as noted by Ichikawa and Terashima (chapter 11). More formal education, in contrast to parent–child learning, would probably reduce the cultural diversity within any one group (see Hewlett and Cavalli-Sforza 1986; and Boyd and Richerson 1985). Societies who share this constellation of traits include Pygmies occupying tropical forests and Hadza and Basarwa in the savanna, and non-African groups such as the Agta of the Philippines (Griffin n.d.) or Batek of Malaysia (Karen Endicott 1979; Kirk Endicott 1988).

What is it about this particular mélange of traits that accounts for the at times bewildering array of diversity (e.g., various Basarwa religious beliefs, or Pygmy ceremony-dances – see Joiris, chapter 10, for the latter)? It is the consequence of what I call their highly egalitarian culture, or of what Guenther (chapter 3) terms the foraging band society (adopting the term from cultural evolutionists). Egalitarianism permeates (and, I suggest, structures) not only the social and political organization, economics, and division of labor of these societies, but also their ethos or world view – in other words, every facet of culture and behavior. How, then, does such an ethos lead to cultural diversity? Egalitarianism promotes individual autonomy because no one, regardless of age or gender, has social or political power or influence over anyone else – that is, no one's opinion takes precedence over anyone else's. Older individuals may be asked for an opinion because they have greater experience, but not because their age or gender separates them or gives them special status (note that, in contrast, Okiek have age sets).

There are many examples of autonomy and age egalitarianism from Kutse. On a number of occasions when I first began my fieldwork, I asked adults who were out of water and unable to fetch any why they did not ask one of their children to get water. Later, after several field seasons, I realized that even if the adult had asked one of the children to get water, more times than not he or she would be ignored. One older man who was ill at the time said, "I asked my son but he refuses to get water for me." I told him that in America a father could order his son to fetch water for him, to which he responded, "That is good but it is not the way we do things here" (he thought it sounded good at the time because he was thirsty). Children are commonly asked to do something and, equally commonly, simply ignore the request, even if the person is yelling at them (this is also noted among the Ju/'hoansi by Draper

[1975:92]). My point is that individual autonomy is not something bestowed on adults only, any more than it is on a single sex.

In contrast, more complex societies (complex because they are made up of more parts) institutionalize inequality by rigid stratification. For example, sociopolitical organization is composed of groups or strata often hierarchically arranged. Economic units are usually stratified, again often hierarchically, by gender, age, and status. Perhaps because there are more divisions, there are more rules regulating with whom one can interact and in what way, depending on such factors as age, gender, status, and ethnicity. Because there are more rules, there is more (or longer) formal education, which encourages greater conformity. The consequences permeate all facets of culture. Architecture is spatially segregated with gender-specific, age-specific, activity function-specific, and status-specific compartments, rooms, or bounded space (the latter can be conceptual, without physical barriers but reinforced by usage; Kent 1990a, 1991a). Even material culture is more complex, particularly in terms of the use of more function-specific objects and gender-associated objects (e.g., power tools or toy guns in North American society might be considered more masculine objects than sewing machines or baby dolls).

Highly egalitarian societies do not partition architecture or the use of space by gender, physically or conceptually, since the differences between males and females, although obviously acknowledged, are not emphasized to the same extent as they are in non-egalitarian societies (Kent 1984, 1990b, 1991a). The built environment reflects the degree of segregation (or segmentation) that exists within a culture, as seen in stratification and hierarchies. In this way, the partitioning of buildings and the use of space within them act as mnemonic devices to reinforce the cultural and behavioral partitioning found in the culture of most complex societies (see Rapoport 1982, 1990).

Why, out of the four general groups highlighted in this book – the Basarwa, Pygmies, Hadza, and Okiek – does the latter stand out as different? This question takes on more meaning when Okiek are compared to some Pygmy groups who are similar in their inter-action, dependence, and linguistic relationship to non-foraging peoples. I suggest the Okiek differ because, on the continuum from highly egalitarian (e.g., the other groups here) to non-egalitarian (such as highly complex societies), they are less egalitarian than the former, although much more so than the latter. Among only the Okiek do we see the presence of a gender hierarchy, with males thought to be superior, an age-set system, ownership of possessions, less sharing of objects and resources, and gender-segregated space (e.g., the men's campfire referred to by Blackburn in chapter 8). This hierarchical system integrates Okiek society; in an analogous way, egalitarianism (and the sharing which fosters that egalitarianism) integrate certain Basarwa and other highly egalitarian societies. Okiek blessings or prayers, for example, are the province of male elders and reinforce their authority in consequential matters such as marriage and dispute cases (Kratz 1988:218). A less egalitarian ethos is visible also in the Okiek fear of affines and witches, where, at least in the latter case, some individuals have supernatural power over others.

Several authors in this volume suggest that with cultural flexibility comes cultural diversity – that is, cultural traits are mutable among the forager societies examined in this book partly because individual and group diversity is tolerated. However, it is perhaps here that the consensus among authors disappears: each comes to the study of diversity from a different perspective. Together, through our diverse approaches, we present a more comprehensive perspective of foraging peoples, past, present, and future, than any one of us could present on our own.

Conclusions

One of the most striking findings in this book is that there is a great deal of variability within groups usually considered to be more homogeneous than heterogeneous. At the same time, there are similarities within the groups that balance their differences. The lesson gleaned is that comparisons are appropriate only when both the differences and the similarities between groups are taken into account. It may be, depending on one's research goals, more appropriate and profitable to compare highly egalitarian societies with other highly egalitarian societies than to compare foragers with foragers merely because their subsistence strategy is similar.

I suggest three basic reasons for the frequently inaccurate portrayals of hunter-gatherers as homogeneous. One is a general lack of knowledge of different groups among the Basarwa and Pygmies. For this reason I insisted that authors ground their discussions in ethnographic detail.

A second failure to recognize diversity results from the rapid culture change experienced by these and many other small-scale societies in developing Third World nations. Even during the brief time I have been conducting research in Botswana (1987–94), change has been so rapid and so encompassing that, had I not witnessed it myself, I would have been skeptical of someone else's description of it. For people not experiencing such rapid change, it sometimes is difficult to conceive that it can occur so quickly. Some researchers are consequently skeptical about descriptions of a people they know today that were written only a decade or less ago. However, we need to acknowledge change and to take advantage of the situation to learn about cultural evolution in the twentieth century. It has been suggested that change is as much a part of culture as people are (Carrithers 1992). While certainly true, the rate of change and what is changing have differed at different times. The type and rate of change experienced by many indigenous peoples around the world during the past one or two hundred years is unlikely to be identical to change experienced two thousand years ago.

The third reason why cultural diversity has not been appreciated stems from the popularity of one or two theoretical orientations that emphasize economics, particularly subsistence strategies, at the expense of other realms of culture. Materialistic theories which claim that economics or material culture are the most important facets of culture, the rest being epiphenomenal, are narrow to the point of obscurantism in my opinion, particularly for small-scale societies where the various aspects of culture are tightly intertwined. It is not surprising that if hunting-gathering is considered the most important aspect of a society, groups will be inappropriately lumped together regardless of other factors such as kinship, religion, linguistics, and social and political organization. Conclusions reached on the basis of only one small aspect of a society are suspect at best (also see Barnard and Widlok, chapter 4, this volume).

Similarly, conclusions about a society formulated from a single theoretical orientation, without the benefits that accrue from studying a phenomenon from a variety of perspectives, are limited. The chapters in this book employ rich ethnographic descriptive data to substantiate their interpretations; they also tend to have a diachronic perspective. All manuscripts were circulated among the authors and cross-referenced as much as possible. Authors were thus forced to consider not only their own data, time period of investigations, and views, but those of the other contributors as well. This encouraged them to evaluate their own data and the data of others in different ways, potentially leading to new insights.

This book advances our knowledge of foraging societies by presenting new data, as well as reinterpretations of previously collected data, within the framework of cultural diversity. Any good book will generate as many new questions as it answers old ones. *Cultural diversity among twentieth-century foragers: an African perspective* represents an exciting direction in forager research, one in which researchers cooperate and collaborate to examine an important issue – cultural diversity. We do not pretend to have all the answers concerning cultural diversity; we do suggest we have some of the relevant questions.

These relevant questions stem from acknowledging similarities and differences within and between groups. Instead of accusing a researcher of being misleading and/or wrong because his or her research findings are different from someone else's, we need to study what and why differences (in addition to similarities) exist. After all, is this not one of the major *raisons d'être* for anthropology – discovering diversity and similarities and explaining how and why they exist?

Acknowledgements

This chapter, and indeed the entire book, has been made possible only through the generosity of our host countries who allow foreign researchers to learn about their people. I would like particularly to thank the Botswana government, especially the Office of the President, Ministry of Local Government and Lands, National Museum and Art Gallery, and the Remote Area Development Office, for permission to conduct research in the Kalahari. Most of the insights contained in this chapter were based on data collected among the people of Kutse. Thus, not only has it been a privilege to be able to work with the people of Kutse over the years, but it has also been a personally enriching and rewarding experience.

I appreciate the time and effort various contributing authors made by reading and commenting on a rough draft. I would like to thank Barry Hewlett, Nurit Bird-David, Mitsuo Ichikawa, Alan Barnard, Rod Blackburn, Mathias Guenther, and George Silberbauer. I also thank Margaret Deith, Denise Elliott, and Marion Blue for editorial suggestions on rough drafts. In addition I thank Jessica Kuper of Cambridge University Press for assistance in turning rough drafts into the polished chapters that follow.

Part I

Southern African foragers

2   Neither are your ways my ways

George Silberbauer

In the search for understanding of any class of phenomena, including cultural diversity, it is necessary to select the members of that class. This is done on the basis of their having in common those characteristics which are judged relevant to the understanding we seek. To assume uncritically either that a quality is shared, or that it is relevant, is to beg this question and thus to frustrate the search. Instead, one must ascertain both the presence of the quality in each of the members and that it is, indeed, relevant to the purpose of the investigation. A trite illustration: as a gardener I might covet my neighbor's delicious raspberries and form a conceit to grow my own. In my tyro's enthusiastic haste I remember only that they are of the genus *Rubus*, and foolishly rush into planting *fructicosa*, instead of *idæus*. In Victoria I will not only be sadly disappointed but will also have to suffer the opprobrium of all about me for having occasioned the further spread of the dreaded blackberry. My error was to assume that shared generic membership was sufficient.

Commonality and relevance become more difficult to identify with confidence when the putative characteristics are those of relationship. Qualities which are important in one relational context may become trivial in another. Characteristics which are desirable for one analytical purpose become anathema for another: raspberries and blackberries are both good food but the latter plant is a noxious weed. In analogous fashion, categories and criteria of their membership change concomitantly with the scale of comparison; when comparing subsistence techniques on a global scale it is likely to be useful to set up a category of hunter-gatherers that includes both the recent-historical G/wi and !Kung. However, the fact that both foraged for wild food-plants and hunted undomesticated animals is, in itself, trivial when these two peoples are compared directly. Within that narrower scope, other categories, such as their respective arrangements for allocating areas in which to gather plants, their styles of hunting, their customary division of meat, might be more informative for comparison. Some of the muddles in Basarwa ethnography and the generalizations drawn from the research stem from neglecting the need to establish clearly the scale and categories of comparison. We are in danger of constructing depauperate stereotypes of the peoples' behavior if we do not take into account the malleability of G/wi and other Kalahari Basarwa cultures and how it enables the people to cope with unusual habitat conditions, or with hostile pressures exerted by the presence of other peoples, government, and other powerful external factors. When confronted by an unexpected example of variability, we should be cautious in ascribing this to a fallacious diversity lest we perpetuate absurdities comparable with the original description of puparia of *Microdon* hoverflies as molluscs (Colless and McAlpine 1970:714).

The concept, hunter-gatherer

The concept, hunter-gatherer, has become somewhat nebulous. In the 1950s and 1960s the G/wi of the central Kalahari were unequivocally hunters and gatherers. They neither cultivated plants, nor kept domesticated animals for food or other products. Their subsistence base was what they found (after well-informed, directive search and/or hunt): esculent plants, prey animals, and, for six to eight weeks of the year, water. Imports were restricted to supplies of leaf-tobacco, soft-iron rod for spear-heads, knife-blades, and adze/axe-heads and eight-gauge fencing-wire for arrow-heads and earrings. If the exchange network which was the vector for these commodities failed, as it did for periods of a year or two, the G/wi substituted bone for metal and *Leonotis* leaves for tobacco. For all practical purposes they were capable of, and regularly practiced, economic self-sufficiency. In short, they were hunters and gatherers because they depended on their hunting and gathering for all their food. Without much thought, we of that era equated subsistence technology with a specific cultural style – it seemed so obvious.

In the 1950s and 1960s there were also cattle-post and ranch Basarwa, whether G/wi or some other people, whether permanent residents or seasonal visitors, who were not hunters and gatherers by this purist criterion. In making strict comparisons of subsistence strategies and sources, it would make sense to exclude them from the category, hunter-gatherer. However, their cultural and social practices were, in most cases, so recently derived from and, in a substantial sense, similar to their own experience of the foraging life, that of their close kin, parents or ancestors, that it furthered ethnographic understanding to include these people among hunters and gatherers. Equating a way of getting food with a style of culture began to show a few cracks and shakes. However, the utility of this extension of the meaning of the term is

apparent when applied to those whose beliefs, world-view, values, social
organization, and – perhaps most importantly – self-image are as close to
those of full-time foragers as were those of Basarwa residents of ranches
and cattle-posts. That these latter maintained close and very active
social links with the desert-dwellers demonstrated the validity of the
classification.

But this only says that a certain set of social and cultural usages
persisted and that the people identified themselves with a category of
others who, in the instance, hunted and gathered. This is no more of an
argument for the validity of the category, hunter-gatherer, than are the
persistence of Greek as home language and membership of the Hellas
Football club and Orthodox Church among Melbourne's population of
Hellenic immigrants reasons for visiting upon the latter the sins of the
unlamented Colonels. The extension of meaning begs the question of
whether or not there is a set of socio-cultural practices – a socio-cultural
style, if you like – that is distinctively that of people who get (or whose
recent ancestors got) their food only by hunting and gathering.

I learned that caution is needed in concluding that people who are
apparently rather remote from their foraging ancestors and their ways
are no longer rightly to be seen as qualified hunters and gatherers. In the
late 1960s many Pitjantjatjara women and men of Central Australia lived
in Adelaide, Alice Springs, and other towns, and on stations. They were
clerks, teachers, mechanics, shearers, cattlemen, domestics, and fruit-
pickers, whose lives appeared identical with those of non-Aborigines
(overlooking the pernicious effects of prejudice and discrimination).
Only the home language distinguished them. Many other Pitjantjatjara
lived on mission and government stations. Their subsistence base was
store-bought foods (see Silberbauer 1972). The bushcraft of these latter
compared poorly with that of the masterly G/wi. Even the best of them
was an indifferent tracker by that virtuoso standard. It seemed to me
that their knowledge and skills, impressive as they were, would not
suffice to sustain the people's hunting and gathering, should they ever
have to rely on them. Then came the Outstation Movement. Many
Pitjantjatjara moved away from the stations, came back from the city
and towns, and managed to live off the bush. It took them some time.
They did not abandon the store-bought foods at once but, quite soon,
the women's and men's bushcraft, knowledge of, and skills in gathering
and hunting were refurbished to the standard needed for comfortable,
secure living. As has happened so often, a little reflection showed me
that I should not have made this mistake. In western society we all
acquire skills that we lose through lack of use. One's tongue grows heavy
in a language left unspoken for a decade or so. Without regular use my

own proficiency in previous trades and professions had declined fast and dangerously. I would not trust myself as a navigator, a firefighter, a flier or a practitioner of law, or even driving a tractor. But a refresher course and a few months of practice brought back tolerable competence; so, also, with the Pitjantjatjaras' hunting and gathering.

It is, or was, commonly the case that hunter-gatherers have low population densities with small residential groups using fairly extensive tracts of land in relation to their size. These groups tend to have egalitarian, rather than authoritarian polities and concomitantly unstratified social organization. Qualification for membership of most of each people's larger groupings (i.e. larger than the household) is inclusive, rather than exclusive. That is to say, the organization emphasis is on how one can find a reason to include an individual in a group, rather than providing the rationale for denying her or him the rights and obligations which go with membership (e.g. universalistic systems of kinship). World-views construed the links between humans and habitats as being close and equalitarian, seldom – if ever – placing mankind at the pinnacle of creation in the manner of the Judeo-Christian construct. Hunter-gatherers' material culture is typically deceptively simple. The inventories of artefacts are small but the design of most items combines low-energy manufacture, use of locally available materials, and versatility of use.

This profile would accommodate many hunting-gathering peoples. I doubt if it would fit any non-foragers. But not all hunter-gatherers (*sensu stricto*, those who live only hunting and gathering) are, or were, true to it. Koniag of Kodiak Island, when the Russians first encountered them, lived by hunting and gathering, had a population density exceeding that of modern suburbia and an exclusive, clearly stratified, complex society – including slaves – and a lavish inventory of specialized, luxury artefacts (Lazenby 1993: personal communication). To be fair, they were as much marine harvesters as they were hunters. But the literature is replete with descriptions of the complex societies of other hunter-gatherers (e.g. Price and Brown 1985).

The profile makes a dubious fit with many of those peoples whose subsistence technology combines hunting and gathering with pastoralism and/or horticulture. It will not suffice to compare the relative proportions of wild with cultivated plant foods consumed, and of hunted meat with that of slaughtered stock, and dub those who score more than 50 percent foragers. On my parents' farm my mother included the fruits, bulbs, and leaves of indigenous plants in her cuisine and our table (and those of our bank manager and urban kin and friends) often bore more kilograms of antelope venison than of beef, pork, and

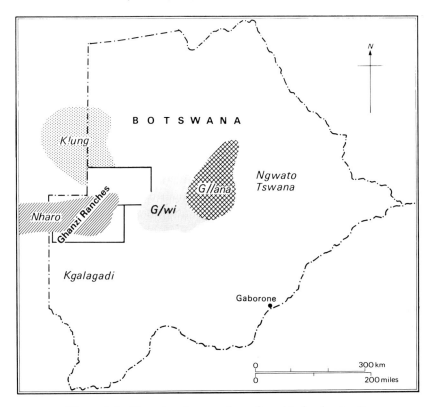

Figure 2.1   Map showing peoples referred to in chapter 2

mutton. Alas, this does not entitle me to claim affinity with my G/wi and
Pitjantjatjara friends as a fellow forager.

In the aspect of ethnicity, hunting and gathering are clearly important
to some. Koories and other Australian Aborigines, many North
American First Nations and many Basarwa include their status (or that
of their forebears) as hunter-gatherers as an element of their distinctive
identity. Some Sydney-side Koories of Redfern, or those of Melbourne's Fitzroy, might be sickened by the prospect of dispatching a
wallaby, let alone eating it, but are very proud of their hunter-gatherer
heritage and see many of their cardinal values and meanings as deriving
from it. For them, as for others, the content of the concept emphasizes
not a subsistence technology but the closeness of kin, the quality of their
relationship with what we call Nature, and other features which provide
definitions of their Truth.

It seems that what we currently mean by "hunter-gatherers" is

people who, wherever and however they get their food, still see themselves as directly connected with their own hunting and gathering
tradition, and for whom that tradition continues to furnish what are to
them significant social and cultural meanings – a cognitive definition,
rather than a mechanistic technological one. Figure 2.1 shows the
locations of the peoples referred to in this chapter.

Cultural diversity

Cultural diversity is the variation in time, space, and ethnicity of
patterns of social and cultural behavior, and the products and meanings
of that behavior. What is selected as significant variation depends on the
purpose of the analysis. To take language as exemplar: diversity of
vocabulary, grammatical form, pronunciation, and inflection are apparent in regional, occupational, gender, and – in stratified societies – class
dialects of what all its speakers recognize as the same language. At some
vague threshold of variation, dialect becomes separate language; those of
us who have worked in the central Kalahari usually refer to G//ana and
G/wi as different peoples, each with their own language. That is a very
low threshold: they are, surely, no more than dialects. I doubt if many –
other than fervent nationalists – would insist that Flemish and Dutch
are truly different languages (which puts the status of Afrikaans in some
doubt), although with some initial difficulty, they are mutually intelligible for much of the way. Setswana and Sesotho and at least the western
dialects of Sepedi (all of which are regarded as separate languages) bear
comparable resemblance to one another.

My point here is that these distinctions are not made on purely
linguistic grounds, nor are they consistent. They are more a matter of
social rather than cultural distinctiveness. Other distinctions which
comprise cultural diversity are comparably muddy, unless there is some
methodological neatness. Diversity can only be detected by a process of
comparison. As I argue below, the scale of the analysis, the criteria of
comparison, and the parameters of relevance should be established and
followed for each series of comparisons.

Plausible explanation of diversity is seldom likely to be definitive;
speculation and more or less informed guesswork are almost always
needed to paper over the gaps in the data, the theory and interpretive
skill, and wisdom. But the need for them is diminished if one can
establish whether or not observed variations are normal to the societies
and cultures under examination. If one concludes that variation is
preponderantly beyond the peoples' normal experience, then causation
must be sought and attributed. It is improbable that a single cause, or

even an integrated set of causes, will be responsible. Part of the explanation will be found among endogenous factors; other changes and differences will be attributable to external influences.

Cultural diversity is a relativistic concept. Unless one is a very meticulous scholar of material culture for whom minute stylistic variation may be important in itself, the validity of identification of cultural variation requires at least some degree of self-distinction in the groups among whom the anthropologist differentiates. In other words, the perceived diversity should be accompanied by social distinctiveness. This is not to say, however, that cultural diversity and social distinctiveness are the same thing: the former has to do with differences in behavior, and the products of behavior, while the latter concerns significant meaning that the people give to such difference. For them it may be a badge of their distinctiveness, an affirmation of their identity, a sad reminder of what they may see as their own inferiority, or simply another instance of the perverse tastes and curious ways of those who are perceived as "others."

The circumstances under which the populations live will influence the categories within which contrasts and similarities are made, noted, defined or classified. Among neighboring bands of autonomous, permanent hunters and gatherers whose interaction is extensive and frequent, sameness and difference might be more easily found, or more clearly seen, by stratifying the population by age, gender, or family groups, rather than simply by band membership. If contact with alien peoples is one of the variables then proximity to, or the nature and extent of interaction with, the foreigners, may be a more useful basis for categorizing than native language. The cultural items which are chosen to measure similarity or diversity are, to some extent, a function of the size of the categories which are being compared. On the microscopic scale of, for instance, households in a G/wi band, fairly small variations in behavior and usage will be regarded as significant. The division of labor between spouses will be compared in much finer detail of task, time, and frequency than if one were to expand the scale by comparing these people with members of a !Kung community. Then the differences between the range and nature of household activities in the two milieux would be too great for there to be much reward in comparing them in the same fine-grained detail.

As in any mode of analysis, the anthropologist's purpose in drawing distinction will also influence the parameters of relevance and, hence, criteria of significance. If, as has been the case with many of us working in the hunter-gatherer field, emphasis is on ecological variables with which conceptually to associate social and cultural behavior, variations in residential patterns of the population may be seen as important. To another, for whom kinship is the focal point or for whom mythology and folk-tales are the pathway to an understanding of behavior, how the population groups itself in time and space may be of peripheral significance. Each approach is valid but, once adopted, each imposes its particular matrix for selection, arrangement and interpretation of data. What I wrote in *Hunter and habitat* when commenting on fellow-workers in the Kalahari still holds good:

> Each of these fieldworkers illuminated the general, as well as the particular aspects of the sociocultural system he or she studied. Whatever the emphasis in the investigation and point of entry into the system, each has achieved and communicated an understanding of the whole. None of us will understand all of the whole, and the variety of emphasis and approach that exists is necessary if we are to fill one another's gaps and clarify perception of sociocultural systems by showing them in the nuances and contrasts of our different perspectives. (Silberbauer 1981a: xvi)

Therefore, although cultural diversity may be an empirical fact, the meaning accorded to it by the anthropologist is relative to her or his perspective and the purpose, scale, and mode of analysis. The value of such conclusions carries the proviso – as I have said – that analytical meaning can be related to (but not necessarily mirror) the meaning which the peoples themselves attach to variation.

It should not be assumed that an anthropologist's remarking of cultural diversity necessarily implies social distance between those who are compared. As I shall show later, some G/wi were ranch-dwellers; others sporadically visited ranches in search of water during drought; many had no direct contact with ranches and continued to live entirely on sustenance gained by gathering and hunting. It is clear that there would have been considerable cultural variation across these three categories. Nonetheless, groups were not isolated from one another. For instance, some siblings were to be found in each, but this did not in any way diminish the conceptual or emotional closeness of their kinship ties; it only engendered sadness that those in the first group had little contact and interaction with those in the last one. Also, many G/wi bands had members who were identified both by themselves and by their band fellows as G//ana (a Nharo and two Kgalagari were also permanent and fully-accepted members). The dialectal differences in their speech were pointed out to me by them and G/wi as "foreign," as were other differences. Although such ethnic cultural differences were readily remarked, they appeared to have no effect on the range and quality of relationships among G/wi and non-G/wi band fellows. Marriage, friendship or hunting partnerships between G/wi and G//ana, and so on, showed no differential distribution nor was there any expectation by any members that it should. Ethnicity in this instance could be compared with the G/wi view of left-handedness. Even if, in industrialized society, we no longer fear meeting a skir-handed man on a Tuesday as an ill omen (Radford and Radford 1980:179), we impose penalties by charging sinistrals more for their irons (golf-, or smoothing-), scissors and vegetable-peelers than right-handers have to pay for theirs. To the G/wi, left-handedness had no such importance and was merely something to remark as "cute" (*tʃwê:*). Plainly it would be an empty or misleading ethnography which recorded only what the anthropologist considered to be significant differences and omitted the people's own view.

When cultural diversity among Kalahari Basarwa (whom I have previously called Bushmen and upon whom others have inflicted that regrettable label, San) is being considered, there are problems in distinguishing between inherent variability, adaptive changes, and the diversity that is a function of ethnicity. (That is to say, what people A does, and considers to be part of its own customary practice, that people B does not do as a matter of course.) What I have noted here as three phenomena are not sharply divided but shade into one another. There is, I think, a tendency to overestimate the uniformity of custom, practice, belief, and attitude among members of a small-scale society. Where the scale is as small as that of a G/wi band there is the expectation that there would be only trifling differences in beliefs; if we are particularly thoughtful we might make allowances for the longer experience that age brings and not be surprised by rather greater differences in knowledge and certain skills. It would also not be altogether strange to find that some individuals showed greater natural aptitude than did others in certain activities. The members of a small-scale society are not automatons, rigidly regimented by the iron authority of custom. Individuality is perhaps more trammelled in its expression than in pluralistic societies and differences in personal circumstances are less, but both factors are responsible for a good deal of day-to-day, and longer-term, variation in both individual and group behavior, and in heterodoxy of belief and attitude.

Description and analysis of the socio-cultural systems of Basarwa who were serfs and/or laborers on cattle-posts or ranches pose the problems of which areas of behavior are to be examined. On a ranch owned by a Motswana or European, Basarwa were socially and residentially separate from their masters. Outside working hours, there were effectively two socio-cultural systems operating: that of the Basarwa and that of the rancher. Furthermore, each ethnic group of Basarwa (e.g. of G/wi,

Nharo, !xõ, ≠xaũ//eĩ) separated itself from any others resident on the ranch, but to an extent less than the distance which stood between Basarwa and rancher.

Inherent variability

The culture of any foraging Basarwa people has a natural inherent variability reflecting the seasonal and annual changes in weather that directly influence the plants and animals on which hunting and gathering depend. Although these changes are imperative in the burden they place on the people, they are non-determinate. Thus, if given only meteorological data, one would find it is increasingly difficult to predict in any but the most general terms what the respective floristic, faunal, and socio-cultural responses would be.

The Kalahari is probably not unusual among deserts in the exuberant variety of climatic extremes with which it assails its inhabitants. However, because of strict seasonality and the absence of relief and, hence, of surface drainage, flood-years in the Kalahari are more marked in their observed effects on flora and fauna, temporarily extinguishing many human and animal food-plants and reviving others after absences of many decades. Such conditions bring about significant and abrupt changes in the subsistence base. Because of the great ecological diversity which surrounds the central Kalahari (e.g. the relative proximity of the Okavango swamps and the Zambesi and Limpopo valleys), there are populations of mammals, birds, and insects which can respond rapidly to changes by migrating into or out of the desert. These will alter the nature and levels of environmental stresses such as hunger and disease. Although major abnormalities of drought, flood, epidemic, or insect plague may occur only once in a human life span, such events and the solutions to the problems they engender, are remembered. The full range of cultural variability may therefore only be manifest over a period spanning two or more generations. This is clearly beyond the observational capability of any fieldworker. My point is that we should be open-minded in our receptiveness to, and interpretation of, historical evidence in the form of vernacular accounts and the records of surrounding peoples and of travelers.

I am unable to accept (Silberbauer 1991) the extreme, over-generalized claims of Wilmsen (1989). Nonetheless, it is commonplace that, for at least the two millennia since Bantu-speaking peoples have been present in the southern third of Africa, Kalahari Basarwa have experienced a great variety of major and minor, direct and indirect, cultural influences from one another and from non-Basarwa. For instance, they first adopted the design of bone arrowheads from far afield (Silberbauer 1965:55) then further adapted them by making modern substitutes from steel fencing-wire. Meanwhile, their population has been ravaged by infection such as tuberculosis, smallpox, and poliomyelitis as their territories have been invaded and usurped by Bantu-speaking and white pastoralists. Basarwa have often shown great ingenuity and resilience in their accommodation of these factors by adapting their own cultural behavior variously to withstand, tolerate, or benefit from influences, while retaining control of what happens to themselves. At other times some have been overwhelmed by the changes – sometimes, apparently, by their own choice – and have lost or chosen to abandon much or all of their social, political, and economic autonomy. With that some Basarwa lost a measure of their distinctive identity, as did other peoples who became incorporated in some larger, more powerful formation.

New and old knowledge

In the 1950s and 1960s G/wi bands were consensus polities. Their theology construed the role of humans and all of N!adima's other creatures as having to devise their own *modus vivendi* within the constraints of their respective capabilities and needs as ordained at the time of their creation. G/wi saw their own culture quite clearly as an artefact of their own design and meaning, with earlier practices having been replaced by new ones. Current practices would continue only as long as they were effective and convenient; if somebody's new idea was seen as preferable, then the band would adopt it. The people were sensitive to tedium and if a feasible personal variation on a too-familiar theme provided relief, it was welcomed even if it was not always adopted by others.

Some variations are immediately obvious. G/wi danced on many different occasions and for differing purposes. Therapeutic dances were performed to exorcise the evil which G//amama showered upon them in the form of mystical, invisible arrows. Women danced as part of their many cooperative games and men danced in imitation of birds and other animals to amuse others and show off their inventiveness and terpsichorean prowess. After I built an airstrip at ≠xade, airplane dances began to appear in the repertoires of some. Later, when a few other fliers and I used the strip fairly regularly, the dancing was refined to reflect the idiosyncrasies of each pilot's style of approach and landing – including embarrassing bounces after touchdown.

Some new experiences were incorporated into existing knowledge with greater difficulty, but the result was a similar seamlessness between the new and the old. Despite my attempts to reassure the people, the appearance of overwhelmingly unfamiliar phenomena like trucks and aircraft initially appeared to stall cognition. Then, after a few hours or a day or two, people would gather and examine the vehicle from a short distance. "We hear you that this thing will not bite [i.e. harm] us but we wish to take its wisdom and know it first." Lacking a concept of machinery, the G/wi saw these things as animate beings which, although under the control of the driver or pilot, moved of their own volition. Their nature and ethology had, therefore, to be deduced before they could be trusted.

The wheels of a truck are clearly its feet. The engine is the heart. Why, then, is it so noisy? It only roars when it runs, that is the manner of all hearts. What when it is silent? Then it sleeps. Does the heart stop then? I cannot know [only half-humorously] – would you creep up on a sleeping lion to listen if its heart is silent and feel if it is stopped? The heart is the motive power for all animals; it must also be thus with *kwene:dzi* (trucks).

Then the train of logic followed the clutch housing and transfer-case, the drive-shaft and through the differential to the axles – these are the sinews and muscles by which effort is exerted and the feet are made to move. There was a departure from the mammalian model: the differential housing was also the *kwene:sa's* (truck's) scrotum and the drive shaft its penis. As the noun has feminine gender (which commonly accords with biological sex) I challenged this interpretation. Came the riposte, "It is clear that a truck is like an hyena, male and female in one." (The female spotted hyena, *Crocuta crocuta*, has an elongated clitoris which resembles a penis, and a scrotum-like sack behind the clitoris, making it difficult to distinguish the sexes.) Four-wheel-drive trucks with two drive shafts and differential front and rear were simply seen as an elaboration of this hermaphroditic theme. I was puzzled when the radiator was identified as the vehicle's lungs, a notion which appeared to me to require an understanding of elementary physics. The explanation was a neat piece of reasoning and included the physics.

See, water is sometimes poured into its water-mouth [the radiator filler, which was distinct from its 'food-mouth', where petrol was poured in] after it has been running. It must be that it has sweated and grown thirsty. You know that when you run the sweat on your chest cools you. Here is the truck's chest and behind, inside, lie its lungs. See how it sucks in the wind when it is roaring from exertion [i.e. the intake of air caused by the radiator fan].

Aircraft were comparably interpreted in terms of *kx'keidzi* (eagles and vultures): both need to take off into the wind, the extension of flaps prior to landing was equated with the spreading of primary feathers, and even those wretched bounces were attributed to over-hasty touchdowns. It all accounted for their experience of these machines and fitted smoothly onto their considerable existing knowledge of mammals and birds. The question of breeding was raised and more or less answered by this comparison – "No man has ever seen the nest of $n \pm a$:tsoma [secretary bird, which is actually a non-breeding vagrant in the central Kalahari]; we do not know if they breed, but there they are – perhaps they live forever for no man has ever seen a dead one either."

The capacity to vary usages without impairing the integrity of the culture is also manifest in the perception and treatment of illness. The Kalahari is not exceptionally unhealthy but I was impressed by the general absence of chronic illness and of long-term sequelae to the fairly severe injuries which were regularly sustained by men, women, and children. Ailments were treated with medicines and/or healing dancing and were a matter of free public discussion. *Materia medica* and their use were also common topics of conversation. It was, thus, not seen as intrusive when I sought to trace medical histories and learn something of vernacular practice. Most complaints were treated by using plant or mineral materials which were readily available and were picked, dug or prepared when needed. Households also carried a stock of remedies which were not easily obtainable (e.g. those which came from plants of restricted occurrence and others of animal origin). Packed away some-where at the bottom of a dilly-bag, these would be brought out after longer or shorter searches and their uses and, where possible, origins explained to me. No two households carried the same range of items and some were found in only very few households. There was also consider-able diversity of belief in the efficacy of the remedies. Scorpions are ubiquitous and I treated people who had been stung by them (there being no vernacular remedy); it was natural that we should then discuss the problems of snakebite – a far less common occurrence. Although some two-thirds of households produced snakebite remedies, there was neither uniformity among the plant materials nor much agreement about the efficacy of any. Knowledge of their origins were very patchy; as every adult is a good field botanist I found this puzzling. It turned out that none had collected her or his own remedies but had obtained them second- or subsequent hand and had forgotten the source, if ever knowing it.

Differences in the religious beliefs of the members of the $\pm$xade band were of no apparent consequence to the people. All gave much the same account of N!adima's creation of the universe and present remoteness from it and its everyday life. But some maintained that adventuring men had come across very tall trees and had climbed them to find themselves in the Sky Country where N!adima and his wife, N!adisa, live with their children. Most dismissed this as fantasy, but without any rancor ("I have never seen tall trees, but perhaps they exist") or distress at the heterodoxy it represented. However, there was no such tolerance of any questioning of the validity of beliefs and attitudes concerning the condign sanctions against blatant blasphemy, greed, destructive fire-setting, and other deeds which would incite N!adima's wrath and bring it upon everybody in the band. The question of overt displays of respect to N!adima and his more notable creations was less clear; some were punctilious in saluting the new moon or praising the baking early summer sun and begging it to hasten its passage through the sky and bring the wet season. "I don't know whether or not it pleases N!adima. I only know that some things make him angry. I know of no way to please him. But let those people do those things – it may do good."

I was confused by the taboos on the consumption by children, young adults, or young women of certain animals' meat. Informants gave different precepts and there was frequent conflict between them and practice. (This may well have been my fault – imperfect knowledge of G/wi ways and language enhances one's natural propensity to get the bull by the wrong horn.) The consequences of transgression of taboos were dire: a girl or boy eating a snake would be expected to sicken and waste away. A young woman would become sterile and a young man would weaken, perhaps fatally. When snakes were, indeed, eaten by them it was only in times which, retrospectively, were described as being of great hardship. When nothing untoward appeared to befall them, desperation at the inclemency of the conditions was both the excuse and explanation of non-operation of the taboo (although it seemed to me that things were far from as desperate as claimed). While their lists of prohibited meats differed, people nevertheless appeared to take the food-avoidances very seriously.

The contrast between what I saw in the 1950s and 1960s and Jiro Tanaka's experience of the ╪xade band a decade later (Tanaka 1980b) is an example of adaptive cultural change which was well beyond the range of inherent variation. During my time with them the ╪xade people's normal residential pattern involved first a series of single, shared camps lasting from early summer (i.e. as early as October, but more commonly starting in November or even December) until the imminent or actual onset of the first frosts of winter (some time between April and late June). After the first frost each household would retreat to isolation in its allocated winter range to await the return of conditions which would permit resumption of band camps. The band occupied a territory of some 900 km² – an overall population density of 0.094 persons per km² –

over which it presumed sole right of allocation of use of the resources. This right was affirmed in word and deed by other G/wi bands, who had occupied their own territories and followed a similar residential pattern-ing. In each shared band camp households clustered in groups which changed with each shift to a new site. I termed these clusters cliques. In the second, much more fruitful half of summer, it was common for one band to visit another in the latter's territory, forming a sort of mega-clique; during the short visit of, perhaps, two weeks, they built huts a short distance from those of the hosts with whom they interacted freely to the evident enjoyment of all. I judged this to be the normal pattern because the people told me that it was and it was what I saw happen in most years. In a rare year of good, prolonged, but not excessive rain followed by a mild winter it was possible for the band to avoid winter dispersal into isolated households – a much-welcomed circumstance. In drought years plant growth was so sparse that a shared camp would have to shift to new resources within a week or ten days. This was seen as tiresome and wasteful of energy. At these times the band arranged itself in several camps, each with a membership approximating that of a clique. There were fairly frequent moves of individual households from one camp to another, reflecting the temporary nature of cliques. Although the people resented and regretted this inconvenience and deprivation of the company of the band's full membership in a single camp, they considered it a normal burden to bear.

Tanaka's study (Tanaka 1980b) of the G/wi centered around ≠xade Pan and the recently equipped government borehole near it. He reported a strategy of residential patterning radically different from that which I had experienced there before the existence of the borehole. I interpret the variation as an adaptation to accommodate a semi-permanent influx from other bands without critical loss of cohesive social organization. This development, triggered by the coincidence of deepening drought and the unprecedented provision of a year-round supply of water anywhere in the Central Kalahari, was not foreseen by those officials who arranged for the supply nor by the G/wi themselves. What is interesting is that the latter were able to extemporize a variation of their customary organizational theme to produce at least a tolerable, workable solution to a problem which they would not nor-mally have experienced or even envisaged. As I see it, they had adapted the device of cliques to form and order more nearly permanent sub-camps, each with a measure of internal autonomy but, together, func-tioning as a much-extended band. Here was not revolutionary cultural variation but something more like startlingly saltatory evolution. They achieved the adaptation without losing social coherence; Tanaka's description is of people confidently and competently managing their relationships.

This situation was very different from that which developed during May of 1964 (Silberhauer 1965:106) when the borehole was sunk and the drilling-crew, with every good intention, gave the local Basarwa free access to the yield during the months that the crew was in the area. When news of this boon reached others, nearly three hundred rapidly gathered at ǂxade. The hodgepodge of kin, friends, and strangers crowded together with plentiful water but with an inadequate and diminishing food supply had neither time nor, apparently, means of organizing themselves. Consequently they faced serious problems of disease, hunger, and social disorder. In the years between this unfortunate experience and Tanaka's visit the G/wi of ǂxade and their fellow Basarwa in the central Kalahari took much thought and were able to handle the next 'pluvial' much more happily.

Basarwa on Ghanzi ranches

In *Bushman survey* (1965:62) I mentioned that there is significant cultural diversity among G/wi but that "shared language and culture give a certain feeling of affinity but not of unity"; concomitantly they distinguished themselves from others with whom they did not feel this affinity. In the context of the present discussion some amplification of this statement is needed. I have already referred to the acceptance of non-G/wi band fellows as equals, even though their different accents and experience were remarked on. In bands whose territories were not too distant from the Ghanzi ranching area the extension of the notion of affinity to those G/wi who lived permanently as ranch laborers was apparent among families who came out of the desert to the ranches in dry years and temporarily settled themselves among their compatriots. The bonds of language were invoked and greatly reinforced when kinship could be established (a highly likely event in view of the universalistic nature of G/wi kinship reckoning). Here was unquestionable cultural diversity. There were three groups of G/wi each representing a different cultural pattern. First are those who remained in the remote parts of the central Kalahari with no direct contact with ranches, cattle-posts, villages or towns. Then there were the desert-dwellers who periodically trekked to the closest, north-eastern ranches because they preferred the lean rations and (to them) limitless supply of water to constant thirst and nagging hunger, even though it meant continuing hunger, boring months with little to do, a time of stilted social interaction, and apprehension at the presence of what they saw as dangerous strangers. Third were the ranch laborers who had learned many new skills but, at the same time had lost some of the traditional ones, the practice of which constituted a large part of the frame of reference for the exchange of goods and services by which many social relationships were established, expressed, and adjusted.

A description of the conditions of ranch Basarwa in the 1950s makes clear the transition from customary band life to that of a temporary visitor or squatter, as they were known.

At that time the north-eastern ranches were nearly all owned and run by members, descendants or kin of the original party of white settlers who had come north from the Transvaal and from Stellaland and Goshen (short-lived Boer republics now part of the Northwestern Province of South Africa) a hundred years ago. According to Martinus Drotsky (1956: personal communication), son of the leader of the trek, an advance party arrived to scout the suitability of the land which Cecil Rhodes and his British South Africa Company were offering them. This party was caught by drought at Kgoutsa, near Ghanzi. The men made a dash across the desert to organize rescue (which seems a singularly futile gesture under the circumstances), leaving the women and children, including Martinus, in the care of the resident Basarwa. Eighteen months later the men managed to return and found that the Basarwa had taken excellent care of their wives and children. Margo and Martin Russell (1979) make no mention of this episode in their carefully researched book. There is some archival evidence in support of it but, true or not, the tale is part of white Ghanzi rancher folklore and has forever put the descendants of the first party (in time, this meant all of the "old" Ghanzi white families) in the debt of Basarwa.

The relevance of this is that in the 1950s it would have been a shameful thing for a rancher to turn Basarwa off his land or refuse to give them succor when hungry or ill, even though the ranchers were themselves far from comfortably off in those days. For a G/wi household in time of drought a temporary move to one of the north-eastern ranches were consequently a fairly attractive alternative to struggling through a particularly harsh, hot, dry, first half of summer in the desert. Food was scarce in either case but a ranch provided unlimited drinking water. If the distance was not too great and the trek not too hard, the move could mean the difference between death and survival but, usually, was that between extreme and nagging discomfort.

The life of a G/wi, or other Mosarwa man or woman in regular employment or simply permanently residing on one of the north-eastern ranches differed in many significant respects from that of one who was a hunter or gatherer in a band. There was the obvious matter of food: on a ranch it was a steady, sufficient, but never plentiful supply of maize-meal and beef or goat-mutton and cultivars like pumpkins, beans, sorghum, maize, and melons grown when summers were neither so dry as to wither the crop nor so moist as to unleash plagues of ground-crickets, locusts, and other all-destroying pests. These were supplemented by thin pickings of small game like steenbok, duiker, and springhare, and food-plants which, because of the cattle's grazing and trampling and the goats' relentless browsing, were present in smaller amounts and variety than were to be found in the desert. Only rarely did herds of larger antelope stray onto the (then) unfenced ranches. Then there would be short-lived plenty as the ever-ready rifles of game-hungry ranchers were used to chase the pasture-consuming, disease-bearing intruders off. (On one most memorable occasion a hippopotamus wandered down from the Botete River; even the hunting-lust of Basarwa, Bantu, and Boer was checked by the poor creature's distress and confusion. Unmolested, but watered at great risk to life, limb, and troughs, it blundered across one ranch after another eventually to perish in the desert.)

The Basarwa ranch hands, servants, and their families depended on the rancher for their living. For their part, White and Colored ranchers (in the 1950s and 1960s there were not yet any Black ranchers) were dependent on the labor of substantial numbers of Basarwa for the running of their labor-intensive enterprises. In the 1950s, before properties were fenced and when about the only mechanical power to be found on a ranch was a motor vehicle, many hands were needed for watering, herding, and mustering stock. Travel was on foot, by donkey, or by horse, and goods were carried on animal-drawn wagons or sleds. Anybody sent on an errand was away for a long time, necessitating her or his replacement by somebody else when other tasks were to be performed.

Great social distance stood between ranchers and workers in their off-duty lives. Despite their interdependence, each group developed its own internal patterns and dynamics of behavior. This separation contrasted with the close, coherent and integrated interaction between employer and employees necessary to farming. There were, thus, three interdependent socio-cultural subsystems: first, that of the Basarwa, which was linked to those on other ranches and, in the case of G/wi and other groups with band connections, to those of the remote desert. Second, that of the rancher and his family. This was linked to the White or Colored rancher community and, through government and commercial structures, to the rest of the country. In the Ghanzi rancher culture Whites and Coloreds lent their distinctive variations to it. Within these two sub-categories, further variation arose from the fiercely individualistic ethos of ranchers and their relative isolation from one another. Thus, although there were many similarities to be found on the ranches, there were also great, and important, differences. The third system was the arrangements by which the ranch was operated. Although differences among these arrangements were limited by the commonality of ranching techniques, the variability found in the other two subsystems exerted its influence. Faced by such complexity, it is difficult usefully to generalize about cultural variability among ranch Basarwa. I have, therefore, distinguished their "off-duty" culture from that of their work. The former was obviously strongly influenced by the circumstance of employment but it was something devised by Basarwa as the means of integrating, or reconciling, their habits and traditions with that circumstance. It was as much "their culture" as was that of a desert band.

Ranch Basarwa lived in sedentary, fairly stable groups. They constructed their own wattle-and-daub huts within convenient distance from bore-hole and homestead. As well as the employees, there were also unemployed friends and kin attached to, and more numerous than the workers, so that most ranches had between thirty and fifty more or less permanent residents. Some had fewer and some had over a hundred.

Although subject to the sufferance of the rancher, they largely ordered their own lives out of working hours. This was by no means a simple matter. Even in the north-west, few ranches had only G/wi workers; Nharo came over from the south-west, ≠xau//ei from the north-west and, in later years, Bantu-speaking Tawana, Kgalagari, and Herero from north, south, and west. Ethnicity was proclaimed by language and reinforced by the disdain which others had for the unassertive G/wi. It was manifest in residential separation, each group clustering its huts a small distance from others. Interaction among the residents of each cluster was more intensive; conversation, sharing, lending, and borrowing of possessions, and mutual child-minding occurred more frequently within such groups than between them. However, if they were to remain as residents on the ranch, the laborers, their friends, kin, and visitors, all had to interact and function as a reasonably cohesive group, despite traditional dislike and suspicion.

If there is to be any order in a group its members should have a tolerable level of confidence in their expectations of others' behavior, and of others' reactions to their own actions. These expectations do not depend upon a milieu of regimented, stereotyped behavior, but are formed from a substrate of formal and informal, enduring and ephemeral structures. Expectations are also guided by peer reaction to the quality of performance of roles within those structures and of the particular structure which is deemed relevant to the specific situation. In combination, all these give reasonable clarity of intended meaning of action, and of outcome. Interpersonal behavior must communicate information (i.e. that which reduces uncertainty) about which set of conventions is to apply in the particular situation and interaction.

Ranch roles did parallel social structure within a band where there was a dense network of mutual dependencies for all activities and needs. Roles were not narrowly prescribed but were negotiated within fairly broad structural principles. Kinship accorded to those within each category certain rights and obligations, the full extent and qualities of which were defined by agreement, often tacitly. Rights and obligations were also subject to other, cross-cutting factors, like respective ranges and levels of skills of individuals and, furthermore, their rights and obligations *vis-à-vis* others. Although many of the expectations arising from these arrangements related to pragmatic needs, e.g. the rendering of economically significant goods and services, their social and affective meanings were commonly of equal, or greater importance.

The meaning accorded to behavior by a particular group is not determinate, but is arbitrary in nature and depends not only on agreement for its establishment but also on frequent affirmation for its maintenance. An "audience" of other band fellows (whether actually present or only in the minds of the participants in the transaction) was therefore necessary both to give and to receive confirmation of the meaning of the interaction and to mediate, arbitrate or explain where uncertainty arose. In the intimacy and relative stability of a band such uncertainty was slight, short-lived or rare, being removed by the ample opportunities provided, and taken for comment and discussion. There was, therefore, a prevailing high level of confidence in a member's expectations of others' behavior, and their responses to her or his own actions. Social life, although fluid and subject to radical change through the circumstances of season, departures and arrivals, birth, death, marriage, and divorce, was generally well ordered.

The "off-duty" social life of G/wi and other Basarwa on ranches was markedly less secure, harmonious, and orderly. The differing usages and values of other, non-G/wi ethnic groups also present on the ranch engendered confusion and conflict. Also, there was the potent fact that services were rendered to, and goods and authority received from, the rancher, which limited the range and meanings of exchanges of services and goods between Basarwa. Furthermore, the rancher's authority was of a political nature (i.e. relating to the individuals or groups that manage matters of public affairs – here those concerning the population

of the ranch – see Fried 1967:20–1) and it also defined the tasks and
services to be done by workers and the criteria by which their rationale,
value, quality, and meaning would be judged and understood.

Skill is a social construct as well as a reference to ability in that each
social group confers more or less specific meaning and varying measures
of prestige upon particular capabilities. An important element in the
web of social order is assessment of both role and the quality of the due
performance within it. Where the criteria of judgment of that quality are
neither fully understood nor controlled by performers, confusion
impairs order. Workers did not share the cultural heritage of the
rancher, had slender and unreliable means of learning his meanings and
criteria (and, sometimes, of acquiring requisite skills) or of negotiating
their definitions. Separated from him by a wide chasm of culture,
values, and, often, language, both workers and unemployed ranch-
dwellers had to conform to unfamiliar standards. They had to fulfil
expectations which were strange to them and learn new tasks if they
were to earn a living and the rancher's tolerance of their continued
residence on the property. They had also to discover the new bounds of
acceptability and relevance of their customary behavior, values, and
meanings and to amend them where necessary, abandoning life-long
patterns of thought and feelings. This had to be done in a reasonably
coordinated fashion if the great range of cooperative work done on a
ranch was to be performed successfully. It was not necessary that all
knowledge should be completely shared. There was a measure of
specialization even among semi-skilled laborers. Domestic work done
by women and older girls was, for instance, rigidly separated from the
outdoor tasks of the men. Among the latter there were those who had
some knowledge of machinery or of the more skilled aspects of fencing
and there were yet others who mainly did stock work. Furthermore,
there was the annual trans-Kalahari trek when cattle were walked the
700-odd km. to the abattoir and railhead at Lobatse. This was hard
work, high adventure, and contact with civilization and strange peoples
and ways. Such experience and knowledge could not be fully shared but,
so that tasks could be integrated, any worker had to have some understanding of what others did. On successful ranches, i.e. those which
yielded a reasonable income and among whose residents a fair measure
of harmony prevailed, it was achieved by frequent and open communication between rancher and Basarwa, and by the latter sharing information among themselves. Such places required a demonstration of the
empathetic skills, patience, and ingenuity of Basarwa and rancher. Some
ranches, however, were dreary wastelands of badly managed pasture,
poor stock, and general poverty with demoralized workers and bitter,

defeated ranchers blaming one another for failure and abrasive relations apparent among all.

There was abundant opportunity for disharmony. Ranch-workers were subject to the authority of the rancher, who had the power to order workers or visitors off his land. In fact this seldom occurred and always had to be done with a measure of perceived justification. Had it not been so, kinfolk, other ranchers, and friends would have murmured their disapproval. Aggrieved Basarwa could have resorted to revenge in various ways such as sabotaging stock or equipment or going to the police with false charges which, even if thrown out of court, would entail a good deal of bother for anybody thus accused. The farmer's authority was frequently invoked as an ostensibly neutral means of resolving disputes, righting wrongs, and dealing with other interpersonal problems. As every rancher had his favorites who could, to some extent, tailor his view of any event or situation by their manner of its presentation to him, bias was often present. Nevertheless, his intervention could be seen as not involving kin or friends in what might be invidious resolution. Many of the problems were insoluble by the means available to the Basarwa laborers because the traditional sanctions were unworkable, or because there were ethnic differences in values and perceptions of the problem. The rancher's solution was seen as binding on all and not essentially favoring any. Susan Kent (Kent 1989b) and Kuper and I (Silberbauer and Kuper 1966) found this same readiness among other Basarwa to turn to outside authority when their traditional band structures had been disrupted and were inoperative or were seen as no longer adequate. As traditional structures functioned in a context of agreement to seek consensus, it is understandable that they should be doubted when there was insufficient confidence in the context of agreement and a more nearly coercive substitute had to be sought. Basarwa, with some justification, saw themselves and one another as threatened by almost everybody else and thus in need of unity against shared dangers. Thus, if A and B could not agree on the respective rights and wrongs of their conflict, or even about the definition of the *casus belli*, they considered themselves better served by perhaps suffering an unjust imposed solution than by intensifying and perpetuating the strife through never coming to agreement over its principles and perhaps entangling other valued relationships in the conflict. Injustice was commonplace but was less evil than worsening disharmony. If tolerable harmony could not be restored by these means the only remaining remedy was for one of the parties to move away to another ranch, which was often a very costly step.

Ranch Basarwa thus found themselves with a good deal less control over their activities and relationships than was the case in band society. In the latter milieu competence in any socially significant activity brought a corresponding measure of prestige. A high level of capability usually meant that the individual was a leader in that particular field, often initiating action and always having due weight given to her or his relevant suggestions and opinions. Use of expertise was a commodity which, when given as a service, was a means of creating, expressing or modifying relationships as well as constituting an economic transaction. In ranch life competence did not always have social meaning for other Basarwa. A ǂxau//ei friend of mine, for instance, was one of the best fencers in the district. In his hands a pair of fencing pliers became a magician's wand as he demonstrated his exceptional intelligence in devising novel uses of this versatile tool. I have learned from, and worked with, many professional fencers in Central Australia and on my own property in Victoria – none of them was his equal. His skill was recognized by ranchers and other laborers but had no significance out of working hours, when he became a nonentity. A reserved man, he had little to offer as company to his fellows. Although he had great know- ledge of field botany and vernacular herbalism, it had been devalued by shop-bought remedies and the distant government health-center. He was one of the few lonely Basarwa I ever knew.

Household relationships were comparably disordered by the partici- pants' confusion and reduced measure of control over them. Spouses were unable to meet complementary obligations because their respective capabilities were limited by the restricted activities and their social meanings of ranch laborers' lives. With almost no game on the ranches unemployed men were not able to hunt and had no access to the animal products which were the raw materials of clothing and many other artefacts. Few of these traditional adult male skills were relevant to ranch life. Unable to provide more than a narrow range of goods and services for which there was, in any case, seldom much demand, men had correspondingly small opportunity for the transactions which were necessary to the traditional conduct of relationships. Women were almost as badly off as there was little that could be gathered – even firewood was a long day's walk away on the longer-established properties where cattle and goats had stripped the unstable sands of vegetation in a wide area around the well or borehole where the huts stood. The resulting imbalance in capability deprived marriage of much of its rationale and reward. Parent–child bonds were also attenuated. Traditional sanctions against familial neglect were negated by the comparative ease with which a defaulting spouse, parent or child could abscond to another ranch beyond the reach of not only spouse, children or parents but also kin and significant others whose opprobrium and actions might otherwise have had a restraining effect. Those who had been deserted were then dependent on their friends and kin, and on the rancher, and were largely bereft of means of reciprocating the goods and services that they were given.

The extent of social disarray varied from one ranch to another, correlating well with the type of relationship between rancher and resident Basarwa. A happy relationship was usually indicated by the fluency of the rancher and his family in the language(s) of the other residents. But facility in another's language reveals more than it hides of the attitude one holds towards the other; some ranchers used their fluency to tighten the noose of the resident Basarwa's dependence on them. However, where the relationship with the landholder was stable and harmonious, Basarwa tended to remain on the one property, extending and consolidating their links of kinship and friendship among themselves. Here systems developed in which work was shared so that no adult was permanently and hopelessly unemployed. The difficulties of devising appropriate goods and services for social trans-actions were alleviated, but never completely removed, in the 1950s and 1960s.

G/wi, G//ana and other central Kalahari Basarwa who made the temporary shift to the ranches in drought years encountered this diver-gence from their own ways of social and cultural practices. A group would only seek refuge among kin, so there was always an element present among the ranch residents to whom they were known and from whom they could take some direction in adapting to the circumstances of life on the particular ranch. Depending on the severity of the season, squatters would wait between two and six months for the onset of the rains and then return to their band territories. Workers and other regular residents shared their meagre fare with the visitors and every-body went hungry. The pleasure of renewing contact with friends and relatives soon waned to be replaced by boredom. Before long there was friction and misery and all were equally anxious for the rains to come and the visitors to go.

However, these drought treks did constitute an opportunity for sharing news and gossip and as a vector for the spread of information about the wider world which was passed on from band to band to diffuse across the central Kalahari. They were also the occasion for a small circulation of population between ranches and desert as a few households decided to remain on the ranches and a small number of others chose to leave with the visitors and return to band life.

Basarwa, cattle-posts, and villages

It is thus evident that, among G/wi and G//ana, there were radical cultural and social differences between those whose whole lives were spent in bands, those who occasionally sought succor on ranches, and those who were permanent residents of ranches. But how is one to categorize these differences and the groups among whom they represent typical patterns of life?

The small but recurrent circulation of population between ranches, trekking bands, and those who remained permanently in their desert territories meant that some individuals and households experienced all three patterns and the total variety became part of their individual culture. To them each pattern was clearly distinguishable from the others, even though several other people might share part, or all of the range of plurality. Among other Basarwa there was comparable circulation of population between bands and the villages and cattle-posts of Bantu-speaking pastoralists in other parts of Botswana and consequent cultural variety. Kuper and I (1966) described the culture and relationships of (mainly Nharo) Basarwa and Kgalagari in Kuli village. Although the village and cattle-post situations were by no means stereotyped, the breadth of cultural variety which we encountered was representative.

The ethnic factor in the adaptations which Basarwa made to ranch, village, or cattle-post life was always apparent in their languages; however many other languages an individual acquired (some had as many as six), fellow native-speakers remained the preferred social circle. Such aggregation tended to produce a measure of uniformity in the subculture of, for instance, the G/wi on a particular ranch. But there was little such uniformity among the G/wi from ranch to ranch. Their culture and social organization (and disorganization) were heavily influenced by the circumstances of the particular ranch: e.g., the extent and manner of the rancher's intentional and inadvertent intervention in their lives, and the mix and proportions of ethnic origins of the Basarwa. There was comparable diversity among Basarwa on cattle-posts and in villages.

The Nharo, whose country ran from the central ranches west to the Gobabis district of Namibia, also worked as ranch hands or were dependent on them. Many lived as serfs in Kgalagari and Mbanderu villages and cattle-posts and others lived on white-owned ranches in Namibia and in the town of Gobabis. In the 1950s the border between what were then the Bechuanaland Protectorate and South-West Africa was unmarked and open, permitting free movement across it. Although generally inclined to be sedentary, many Nharo chose to explore. Some traveled to avoid vengeance, justice or irreconcilable conflict. A few followed the peregrinations of their employers. All, to greater or lesser extent according to their circumstances and needs, learned and adopted what they encountered of Nharo cultural variations.

The range of circumstances to which Nharo had to adapt was even more varied than that of the G/wi. Guenther (1976, 1979b, 1986a, b) has described these with great insight and knowledge. Bantu cattle-posts and villages presented a pastoral technology quite different to that of the ranches and, very importantly, another set of attitudes to Basarwa. Kuper and I (1966) concluded that the relationship in the study village was one of masters and serfs; it appeared to be typical of the area. Bantu-speaking masters had more extensive rights over, and obligations towards, their serfs than ranchers had over their laborers. The life of Nharo serfs were intruded upon to a greater extent. Some conflict of laws occurred here; some of the *de jure* and *de facto* rights which, for instance, Kgalagari law and custom conferred on masters were intolerable to the statutory and Roman-Dutch law of the Protectorate. Although this may sometimes have curbed excess, it surely added to the uncertainty and confusion facing Basarwa. These were further exacerbated by the fact that a black policeman might react to a Mosarwa's complaint in one way, and a white police officer or adminstrator in a quite different manner. (This is not to cast calumny on the Details and Non-commissioned Officers of the Bechuanaland Protectorate Police – they often achieved justice by wise negotiation and mediation without recourse to law. The B.P.P. had more merit and less evil than any other police force that I have encountered.)

Across the border in South-West Africa (now Namibia) ranching practices were more modern and commercially oriented. Labor was a commodity for which payment was made only for as long as it was satisfactory to the employer. Basarwa were regarded as poor workers and were treated accordingly. Here, as everywhere in southern Africa, society generally considered them to be inferior human beings and few ever stood up in their defence. Nevertheless, the Mandated Territory offered cash wages and the excitement of greater sophistication, even rudimentary schooling, and some Protectorate Nharo explored these benefits for shorter or longer periods. Missionaries introduced Judeo-Christian doctrine which merged, unequally and more or less unconformably, with vernacular belief to add to Nharo cultural variety.

This range of cultural diversity was not shared by all G/wi, G//ana, Nharo or other Basarwa. While there might have been close bonds of affection between a domestic servant and her sister in a remote band, the former's knowledge of homestead layout, routine, foods, and their preparation would not have been shared by the latter and the sister on the ranch would have lost much of the knowledge and skill of desert living. However, each would have unequivocally considered herself to be G/wi. The anthropologist who sets up categories for the purpose of cultural comparison would clearly be wrong in generalizing to all G/wi women a competence in Ghanzi Afrikaner homestead domestic science. It may be more helpful to acknowledge cultural plurality in which there are mutually exclusive elements (i.e. A possesses X cultural attributes, B possesses attributes Y; A does not have Y and B does not have X). However, the variability of adaptations to band, ranch, town, village, or cattle-post life indicates, first, that there is nothing determinate in these circumstances and, second, that one would require a separate category for each band and ranch. No doubt the accumulation of these minute data would impress somebody but, as an end in itself, taxonomic combing with such fine teeth looks like idiot meticulousness. Anthropology's task is to *explain* human social and cultural behavior – and its variability – and does not end with mere recording and typology.

Relativism and rationality

Explanation of variation across the G/wi spectrum of remote and trekker bands and the G/wi-occupied ranches must extend beyond the bounds of purely G/wi society to include the "alien" factors. But this does not, in my view, entail adopting the World System perspective. However powerful and inexorable the influences to change may be, they are not determinate in the sense that they will invariably produce precisely the same effect. Those upon whom the influences are exercised perceive and respond to them in the light of their own cultural knowledge and other resources, imparting distinctiveness to the outcome. Even something as culturally overwhelming as slavery was not determinate; slaves of the Dutch East India Company at the Cape of Good Hope led lives which differed from those in Batavia or in Holland (see Ross 1983). In the central Kalahari the external factors of change must be understood *as the G/wi see them*. Unless this is done the anthropologist has no recourse other than divesting the people of their rationality or, *faute de mieux*, of imposing her or his own rationality on them. Neither position is tenable. Evidence of the rationality of G/wi thought is at least as persuasive as is that of western thought but it also indicates that the respective styles of reasoning do not always arrive at the same conclusions, i.e. that G/wi (G//ana, !Kung, Nharo, or whatever) rationality is somehow different.

As a recidivist cultural relativist the suggestion of difference comforts rather than alarms me. Any logical structure that is to be more than a completely abstract notion – is to be employed in rational thought – must rest on one or more assumptions. The structure must be consistent with the assumption(s) but cannot be used as proof of the validity of the latter. It is commonplace that perceptions and interpretations of experience differ and are, to a considerable extent, learned, and that such learned perception and interpretation are often culture-specific. Furthermore, the products of such culturally learned perception and interpretation are partial in that both processes select certain aspects as significant and reject others. Thus, as a lay suburbanite, I might look upon an afternoon thunderstorm simply as a thing of beauty, thinking only of its colors and awesome symmetry of form to which lightning and thunder merely lend dramatic embellishment. Then, as the first drops slash about me, I may belatedly anticipate an imminent deluge from which I had better seek shelter. A meteorologist, however, might ignore all the Gainsborough gold and perceive this cumulonimbus and predict its future activity in terms of fluid mechanics, differences in pressure, temperature, and humidity, and characteristics of the surrounding air masses. Lightning would be a matter of charged particles and, perhaps, debates about their polarity. In the central Kalahari a G/wi would tell me about the mystical leopard in the thunderstorm, that lightning is the flashing of its eyes and thunder its growl, then give me a forecast framed in terms of leopard ethology. The respective sets of assumptions about the nature of thunderstorms are hopelessly at variance from each other. But the G/wi, the meteorologist and I, on hearing each others' explanations of how we applied logic to those assumptions, would agree about the validity of that logic and recognize it as common to all of us. This is not to say that each set of assumptions is of equal validity and of equal explanatory and predictive value. My lay perception, founded on generous ignorance, might leave me struck dead by a bolt of lightning. (My late mother, who had much experience of lightning but inclined to a non-conformist interpretation thereof, would have insisted that it was because I had recently been talking on the telephone.) Although so different, the constructs of both the weathermen and the G/wi would have warned me against standing out in the open, particularly if near or under trees, once the storm came within a certain distance. Each would, in all probability, have given accurate indications of the storm's movements over the following two or three hours, the amount and intensity of rainfall, and the frequency of flashes of lightning. My assumptions (and, I suspect, my mother's) about the nature of thunderstorms would have been quite unable to inform me on these matters. Unless I came to know the assumptions of the Mosarwa and the meteorologist, I would have had no way of following their logical applications of them and might have taken their conclusions to be either lucky guesses, groundless opinions (i.e. non-rational) or superstitious nonsense (irrational).

The G/wi interpretation of their experience of motor vehicles, described above, illustrates recognizably valid use of logic. Although founded on the mistaken assumption that the trucks were living creatures, G/wi reasoning reached conclusions which – however much in conflict with our notions of automotive mechanics – satisfactorily met their particular needs to accommodate the experience of vehicles in their lives and explain and predict the behavior of the trucks. By contrast my interpretation of my experience of precognition among Basarwa is based on the assumption that the phenomenon does not exist so I am left in a state of logical paralysis, unable to meet my, or anybody else's, explanatory needs.

To explain G/wi culture, in whatever context we encounter it, we are surely required to come to know and understand their assumptions, their perceptions of experience, and their interpretations of it so that we can follow the logic by which they link phenomena together in systematic relationships to make sense of experience and act purposefully in the light of it. Otherwise we will be unable to explain their social and cultural behavior and its variations within those contexts.

The epithet, Basarwa

Understanding the logic of the G/wi is assisted by some knowledge of their history. In the four decades since the 1950s Botswana has experienced growth in its population; communications have improved and the relative isolation of Basarwa and of other groups in the central and western parts of the country has been largely broken down. Earlier cultural contacts have intensified and diversified and the intended and inadvertent consequences of government action and inaction have done little to foster among Basarwa a sense of valued ethnic identity which might otherwise have enabled them to join together to absorb and adapt to these influences while maintaining their own cultural and social integrity. This is not to argue for their having been left in isolation and "pristine primitiveness." Had they been given choice and the means of voicing their preferences, and had they then elected to remain as hunter-gatherers or poor and deprived ranch laborers or serfs, it is doubtful that the exercise of these improbable preferences would have been feasible. What I am saying is that they were given very few choices, had few means or opportunities for formulating and voicing choice, and virtually no power to influence their own fate. The outcome is a wide diversity of cultural and social practices. But it is a fragmented diversity with fewer and fewer cultural meanings common to, and shared by, those who were previously mutually recognizable as kin, friends or potential friends because of their shared language. Their future may bring a complete loss of cultural identity or, as Australian Koories, Murries, and other Aborigines, and First Nation peoples in North America, are doing. Basarwa peoples may wish, and may be allowed, and may become able to gather enough strength from one another and from competent sympathisers to forge a new identity and to connect it coherently with their roots.

Attributing cultural variability among Kalahari Basarwa to ethnic distinctiveness raises the question of the validity of grouping the peoples together in the category, Basarwa. This category – or its misuse – has caused as much mischief in anthropology as has that of Pygmy (see Barry Hewlett's plaint in this volume). Both are inventions of aliens and are about equal in their lack of precision and meaning. The category, Basarwa, was coined by Tswana and other Bantu-speaking people, from the root *-sarwa* or some other derivative of the hypothesized Proto-Bantu *-twa*. This category has been reinforced by Europeans referring to them as Soaqua, Sonqua, San, *Bosjesmans, Boesmans, Buschmänner, les Boschimans*, Bushmen or Basarwa. There is no vernacular term which denotes more than one group (e.g. !xô, G/wi, G//ana). Almost all of these are terms of self-appellation. There are genetic links among the various groups which, although never close, and sometimes quite distant (see Harpending and Jenkins 1973; Nurse and Jenkins 1977), are stronger among the Basarwa generally than between them and any other element of the population. Some of these links are expressed as physical resemblances, e.g. stature, skin color, eye shape. Like the physical make-up of other population groups, these are commonly the basis of classification. Such classification is innocuous in itself but becomes pernicious when accompanied by false attribution of behavioral correlates like intelligence or innate morality, or as the reason for exclusion from access to the rights, privileges, and pleasures enjoyed by others. Physical resemblance is, however, neither a necessary nor a sufficient condition for cultural similarity.

The click consonants which occur in the languages of all Basarwa groups (although the full range does not occur in all languages) excite much attention. These are not unique to Basarwa (and Khoi) but are also indigenous to Hadza and Sandawe of East Africa. Some click consonants are also found in Nguni languages (e.g. Zulu, Xhosa, Swati), Sotho, and some of the South-western Bantu languages, apparently having been acquired from Khoi and Basarwa. That two voiceless clicks

(/ and //) occur in European languages (e.g. English, Afrikaans) as interjections is hardly relevant here. The rarity of clicks as an indigenous feature of phonetic and phonemic structures led many to assume a common origin of all click languages. This may be so but the origin is now so remote as not to be reflected in any significant incidence of correspondence of the sounds and meanings of words not only between Southern and East African languages in which clicks occur, but also among the major families of languages spoken by Kalahari Basarwa (Traill, 1978a), precluding any test of the hypothesis. (Within each family, however, there are lexical and grammatical similarities which are often close enough to make some languages mutually intelligible.) The presence of indigenous click consonants is therefore not, in itself, a basis for categorization.

Ample archaeological evidence links ancient cultural and physical remains in the southern third of Africa to modern Basarwa sufficiently closely to suggest their ancestry. Combined with the genetic evidence this appears to justify formation of a category of people whose ancestors, or who themselves, lived as hunters and gatherers in the southern third of Africa, including the Kalahari in what is now Botswana. There is a long history of the use of bows and arrows; of digging-sticks; ostrich eggs (whole for holding water, pieces for ornamental beadwork); game hides for blankets, skirts and breechclouts; and of brush windbreaks and roughly thatched huts for shelter by all groups. Some – but by no means all – made beautiful engravings or paintings on rock surfaces or etched ostrich eggshells. That is about the extent of shared characteristics beyond which cultural generalizations about Kalahari Basarwa are of dubious or no validity. As Barry Hewlett shows in his chapter, the extent of characteristics common to forest foragers is comparably narrow.

The whirligig of fashion still spins; until about the 1970s we aliens referred to them as Bushmen, encompassing all pre-Bantu southern Africans who were not Khoi-khoi. Then came the ill-chosen term, San. In the 1980s the Botswana Government chose Basarwa as the name for those of its citizens who had been categorized as San. Bushman had been rejected because of its perjorative use in Afrikaans (*Boesman*) in reference to those who, in South Africa, were termed Colored. (A broad category, it included descendants both of Southeast Asians brought to the Cape by the Dutch East India Company and of those who were called Bushmen. They deeply resented being called *Boesmans*.) Now, in post-apartheid South Africa, some of relevant descent in the Western and Eastern Cape, and Northwest provinces, have chosen to identify themselves as Bushmen, or *Boesmans*. We may, perhaps, return to Bushmen as the label for this inexact category of ours.

Cultural diversity among Basarwa peoples

Beliefs

Belief systems vary significantly. In the 1950s and 1960s G/wi theology depicted a creator of the universe whom one might, perhaps simplistically, characterize as a god of order. N!adima lived in the Sky Country with his wife, N!adisa, and their children. He was not only physically remote from the inhabited world, but also held himself aloof from it for most of the time. He had created the universe as a self-regulating system in which – as I have said – humans, animals and other life-forms had to devise their own *modus vivendi* within their capabilities and needs bestowed at the time of their creation and without disrupting natural (i.e. N!adima's) order. Humans were sufference tenants in the inhabited world, neither greater nor less than other creatures. He would sporadically intervene to harm or destroy some person of whom he had "grown tired" or to punish those who had offended against the order of his creation. Less frequently and unaccountably he would help somebody. There were no acts of worship, prayer or sacrifice by which people could influence him favorably but all took care to make clear their respect for him (and, by extension, his more powerful creations like the sun) so as to preclude the inference of impiety.

G//amama was the other supernatural being. He could assume many forms, appearing as a willy-willy or dust-devil, as a rampaging lion or leopard, or secretly as an invisible presence. He was powerful, but not invincible, and his constant attempts to harm people could often be frustrated by measures which they had discovered or invented for themselves. These include prophylactic avoidance of vulnerability (e.g. a man's not hunting while his wife was menstruating), herbal and other medicinal treatment and trance-dancing to prevent, or overcome, the ill effects of G//amama's doings. On more than one occasion self-protection extended to the severely pragmatic solutions of beating off the attacking lion or leopard. As I have mentioned, herbal remedies were used for treatment of snakebite and other injuries as well as illnesses. Plant materials were also introduced into tattoos during girls' menarchial and boys' initiation ceremonies to imbue them with good qualities. Hunters, too, were periodically tattooed to maintain their strength, eyesight, and cunning. The concept of magic is too imprecise in anthropology to enable one to decide whether these practices were generically different from therapeutic herbalism. Informants did not distinguish between them and I am inclined to conclude that the G/wi had little or no magic. Certainly they did not practice sorcery. They had knowledge of others' sorcery but dismissed it as delusion. ("It will harm you if you let it into your heart, like any other fear. If it does not enter your heart it cannot hurt you.")

In G/wi belief a post-mortem spirit remained near the grave for about a year, gradually losing power as it became incorporated in the underworld of monsters and others' spirits. A spirit of one who had recently died was lonely and angry at being wrenched from the society of kin and friends and sought company. Thus it was that such a spirit could "rob a person of understanding," stealing the living spirit and leaving its owner witless and incapable. This was prevented by simply avoiding the vicinity of the grave for a year or longer after the funerary rites but, if it were to happen, there was no known remedy and the victim would die from starvation or accident, not being able to eat or exercise the simplest self-care.

G/wi had some belief in precognition. Pricking, or itching, in various regions of the body indicated the imminent arrival of a relative (a specific region for each kin category) and on rare occasions N!adima would inform people of the future in their dreams. These beliefs were clearly distinguished from what we would class as purely rational calculation of future events, states, and outcomes which was the basis of planning of joint and individual action.

All G/wi practices and beliefs had their equivalents among other Basarwa. Nharo had a system of precognitive dream interpretation in which the deity had no part. Ability was given only to some, but was accepted by all. It was elaborate and covered the whole variety of life. Among dream interpretations which I observed, I exhaustively investigated three instances and could find no scientifically acceptable explanation of their detailed accuracy.

!Kung beliefs differed in many respects. From the ethnographers (see Biesele [1976]; Lee [1984]; Katz [1982]; and Marshall [1976]) I have formed the impression that these people lived in a state of greater fear and higher anxiety than did the G/wi. The former's world view seems to have been one of uncertainty and constant threat (understandable anywhere in the Kalahari, which is seldom a predictable or clement environment for people), leaving them less confident of their own ability to cope with its dangers. The high god and low god, G//angwan!an!a and G//angwamatse, were, respectively, creator and trickster – roles comparable with the G/wi N!adima and G//amama – but that is about as far as resemblance went. The !Kung identities were linked mythically with animals in roles which were unrelated to the G/wi tales and their characters appear also to have been quite different. !Kung *g//angwasi* were also post-mortem spirits, but had mobility and other capabilities not shared by G/wi spirits of the dead. Both were malevolent but the !Kung spirits acted purposively and were responsive to the behavior of the living. The !Kung concept of *n/um* as a personal essence of humans, creatures, and things – the "boiling energy" or Katz's title – a power to be developed and harnessed by healers and others, was unknown to the G/wi. Both peoples had trance dances which were medicinally and socially therapeutic but G/wi dancers gathered their power from the other participants. They had to learn how to do this, but the power was not essentially a personal one. Outwardly both peoples' dance performances were alike – women sat in a circle, singing and clapping, while men danced round them until one or more fell into a trance. !Kung dancers did their curing while in the trance; G/wi men fell into a trance once they had gathered the ill from others and then had to be revived by their fellows, an act which dispelled it harmlessly into the night.

Residential grouping

The social organization of !Kung camps differed from that of G/wi bands, allowing that both peoples congregated in fairly small numbers within areas containing the necessary resources of food plants, wood for heating, cooking, and artefacts (including housing), prey animals, water (when available), and space. Although Lee (1984:61) has reservations about the instability of camps prior to the 1960s and his decade of research, it seems that !Kung were always much more mobile between camps. They either visited or changed camp membership much more frequently and readily than did G/wi. Lee ascribes the mobility which he observed more to conflict-avoidance than to any other cause, but emphasizes that shortage of food and imbalance in the age-structure of a camp's population were also imperative causes. This meant that !Kung could manipulate the human resources of a camp's area, its *n!ore*. Such mobility was a rare luxury for the G/wi who changed band membership much less frequently and switched human resources around after much longer intervals, when the process of forming a new band was initiated.

Conflict

Perhaps because practitioners were never able to arrive at and agree upon criteria of comparison, the culture–personality connection is a taboo topic in anthropology and it is woefully unfashionable to fancy that one can discern differences in personality between societies. I do not subscribe to the Modal Personality notion but I do fall into the forbidden solecism of finding an "atmospheric" difference between groups of, say, Canadians and Australians, South African English-speaking and Afrikaans-speaking whites, Batswana and Basotho. Admitting the gross subjectivity of these impressions, I accept that any society's population probably contains the same range of personality types as does any other. However, I also think it likely that each society differentially encourages or discourages certain ways of expressing one's feelings. The French are said to be excitable, more so than New Zealanders. Rather than a theory which has all Kiwis born with low-octane genes, I incline to the view that their social meanings accord the same weight to a murmur that the French do to a roar.

In the light of that digression I interpret !Kung ethnography (and my slight acquaintance with !Kung) as one in which antagonistic sentiments were more freely and intensely expressed than within G/wi bands. There were plenty of G/wi with low flash-points and tender vanities but the unguent of close attention was always to hand to comfort the affronted – it was not necessary to stage an impassioned display in order to be heard. Conflict-resolution was a serious pursuit in a band and there were many ways of achieving it. Physical violence was deeply feared and polluting to all who witnessed it. Bruises were the most serious intentional injuries that I saw. These were rare and very shameful. Verbal abuse – exuberant, torrential, and splendidly inventive – sufficed on most occasions. (My observations appear to be at odds with Knauft's [1990:1014] conclusion, "under previous nomadic conditions . . . those aggressive incidents which *did* occur were relatively likely to result in death.") The few obstinately insoluble conflicts that I heard of or saw were construed as being due to the intractability of one of the parties, who was then eased out of the band (see Silberbauer 1981a:173–4). !Kung also had devices for resolving conflicts, but appear as well to have been fairly ready to come to blows. If this did not end the matter, one of the parties would likely move to another camp.

Kinship

Kinship was equally important as an organizing principle for the !Kung as for the G/wi but, although both are universalistic (a characteristic not unique to Basarwa), there were significant differences between the two systems. Terminologically !Kung was of an "Eskimo" type, i.e. parents and children are distinguished from other kin, father from father's brother(s), mother from mother's sister(s), siblings from cousins and offspring from nephews and nieces. The G/wi terminology was "Iroquois": there was structural equivalence of father's sister and mother's brother and formal equivalence of same-sex siblings. It yielded a small number of distinctive categories, some of which were very broad in their scope. !Kung personal names were gender-specific (32 female names and 36 male names) and were bestowed by rules of kinship – a first-born girl named for her father's mother and a son for his father's father and second children named for the corresponding matrilateral forebears and subsequent ones for father's, then mother's siblings. Shared names implied kinship analogous with the link between oneself and the person for whom one was named. Terminologically the kinship circle was divided into joking, and avoidance-respect categories (a feature common to many peoples around the world, including G/wi). In principle one's name-relationship would accord with the categorization of the person for whom one was named. In practice this resulted in many an *impasse*: potential spouses were placed in a prohibited category, a name-relative would belong to both categories, depending on how one reckoned the link, etc. An overriding principle allowed the senior of the two involved in the jam to define the working kinship category. Lee's discussion (1984:61–73) clarifies what is a complex and wonderfully ingenious system of negotiating the interpretation of rules so as to order relationships coherently.

Personal names

G/wi had no name-relationship. Personal names were bestowed to mark some event or circumstance associated with the mother's pregnancy or the birth, e.g. Stint-Me-[of-Tobacco], whose father was insufficiently generous to his mother; Laughing-Steenbok, whose father had a ludicrously unsuccessful hunt (by no means the only one, poor man! – his name is Elephant-Knees because of their wrinkles). The birth of Guineafowl-Peeks was watched by one of these birds displaying unwonted curiosity and boldness. My own name translates as Bluebells. This does not mark my parents' botanical lyricism but derives from the resemblance between the G/wi name for the plant, *dzaundzi* (a plural, feminine noun which becomes a masculine, singular one, Dzaundzima), and Georgie, which the G/wi overheard the poet, Joe Podbrey, call me in unpoetic moments to infuriate me when he visited me in the central Kalahari. (This led to enough tasteless jokes in English; I am grateful they never latched onto Georgie-Porgie, which would have become Dzaundzipa:dzi – He-Bites-Bluebells.) With such freedom of association and absence of gender-specificity it would have been a very rare occurrence for two persons to have had the same name. I could not discover an incidence but it was a hypothetical possibility. I was told that the consequences would have been very difficult; the two people would have shared an identity; they would have to become the same person and, unlike !Kung name-relatives, be linked by much more than kinship.

Perilous, and prudent generalizations

The social, ideational, and mystical contexts of G/wi and !Kung life were clearly very different, allowing very limited direct generalizations from one people to the other. There is, however, a greater potential for indirect generalizations in which different forms of cultural and social behavior are shown to be functionally equivalent responses or adaptations to analogous problems faced by the peoples who are being compared. Here, as elsewhere, one must take into account the vernacular perception and experience of what the anthropologist identifies as a problem. If this is not done the researcher is in danger of overlooking aspects of which she or he is unaware, or takes for granted in her or his native culture. (To illustrate: we metropolis-oriented westerners have an ethnic impediment in understanding the intimacy of band life and how it extends and intensifies interpersonal perceptiveness; not comprehending the vernacular delineations of privacy, we may lack insight into the complexities of the conspiracy of tactful silence about the products of heightened perception.) Alternatively, the researcher's own cultural background may incline her or him to accord for greater importance to something than do her or his Basarwa mentors (what a cow'rin', tim'rous beastie I become when the lion roars!).

It is for the anthropologist to make the indirect, or second-order comparison and find functional equivalents to compare. Informants can provide the data from an emic perspective but they are unlikely to have the comparative viewpoint and it is not their task to transform these data into the etic. This transformation is of two sets of quite disparate statements into a third, with common values. (Thus, as a dedicated pipe-smoker I am miserable if unable to obtain my particular mix of tobacco. Cigarette-smokers are addicted to their brands and would choke on my pipe. My physician, obsessed by the current genesis-myth of lung troubles, notes only that I, and the others in her sample of coughing, wheezing patients smoke so many grams per week, with no regard for brand or whether it is in the form of cigars, cigarettes, or pipe.)

Two comparative studies of Basarwa settlement patterns, those of Alan Barnard (1980a, 1986a, b) and of Susan Kent and Helga Vierich (1989), illustrate the fruitfulness of this strategy. Barnard has taken his informants' perceptions of their circumstances, and has taken the data of other ethnographers in a comparably emic context and has abstracted each of these sets to their highest common functions. That abstraction constituted the transformation which enabled him to make legitimate, second-order comparisons. What he did *not* do was first to impose lowest common denominators on the data by assigning his own values to them.

Kent and Vierich proceeded in similar fashion; their research data focused on Kgalagari, G/wi, and G//ana settlements and whether these were of short, medium or long anticipated duration. Anticipated length of stay, in all its variety of conceptualization and expression, was an element of vernacular reality which they abstracted into the three categories and then aligned them with three more (etic) categories of actual length of settlement. They concluded "that anticipated mobility is a primary variable in site spatial organization" (1989:115) which overrides ethnicity and subsistence strategy. I was initially surprised by, and sceptical of, their hypothesis but, on reflection, their finding makes good sense; people *do* dispose themselves differently when they expect their neighbors to be next door for a short, medium or long time. Functional equivalence is fairly easily and confidently established; three-stage comparisons can be conclusively demonstrated in G/wi, G//ana, and Kgalagari speech and practice so, although "short" may imply four to ten days for the first two and up to three weeks for Kgalagari, the three peoples distinguish clearly between that, medium, and long periods.

Another area of equivalence is in the social meaning of the spacing of huts. When all huts are within sight and hearing, for yours to be closer to mine than to any others' expresses, and creates in us and others, the expectation that our relationship is, and will be, such that our inter-action will be more frequent and intense than that between either of us and others. Furthermore, this statement is more definite, more emphatic where the settlement is of long anticipated duration than if intended to be of shorter time. It is comparable with two people moving closer together at a cocktail party – it has symbolic meaning of wishing to share each other's company more closely than that of others. It also has the pragmatic utility of allowing the pair to probe for soul-siblinghood by remarking the awfulness of the other guests and the host's canapes without broadcasting it to the whole room. But there is no long-term commitment in this informal choreography. The conversation and a beautiful friendship might be cut short by the discovery that one of the two is the hostess, responsible for all the canapes and half the guests. Or it might flourish in bitchy venom-dropping and eventual departure together, which *does* hint at a measure of commitment.

John Yellen's careful description of residential spacing among the contemporary !Kung (Gould and Yellen 1987) presents another facet. By the time of which Yellen writes, these people had become much more nearly sedentary than in Richard Lee's description of the 1960s. They had also acquired more material goods and the notion of private property had become much more weighty. Residential spacing was more distant than in the past. My interpretation is that there was not yet a complete accommodation of privatization and that there was a residue of old-fashioned shame over the failure to share (entailed by privatization). It would make sense to place more distance between me and my neighbor if I felt rather uncomfortable about having her or him constantly gazing at my unshared wealth. This negates the convenience factor of Kent and Vierich's camps, in which it is handy to have my intimate social circle very close at hand. It does not, however, invalidate Kent and Vierich's conclusions, which apply to a people as yet without wealth.

Simple, direct comparison of these cases would not inform understanding but, by taking social factors into account, one could venture a generalization from Kent, Vierich, and Yellen's discussions. Settlement space in the relevant areas of the Kalahari is free in the sense that it costs no more to occupy a hectare than it does to take up ten square meters. If, then, residential space and intervening privacy-distance are free, why are camps not more extensive than they are? (Exception must be made for those instances shown by Kent and Vierich where the camp is fenced. Total camp space is then paid for by the cost of erecting the perimeter fence, which is quite a lot of work.) Why do the people not put even more privacy-space between their residences than has been reported? Those questions are answered by the ample evidence in these and other ethnographic descriptions of all four peoples that social interaction is generally valued for frequency and variety. One might, therefore, conclude that people will seek to maximize opportunity for, and convenience of, interaction by close spacing of their residences except where rivalry, jealousy or enmity diminish the benefits and the desire for closeness.

Testing this general hypothesis would leave the investigator with the Herculean tasks of identifying the push–pull factors, discovering their relative values for the people concerned, and then arriving at some common measurement of those values (other, of course, than privacy-distance, which expresses their sum). The neatness of such plane-table social surveying is, alas, prone to messy complication. In the 1950s a potent, but not determinate factor in the disposition of huts or shelters in a G/wi band camp was the availability of suitable shade-trees. The band had quite wide latitude in selecting the campsite even when there was the powerful gravitational pull of something like a waterhole or a generous stand of esculent plants. If one array of trees did not suit, there were others within a kilometer radius that would be preferable, but none would perfectly accommodate the placing of huts in exactly the arrangement that the people desired. The outcome was that they compromised, squeezing and pulling their current ideal to make the best fit in the best site. Human brains can do it very well, but this kind of intuitive nudging of the weights on the scales of decision does not readily translate into pretty algebra.

Cultural comparison and cultural change

Describing Basarwa social and cultural practices with fair accuracy and reasonable completeness is a very skilled and difficult undertaking. Clearly, it is necessary to describe and analyze the particular before one can venture into comparison and generalization. Without detailed ethnography there is no foundation on which to erect the structures of generalization from which come further understanding of human social and cultural behavior. This is not to say that they cannot proceed until all ethnography has been completed; comparison and generalization feed ethnographers with further directions of enquiry, and progress in explanation comes from both modes of investigation. But in anthropology we are in some difficulty in making comparisons. The objects of comparison must differ to some extent for, were their properties identical, there would be no point in comparing them (e.g. 10¢ coins of the same country struck in the same year). However, comparisons can only be made among objects which share one or more properties (e.g. that, despite their different denominations, they be coins of the same country). Also the comparison must be made for the same purpose, i.e. one relevant to the situation. (While counting the change in my pocket to see whether I have sufficient for my busfare is not a good moment to keep the driver and other passengers waiting as I drift off in numismatic contemplation of the relative aesthetic merits of South African, Australian, and Canadian coins that recent globe-trotting might have left me with.)

The ethnographic literature provides ample evidence of difference. The difficulties arise in identifying the properties that are common to the groups which are to be compared. Here we may usefully start with the venerable anthropological view of society and culture as humans' principal survival strategy – as being the main means whereby we provide our own, and others', life-support systems. H.-J. Heinz (1966),

Lorna Marshall (1976), Richard Lee (1979, 1984), Richard Katz (1982), Jiro Tanaka (1980b), and I (1965, 1981a) have all taken an essentially functional (and not Functionalist) perspective in describing, respectively, !xô, !Kung or G/wi in that we sought to show how elements of the cultural and social patterns fitted together as means of the peoples' survival. (This is not all that these books say – society and culture have many other aspects which excite study and demand explanation – but, implicitly or explicitly, it is their, and much of anthropology's, common frame of logic.) The functional equivalence of the respective cultural and social elements in contributing to, or detracting from, each group's survival is one of the common currencies of valid comparison. Comparing functional equivalents is a complex procedure for elements do not all directly foster or impair survival. Also, a people's consciousness is not constantly directed towards stark consideration of the survival value of their activities. However, the analytic strategy of general systems theory does provide a means of coherently translating ethnographic detail into variables to which can be assigned values of differing weight, sign, and vector quantity/quality with reference to the nominal goal of survival (N.B. *not* preservation) of the socio-cultural system and its population of practitioners. Cultural and social change are accounted for as positive or negative growth, development, and/or adaptation, not only to changing ecological, economic, and ideological and political environments, but including those adaptive changes which enhance or reduce efficiency. Today the only neat and tight equations yielded by this approach will be spurious. Any given socio-cultural system confronts anthropology with more variables than can presently be counted, let alone accounted for. Until we and the mathematicians get together and devise something better, we must struggle with an untidy mess of the quantitative, the qualitative, and the gut-felt.

Explanation of causality is still an unresolved (and largely neglected) problem in anthropology. Perhaps we have progressed beyond the Newtonian-mechanical notion of Radcliffe-Brown's *A natural science of society* (1957) but only really to the realization that socio-cultural causality is a horse of another hue – if, indeed, it is a horse at all (*cf.* Kaplan 1964). Certainly simplistic determinism and reductionism will not serve for phenomena as complex, and as highly charged with redundancy, as are socio-cultural systems. It seems more likely that we are dealing with a probabilistic causality in which a calculus of the relevant factors and their values will yield an actuarial ranking of possible outcomes. Too often our naivety is like that of the mythical Joe Blow, who always carries an umbrella to keep him dry and points to the cloudless sky as proof of the efficacy of the measure. Although observers may see environmental factors as imperatives which impel action there is not, in fact, the determinate causation that is implicit in relying solely on them as *explanans*. It is correct, I believe, to argue that there is a functional fit between what Lee (1984:22) has felicitously termed the hierarchy of water sources and a pattern of summer dispersal and winter congregation in a part of the Kalahari where relatively large and reliable supplies of water exist in a few locations during winter, but there are much more numerous, dispersed supplies to be found during summer. I have described (Silberbauer 1965, 1981a) an opposite G/wi habit of winter dispersal and summer congregation in a habitat which had drastically reduced food supplies and *no* water during winter. I argued that this circumstance constituted a pressure on the people to lower localized population density (and, hence, the rate at which local food supplies were exhausted) by dispersing to household-sized winter camps. Clearly the two responses to the respective sets of conditions were good ones in that they worked – !Kung and G/wi survived. It may be inferred that the people chose what they saw as the best responses. In all candor, let us recognize that none of us in anthropology knows enough to judge whether or not it *was* the best. Perhaps in small-scale societies with their very efficient networks of communication of ideas and needs people *do* know what is best for them and do not blunder around in marginally successful or failed experiments as we do in our large-scale, semi-incommunicado society. But there are no grounds for arguing that these two cases represent the *only* solutions, which is a necessary condition for determinate causation. (In choosing this example I am not implying that Lee argued environmental causation – he did not.) There were other options. !Kung could have dispersed in winter and survived on plant juices as did the G/wi. It is probable that there were drought years in which they had to, but it looks as if the social fabric of the time of which Lee wrote would have been severely strained by this. There is the cautionary instance of the G/wi adaptation which Tanaka (1980b) described and to which I referred earlier; !Kung social versatility and ingenuity may have been equal to the challenge.

I and, perhaps, others felt the temptation when first going into the Kalahari to assume fallaciously that hunter-gatherer society and culture were static and that what I found had been that way for untold eons – *sub specie aeternitas*. I was smartly put on the path of righteousness by my informants' frequent references to knowledge, skills, and practices of the *G//ô:khwena* – the Old, or Great People – which they, contemporary G/wi, had abandoned or lost, and of new culture which they had invented or discovered. Archaeological evidence showed the antiquity of some items still to be found in the people's current technology. It was easy to stumble into the false syllogism that everything else in their culture had been retained without change. At best this stemmed from unrecognized ignorance of the people's history. At worst it can be symptomatic of crapulous adherence to a spurious evolutionism and its connotations that the people achieved their potential in the distant past and have remained stuck to the ceiling of that cellar ever since. That would be an improbable state of affairs; Dansereau's "law of the inoptimum" states that "no species encounters in any given habitat the optimum conditions for all its functions" (Dansereau 1957:257); neither will any people devise a socio-cultural system which constitutes an optimal adaptation to their habitat. (Blurton-Jones, in commenting on a draft of this paper, challenged the appropriateness of "optimal" in this context. His view is that, rather than choose the "best-on-balance," they make do with "least-worst." He also asked me to suggest a term for the latter; I offer "parvulopessimal" – perhaps nourishing; certainly indigestible.) For the G/wi, or any others, to remain content without seeking to improve the efficacy and efficiency of their arrangements, knowledge, and practices implies their incapacity to do so – that some factor had stunted their adaptive capability, leaving them in an evolutionary *cul de sac*. Additionally, the fallacious *"aeternitas"* view implies an enviable but, alas, impossible condition in which no knowledge or skills were ever lost and therefore never needed to be replaced. There is no evidence of the existence of a factor which might have debilitated their adaptive capacity. There is ample evidence that Kalahari Basarwa experimented as readily as did others, forgetting, discarding, inventing, and discovering knowledge, cultural items, and social formations. Archaeology can only directly inform us of material cultural remains, say much of how they were employed, and make indirect inferences about other aspects of cultures and societies in the past. But it can seldom tell of *all* the ways in which a tool, weapon or other artefact was used. Thus, unless handles of both applications survive, archaeology is unlikely to be able to tell us that a G/wi axe-blade was customarily rotated 90° to become the blade of an adze. We are even less informed about the non-material aspects of past cultures. This is not to castigate archaeologists. It is to remind anthropologists of the limitations of the archaeological record and its interpretation and to indicate the flaws in *"aeternitas"* reasoning.

Nevertheless, some cultural and social practices *do* persist. It is as rewarding to enquire into similarities and lack of change as it is to examine variety. We are confronted by the fact that, although the majority of the world's societies abandoned foraging and chose ways of life other than hunting and gathering, many Kalahari Basarwa did not.

They experimented, invented, and borrowed. They forgot, and lost skills. Some circumstances favored them and they were sorely buffeted by others. In response to all this they changed their cultures innumerable times in countless ways. But their foraging strategy persisted. The stock-raising Khoi and the Bantu-speaking, European, and Asian immigrants into the southern third of Africa all demonstrated the capacity of the habitat to sustain pastoralism, agriculture, and modern industry. Wilmsen (1989) has argued at length that all Basarwa had earlier abandoned hunting and gathering but some were forced back into intermittent foraging. His thesis has been rejected by several workers (e.g. Harpending 1991; Silberbauer 1991; Solway and Lee 1990), some of whose field experience was of Basarwa who lived only by hunting and gathering.

G/wi informants and I often discussed the choices before them; those who lived permanently in the Central Kalahari Reserve always expressed their preference for their way of living. G/wi living permanently on ranches were distinctive in much of their culture and perforce interacted more with other ranch Basarwa than with their desert kith and kin. But, as I have said, this did not distance them socially or affectively from the desert people in ways, or to the extent, that one might have expected. Seasonal trekkers in search of water were not distinguished at all by their band fellows. There was, therefore, not any apparent stratification which might have led either the trekkers or the permanent desert-dwellers to see themselves as distinctive and thus bounded by a sense of tradition, or damned as desert pariahs as part of a distinctive identity which might have kept them from joining ranches or cattle-posts.

Those who trekked to ranches in times of drought were always pleased to get back to their desert territories, and the ranch-dwellers professed a nostalgic longing for band life. Those who made the drought trek to the ranches did so out of desperation. It is clear that hunting and gathering did not persist because foragers were forced into it by their inability to do anything else. They had the opportunity to go to cattle-posts or ranches. Some did so, either permanently or temporarily. For the latter, and for those who remained in their territories, their customary social, political, and economic arrangements that constituted independent band life were more attractive and rewarding than were the alternatives that ranch or cattle-post offered. Wilmsen's hypothesis that the hunting and gathering life was the last resort of a redundant, dispossessed *Lumpenproletariat*, discarded by their pastoralist Bantu-speaking masters, is made improbable by those Basarwa who chose autonomy in their bands, and who returned to their territories despite the hardships.

3   Diversity and flexibility: the case of the Bushmen of southern Africa

Mathias Guenther

The Bushmen of southern Africa are known primarily through the !Kung, specifically the Ju/'hoansi (or Zhu/'hoasi) of the Dobe and Nyae Nyae regions of Botswana and Namibia. The reason is the prolific, much-cited work of the ethnographers working among the !Kung. It has made of the latter one of the most high-profile foraging societies of the world and a paradigmatic representative of such societies within anthropological work on hunter-gatherers generally. The !Kung ethnographers who come to mind readily are the members of the Marshall family, who have worked with and filmed the !Kung at Nyae Nyae in Namibia since the 1950s, and the various members of the "Harvard Project," in the Dobe area just across the border fence in north-western Botswana (Lee 1976a, 1979). The work of Richard Lee, the coinitiator of the Dobe project, is featured in virtually every anthropology text and reader, and his *The Dobe Ju/'hoansi* (1993), which was first published nine years ago, is one of the best-selling titles in the Spindler Case Studies series and has just appeared in its second edition. To many an anthropology student and professional the Bushmen tend thus to be equated with the !Kung, specifically the Ju/'hoansi. As shown in chapter 5 of this volume, the Mbuti hold similar limelight status within Pygmy studies, equally obscuring the diversity of this group of African foragers.

Stemming from this ethnographic conflation, a second conflation is found, a conceptual one, within Bushman anthropology: the treatment of the Bushmen as exemplars *par excellence* of the small-scale egalitarian band society with the foraging (or communal) mode of production. The reason is that the key architect of this model, Richard Lee, has developed this conceptualization of band society within the context of the Ju/'hoan !Kung, to whom it is appropriate. The question that must be raised is the extent to which this classic band model can be said to apply to the Bushmen generally.

Looking beyond the !Kung at the two dozen or so other Bushman linguistic groupings that are and were found over southern Africa (Figure 3.1), one is struck by the extreme variability of Bushman social

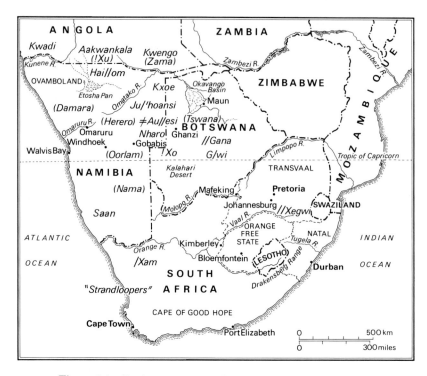

Figure 3.1   Bushman groups of southern Africa (names in brackets indicate non-Bushman tribes)

formations. Economies, societies, and polities come in all shapes and sizes, from small (a dozen or so strong), to large (in the hundreds), loose to tightly organized, and acephalous to politically centralized. The common denominator to all this socioeconomic diversity is that the people it applies to are or were Bushmen, linguistically and ethnically (that is, by self-designation and designation by neighboring groups).

All of this diversity has escaped general notice, however. As noted above, the reason rests partly on the !Kung-fixation of people working amongst, or interested in, the Bushmen, and partly on the tendency of most of the Bushmanologists each to describe and analyze "his"/"her" own group, rather than undertaking comparative studies of several groups. The latter focus was assumed only recently, primarily by Alan Barnard, who, after publishing the occasional paper with that perspective, on spatial organization (1979, 1986b),[1] kinship (1987), and religion

---

[1] Also see Heinz 1972, Cashdan 1983, and Guenther 1981a for other comparative treatments of the topic.

(1988),[2] has recently published a comparative ethnography on the Bushman (and Khoi Khoi) peoples (Barnard 1992a). Another recent regional comparative study, which focuses on the themes of sociopolitical diversity amongst Kalahari Bushmen and the structural flexibility of their social organization, is by the editor of the present volume (1992).

My chapter has two principal tasks, one descriptive, the other analytical. First, in the spirit of setting the record straight on the overly homogenized and "totalizing" presentation of Bushman social organization, I will document the wide range of diversity displayed by Bushman society and culture. Second, I will attempt to explain this diversity, in ecological, historical, and social-structural terms. How this diversity affects, and is affected by, anthropological theory in Bushman studies is the theme of the discussion that follows these two sections. Here, I will deal with two points: one, some of the implications of Bushman diversity as regards the revisionist Kalahari Debate; and, two, whether the Bushmen's remarkable social and cultural diversity might be a reflection of their study by such a remarkable number of researchers.

Diversity of Bushman society

Diversity is evident in all systems of Bushman society and culture, from subsistence patterns to religious beliefs. In addition to "classic" foraging (such as exemplified by the !Kung, G//ana, G/wi, and Kxoe), big game-hunting was a subsistence pattern that more than a few Bushman groups of the past appear to have followed. They constructed game pits up to 3 meters deep, to which they drove game through rows of shrub or stone fences; their efforts were on a scale "the undertaking [of] which would have excited astonishment in far more civilized nations," as Galton (1889:106) exclaimed, in the racist tones that were his and his era's wont, when coming across such an installation in Hei//om lands in north-central Namibia.[3] Other groups who practiced this style of hunting included some of the Cape Bushmen, especially around the Drakensberg (Harris 1852:257; Hahn 1870:103), and the !Kung-speaking =Au//eisi and the Nharo of Ghanzi prior to the depletion of game in the region by ivory-hungry black (Tswana), yellow (Oorlam-Nama), and white hunters (Andersson 1856:374–7; Passarge 1907:10, 57, 65–7, 75–81, 114; Lau 1987:91). At the Okavango and Lake Ngami

---

[2] See also Schmidt (1989) and Guenther (1989) for comparative treatments of Bushman folklore, and Guenther (1992) for a comparative analysis of witchcraft.

[3] See also Serton (1954:65–6) for McKiernan's description of the same feature in the same general region.

(the Kanikwe, for example), or Lake Chrissie (the Tloue-tle or //Xegwi) in the eastern Transvaal, Bushman groups organized collective antelope hunts consisting of all of the menfolk of one or two bands. After surrounding a strategically located stretch of swamp or flooded section of a river, the men drove the encircled animals into the swamp and killed the immobilized antelopes with spears or harpoons (Gusinde 1966:171; Potgieter 1955:22–3). Hahn describes group hunts of two to three hundred men, driving game for kilometres down a converging row of burnt-down tree trunks, in the mouth of which a deep, staked pit had previously been dug (Hahn 1870:105).

Similar high-yield hunting techniques, by large hunting groups consisting of as many as eighty men, were employed by some Khoi-speaking people to the west, specifically some Nama groups and the Nama-speaking (Berg)Dama(ra) (Andersson 1856:377; Hahn 1985 [1859]:1149; Lau 1987:4–5, 10–11, 57), as well as the Tswana to the east (Smith 1975:267; Livingstone 1860:21–2). Passarge (1907:78–9) suggests that the latter Bantu-speaking group may have derived this technique from the //Aikwe (Nharo) Bushmen and one may speculate that the other two non-Bushman groups may have learned the techniques from Bushman neighbors as well.

Along coasts, rivers, and lakes Bushmen could be found, heavily dependent, in classic Mesolithic fashion, on marine, riverine, or lacus-trine resources; fishing techniques utilized, in some instances, were boats, weirs, and large cone-shaped fishing baskets placed in long rows in the reeds lining the river banks, or between rocks in the river's current (Alexander 1967 [1838]:237–8; Moffat 1969 [1842]:55; Hahn 1985 [1860]:1189, 1870:104; Stow 1905:92–3; Dornan 1925:106–9). Examples of such groups are the enigmatic "Strandloopers" of the Cape or Namibian Atlantic coast (Szalay 1983:68–97; Vedder 1934:3; Smith and Kinahan 1985), the "River Bushmen" of the Okavango, such as the afore-mentioned Kxoe-speaking Kanikwe, as well as other Eastern Khoe Bushmen living in the Okavango-Ngami-Botletle drainage system or along the Nata (Gusinde 1966; Heinz n.d.; van Hoogstraten 1966; Cowley 1968; Hitchcock 1987b; Barnard 1992a:122–5), and the little-known "Lake Chrissie Bushmen" of the Transvaal (Potgieter 1955; Toerin 1955).

As emphasized in the current revisionist debate (Wilmsen 1989:71–7, 91, 95, 112, 239–44, 295–8; Wilmsen and Denbow 1990) – and, on occasion, *over*emphasized (Lee and Guenther 1991) – herding and plant cultivation were subsistence patterns that could be found in many a Bushman group of past generations and centuries. As shown in this volume (chapters 5 and 6), the Kutse and Hua Bushmen of the eastern

Kalahari today include agropastoralism within their subsistence strate-gies. As in the past, herding and cultivating tend to be marginal or sporadic elements of the subsistence economy, supplemented with, or supplements to, foraging and hunting. Herding was established especially amongst those Bushman groups who had lived in dependency relationships with Bantu-speaking or Nama herders (Almeida 1965:23; Silberbauer and Kuper 1966; Wilson and Thompson 1969:63–4, 156; Solway and Lee 1990; Wilmsen 1989:98–101; Wilmsen and Denbow 1990).

Trade patterns are varied as well, ranging from *hxaro*-type exchange based on generalized reciprocity, to barter, primarily with Bantu-speaking partners (Hahn 1985 [1857]:1034; Solway and Lee 1990; Williams 1991:88; Wilmsen 1989:116, 119, 185–6). The commodities exchanged in the latter form of trade derived from the hunt (animal skins, ostrich feathers, ivory, ostrich-eggshell beads) and, for the last decades of the nineteenth century, linked some of the Bushman groups to the mercantile world system (Wilmsen 1989:105–29). This was the case especially with respect to those Bushman groups living near Bantu-speaking overlords, who tended to be the middlemen in this trade in Kalahari goods produced by the Bushmen and sought after in the West, in exchange for western-derived goods carted in by the white traders. There was at least one group of Bushmen, the Hei//om around Otavi and Etosha in Namibia, whose commodities were not game animal products. Instead, they traded copper and salt cakes, with Ovambo trade partners covetous for their wares. The copper ore was mined by the Bushmen, at an annual production rate of 50 to 60 tons, from mines over which they claimed exclusive ownership and the location of which they kept secret. It was exchanged primarily with the Ovambo, to the north, for corn, tobacco, and calabashes (Hahn 1985 [1857]:1025, 1027, 1034; also see Vedder 1934:502; Wilmsen 1989:117). An entirely different pattern of Bushman mining – as migrant laborers in the gold mines of the Wit-watersrand – appears in chapter 5 of this volume, as one of a number of economic options and socioeconomic changes of the Kūa Basarwa.

Spatial organization varied extensively (Barnard 1979, 1986b, 1992a:223–36; Cashdan 1983), with some groups being widely dispersed nomads (Saan, !Kxo) and others densely settled (Nharo), at times in permanent villages ("Kwadi"). As shown by George Silberbauer (chapter 2, this volume) and Alan Barnard and Thomas Widlock (chapter 5), for the =Xade G/wi and the Namibian Hai//om and Ghanzi Nharo, settlement patterns vary even within a single Bushman linguistic group, as a result of differences in adaptive strategies to variations within the ecological and social environment of its constituent bands or band clusters. The transhumant concentration-dispersal pattern which is evidently the most common and most characteristic form of spatial mobility may bring people together in multi-band aggregations in either the dry winter (!Kung) or the wet summer (G/wi). As George Silber-bauer suggests in chapter 2 (see also Barnard 1979, 1986b), these alternatives are two of a number of possible adaptive options for dealing with the problem of winter drought.

Social organization also varies from group to group in both specific social institutions and the basic social structure. Regarding the former, one can point to marriage, postmarital residence patterns, and kinship terminology, all of them varying widely, as so cogently demonstrated by Alan Barnard (1992a, especially chapter 15; also see chapter 2 this volume). Joking and avoidance relationships are typical but not univer-sal kin categories and the well-known namesake relationship is a very rare pattern found primarily amongst the well-known !Kung. Political and religious status differentiation is another variable aspect of Bushman social organization (Barnard 1992a, especially chapter 13). The shaman-like medicine men were professionalized and organized amongst some groups (such as the nineteenth-century Cape /Xam [Hewitt 1986:287–99] or the Ghanzi Nharo [Passarge 1907:108–9; Guenther 1975, 1986a:262–9, 288–9]), whilst amongst other groups, such as the Nyae Nyae !Kung, "it is rare to find a man . . . who is not a medicine man" (Marshall 1965:271).

The political role of headman may vary with respect to the degree of power it entails, from virtually none – the "Common Bushman" (i.e. !Kung or G/wi pattern) – to formidable. Power also varies according to whether it is achieved, through personal success and charisma, or ascribed. In the latter instance headmanship would usually be patri-lineally bequeathed, as is or was the case, for instance, among the !Kung-speaking Aakwankala (or !Xũ) of Ovamboland (Williams 1991:86), the !Kxo (Heinz 1994:76–101), or the early Nharo of Sandfon-tein at the Botswana–Namibia border (Bleek 1928:36). The status of headman is usually held by a man; as discussed elsewhere (Guenther 1983), the reasons have to do with the hunt, a subsistence activity with political potential. However, on this score, too, there appear to be exceptions. For instance, amongst the !Kung, whose "*k'xau n!asi* [headman] are as thin as the rest" (Marshall 1976:194) and who are devoid of regalia or special honors or tribute (see also Lee 1984:89), women, too, can be headmen, according to one ethnographer (Lee 1979:344–9). It should be noted, however, that another !Kung researcher (Marshall 1976:194) states categorically that such could never be the case amongst the Nyae Nyae people. She draws a distinction between "owners" of *n!ores* and headmen of bands; the former can, and the latter cannot, be women.

With respect to the basic social structure, Bushmen were organized in bands that were variations of the classic !Kung mold; that is, they were loose, fluid, open, non-territorial, egalitarian, and uncentralized. Some, like the Nama-speaking Saan of central Namibia (Trenk 1910; Vedder 1934:25; Barnard 1992a:218–19), were extremely fluid, open, and loose; others, such as the !Ko (or !Xo) of central Botswana (Heinz 1994, 1972; Barnard 1992a:64–8), were more closed, and were structured spatially and socially. However, Bushman groups could also be found whose social organization was diametrically opposite to the loose and egalitarian band. Almeida (1965:17, 21–2) describes some Angolan Bushmen (such as the dark-skinned, Kxoe-speaking "Zama" or "Kwengo"), who lived in palisaded villages, ruled by chiefs who are recipients of tribute paid in cattle, goats, and dairy products. The reason Almeida refers to these decidedly non-foraging, non-egalitarian people as "Bushmen" is their click language, as well as ethnic self-designation and certain phenotypal traits. The Nharo and = Au//eisi were described by Passarge as having been a fiercely militaristic tribe of warriors who paid tribute to, and were led by, a tyranical chieftain named D = ukuri (Passarge 1907:114–20; Guenther 1991), and traces of centralized political authority were found by Dorothea Bleek (1928:36–7) as well as by myself, when she and later I visited the Nharo, one and two life-times later, respectively.

It is not clear from the ethnographic and ethnohistorical records what prompted this elaboration of male power amongst these Bushman groups of Angola and Botswana. As I have suggested elsewhere (Guenther 1991), the encroachment of Nama and Tawana states into the eastern and western regions of Ghanzi, coupled with a robust and independent foraging economy that was based on big-game hunting and external trade in game products (including ivory), may have been the decisive historical and economic triggers to bring about this change in the political complexity of Nharo and = Au//ei society.

Such a political process was most evident amongst the Bushmen of the Cape of early colonial times, as they resisted, with the fiercest determination, the onslaught of various agropastoral settler groups into this environmentally bountiful region of southern Africa. The land provided rich pastures for both game and stock animals, resulting in acute competition for the same grazing lands amongst the indigenous Bushmen and the incoming herders. As a result, settler hostility and Bushman resistance were the more intense (Schott 1955:133–7; also see Anthing 1863 and Ellenberger 1953 which document the atrocious, frequently genocidal actions of the European settlers against the Bushmen). As revealed by the historical record (Marks 1972; Szalay 1983:170–9), this condition of intense and prolonged settler hostility set in motion the same process of political mobilization and militarization as would occur, at a later time and on a smaller scale, in Ghanzi, as well as in South-West Africa (Kaufmann 1910; Seiner 1913; Wilhelm 1954) in colonial times.

In the Cape, this process consisted of the consolidation of a number of Bushman bands, while others joined up with Nama, Griqua, or Xhosa, as allies or client soldiers. In this way, Bushmen, along with their allies, were able to muster fighting forces up to 1,000 strong. Some of them were mounted on horses and armed with rifles, both of which were stolen from the Boer settlers (Szalay 1983:179). Hit-and-run guerrilla raids became outright wars, terrorizing the white settlers and earning the Bushmen and Khoi the reputation of "banditti" and brutal savages (Guenther 1981b). Their leaders were war chiefs (the so-called "Captains"), who were similar, in power and political *modus operandi*, to the Ghanzi Bushman =Dukuri. Some were escaped Nama or Colored slaves, servants, or soldiers who had fled into the mountainous hinterland, inveigled local Bushman bands to follow them, and led lives of banditry (Szalay 1983:173). German colonial officers reported similar events about the north-eastern regions of their newly acquired colony of South-West Africa. Their reports mention bellicose "hordes" of Bushman raiders, up to 350 in number, led by fierce !Kung "Captains" – such as the notorious Namagoroub around Grootfontein (Seiner 1913:302) – who executed raids against Herero or European settlers.

In the domain of religion, variation abounds, "not merely from one tribe to the next, but also from individual to individual" (Hahn 1870:84). This feature struck Theophilus Hahn as the characteristic trait of Bushman religion, as opposed to the religion of the Hottentots (Khoi Khoi), which in Hahn's estimation was more streamlined. It was because of its high degree of amorphousness that he referred to Bushman religion as "wildwuchener Aberglaube" ("wildly rank superstition") (Hahn 1870:84). As I have shown elsewhere (Guenther 1979a), the range of variation is especially marked with respect to belief, while ritual, the socially enacted element of religion, is (for this reason perhaps) more standardized. Yet, despite all of the interpersonal and intergroup variation, there are a number of broad, common elements in the religion not only of the Bushmen but of the Khoisan peoples in general, such that it is possible to speak of a "Khoisan religious tradition" (Guenther 1989:33–6; also see Schapera 1930:160–95; Barnard 1988, 1992a:251–64).

All groups appear to have the trance curing dance; however, there appear to be some regional stylistic differences in its format. Whilst the women's chanting provides the only musical accompaniment for the dance amongst contemporary Kalahari Bushmen, it appears that Cape Bushmen, in addition to the women's voices, also used wooden, water-filled drums (Hahn 1870:121). I also noted considerable variation in the dancers' performance styles as virtually every dancer had his own, highly idiosyncratic ritual routine (Guenther 1986a:256–7). As for the singing of the women, whilst in perfect time, it is such "that no two in a chorus hit the same note, though the general burden of the tune is kept up . . . [moreover] all go up together, and all go down together, each hitting any note they please" (Bleek 1928:22).

Initiation rites, too, show similarities and in most groups menarcheal rites are more elaborate than male initiation. The exceptions would seem to be the !Kxo (Heinz 1978) and the Bantu-influenced !Kung-speaking Aakwankala of Ovamboland (Williams 1991:87) or the !Kung-speaking Kwadi of Angola (Barnard 1992a:32), who have elaborate male transition rites. Witchcraft and sorcery are generally absent or inchoate. Regarding the latter, however, there are some groups (such as the !Xam, Kxoe, and Nharo) who have or had a complex of sorcery and even, possibly, a form of witchcraft (Guenther 1992).

It is possible that elements of these "black arts" were derived from Bantu-speaking neighbors whose culture contains a fully-fledged witchcraft and sorcery complex (Guenther 1992:99–101). Long association with Bantu-speaking neighbors may likewise account for the presence of a number of other ritual patterns amongst a number of Bushman groups which deviate from the "Common Bushman" mold: circumcision at male initiation among the Aakwankala (Williams 1991:87) and the Kwadi (Barnard 1992a:132); the "sacred fire" among the Hai//om (Barnard 1992a:214, 215); certain divination techniques among the Nharo (Guenther 1986a:251–2); elements of totemism among the Eastern and Northern Khoe Bushmen (Cashdan 1986:147–8, 168–70; Barnard 1992a:125–6), such as the "Masarwa" or Hiechware (Dornan 1917:53); elements of ancestor worship among the Aakwankale (Williams 1991:87).

Like other hunter-gatherers, the Kalahari Bushmen were and are foragers as much for ideas as for *veldkos*. In this regard they are like other hunter-gatherers, such as the Batek of Malaysia, the foraging group amongst whom Kirk Endicott (1979:221) coined this most apt *bon mot*. The propensity for adopting and adapting new ideas and influences that reach the Bushmen from the outside, in ways that enable them to "withstand, tolerate or benefit" from them, is held by George Silberbauer (chapter 2, this volume) to be part of the Bushmen's general "resilience and ingenuity." It is an important element of the cultural diversity, social malleability, and ecological adaptability of the Bushmen.

Regarding belief, cosmology, and expressive culture, one basic distinction is between Bushman peoples who painted and those who did not. The former were the now vanished Bushmen of the Cape, the Drakensberg, the Brandberg of Namibia, and the Tsodilo Hills of Botswana, the latter the Kalahari Bushmen. The artists, in turn, were divided between those who created primarily rock paintings and those who produced engravings.[4] However, the general cosmological and symbolic orientation of both – and all – types of Bushpeople seems to be basically the same: a primal, inchoate order of existence that preceded and was, in some ways, the reverse of the present order, which was populated with therianthropic beings, as well as with humans lacking in "customs" and with the all-pervasive trickster (Guenther 1989:31–3). This basic core of beliefs is very general, however; and within and between groups one notes "a wonderful muddle of religious ideas" (Bleek 1928:25) because of a striking absence of standardization of belief, especially regarding the *personae* of one or both of the two central divinities (Guenther 1979a; Barnard 1988, 1992a:251–64; see also chapter 2 of this book where George Silberbauer describes the variation in the beliefs of the G/wi and the !Kung).

Looking at contemporary Bushmen, we find that they live within a variety of acculturative situations, giving rise to a high degree of diversity: farm Bushmen as seasonal, migrant, or permanent, sedentary wage laborers on ranches owned by white or non-white ranchers (Figures 3.2–3.5); clientage with a *mafisa*-style cattle loan arrangement with Bantu-speaking agropastoralists; government-employed, rural or urbanized; reserve- or government-settlement attached Bushmen; marginal pastoralists or petty entrepreneurs; conscripts in the South African army, and others (Budack 1980; Childers 1976; Stephen 1983; Guenther 1976, 1977, 1986a, 1986b, 1986c; Hitchcock 1982a, 1982b, 1985, 1987a, 1987c; Hitchcock and Ebert 1984; Hitchcock and Holm 1985; Biesele *et al.* 1989; Lee and Hurlich 1982; Hurlich and Lee 1979). All of the other Bushman chapters in this book describe Bushman groups who live their lives in one or another, or several, of these social contexts. Therefore, sociopolitical and economic elements are added to what was previously primarily an environmental ecosystem, thereby requiring an exceptionally wide range of adaptive, resourceful, and opportunistic responses from today's Bushmen. The case of the Kūa

[4] The literature on Bushman rock art is vast; general survey works are Cooke 1969; Rudner and Rudner 1978; Lewis-Williams 1981; Lewis-Williams and Dowson 1989.

Figure 3.2   Nharo farm, Bushman village, Ghanzi District, Botswana
(M. Guenther)

Figure 3.3   Nharo farm, Bushman women, Ghanzi District, Botswana
(M. Guenther)

Figure 3.4   Farm Bushman homestead, Ghanzi District, Botswana
(R. de Hoogh)

Figure 3.5   Nharo farm Bushman family, Ghanzi District, Botswana
(R. de Hoogh)

Basarwa (chapter 5) describes an impressive number of these responses, as well as their effect on shaping the cultural diversity of the people who employ them. It is a striking ethnographic illustration of the resilience and adaptability of the Bushmen to changes in their natural and social environment.

Diversity and flexibility

The diversity of Bushman society and culture is a function, I would argue, of two basic dynamic factors, one internal, pertaining to social organization, the other external, pertaining to the ecological and historical settings within which the diverse Bushman groups have been situated and to which they have had to adapt. The first factor is the institutional, structural, and personal flexibility of the Bushman society, culture, and individual; the second is the variability of the ecological and social-acculturative contexts in which Bushmen have lived over the centuries and are still living today. These two factors are mutually reinforcing because the diverse ecological and historical contexts have, for many generations and to the present, activated the institutional and structural flexibility of Bushman society which, in turn, has rendered that society the more ecologically and socially adaptive.

With respect to the latter point, the Bushmen, in the course of the past two millennia, have come to occupy a wide range of different environments – from lush grasslands in the southern Cape, to well-watered or arid mountain lands in the Drakensberg, north-western Cape, and Brandberg. The arid lands inhabited by Bushpeople range from hospitable, with reliable supplies of permanent water (such as the Ghanzi ridge or the Dobe region of Botswana), to inhospitable, without any surface water for months at a time (such as the Namib or the central Kalahari). Some lived at the coast, others by rivers, lakes, or swamps. In terms of historical contacts and social contexts, the Bushmen have been contacted, more or less pervasively and more or less aggressively, by a wide range of people and cultures with whom, to varying degrees, they traded, intermarried, or fought, or by whom they were subjugated, or whom they themselves drove out or conquered. These contact situations were sometimes acculturative, adding new cultural material to some Bushman groups – possibly witchcraft patterns and (as seen above) other elements of religion, especially in the area of myth and folklore (Guenther 1989:41–50; Barnard 1992a:261). In other situations the contacts were, to lesser or greater degrees and for shorter or longer periods of time, transformative, bringing about certain structural changes within Bushman society, such as sedentism, agropastoralism, clientage, or militarism.

However, throughout these ecologically or politically engendered changes, Bushman society appears generally to have retained its cultural integrity and its capacity for social reproduction. What has been retained, basically, is the foraging band society, both its infrastructural mode of production and its superstructural ethos. As seen from the multiple and multiplex manifestations of Bushman societies in a variety of ecological and historical contexts that were detailed above, the band evidently is a social-structural theme that is playable in many variations. The reason for the protean adaptability of the Bushman band is the inherent flexibility of Bushman social organization and values, beliefs, and ideas.

Flexibility is all-pervasive within Bushman social organization: in composition the society is fluid, with members coming and going at all times (Lee 1976b); it is open with respect to territorial and group affiliation (Lee 1976b; Guenther 1981a); it is loosely corporate with respect to ownership of land or other resources (which include very little property) (Lee 1981); it is slack in its political organization (Lee 1982; Silberbauer 1982). Interpersonal and gender relations are not structured by any hierarchical order but are egalitarian (Lee 1979; Barnard 1980b; Guenther 1983) and there is a virtual absence of craft specialization, except for a basic division of labor by sex. The latter, however, is by no means exclusive, as exemplified by men frequently being engaged in gathering and child-rearing. As for hunting, women occasionally set traps at Kutse (see chapter 6) and, on rare occasion, a woman may be engaged in sporadic hunting (Draper 1976; Heinz pers. comm.; Shostak 1981:93, 244).

A number of social institutions are flexible *sui generis*, a result of (or, possibly, a cause for) what Silberbauer (1981a:185), writing about the G/wi, refers to as the "organizational lability" of society. Neo-locality and highly classificatory (indeed universalistic) kinship systems are both social patterns that "obscure genealogical detail" (Silberbauer 1981a:174). Absence of status differentiation and vaguely defined leadership and ritual specialization, unstable, tenuous marriages in early to mid-adulthood, and loose and informal child-rearing practices are all social institutions that furthermore allow for "ad hoc distortions of formal structure," using, yet again, Silberbauer's apt formulation (Silberbauer 1981a:147). They allow for a wide margin of individual action as none is an institution or practice based on cut-and-dried jural rules but, instead, all are tentative and open-ended.

Individual men and women enjoy a high degree of personal autonomy within Bushman society (Guenther 1992:94–5; also see Gardener 1991 for a discussion of this feature in foraging societies generally). Each individual in this small-scale egalitarian society is self-assured and self-directing; what characterizes individuals' personalities is, in Woodburn's words (1982:438), a "lack of dependence on specific others," amongst people who lead their social lives "without dependencies or commitments to kin, affines, or contractual partners." Lack of craft and ritual specialization, in a culture of which the material and mystical elements are accessible to everyone, further contributes to the development of personal autonomy. Presumably, autonomy of self would also foster a marked degree of individualism, as well as individuation (or self-actualization, in a context of a homogeneous, non-alienating culture) (Service 1979:75). Individuals enjoy considerable freedom of movement and the sense of solidarity they experience toward their own band is probably fairly loose. This they may readily leave, for longer or shorter lengths of time, upon marriage, in the event of an impasse in a quarrel, or for no other reason than whim.

Thus, we see Bushman men and women living their lives within a culture that contains beliefs and values that are variable, flexible, and undogmatic. The institutions and the structure of their society are loose and its organization is fluid. Such a society, I submit, renders the individual footloose and fancy-free, so much so that nomadism and foraging are, in fact, more than subsistence strategies. Mobility is a cultural mind-set that makes peripatetic wanderers out of the Bushman men and women, with an "inability to sit quietly in a room" (as Pascal put it, gloomily and in the spirit of Neolithic chauvinism, as he saw man's urge to wander as the root cause of mankind's troubles). And, as mentioned above, it makes the wanderers forage also for ideas, which they adopt and adapt, as they come in contact with neighboring or incoming groups (unless the latter were of hostile intent, in which case the Bushmen have usually responded in kind). This penchant for mobility of autonomous individuals who, because of their loose attachment to an open group, are free to yield to its urgings, is thus a key reason for Bushman cultural diversity.

Apart from institutional and individual flexibility, there is one other structural feature of the classic Bushman band society that renders it flexible and adaptable. This is the multiple-tiered structure of that society. Formally and ideally, Bushman society consists of at least two, and in some instances (such as the !Kxo, Nharo, and G/wi, as well as, it would seem, the Kūa Basarwa), three basic levels of organization.

The first is the individual household, or nuclear family. The second is the band, or "camp," as Richard Lee (1979:56) prefers to call it – "because of the misleading formal connotation of the term *band*."

The third tier is the multi-band aggregation; Alan Barnard suggests it be termed "band cluster" (Barnard 1992a:65); other ethnographers have referred to it as "band alliance" (Silberbauer 1965:76, 1972:302–4, 1981a:178–90), "band nexus" (Heinz 1994:98–110), or "camp cluster" (Vierich and Hitchcock, chapter 5, this volume). This third level is more or less well defined among some groups, forming either "coherent units" (akin to a Kūa "community," Vierich and Hitchcock, chapter 5, this volume) or named groups with recognized membership (Barnard 1992a:138). Intermarriage and reciprocal access to one another's resources were the basic ties that forged these somewhat inchoate "alliance networks." While structurally incipient, these supra-band units are nevertheless more than etic categories; the Nharo call them *n!usa* (Barnard 1992a:138; see chapter 4) and the !Kxo, *n/u tu* (Heinz 1994:98–100; 1979), terms that, respectively, emphasize common territory and common group membership. While absent as socially or semantically defined categories from other Bushman linguistic group-ings such as the !Kung, it could be argued that supra-band units are an implicit structural component of Bushman society generally, because of the universal concentration-dispersal dynamic, resulting in the annual aggregation of bands, sharing resources, information, spouses, and ritual (Lee 1979:364–9).

The individual household is defined by the hearth and, in the rainy season, the hut around which each family sleeps and eats. Its members are the recipients and consumers of the plants gathered by a woman. During the rainy season, when food is plentiful, this unit may move about, foraging and hunting along its way. The band, for all its structu-ral amorphousness and fluidity with respect to group membership, is consolidated for much of the rainy season. The core members of such "camps" – siblings with spouses, children, and parents – are the "owners" of a band territory. The headman typically holds a loosely defined authority position and is the spokesman for the group (for example, in dealings with neighboring or visiting bands). As noted above, the multi-band unit is the group that normally aggregates, more or less regularly, around the few waterholes that yield water throughout the dry season. Intermarriage, exchange, common performance of ritual (trance and male initiation) are intergroup actions amongst band-cluster members that instill a certain degree of common purpose amongst the constituent bands and their members (Lee 1979:364–9; Barnard 1992a:44–5).

As I have argued more fully elsewhere (Guenther 1986a:292–4), the fact that Bushman society is made up of three potentially autonomous social groupings renders this society both flexible and adaptable. If ecological social, or historical conditions warrant it, the family unit may become the social unit within which people spend most of their social lives. Examples of precipitating circumstances to render this sub-band unit the operative social division might be a persistent drought that forced the split-up of a band, or a serious quarrel alienating one family from the rest of the band and leading it to leave the main group. Such fragmented sub-bands could become the precariously permanent social formation of a group (for instance the now vanished Saan of the Namib). Ghanzi farm Bushman groups today (that is, at the time I did fieldwork, in the late 1960s) are frequently fragmented into nuclear family units because of the employment practice of small-scale Boer ranchers, who may be able to hire only one or two laborers. On the poorer farms, usually only his immediate dependants may stay with an employed Bushman laborer, and the amount of the weekly rations the farmer hands out may be measured in terms of a nuclear, rather than extended, family (Guenther 1986a:294).

In other circumstances, such as encroachment by aggressive settlers, as in the Cape, South-West Africa, and Ghanzi in colonial times, the multi-band group, traditionally loose as a social and political unit, may become the permanent and prominent organizational structure. Such a development may be galvanized by a certain individual, a trance dancer (Guenther 1975; 1986a:288–9) or a headman, such as the above-mentioned "mighty =Dukuri" of the //Au=ei of nineteenth-century Ghanzi, or the "dreaded Namagorub," "paramount chief" of the !Kung or northeastern German South-West Africa (Seiner 1913:302). Such leaders expanded their authority well beyond the narrowly confined limits of traditional Bushman headmanship, in part, perhaps, by drawing also on the afore-mentioned power potential that is inherent in the male hunting role. Other leadership figures, especially during colonial times, were outsiders who typically were partially westernized Khoi or "Basters" from Cape Colony (Szalay 1983:173; Guenther 1991).

Flexibility and cultural autonomy

The supremely flexible and adaptable quality of Bushman band society, ethos, and personality explains, I suggest, the rich diversity of such societies and, at the same time, why so many of these people have basically retained their cultural integrity and their social autonomy throughout centuries and even millennia of contact with encroaching and encircling settler groups. In the course of this contact some have lost their independence and have become the marginal underclass of more powerful, hegemonic agropastoralists. Others may have become so transformed, through stock ownership or sedentism, that egalitarianism and reciprocity have eventually given way to social hierarchy and centralized power. Both or either of these developments are claimed by the "revisionists" to have happened to all of the Bushmen of Namibia and Botswana (Wilmsen 1989; Wilmsen and Denbow 1990).

However, given the resilience, plasticity, and adaptability of band society, looks may be deceiving. That is, a specific Bushman society displaying one or several non-foraging traits – say, stock ownership or prolonged aggregation, trade with or labor for whites or blacks, patrilineality or inherited headmanship – may at the same time be capable of retaining its basic stamp as an egalitarian band society, in terms of its overall structure and ethos. Such was my own conclusion (Guenther 1986a:286–95) about the heavily acculturated, farm Bushmen of Ghanzi of the late 1960s, who, for some three generations, had been involved in farm labor, sedentism, an engulfing cash economy, reduced gender equality, incipient professionalization of the trance dancer, and craft specialization, as well as a number of other changes. I concluded, however, that these developments "neither singly nor in combination have brought about anything like a transformation of Nharo society or culture . . . The band remains the basic social structure and the sharing ethos, despite being challenged by the new values of negative reciprocity, is still basically intact" (Guenther 1986a:289–90).

One basic point of criticism against the revisionists' claim is that they too readily dub a certain Bushman group as tarred with the state brush and as incorporated within the regional state hegemony. Their claim may be made on the basis of just a few trade goods, a few head of stock, or certain hierarchical or political tendencies that they come across with respect to a specific Bushman group (Lee and Guenther 1991, 1993). As argued in this chapter, the structure, institutions, and ethos of Bushman society have sufficient stretch to incorporate the occasional oxen, the occasional spell of sedentism or clientage, and the presence, within social organization, of an external or internal power elite, such as Bantu overlords or Bushman Captains and *n!ore*-owners.

The Bushmen, and the egalitarian society they live in and by, have been around in southern Africa for a long time. Throughout the history that coursed through these millennia of time – of drought cycles and starvation, migrations, settler immigrations and emigrations, raids, resistance, conquests – the structural and ideological muscles of Bushman society have stayed supple and strong. In some regions of southern Africa this strength was broken and the band society became transformed and its dynamics no longer were directed against the state but embraced it. However, in others that strength was retained, allowing Bushmen groupings here and there, and in a diversity of economic and social patterns, to remain independent and to resist the pressure or lure of agropastoral state society.

Is Bushman diversity "real" or "made"?

In endeavoring to explain the causes for Bushman cultural diversity, I have thus far considered them in objective terms, that is, the environmental, historical, and social-structural conditions that shape the society and culture of the people. Before ending this examination of diversity it would be appropriate also to consider subjective factors, ones having to do with the various methodological, theoretical, and ideological approaches of the investigators, to see whether the diversity of the entity investigated may be a reflection or projection of these approaches. Chapter 4 also gives consideration to the "methodological diversity in anthropological approaches" to Bushman societies, as a factor of cultural diversity among African foragers.

This line of inquiry is especially relevant in the field of contemporary Bushman studies, I think, for two reasons. First, contentiousness is created by the current postmodernist climate of the discipline. It has recently been felt in the field of Kalahari studies and is reflected in one of the key issues of the current revisionist debate, that the Bushmen have been "made" into Rousseauian "icons" of pristinism and archaism. This charge has created a veritable "crisis of representation" in contemporary Bushman studies, in the estimation of one researcher (Lee 1992a). The second reason for considering approaches is because an unusually large number of researchers – approximately 130, according to John Hudleson (1993) – have studied the Bushmen over the past four decades, rendering this people one of the most studied small-scale societies of the world. They have brought to their work a range of research problems and conceptual approaches – from "primal monotheism" in the early days, through human ethology, cultural ecology, studies of kinship and social change in the 1960s through 1980s, to political economy in the 1990s (Hudleson 1993). Is the extraordinary diversity of Bushman culture, perhaps, a reflection, simply, of the fact that an extraordinary number of researchers have described and analyzed it, from a variety of theoretical perspectives?

I think not. Notwithstanding the proliferation of researchers and approaches, the theoretical underpinnings of the majority of these studies were those of cultural ecology, the paradigm forged to large measure in the context of Bushman ethnography. This applies especially to the work of Richard Lee, ever since he organized (with Irven DeVore) the influential "Man the hunter" conference in Chicago and published the book with the same title (Lee and DeVore 1968). The work of the "Harvard group" followed the same research program, exploring each and every infrastructural parameter of Bushman social organization, both ethnographically and archaeologically. Even !Kung ritual, belief, and oral traditions were analyzed in ecological, adaptational terms, as "foraging ideology" and symbolic labor (Biesele 1993). The latter concept was employed also by Lewis-Williams (1982), in his work on Bushman rock art and the trance dance. Much of the work of other researchers outside the Harvard/Dobe/!Kung circle was of the same theoretical bent, such as that of Marshall (both the ethnographer Lorna and the film-maker John), Silberbauer, Barnard, Cashdan, Heinz, Hitchcock, Kent, and others. It pervades the theoretical approach even of Wilmsen, the chief spokesman of the revisionists, which one reviewer has aptly summarized as a blend of "an older ecological base [with] strong traces of dependency theory, neo-Marxian modes-of-production theory, 'world systems' theory, and a political economy of urban bias" (Shipton 1991:756).

Thus, while there have been well over a hundred researchers afoot in the Kalahari, the theoretical approaches with which they studied their subjects have been very much less numerous. This would suggest that such cultural diversity as one does find in the field of Bushman social organization across the Kalahari and beyond is a social reality and ethnographic fact, and not an academic distortion, created through theoretical fragmentation. Its ethnographic validity is underscored by a number of other considerations about the methodological and analytical operations of the ethnographers who have worked in the Kalahari over the past four decades.

One of them, deriving from the fact that there are more Bushman researchers than Bushman linguistic groupings, is that one and the same Bushman group has been and is being studied by more than one researcher. This is a salutary circumstance as it makes possible corroboration of descriptions and analyses of the same group. When the diverse researchers work independently, rather than as members of a team or of an ongoing project (as at Dobe), the corrective effects of such multiple research projects are the more enhanced. This can be said, for example, of the Marshalls and Lee and other Dobe workers, all of whom have worked amongst the Ju/'hoansi (!Kung), of Silberbauer and Tanaka, and Tanaka and Cashdan, both sets of researchers studying, respectively, the G/wi and the G//anna, as well as of Guenther, Barnard, and Steyn, all three of whom worked amongst the Nharo.

I think the relative reliability of ethnographic data, and the likelihood that they would correspond to the signified sociocultural reality, is due to another factor, one of an academic-political nature: conferencing. Bushman researchers, as well as hunter-gatherer researchers generally, engage in this mode of information exchange to a large extent (Barnard 1983:194–5). Akin to the socioeconomic life of the people they study, their academic life is one of biennial, week-long aggregation, at a suitably exotic venue (and never far from a permanent, high-yield water hole), and, following this period of dense intellectual interaction, dispersal, back to their respective home universities. The purpose of these gatherings is to discuss and monitor one another's ethnographic work, as well as to coordinate and streamline the theoretical directions of research and to present, for criticism or corroboration, new empirical and analytical insights. My impression of these gatherings – most of which also yield published volumes that disseminate the data and analysis beyond the confines of each conference – is that they have the effect of enhancing the quality of fieldwork and the accuracy and explanatory power of the research concepts and designs. Each new study is presented to, and its data and analysis are vetted by, this forum of fellow researchers. At its best, all this acts as a "quality control" mechanism on the work that is produced; at its worst, it could lead to the entrenchment of a certain notion or paradigm, when the gathering of scholars turns into an "old boys/girls network" that perpetuates old and cherished doctrine. While some academic conferences may deserve such cynicism (*viz*. David Lodge), my impression from the hunter-gatherer conferences I have attended is that these scholarly happenings have not as yet fallen into this rut.

The diversity of the Bushmen is thus a matter of fact (rather than of academic fiction or projection), exemplified and corroborated by numerous, high-quality ethnographic studies. The element of diversity of the Bushmen, as well as other hunter-gatherers of Africa and beyond, and the careful study of comparison, regionally and beyond, is an important step toward identifying the structural and functional parameters and prerequisites of non-food-producing societies.

The analytical focus and research strategy, of diversity and flexibility and comparison, should take center stage in the theoretical examination of Bushman and hunter-gatherer society. It holds the potential for resolving some of the longstanding theoretical problems in the field, as well as more recent ones, such as the revisionism debate. An example of the former, which can be elucidated only through careful consideration of diversity and comparison, is the "definitional problem," that is, coming up with a model for hunter-gatherer society that is broad enough to encompass all cases, while also being specific enough to capture what distinguishes this societal type from others.[5]

A focus on diversity and comparison offers a way out of the stalemate in which Bushman researchers find themselves with respect to the revisionism debate currently holding center stage in the theoretical discussions of Khoisan researchers (Barnard 1992b). After almost a decade of argument and counter-argument – much of it in the pages of *Current Anthropology* (Solway and Lee 1990; Wilmsen and Denbow 1990; Lee and Guenther 1991; Silberbauer 1991; Wilmsen 1993) – and a remarkable degree of tolerance of error on one (the revisionist) side (Lee and Guenther 1993), the Kalahari Debate appears to have become stuck in a groove.

I am in agreement with Susan Kent when she identifies the "failure to acknowledge the cultural diversity that characterizes Basarwa society as a whole" (Kent 1992:45) as one of the principal issues clouding the debate. Looking at the Bushmen as a regional totality, over space and time, we find groups that fit both the "traditionalist/isolationist" and the "revisionist/integrationist" positions, as well as numerous positions in between. The fact that there is evidence for both positions makes them complementary, rather than opposed. The new research strategy in Bushman studies should thus be one of synthesis, not polarization, of these two types of social and theoretical design (Lee 1992).

---

[5] For the most recent attempts at arriving at a definition of the category hunting-gathering society see Gardener (1991) and Rao (1993). The focus of the former (dubbed by Gardener the "individual-autonomy syndrome"), in the "classic" mold of social and ecological anthropology, is on the individual in relation to the group. The latter (the so-called "peripatetic niche") is formulated in the revisionist terms of political economy.

4   Nharo and Hai//om settlement patterns in comparative perspective

Alan Barnard and Thomas Widlok

Introduction

This book is not only about cultural diversity. It is also, inevitably, a textbook on the methodological diversity in anthropological approaches. Here we offer an example of one approach that, we believe, can help to clarify issues inherent in social change and regional variation alike. It is based loosely on the idea of regional comparison (see Barnard 1992a).

The strength of our approach is twofold. First, regional comparison is, by definition, a form of controlled comparison. Secondly, comparison of variation within and between two groups enables us to go beyond surface reasons for similarities and differences. Indeed, the study of Khoisan settlement patterns is one field in which regional comparison has been shown to be fruitful (see, for example, Barnard 1979; 1986b; Cashdan 1983; Guenther, chapter 3, this volume). Our problem here is analogous to that confronted in the classic works on the developmental cycle of domestic groups (e.g., Goody 1958). What appears at first to be random variation can, upon closer examination, be seen as part of an unfolding pattern of patterns. Just as domestic groups expand and contract with births and marriages, and with deaths and divisions, so too do hunter-gatherer bands. Relative size and composition depend on a complex of factors, including season, availability of resources, and outside pressure.

In this chapter, two groups are described (see Figure 4.1). They live more than 500 kilometers from each other and are not in contact. They have different environments and are incorporated in two different nation-states. They speak mutually unintelligible though related languages. A comparison between Hai//om settlement patterns taken as a whole and those of the Nharo taken as a whole shows that the establishment of commercial farms can have quite different effects, although the process appears similar on the surface. The effects depend on rights to land, options for movement, and access to political power. By the same token, some very similar transformations can be observed in

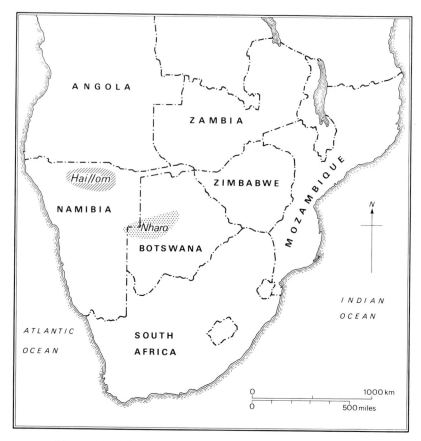

Figure 4.1   Nharo and Hai//om areas of Botswana and Namibia

processes of aggregation. The perceived "unsettledness" of Bushpeople has been a cause of concern for those who came to control and govern them. The transformations in settlement patterns represent attempts by Nharo and Hai//om to come to terms with the pressures from such dominant population groups.

There are distinctive forms of settlement for the Nharo and Hai//om. These are linked to social, political, economic, and environmental contexts. The relations between types of settlement and those contexts illustrate parallels as well as differences between the two groups. They also partly reflect the similar seasonal cycle, especially in past times when subsistence depended entirely on hunting and gathering. Both groups endure very dry winters (July, August, and September being especially difficult) and summers of sporadic rainfall (January usually being the wettest month). The emphasis here is on the diversity found in the late twentieth century, though similar processes operated in earlier periods too. Both groups have been subject to the incursion of Bantu-speaking populations from the early nineteenth century and to the dispossession of much of their land by white farmers since the 1890s.

The Hai//om material was collected by Widlok during his field research in Namibia in 1990 to 1992. A more detailed account is given in his recent Ph.D. thesis presented to the University of London. The Nharo material was collected by Barnard in 1974 to 1975, 1979, and 1982 (cf. Barnard 1980a). The chapter itself was planned during Barnard's visit to Widlok's research base in 1991 and completed after further field research by both authors in 1993.[1]

Nharo settlement patterns

The Nharo (also called Naro or Naron) live in the central-western Kalahari, mainly within the Ghanzi farms of western Botswana.[2] This is a vast area which has been occupied by white settlers since 1898. The area is diverse in style of ranching, in ethnic composition, and in the degree of acculturation experienced by different groups. A 1976 government survey estimated the total farm population to number about 7,700, of whom 4,500 were members of these former foraging groups (Childers 1976:20); the population today is no doubt higher (see also Guenther 1979b:45–53; 1986a:1–10). The Nharo who live outside the ranching area include a number who are attached to cattle-posts of the Bantu-speaking Kgalagari to the west, and some who live south of the ranches, notably at the government settlement scheme of Hanahai.

Although the former foragers of Ghanzi are diverse in origin, they are frequently in contact. The Nharo are the main group and, together with their northeastern neighbors the Ts'aokhoe, they make up the western "Central Bushman" branch of the Khoe linguistic group. The ≠Haba,

[1] Widlok's research in Namibia was made possible by a University of London Post-graduate Studentship, as well as financial support from the University of London Central Research Fund, and the James A. Swan Fund of the Pitt Rivers Museum, Oxford. Barnard's field research in Botswana was supported by grants from the Swan Fund, the Department of Social Anthropology and Centre of African Studies of the University of Edinburgh, and the US National Science Foundation (BNS-8023941). Barnard's research in Namibia was supported by grants from the Nuffield Foundation, the Swan Fund, and the University of Edinburgh (Munro Lectureship Committee, Tweedie Exploration Fellowship Committee, Committee for African Studies, Travel and Research Committee, and Department of Social Anthropology).
[2] In this chapter, the terms "farm" and "ranch" are used synonymously to refer to the commercial enterprises in the Kalahari that owe their economic basis to cattle-keeping. These are similar to "ranches," as that term is employed in a North American context, but the word "farm" is the more common in southern Africa itself.

G/wikhoe, and G//anakhoe are Khoe-speakers too, closely related to the Nharo and distantly related to the Hai//om. They live mainly to the east, and many are found in northeastern parts of the farm block living along with Nharo. The !Kung-speaking ≠Au//ei are found in the northwestern part of the Ghanzi farms. The !Xõ have yet another origin, having come from vast, sparsely populated areas to the south. Although their own language is distinctly different, most !Xõ in the farm area speak Nharo fluently. Culturally, all these groups are similar, for example, in traditional religion, sharing practices, and hunting methods, though settlement patterns in their places of origin sometimes differ profoundly. For example, !Kung-speakers until recently aggregated in the dry season and dispersed in the wet season; G/wikhoe and G//anakhoe dispersed in the dry season and aggregated in the wet season (Barnard 1979; 1986b). All these groups have been undergoing changes since the 1960s when intensive field research began, and indeed periods of intensive change have taken place in the presence of observers in earlier times too (see, for example, Passarge 1907).

≠Aa: a semi-traditional Nharo band

≠Aa is a Nharo settlement in the Hanahai valley. It lies between a large farmhouse settlement, about 6 kilometers away, and the communal lands south of the farms. The people of ≠Aa live partly as hunter-gatherers and partly as herders; they have close kin both at the farmhouse settlement and in the communal lands. The average population during Barnard's ten-month stay there in the mid-1970s was about twenty, though this varied from month to month.

The farmer who then leased the site kept cattle there, but he visited only once every month or two. He employed one Nharo resident to switch on the petrol-driven borehole engine which ran water into the cattle trough. The borehole, about 30 meters from the camp, provided a year-round supply of water. Other than that, both the cattle and people were left to look after themselves. On rare occasions, two of the men did odd jobs for the farmer, such as mending fences or driving cattle. Maize rations distributed to the farmhouse workers frequently found their way to ≠Aa, and some ≠Aa people owned goats and chickens. Even so, gathering and hunting remained the primary subsistence pursuits. The inhabitants did no gardening, but preferred to forage and to maintain the residential flexibility which foraging allows.

The land near ≠Aa is not extremely rich in resources, but edible roots, tubers, and berries are available. Food-gathering takes place in groups of two to five women, and the ethos is one of cooperation rather than of competition. Men most often hunt in pairs, although sometimes several will hunt together. Meat is widely distributed, whereas vegetable food normally remains within the nuclear family. The Nharo of ≠Aa maintain close ties with others of the N//ua//xe band cluster. Band membership changes from month to month, and visits between ≠Aa people and members of other bands are exchanged nearly every day. The most frequent bands visited are those occupying the area around the nearby farmhouse settlement. Because of the inexhaustible supply of water at ≠Aa, the inhabitants can remain there all year round. In the valley near the farmhouse there is also a permanent natural waterhole which is used for bathing. In years of exceptionally good rain, it can be 2 meters deep at its deepest point and up to 50 meters long and 20 meters wide.

The number of huts in use varies according to the number of residents. At one period of stable band membership, there were 21 residents and 7 huts. The band is composed of individuals of several generations and ages. Sometimes, though, members of one or other informal age group reside elsewhere, leaving the age structure much less uniform. During the period of Barnard's fieldwork, ≠Aa was to some extent an old people's band. This may have partly accounted for its traditionalist ethos.

The Old Grimmond Place: a multi-ethnic community

The Old Grimmond Place marks the center of a mixed community in the middle of the Ghanzi farms. At the time of Barnard's study, the farmhouse itself was uninhabited. The absentee landlord visited only once every two months in order to pay his workers. The ethnographic present described here is 1975.

The Old Grimmond Place consists of two separate settlements. In effect these two settlements function as a single community. The smaller lies in the shadows of the farm buildings, while the larger lies in a heavily wooded area about 2 kilometers to the north. Each has its own borehole. The person nominally in charge of both settlements is Rapedi, a Tswana man who is married to K'waba, a Nharo woman who is the focus of the family grouping residing near the farmhouse. Both K'waba's son-in-law and her son are employed by the farmer, but they supplement their meager wages by hunting inedible carnivores (mainly foxes and jackals) for their skins. The residents of the outlying settlement include a pair of elderly female cross-cousins and their relatives by marriage and descent.

Perhaps partly because of the scarcity of wild foods and partly because of the diverse ethnic make-up of the two settlements (they include

Tswana, ≠ Haba, G//anakhoe, and Ts'aokhoe, as well as Nharo), there is no clear concept of a "band territory" here. A number of individuals have strong ties to Nharo and Ts'aokhoe who live on surrounding farms, and exchanges of visits are frequent. Even so, the kinship and friendship ties across the farm boundaries are less evident than the ties between the two settlements of the Old Grimmond Place.

The Old Grimmond Place differs from ≠Aa in two important respects. First, the Old Grimmond Place consists of individuals from several different ethnic groups and places of origin. They mix freely and have intermarried. The residents retain strong senses of their respective ethnic identities, though language differences are slight. Secondly, the people of the Old Grimmond Place do not regard themselves as the owners of the land they inhabit. No individual has a claim to aboriginal ownership of the settlement area, since all of the older individuals come from elsewhere.

Rhodes' farm: a commercial ranch

Rhodes' farm is a large commercial ranch. When Barnard surveyed it in 1975, the manager was a relative newcomer and had little tolerance for squatters. When spotted, individuals who were not either workers or members of their nuclear families were asked to leave. The workers earned much more than those at ≠Aa or the Old Grimmond Place, but they had to pull their weight in order to stay on the payroll and remain on the farm.

In 1975, twelve people were residents at the farmhouse settlement. Most were Tswana brought in from other parts of the country. The farmer hired them in preference to local Nharo because, as he put it, Tswana have less of a tendency to wander. The farm then had eleven outlying boreholes, each the center of one of the cattle-posts. In addition to wages, workers would receive maize meal, sugar, tea, coffee, and tobacco. Some owned goats and chickens, and a number made curios for sale at the shop in Ghanzi, less than 30 kilometers away.

Unlike many of the larger ranches, Rhodes' farm does not have separate settlements for each ethnic group. Such *de facto* segregation, where it does occur, involves individual groups who reside in a circle of huts with their kin – one circle containing Nharo, one circle G/wi, and so on. True to its commercial ethos, Rhodes' farm avoids this kind of grouping in favor of a seemingly random, non-circular arrangement. Only the G/wi and G//ana maintain separate camps, apparently because of their more traditionalist ethos. The Nharo live mixed with Tswana and Kgalagari. Through the intermarriage of their parents, many claim membership of more than one ethnic group, though most in this situation choose to be identified as Nharo, who are the traditional inhabitants of the site.

There were twelve occupied dwellings at the farmhouse settlement at the time of the survey. Most of these were "traditional" Nharo huts, with roofs. Most of the cattle-posts were located on a circular road. Huts there were variously of traditional style (the most common), of Kgalagari style, or of sheet metal. Typically, settlements contained one or two employed men and their families.

Residents of both the farmhouse settlement and the cattle-posts come mainly from outside the farm. Individuals and families move from borehole to borehole as work requires, and they do not develop the ties that characterize settlements elsewhere. They lack both the close association with the land found at ≠Aa, and the community spirit of the Old Grimmond Place. The outlying settlements are small and generally have neither Nharo names nor community identities.

Diversity and continuity in Nharo settlement patterns

Clearly, the settlements described here are very different places. Our isolation of one borehole settlement in the case of ≠Aa, two in the case of the Old Grimmond Place, and several in the case of Rhodes' farm reflects our own perceptions of the significant level of socio-territorial organization in each case. But to a great extent, these units also represent indigenous perceptions of community and of land use. All the areas include "bands" in the sense that each settlement may be referred to as a *tsousa*, the traditional word for "camp" or "band location." Similarly all exist within a large territorial framework, though the boundaries of traditional band clusters are somewhat obscured. The traditional word for "band clusters" is *n!usa*, and this is a term heard often at ≠Aa in reference to ≠Aa's place within the N//ua//xe *n!usa*. The term sometimes also means simply "land" or "country," and all of the farming area and parts beyond can thus be said to be the *n!usa* of the Nharo people as a whole.

The socio-territorial organization associated with ≠Aa is not typical. It probably represents a form of territorial organization more common before the settlement of Ghanzi by whites, or at least before the extension of freehold tenure in the 1960s (cf. Russell and Russell 1979). The Old Grimmond Place, although made up of members of several different ethnic groups, is similar to ≠Aa in some respects. Inhabitants participate in traditional activities like hunting, gathering, sharing, and visiting, and hold frequent medicine (trance) dances. Each settlement is intralinked by ties of kinship, friendship, and clientship, independent of

Figure 4.2   Nharo: permanent settlement, 1974

relations with the absentee rancher. Rhodes' farm is rather different. In contrast to the kin-based networks of the other two settlements, Rhodes' farm *is* very much farm-centered (Figures 4.2 and 4.3).

Still, there are some similarities between all the settlements. All have a mixed economy, with some hunting and gathering, and some trade or wage labor. One government survey (Childers 1976:53–8) found that nearly 90 percent of farm Bushpeople do some food-gathering and that over 22 percent hunt at least once a year. Even at Rhodes' farm, there is still some hunting and gathering, as indeed there are some unemployed squatters. Another similarity is the presence of livestock other than that owned by farmers.

The significant differences between the three settlements stem from two main factors: ethnic composition, and the association between the land and the people. With the expansion of large farm holdings by wealthy ranchers, earlier forms of socio-territorial organization are giving way. In the future, people of diverse ethnic background will be brought into greater proximity wherever employment opportunities exist, and those without employment will become more marginal. The marginalized may well drift towards population centers such as Ghanzi township, D'kar, and Hanahai (Figure 4.4). Indeed, when Barnard last visited the area in 1993, there were strong signs of this happening.

Hai//om settlement patterns

The Hai//om live mainly in commercial farming areas around Tsumeb and Grootfontein and in communal areas of northern Namibia (where they are also known as ≠Akhoe). Some live in close association with Damara or Owambo herders; others stay in more outlying areas or, increasingly, in population centers. The total Hai//om population is about 11,000.

Botos: subsistence foraging on communal land during crop season

Botos only became a long-term dwelling place just over a decade ago, when Kwanyama-speaking (Owambo) farmers moved there from near the Angolan border about 80 kilometers away. Hai//om claim that this place has no Hai//om name except "Botos," which is derived from the original Owambo name. The area served as a hinterland for Owambo hunting expeditions from the Ndonga kingdom and as a refuge for members of their royal clan in the course of power struggles (Williams 1991:142).

At present, the main attraction of Botos lies in the opportunities for work, income, and exchange with the local Owambo. Work is available during the entire cycle of millet or sorghum growing, from the clearing of fields in December and January up to the harvesting and threshing, which ends in May or June. During that time, water is available in waterholes, and the local Owambo provide the workers with food and drink. Hai//om spend much more time working in the Owambo fields than in their own, and the crops in their own gardens suffer. The Hai//om do not own livestock, but the nearest Owambo homestead is only 500 meters away and the cattle and goats of the Owambo graze in the surrounding forest.

The huts are arranged in two sites, separated by about 60 meters and surrounded by a fence. They are built in Owambo style: a circle of

Figure 4.3   Nharo: at a farmhouse settlement, 1979

wooden poles with a thatched roof on top. In the southern site, the hut
occupied by the oldest man lies in the east, next to a shady place where
people sit during the day, do handicrafts like wood-carving, and where
the mortar is placed for stamping millet. The fireplace in the west is
made in the style of the Kwanyama *olupale*. In a Kwanyama homestead
this is the place where the owner receives visitors.

Figure 4.4   Nharo: building a permanent hut, 1982

The Hai//om have a number of names for this fireplace, including *orupare* (visitors' place), *hos* (meeting place), and *!khais* (men's fire). At Botos it is also called ≠ *khoa-ais*, literally "elephant's place," referring to the medicine trance dance that is associated with the elephant. During the medicine dance, men are seated around the *!khais* (≠ *khoa-ais*) while the women and children gather around a second fire a few meters to the east. Women usually do not sit or cook at the *orupare* or *!khais*. In the northern settlement, the cooking and eating place of the women and children is exactly opposite. Men either sit at a separate fire, or they have plates of their own. Although probably introduced from surrounding agro-pastoralists, this gender division and east–west axis has been characteristic of Hai//om settlement for some time, as evidenced by descriptions by the early ethnographers (e.g., Lebzelter 1934:80–8; cf. Fourie 1926; 1928). During meals, visitors from another hearth would be offered a share, but in most cases they would return to their own fires to eat. Uncooked foods (above all, mangetti or mongongo nuts) are widely shared. During the most labor-intensive period, food is often prepared in the Owambo homestead and consumed at the end of each day by the whole local group, regardless of their work effort. The same is true for beer that is given out as payment.

The permanent huts in the northern site are inhabited by a married couple, the husband's widowed mother, and the eldest daughter and her husband who is doing brideservice. The southern site has a hut for the widowed eldest man, a son of his with his wife and children, and two widowed women. There are temporary dwelling places in both sites for visitors. In its general layout, the settlement resembles an unfinished Owambo homestead or cattle-post. From an Owambo point of view, therefore, the settlement is that of a *kwankala*, a poor person, which in fact is a term frequently used by the Owambo to describe Hai//om and !Kung. From the Hai//om perspective, this kind of settlement (particularly when it has a fence and special-purpose huts) is often covered under the same term as an Owambo homestead: *!naos*. This Hai//om concept implies a more clearly bounded entity than the term //*gâus* or "band."

!Gai ≠ nas: subsistence foraging on communal land during the dry season

In July, the Botos community moves to !Gai ≠ nas, which they regard as their original waterhole, and where another //*gâus* of Hai//om, with whom they are closely related, stay for the whole year. Lack of water (the nearest water source is 10 kilometers away) is given as the reason for moving from Botos, though for several weeks the Hai//om will have fetched water over that distance and will do it again when they return to Botos in December. Before reaching !Gai ≠ nas, they stay for two weeks at a mangetti grove about halfway between the two sites – with the nearest water source a two-hour sturdy walk away, at !Gai ≠ nas. Thus the crop season and the availability of wild food seem to be more decisive factors for dwelling at a place than is easy access to water.

Each year at !Gai ≠ nas a new campsite is chosen a few hundred meters from that of the previous year, and about the same distance from the other Hai//om //*gâus*. There small grass huts are built, while there are only small windscreens at the interim camp. There were altogether twelve small grass huts at !Gai ≠ nas at the time it was surveyed. At this time of year Hai//om have hardly any work to do for the neighboring Owambo, except gathering grass and cutting poles for house construction. Therefore, they rely on other forms of income. Hunting, by bow and arrow, is at its easiest, since trees and bushes have few leaves. Nevertheless, hunting returns in the area are low, and gathering provides the bulk of the diet, with many fruits becoming ripe during the dry-season months during which !Gai ≠ nas is occupied (Figure 4.5).

/Gomais: aggregating at a service center

Due to the abundance of the mangetti nut, /Gomais (literally "mangetti place") has been a center of Hai//om settlement for as long as oral history recalls. At least since the beginning of this century, Hai//om from farther north, particularly men, have stayed at /Gomais for certain intervals, either to look for a wife or to find work on the neighboring farms. In 1979, the area was developed as a large ranch operated by the First National Development Corporation (FNDC), a semi-state development enterprise. Its present high population of over 200 at the central cattle-post is a result of the recent war in the area (1978 to 1989). Hai//om were told by the South African Defence Force, who were then operating at Hai//om places to the north, that they should leave those areas and gather at /Gomais unless they wanted "to be shot together with SWAPO."[3] While the area was only seasonally occupied before the establishment of pumps, it has been a permanent Hai//om settlement since the 1970s.

Some 14 Hai//om men have found work with FNDC, doing livestock management, including fencing and pump maintenance. They are well paid in comparison to laborers on privately owned farms. One of the central differences is that to be a worker or part of a worker's core family is not a condition for staying at /Gomais. Hence the population is higher than on the private farms. There are also other sources of income. Mangetti and a variety of other wild foods are available throughout the year. Also, the Church operates a school and offers occasional food distributions. Finally, there are about 40 Owambo (mostly workers and their wives) who distill and sell alcohol on a large scale. This is a potential source of income for some Hai//om, and a source of social disruption for all of them.

Gardening is limited, since the area for use by the Hai//om is small and fenced. The food return is therefore very low. Gathering food, either for own consumption or for sale to the Owambo, takes up much more time. In many instances, the payment for food is either liquor or money later used for purchasing liquor. In contrast to the Owambo "location" some 100 meters away, no housing is provided for the Hai//om. Instead, the workers have access to materials such as wooden poles, old cattle-feed bags, and corrugated iron, out of which they

---

[3] The war was fought between forces of the Republic of South Africa, which controlled Namibia from 1915 until 1989, and those of the South West Africa Peoples Organization (SWAPO). Since independence in 1990, Namibia has had a democratically elected parliament with SWAPO as the majority party.

construct square houses. Only workers build such houses, which are in the same style as those of workers on commercial farms. All other Hai//om at /Gomais build either Owambo-style houses or grass huts.

The distribution of huts corresponds to the three groups of Hai//om, differentiating themselves with regard to their places of origin: a group of about 100 people from about 70 kilometers north (not far from Botos), a second group from about 25 kilometers northeast (50 people), and a third group from places to the south or from /Gomais itself (50 people). Each group builds its huts in that part of the settlement that is in the direction of its place of origin. Due to intermarriage and individual preferences and conflicts, there are some exceptions to the rule, but people recognize each other as belonging to the same //gâus (band) and refer to the identity linked to that //gâus in their discourse (for example, blaming members of a particular group for being "primitive," for heavy drinking, or for causing disruption in the community). Most Hai//om at /Gomais regard it as their permanent dwelling place, and only a few move seasonally back to their former areas. Yet this does not inhibit movement within camps. Reasons are manifold, but social conflict is usually behind such moves. As among other "Bushman" groups, huts are also abandoned or moved in the event of death in the hut itself. Out of 89 huts and shelters recorded at /Gomais in 1990, all but 16 had either been destroyed or moved in the course of one year (Figure 4.6).

The cattle outposts provide another opportunity for movement in the case of conflict or economic strain. Temporary camps there are taken up to gather wild food, while residents continue to enjoy features on the service center, such as easy access to clear water. Outposts are visited at all seasons, and the time spent on a post will vary from a few days to several months.

//Ausis: wage labor on a commercial farm

//Ausis is a commercial farm some 20 kilometers from /Gomais. It was among the first farms to be established in this area at the beginning of this century. Only in the late 1950s was the entire farming area fenced in. Since there were hardly any Owambo settlements in the southeasterly part of the Owambo region at that time, farm workers were recruited among the local Hai//om and others who came from places as far as Botos. Individual Owambo and Kavango contract workers came in small numbers and in many cases married Hai//om women. The children were usually brought up as Hai//om. During the war, the employment of Hai//om was fostered; many farmers regarded Bushpeople as more loyal than Owambo or Kavango. After the war, a different tendency emerged that resembles the Nharo case described above (Rhodes' farm): farmers now value the "good reliability" of Owambo and Kavango workers in preference to the "poor reliability" of the Hai//om.

At //Ausis, workers have only limited freedom to build their huts how and where they want. Farmers usually provide limited space for construction. Some require their workers to build houses of provided material (usually no grass but poles and corrugated iron sheets) and to space houses a specific distance apart. Some Hai//om workers of long residence are now also provided with stone houses. The farmer built a stone wash-house for the use of all workers and their dependents. However, only the men used it; the women, at the men's insistence, constructed their own individual washing enclosures some distance from the huts.

In contrast to the houses at /Gomais, those at //Ausis all have front yards a few meters square, with surrounding walls made of corrugated iron and wooden poles. This enclosure is called a *hos*, the same term used at Botos for the men's fireplace. Instead of one *hos* as in Botos, every house at //Ausis has one. This fragmentation of the communal *hos* and the enclosure of the *hos* belonging to the core family suggest that individual core families become more isolated as they gain importance on the commercial farms (such status may arise, for example, from the ability to distribute rations or grant residence rights). From the Hai//om perspective, the main problem with work on the farms is the fact that farmers are very reluctant to allow in anyone who is not a worker or an immediate kinsman of a worker. Many farmers run their farmers with as few as three or four workers.

The primary economic unit of production, sharing, and consumption is the nuclear family, and private ownership of more valuable goods is tolerated. Some workers at //Ausis own donkey carts, bicycles, and water hoses, which are loaned to others. Here, unlike in other settlements discussed, individuals write their names, initials, or signs on cups and dishes to mark ownership. A few workers even have bank accounts, which are managed by the farmer. Nevertheless the theoretical principle of universal kinship prevails, as all Hai//om workers on the farm are labeled with kinship terms (cf. Barnard 1978).

Diversity and continuity in Hai//om settlement patterns

In all four examples, economic and residential changes that have been forced upon the Hai//om have made changes in settlement patterns inevitable. But it is important to note that these changes also involved choices made by the Hai//om who, consciously as well as unconsciously, made shifts in their complex social practices. The case studies show great flexibility in adapting to new economic conditions with regard to the size and composition of a settlement, the time span of occupation, and the construction and inventory of houses.

We may note that the flexibility in settlement patterns accompanies flexibility in terms used by the Hai//om to conceptualize the socio-political units involved. There is a straightforward term for "place," *!as*, which is not problematic in general conversation since it refers to any point in space whether inhabited or not. Looking more closely, one realizes that the definition of the *!as* is altered according to the specific situation. For example, a given settlement may be referred to as a *!as*, or a unit within such a settlement may be a *!as*. Also, one and the same place might receive different names according to function. !Gai ≠ nas has three names. It is !Gai ≠ nas (probably its oldest name) for those who return there regularly to live on wild fruits. It is called Inkete (from the relatively recent Owambo name) by those who stay there all year long and live in close association with the Owambo. And it is //Khana/khab for those Hai//om who are not part of this band cluster but who move through the area when visiting other places. This name is derived from a plant that grows near the permanent waterholes at this place, and these waterholes are particularly relevant to the travelers.

Similarly the category *//gâus* has now at least three levels of meaning. In a very basic sense, especially in a settlement composed of just one core family, the people living in the main hut (or *oms*) might be regarded as a *//gâus*. In a somewhat wider sense, *//gâus* refers to a circle of huts belonging together in the sense that they form a hearth group. Informants may disagree about the boundary of such a *//gâus*. In its widest sense, *//gâus* refers to those people who come from one place. Hence large population centers are divided into several *//gâute* (*//gâus*, plural), since they consist of groups that come from several places. Hence this key term can be said to have three meanings: "home," "family," and "band."

There is a parallel in the way the term *!nus* is used. It is cognate to Nharo *n!usa* and is widely used to designate the land of a "band cluster." However, those Hai//om who have not grown up in a band type of social organization apply the term in a more vague sense, usually to refer to the lands that they know, they like, or they have stayed within for some time, regardless of their actual origin or the association of the land with a group of people. Another meaning of *!nus* which has gained currency since Namibian independence is "nation state." While *!nus*

Figure 4.5   Hai//om: dry-season settlement, 1991

has always been used to conceptualize other countries (the land of the Owambo, that of the Germans or the English), it is only now, fostered by radio broadcasts, that the term has been recognized by the Hai//om as being applicable to Namibia as a whole.

Yet flexibility does not occur only in the outward appearance of settlements or in the categories associated with them. There are also structures and practices that are recurrent, though nevertheless undergoing transformations. Kinship is used to define a person's place in a settlement. In the settlements on communal land, kinship ties are closest, while in others classificatory kinship predominates. Sharing and egalitarianism are kept as values but narrowed down, in practice, at centers and on commercial farms. Movement remains an important social tool of conflict resolution in all settings despite varying outside pressures that can inhibit mobility. Frequent intracamp movement at the centers can be paralleled to the prevalent intercamp movement in other settings. There is a meta-variation here: the transformations of patterns between exemplary settlements resonate in the ways in which these transformations occur. Thus Hai//om settlement is characterized not only by diversity of form at any one time, but by variation in its dynamic aspects as well.

Comparisons and conclusions

In terms of dependence and independence, the Nharo and Hai//om have a variety of settlement patterns, based variously on isolated bands, client communities near villages and cattle-posts, communities associated with government settlement schemes, and communities sharing land with commercial ranchers. Individuals can move freely from one settlement to another, and therefore move from one "pattern" to another. Indeed, the patterns change through time and are related, sometimes in an evolutionary sense (as when a structure like that of ≠Aa is transformed into one like the Old Grimmond Place) and sometimes in a cyclical sense (as when a structure like that of Botos becomes one like !Gai≠nas because of the seasonal fluctuation in resources).

In the Nharo case, an evolutionary trajectory is particularly visible. In the Ghanzi ranching area, at least three specific forms of local organization are discernible – each corresponding to one of the three cases described here. There are semi-traditional bands such as ≠Aa, in which traditional band structure is maintained. There are multi-ethnic communities such as the Old Grimmond Place, with Nharo who work as laborers or live as squatters, no longer recognizing ownership of the land they inhabit. There are also commercial ranches, such as Rhodes' farm, on which Nharo live in very small and socially unviable groups.

Hai//om settlement shares with Nharo this trajectory, but the situation is more complicated. Diversity occurs in relation to degree and type of contact with outsiders, and individuals may have a variety of options, or be forced by outside pressures, to adopt one form of settlement pattern or another. At the micro-level, even "traditional" Hai//om village life seems to be a blend of hunter-gatherer subsistence strategies and Khoekhoe (Nama/Damara) and Central Bantu notions of the village hearth (or separate hearths for men and women). At the macro-level, Hai//om settlement is based on a diversity of resource bases, including water, bush food, and opportunities for employment.

Among both the Hai//om and the Nharo, strategies for exploiting opportunities are conditioned by a persistent foraging ethos. This ethos pervades these societies, even where hunting and gathering *per se* have ceased to be the dominant modes of subsistence (cf. Barnard 1993; Kent, chapter 5, this volume). The flaw in a categorical distinction, say, between "farm Bushpeople" and "traditional Bushpeople" becomes apparent when we realize that one person, or members of one family group, move between farms, population centers, and other places either seasonally or at specific times of their lives. It is as if the structures themselves are out there to be foraged; or, in Bourdieu's (e.g., 1977) terms, the *dispositions* available for exploitation make up a *habitus* of possible forms of settlement. This cultural "environment" parallels the natural one in its openness to manipulation, either by outsiders who aim to transform it or by foragers who live within it. The range of diversity is very wide indeed, as the opportunities for "foraging" in its widest sense are seemingly unlimited in scope, though not of course in material yield.

Silberbauer and Guenther (respectively chapters 2 and 3, this volume) have shown, across a wide spectrum of social life, the diversity that exists between southern African foragers generally. Both have remarked on the importance of flexibility of these cultures and their social systems, and on the ingenuity of their people. We hope to have shown here that this flexibility is just as prevalent at the micro-level (that of the family or band) as that at the larger, cultural level. The various forms of settlement are fashioned not so much consciously as by the interplay of individual and group choice and constraint within trajectories of seasonal changes and social transformations. At certain points in these trajectories, one settlement pattern becomes another. The idea of a "threshold of abundance" that, as Barnard (1992b:140–3) has argued, reverses the trend toward territoriality, could equally be applicable as an agent for the cyclical transformation of a settlement like Botos to one like !Gai ≠ nas. It could also help explain the directional transformation of a pattern like that exhibited by Botos and !Gai ≠ nas to one like /Gomais or //Ausis.

In our descriptions above, we have excluded certain constellations of settlement. Urban settings have not been included, since the authors have not researched the urban areas, and indeed very little is known ethnographically about them. Since the arrangement of urban settlements in Namibia has in the past been very regulated, there has as yet been little urbanization of former foragers and it is unlikely that specifically Hai//om settlement strategies would be apparent. Relatively urban Nharo settlement has long occurred and is now growing in the township of Ghanzi. In the 1970s, Nharo settlement there was mainly confined to the outskirts of the town, where both temporary and long-term inhabitants lived by a variety of means: regular employment, occasional labor, prostitution, begging, and urban foraging. Today, Nharo are settling in the town itself. In other places, such as D'Kar (itself a densely populated farm) and Hanahai, larger Nharo populations are moving in from the farms where they are no longer welcome or cannot find adequate sources of food, desired social amenities, educational opportunities, or other attractions of "modern" life.

There are subgroups of Hai//om living in the western Owambo region, as workers at tourist camps in the Etosha Game Reserve, and in

Figure 4.6   Hai//om: permanent settlement, 1991

the farming districts south of Etosha where they live in close relation with Damara. Similarly, many Nharo live in association with Kgalagari and Herero in western parts of the Ghanzi district of Botswana (see also Silberbauer and Kuper 1966; Steyn 1971). Indeed, some also live across the border in the Gobabis area of Namibia, on white-owned farms which are similar though often less densely populated than those of Ghanzi. Variations from the patterns suggested in this chapter are to be expected in such places, and further research is needed to find out exactly what these variations are.

Nevertheless, from the examples covered here it is clear that great variation in socio-spatial organization exists even among the Hai//om and Nharo with relatively similar subsistence strategies. The range of variation is not dissimilar to that among other hunter-gatherers in Africa (cf. Blackburn, chapter 8, and Ichikawa and Terashima, chapter 11, this volume). Its causes can be found in a complex of environmental, economic, political, and cultural factors. These are revealed through a comparable diversity in methods and interests, for example through the study of relevant aspects of subsistence ecology, relations between ethnic groups, and kin relations between and within settlements. All of these impinge on each other. By focusing on just two related foraging groups, we hope to have shown the form such diversity *can* take, and to have highlighted comparisons which may help us to understand the relation between the range of environmental and social factors that induce different kinds of settlement. There are also continuities between Nharo and Hai//om areas, as indeed there are across the range of African societies considered in this book. All are worthy of future comparative research.

The comprehension of diversity requires an ability to delve into a wide range of theoretical specializations, and sometimes to approach the problem with the methodological tools of a genealogist, an ecologist, and a diplomat, all at once. No single area of interest is adequate to explain the range of diversity, either between two groups of African foragers, or even within a cultural unity such as those represented by the Hai//om or the Nharo.

5   Kūa: farmer/foragers of the eastern Kalahari, Botswana

Helga I. D. Vierich and Robert K. Hitchcock

Introduction

Indigenous peoples, especially hunter-gatherers, are often viewed by governments as static, incapable of initiating major changes on their own. Prisoners of their own supposedly conservative values, they are perceived as being affected primarily by forces external to their societies.

Contemporary anthropologists, however, see hunter-gatherers as dynamic societies that have had to adapt to complex sociopolitical, environmental, and economic conditions (Leacock and Lee 1982; Lee 1992a; Ellana 1993; Burch and Ellanna 1994; Kelly 1995). The foragers of today, especially those in Africa, have to be understood both in light of their own histories as well as their involvements with non-hunter-gatherer groups, from subsistence farmers to colonial and post-colonial governments (Wolf 1982; Woodburn 1988; Wilmsen 1989; Gordon 1992). Exchanges between African hunter-gatherers and non-hunters were common throughout Africa, although the degree to which these reciprocal relationships were institutionalized varied tremendously.

The success of African foragers may be attributed to their flexibility: their ability to avoid extensive involvement with the state on the one hand, and their willingness to work with state agencies on the other, to shift back and forth between foraging and food production, and between dependency on government handouts and self-sufficient economic activities. Not least among the flexible responses to environmental or social stress is mobility, which allows areas where foraging has taken place to regenerate, enables population size to be adjusted to resource availability and to the distribution of other groups in the area, and provides a means of responding to internal social stress or of resisting political domination by other groups (Lee 1965, 1968; Hitchcock 1982a, b; Kelly 1983, 1995; Kent and Vierich 1989). In order to illustrate how these processes were played out, data are drawn from a population of farmer/foragers in the eastern Kalahari Desert of the Republic of Botswana in

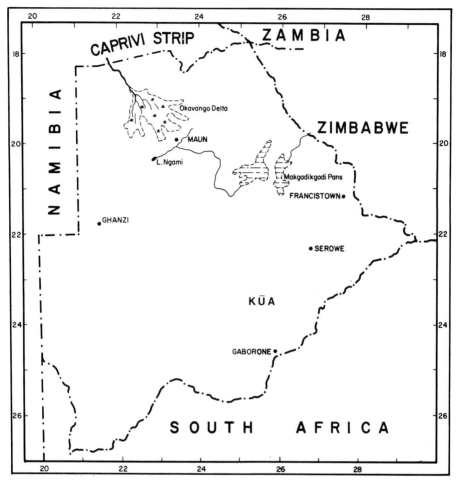

Figure 5.1   Map of Botswana showing the location of the Kūa in the
southeastern Kalahari Desert

southern Africa, the Kūa. This chapter assesses the sometimes complicated but generally effective adaptive strategies of the Kūa, a population
that has moved into and out of foraging and farming activities for
hundreds of years.

The Kūa of the eastern and southeastern Kalahari Desert

Ethnographic fieldwork was carried out among Kūa populations in the
eastern and southeastern Kalahari Desert region of Botswana between

1975 and 1982 (Figure 5.1). Research efforts centered on a population of about 950 Kūa in the Ngware area of northeastern Kweneng District and on approximately 1,800 Kūa in the western sandveld region of Central District (Vierich 1977, 1981, 1982; Hitchcock 1978, 1980, 1982a, b, 1987c, d; Bartram 1993). There were at least 2,000 Basarwa (Bushmen, San) in the entire Kalahari Desert portion of the Kweneng District. Of these, over 1,000 were Kūa. The rest came from a number of other groups, including !'Xoo, Tsassi, and Eastern /'Hua (Vierich 1977, 1981). These people shared an area of approximately 15,000 km^2 with over 6,000 Bakgalagadi and some 10,000 head of livestock.

The Kūa possessed many of the characteristics of other Botswana Basarwa populations such as the G/wi, G//ana, and Ju/'hoansi (!Kung) (Lee 1965, 1979; Marshall 1976; Silberbauer 1981a; Barnard 1992a; Guenther, Kent, this volume). Social units tended to be small, and they were made up of several families linked through kinship, marital, economic, and friendship ties. Groups aggregated and dispersed, depending in part upon resource availability and social relationships among members. Organization of labor was structured along lines of gender and age. The Kūa were also egalitarian, with decisions being taken on the basis of general consensus (Vierich 1981; Hitchcock 1978, 1982a, b; Valiente-Noailles 1993).

Kūa groups have been on the fringes of an agropastoral economy for centuries. It was found during the course of our work that Kūa have not undergone a gradual socioeconomic shift from foraging to farming, as might be expected, but rather have employed an opportunistic, flexible set of adaptive strategies in which they hunted and gathered some of the time and worked for farmers and herders at other times. This optimal shifting from one strategy to another was partly a function of their extensive kinship networks and patterns of reciprocal visiting. In many cases there were close kinship links between people in wage labor and those still living traditionally. Indeed, individuals and families passed through a whole spectrum of activities throughout the course of their lives.

The environment of the Kūa

Some of the environmental features of the region within which the Kūa resided included low to moderate rainfall (400–600 mm) which was highly variable in both space and time, dune ridges and open rolling countryside supporting tree-bush savanna vegetation, and a wide variety of habitats containing an array of wild and domestic animals. Apart from springs, which are rare in the southeastern Kalahari, the only naturally occurring sources of surface water were pans and pools filled during the rains. Many pans were found along fossil river valleys in the northeastern Kweneng; these tended to hold water for periods varying from several days to several months each year.

These fossil river valleys in the southeastern Kalahari were crucial in the adaptations of both human and faunal populations. Game was drawn to the pools that formed during the rains, as well as to the nutrient-rich plants on the edges of the valleys and near pans. Sometimes game and livestock licked salt and other minerals in the valleys. Kūa sometimes constructed hunting blinds in the vicinity of pans, from which they ambushed game animals as they came down to drink.

In addition to the natural sources of water, there were approximately thirty boreholes in the area, of which seventeen were functional during the study period. Many of the small pools in remoter areas where people were not settled permanently had been deepened by hand. In areas lacking surface water there were sipwells, places where people were able to suck water out of the ground through a straw; these water sources were generally located in fine white sand on the side of a river valley near a pan or pool (Vierich 1981:47).

There is evidence of long-term and short-time environmental cycles in the Kalahari which have affected populations residing there. Wet periods saw groups of agropastoralists moving deeper into the Kalahari, while dry periods were characterized by a reduction in population, particularly of those involved in farming and herding. During the 1973–8 rainy cycle in the southeastern Kalahari, Bakgalagadi populations expanded their agricultural settlements along the river valleys. Whereas there was only one Kgalagadi household plowing at Mazane in 1971, there were no fewer than twelve in 1978. Of these households, all but one were originally descended from people who had retreated from locations much deeper in the central Kalahari during the 1933 drought.

After the drilling of boreholes in the southeastern Kalahari, people had more places for water in droughts and during the dry parts of the year. In the late 1970s, most of the boreholes in the northeastern Kweneng District were being used in this manner; in fact, boreholes dug in cattle-post areas were giving rise to new villages as more and more people moved into these places rather than going to established villages.

Many of the Kūa, like the Bakgalagadi, followed a kind of transhumant pattern, though they tended to move deeper into the Kalahari from October to May, obtaining their water from small seasonal pools or wild plants. This meant that when the Bakgalagadi moved out to the agricultural areas during November and December, the Kūa population there was relatively low. From late April onwards, however, many Kūa moved back to the vicinity of permanent water points and agricultural areas. In those periods when agropastoralists encroached on the sandveld, the opportunities for cooperation and the risk of competition between the hunter-gatherers and other groups both increased. When agricultural activities expanded, foraging families sometimes approached farmers to ask for employment in exchange for food. Such contacts initially were highly seasonal and informal.

In some areas in the Kweneng District, up to 70 percent of Kũa women were employed by Bakgalagadi farmers to help during the bird scaring, harvesting, and threshing phases of the agricultural cycle. In late May, early-ripening crops such as melons, beans, and maize were available and people took advantage of the employment opportunities this offered. Sorghum and millet were harvested in late June through July. Local women worked for farmers in a system known as *majako* in which they received a portion of the crop produced in exchange for their labor. This system was organized in such a way that Bakgalagadi farmers sometimes employed members of the same Kũa family as *majako* laborers from one generation to the next. In most cases, however, *majako* contracts were not on-going. Frequently, the contractual arrangements were made on a short-term basis between individuals who did not know each other previously (Vierich 1981). Thus, the arrangements were essentially along the lines of employers and employees.

Socioeconomic, environmental, and political changes in the southeastern and eastern Kalahari

The recent history of the southeastern Kalahari has been dominated by four major developments. One has been the establishment of new water points. The second is the change in land use and tenure accompanying shifts in land management and allocation practices and the commercialization of the livestock industry. The third is the expansion of commercial trading in the region, particularly during the latter half of the nineteenth and the early twentieth centuries. The fourth development is the increase in labor migration to towns and villages in the east and south, as well as to the South African mines. With some recent exceptions, all of these developments have been, on the whole, financed, engineered, and based on technology from outside the region.

Permanent water

The availability of year-round water supplies in what formerly were remote areas lifted the major constraint on agriculture and livestock production, and served to prolong periods of residential stability. The existence of a borehole appears to be a prime factor in the amalgamation of previously scattered residential groups of Basarwa and Bakgalagadi into new villages. Contacts between the hunter-gatherers and agropastoral populations become more frequent, more prolonged, and have a tendency to produce greater economic disparity. Relationships formerly based on independent seasonal interactions become more permanent, involving greater dependency on the part of Kūa employees and more control and power on the part of the agropastoral employers. It is likely that the development of patron–client relationships represents an institutionalization of early, sometimes troubled, contacts between the two different types of societies (Russell 1976; Vierich 1981; Hitchcock 1987c).

The first borehole in the northeastern Kweneng District was established in the Ngware area in June 1929 at Khudumalapye and was equipped with an animal gear pump. The 1950s saw a major increase in borehole drilling, particularly by private individuals, generally near existing pools or pans in river valleys, transforming those areas within a few years from rich foraging environments into areas of heavy livestock and agricultural use. These new water sources had a profound effect on the Kūa. Groups already living in areas where boreholes were drilled completely changed their seasonal mobility patterns. Whereas they had formerly spent the dry season in progressively smaller and smaller camps, once water points were available they began to aggregate around them in larger numbers. Some people were employed as herders (*badisa*), and they and their families settled more or less permanently near the water points. Thus, the introduction of boreholes changed both mobility patterns and the size and structure of social units.

There are a number of factors that condition group size in the Kalahari Desert. A crucial determinant of the numbers of people per group is resource density. Wild resources in cattle-post areas were reduced significantly in those regions where stocking densities were high, partly because cattle tend to consume many of the same resources as people, including Grewia berries, vines containing beans such as *morama* (*Tylosema esculenta*), and water-bearing melons (Hitchcock 1978; Brandenburgh 1991). Trampling compacted soils and reduced vegetation cover in the vicinity of water points, a process which in turn raised soil temperatures and reduced biological productivity. In addition, the expansion of cattle numbers led to localized reductions in the numbers of wild animals, especially mobile grazers such as hartebeest. It is also likely that heavy grazing pressure and woodcutting around village settlements, both for building materials and for firewood, has had a deleterious effect on the water table in the southeastern Kalahari, which has dropped significantly over the past 30 years.

As resources declined, people either had to leave the area or, alternatively, had to become more dependent on handouts or to seek wage employment in order to raise the cash to buy manufactured food. Limited resources affected traditional band sizes, causing a reduction from an average size of twenty-five to thirty persons to groups averaging five to ten people. Consequently, there were fewer multifamily bands in the southeastern Kalahari than there were previously; the majority of groups consisted of nuclear families or female-headed households. The subsistence of these groups was derived wholly or mostly from employment income, supplemented with wild foods. One problem with the change in group sizes was that the number of laborers available to pursue hunting and gathering activities declined, thus causing further disruption of foraging strategies.

We found during the course of our research in the eastern Kalahari that the Kūa camp, because of its generally small size and the fluidity of its membership, was a difficult unit of analysis. Rather than use arbitrary units, we decided to use groups of camps or "camp clusters" which appeared to be coherent units, akin to a Kūa "community" (Figure 5.2). In 1977–8 there were ten major camp clusters in the Ngware area of the northeastern Kweneng (Vierich 1981). They ranged in size from 72 to 129, the average being 95 people. The overall average for the thirteen intact groups was 24.23 persons.

Social arrangements in most hunter-gatherer societies were fluid and could be somewhat confusing, but certain regularities did exist. Among the Kūa of the southeastern Kalahari, dry-season camps, whose occupants relied primarily upon hunting and gathering, contained eleven to twelve people. In the rainy season, there were groups of up to forty people, tripling the average size of camps. Although there was a great deal of variation throughout the year, Kūa camps containing more than thirty people were rarely recorded except during the rainy season.

In all the Kūa clusters, there were dry-season aggregations, usually of camps that were near water points, and rainy season dispersals. These patterns did not always involve the same degree of mobility for all of the households, nor did they necessarily correspond to the waxing and waning of camp membership. A century ago, the only permanent water points in the southeastern Kalahari were springs at a few locations such as the Lephepe Pans, Khudumalapye, Boatlaname, and Boatlapatlou. The Kūa would utilize these places as the dry season progressed.

It appears that for at least fifty years and possibly longer, most permanent water points in the southeastern Kalahari have been heavily

Figure 5.2   Kūa campsite in the eastern Kalahari Desert, Botswana, showing linear arrangement of huts

settled by Bakgalagadi (Vierich 1981; Hitchcock and Campbell 1982). Consequently, the Kūa have not been able to utilize the pattern employed by the Ju/'hoansi, who lived near a water point and exploited a hinterland within a two-hour walk (Lee 1965, 1968, 1979). The exceptions have occurred in those instances where a new borehole had been drilled but the cattle had not yet ruined the range.

Permanent water sites suited the Bakgalagadi, whose economy consisted mainly of raising livestock and growing crops, supplemented by hunting and by collecting wild plant foods (Vierich 1981; Hitchcock and Campbell 1982). Although their foraging was limited, hunting included the use of horses and dogs, as well as spears and guns. After the harvest in July, most of the Bakgalagadi moved back to their dry-season quarters in villages with year-round water supplies.

The Bakgalagadi rarely moved more than 15 kilometers from the water points in order to plow their fields, and during the post-harvest dry season from July to late November, 80 percent of the Bakgalagadi lived within 5 kilometers of a permanent water source. The Kūa, on the other hand, usually did not live so close to a water point unless either it had a very small Bakgalagadi population or they were long-term clients or employees of a farming family. During the period from mid-September to late May, in places with high livestock densities, 50 to 70 percent of the Kūa lived at least 10 kilometers from the water points, which placed them beyond the zone of the most severe overgrazing.

In the 1970s the Kūa had at least two different patterns of aggregation and dispersal. Near water points that were not surrounded by too much thorn bush, there were clusters of camps containing between twenty and forty people. These tended to occur at new boreholes where the cattle had not yet had much impact. In the rainy season, these large camps split into smaller units of ten to twenty people, with some groups remaining near the boreholes while others moved out to forage at seasonal pools.

The second pattern was one in which there were people who never camped closer than 12 to 15 kilometers from permanent water points. In these cases, the water points were heavily overstocked. Most of them were old boreholes or wells which had been in operation for between twenty to fifty years. On such heavily overgrazed boreholes, Kūa winter groupings consisted of smaller camps clustered within an area between 8 and 15 kilometers from the water point.

These two patterns were affected significantly by drilling and stocking of a borehole. As stated above, Kūa mobility was reduced, with people settling for months or even the full year on the water point. However, traditional group size no longer was based on seasonal rounds or the availability of wild foods. People became dependent on alternative sources of food. Thus, with the introduction of boreholes, the home areas of the Kūa acquired a new and critical resource: abundant and year-round water. They also gained a new set of resources in the form of employment opportunities and goods such as milk and maize meal (Figure 5.3). The initial response to this new set of conditions was an upsurge of visitors from other places lacking permanent water. The changes in group sizes had serious socioeconomic implications, particularly in terms of social conflict.

Kūa land use and land tenure

The Kalahari Desert, like other parts of southern Africa, was divided by the Basarwa into a series of named localities, or territories, which people claimed rights to on the basis of birth, group membership, inheritance, or marital ties (Heinz 1972, 1979; Hitchcock 1978, 1980; Cashdan 1984a, b: Wilmsen 1989). The Kūa referred to a territory as a *no*. Most *nos* were named after a particular geographic feature such as a pool, a ridge, or a grove of economically important trees. Others could be

Figure 5.3 Kũa boys watering cattle from a hand-dug well in the eastern Kalahari Desert, Botswana

named after a particular event that had occurred there, such as an important hunt or a mass starvation. The territories in the Ngware area usually contained a seasonal pool in addition to fuel, grasses, and other wild resources. These areas had boundaries which were only vaguely defined and in some instances overlapped. Occasionally, there were areas of "no man's land" or neutral places between the territories.

In most cases, the area used by a particular group during the year was larger than their specific territory. This was due in part to the fact that individuals inherited rights to at least one, but more often two, *nos* from their parents. Individuals also had access to one or two areas where their spouses had birth or inheritance rights.

Within the overall range of a band or camp cluster, there were seven to ten *nos*, each of which was "owned" by particular people, usually a group of siblings who comprised two or more households. These units consisted of two or more people who shared a hearth and ate together most of the time. The eldest member of the "owner" family was called the /*kae iha*. It was to this person that an individual had to go in order to seek permission to use a *no*. Different kinds or proportions of key resources – water, esculent plants, wild foods, and fuel – were found in each *no*. Some *nos* lacked permanent water, and people used them primarily for gathering or hunting purposes. Within the range of each major camp cluster using a series of *nos* there was at least one major cattle-post area or agricultural area.

The mechanisms of reciprocal access to resources mediated access to new employment opportunities afforded by the increased numbers of cattle-posts and agricultural activities. A few *nos* had been so taken over by cattle-posts and Bakgalagadi settlements that they were used almost entirely for employment purposes rather than for foraging.

At new boreholes, seasonal employment in agriculture and cattle-herding might be balanced by exploitation of abundant foraging resources, thus allowing large camps to settle semi-permanently nearby. At older boreholes, however, human and livestock populations have led to a decline in wild plant foods and game.

Taking the various settlement and subsistence patterns into account, it is possible to divide Kūa groups into a number of categories. One must remember that these categories are not mutually exclusive and that there are shifts in strategies among households and camps over time. The Kūa can be categorized as follows: (a) full-time hunters and gatherers, (b) part-time hunters and gatherers, and (c) people involved in the agropastoral economy.

Data on hunter-gatherer and cattle-post populations in the east-central Kalahari reveal that there were 710 mobile foragers (20.12 percent), 1,576 part-time hunter-gatherers (44.66 percent), and 1,243 sedentary agropastoral people (35.22 percent) out of a total of 3,529 people (Hitchcock 1978). Among the Northern Kūa, 6.8 percent of the population was involved in agriculture in 1977–8 (Hitchcock 1982a).

Similar patterns were noted in the southeastern Kalahari by Vierich (1977:12), who identified three categories of people among the 2,500 she counted: (1) dependent people, characterized by complete loss of hunting and gathering as a way of life and who usually were found near compounds or prominent families of Bakwena or Bakgalagadi (23 percent); (2) semi-dependent people, characterized by individuals supporting themselves mainly by foraging but supplementing their subsistence by working either regularly or seasonally, sometimes around settled villages (54 percent); and (3) independent people, characterized by full-time hunting and gathering, residential mobility, and occasional planting of gardens and herding or working as agricultural laborers sporadically (23 percent).

Kūa camps often consisted of individuals or families pursuing different strategies at the same time. In some cases, one member was doing *majako* labor while another foraged. In other cases, a group might be completely dependent upon wages and food gained through employment, but might fall back on foraging during a drought. A comparison of the percentages of full-time hunter-gatherers in the northeastern Kweneng reveals that 33 percent of all camps were foraging in December–January, 1977–8, 10 percent in May–July, 1978, and 60 percent in the May–July period of 1979, a drought year (Vierich 1981).

Frequent shifts in strategy were facilitated by marital and reciprocal visiting ties. During the period from May to September, most people had at least one close relative working for agropastoralists. If an individual visited such a relative, he or she was sometimes hired to work in the agropastoral economy. Thus, a network of kinship ties helped people gain access to employment. Conversely, an individual might leave his or her employment or be laid off, thus prompting an extended visit to relatives in a foraging camp. The same network thus provided access to a kind of "unemployment insurance" or "self-employment insurance." It should be stressed that this is not a new device; it is an old hunter-gatherer tactic with a new twist.

In addition to droughts, Botswana has been plagued by outbreaks of livestock diseases, including rinderpest and hoof-and-mouth disease (also called foot-and-mouth disease). In 1896–7, rinderpest was responsible for killing the majority of the livestock and substantial numbers of wildlife in Botswana. One response to this situation was the construction of a cordon fence to prevent movement of diseased animals. The threat of outbreaks of hoof-and-mouth disease led to the implementation of additional fencing and livestock immunization projects, especially in the 1950s. Efficient veterinary programs, coupled with an expansion in the number of water points and favorable world beef prices, contributed to a sizable increase in the region's livestock herd.

Fences had a major impact on wildlife populations, whose migration routes were disrupted and who were cut off from access to water and grazing. Large numbers of wild animals died along the Dibete cordon fence between the Kweneng and Central Districts north of the Ngware area in the late 1970s and early 1980s. Similar die-offs occurred along the Makoba fence in the east-central Kalahari and in the area along the so-called "tail-end" fence along the northeastern boundary of the Central Kalahari Game Reserve (Hitchcock 1978; Owens and Owens 1980, 1984). Sometimes people would scavenge meat from the animals that had died along the fences, but the nutritional returns from this strategy were low because the quality of the meat was poor since the animals had died from thirst, stress, and starvation.

Kūa in the cattle-post areas also suffered as a result of decisions made by the government's Department of Animal Health and the Department of Wildlife and National Parks: herders whose cattle wandered too close to the veterinary cordon fences were beaten by fence guards; veterinary teams had the right to shoot any wild animals that they considered a threat to the fences or to the cattle in the area, and all hunting in the area was banned. These decisions affected both the nutritional status of Kūa and their relations with government officials.

The hunting issue was perhaps the thorniest one the Kūa encountered. The people on the cattle-posts were afraid to hunt openly since many of them had been arrested in the past or at least had had game and skins taken from them. An analysis of arrest records indicated that those charged with hunting violations were usually not cattle-owners but rather the poorer people on the cattle-posts, usually part-time or full-time hunter-gatherers.

In the early to mid-1980s many Kūa moved into settlements in order to gain access to drought-relief food, water, and employment opportunities. The government contributed to this process by encouraging people to settle down and live in villages. A major reason for this establishment of settlements by the government for Kūa and other rural people was that it was seen as a means of providing social services in centralized areas (Hitchcock and Holm 1993).

Settlement of mobile groups was also seen as a strategy for facilitating the process of land reform in Botswana. In 1975 the Government of Botswana announced a major land reform and livestock development effort known as the Tribal Grazing Land Policy (TGLP) (Hitchcock 1978, 1980). Having hunter-gatherers in the area could potentially have proved problematic for those individuals and groups seeking grazing rights. In the period between 1975–6 and 1979–80, surveys were undertaken in the sandveld areas in order to ascertain the numbers of people who would be affected by the establishment of commercial cattle ranches (Vierich 1977; Hitchcock 1978, 1980). One result of these surveys was the decision to set aside land for communal usage, as was done in the case of Diphuduhudu, a 40,000 hectare remote area dweller (RAD) settlement in the northeastern Kweneng which has a borehole, primary school, and health post (Mazonde 1992).

In the northern Kweneng District and western Central District, several dozen ranches were demarcated and allocated to individuals and small groups of cattle-owners under leasehold tenure. Resident populations of Kūa and others who did not have water rights were required to move out of these areas. Traditional tenure rights were not observed in the process, although some efforts were made to ensure that the new communal service centers being established for people were in areas occupied traditionally by Kūa. Some of the Kūa who left the areas went to towns while others joined relatives in their camps near cattle-posts and villages. Again, the increased population densities contributed to environmental degradation and impoverishment. While some of the groups who were dispossessed sought compensation payments, none of them received more than a token amount of money for reconstructing their homes and other facilities.

Commercial economic impacts

Another factor in socioeconomic change in the southeastern and eastern Kalahari was the introduction of a market exchange system. In the mid-nineteenth century, the establishment of a market for wildlife products, especially skins, furs, and ivory, helped contribute to a process of overexploitation by hunters, both indigenous ones and Europeans (Parsons 1973, 1977; Hitchcock 1987c; Solway and Lee 1990). By the latter part of the nineteenth century, large numbers of skins and tusks were being sent to Europe and Asia (Parsons 1973).

In the twentieth century, sales of meat and craft items to villagers, tourists, shops, and the government buying agency, Botswanacraft, provided important sources of income for Kūa. The Kūa frequently used furs and hides as a medium of exchange. Economic transactions consisted of selling the skins for cash, either to local shopkeepers or to individual Bakgalagadi. The cash was then used to purchase foodstuffs, weapons, tobacco, blankets, and European clothing (Vierich 1981).

Northwest of the Ngware area are the Khutse Game Reserve and the Central Kalahari Game Reserve, which together make up one of the largest conserved areas on the African continent. These reserves were established primarily to protect habitats and wildlife, but in the case of the Central Kalahari, people's foraging rights were also maintained (Silberbauer 1981a; Hitchcock 1988). In some cases Kūa had access to employment opportunities there. At the Department of Wildlife and National Parks camp outside the Khutse Game Reserve, people sometimes did odd jobs for game scouts or posed for photographs and did dances and demonstrations for tourists (Vierich and Hitchcock 1979).

There is no question that some members of Kūa groups were poverty-stricken and thus particularly vulnerable to the effects of environmental and socioeconomic change. Kūa populations in the southeastern Kalahari experienced a fair amount of stress during the drought periods of the early 1960s, 1973, 1979–80, and the early 1980s (Hitchcock 1978; Vierich 1979). While there were few well-documented instances of death from starvation, substantial numbers of people in rural areas were forced to supplement their subsistence through government food relief supplies. Food-for-work and, later, cash-for-work programs were established in order to provide people with sources of food and income. In 1979, a special drought relief program was instituted for people in remote areas after two districts reported severe malnutrition among Basarwa (Vierich 1979). This effort was hampered initially by the fact that many government officials felt that the Kūa and other Basarwa were not in need or deserving of assistance. While the relief programs that were eventually implemented undoubtedly alleviated some of the suffering in rural areas, they also tended to encourage a degree of dependency (Vierich 1979): in the mid-1980s it was estimated by the Norwegian Agency for International Development (NORAD) that remote-area dwellers depended upon food relief for up to 80–90 percent of their subsistence (Gulbrandsen, Karlsen, and Lexow 1986:1).

In all employment and commercial exchange situations, the majority of Kūa were seen as involved in a flexible labor market which had been generated by the encroachment of the agropastoral and capitalist economy of southern Africa. Very few people were involved in long-term dependency relationships with particular Bakgalagadi or Tswana. In the southeastern Kalahari, there were only four cases where Kūa were living with the Bakgalagadi "master" or local headman.

Relatively few Basarwa have sufficient resources to be completely independent pastoralists, agriculturalists, or wage laborers. Farmers in Botswana employ Basarwa labor in situations that range from occasional piecework to complete incorporation into patron–client or employer–employee-type arrangements (Hitchcock 1978; Biesele *et al.* 1989). The problem is that laborers are usually given relatively little recompense for their work. Monthly wages average between about 10 to 20 Pula (about US $5–10). Some herders get paid in kind, sometimes in the form of a cow a year in a system known as *sejara*. In return for their efforts, the Kūa are admitted to the lowest rung of the larger socioeconomically stratified society, a position from which it is difficult for them to move much higher (Hitchcock 1987c).

Mine labor among Kūa

One of the ways Kūa have adapted to socioeconomic changes in the eastern and southeastern Kalahari is through taking advantage of new opportunities. An example of opportunistic behavior was the decision on the part of some Kūa men to engage in labor migration to the mines of South Africa. Until the 1950s, relatively few Basarwa were recruited for work in the mines in the Kalahari. Decisions were made to expand the recruitment activities of the Witwatersrand Native Labor Associations (WNLA) in the late 1940s and early 1950s (Taylor 1978).

Subsequently, 83 Basarwa men were recruited in the Molepolole area in 1953 (Taylor 1978:109). One problem with Basarwa recruitment was that the families of the miners were left without enough men to hunt for them. Nevertheless, labor recruitment continued among Kalahari residents, in spite of the fact that some local administrators felt it was harmful (Taylor 1978:109).

Labor migration to the South African mines was a significant factor in the economy and social system of the Kūa. In some groups over 20 percent of the adult men were reported to be at the mines between 1976 and 1979. While men were absent at the mines, however, remittances were not received by their families, in part because of their inaccessibility and relatively high mobility. Sometimes Kūa claimed that Bakwena and Bakgalagadi took their money, stating that since they were Basarwa their property could rightfully be claimed by their *mong* (master).

The households which had men involved in mine labor were often those in which other members were herding cattle and doing *majako*. There were only ten households out of 130 (7.7 percent) in which no other members had employment save the young men who had gone to the mines. A further eight households (6.2 percent) which had miners also had women doing seasonal agricultural labor. Sixty percent of all miners came from households in which more than one member was employed in a combination of herding and agricultural work. This suggests that going to the mines and participating in other kinds of economic activities among the Kūa is related to sedentism and an increasing need for cash to buy goods to replace those that households are no longer able to obtain through foraging.

Conclusions

In the eastern and southeastern Kalahari, the farming economy is one of risk. Any human adaptation that includes agriculture must incorporate fallback strategies in case of crop failures. For most agropastoralists in southern Africa today, these fallbacks consist of livestock sales, migrant wage labor, and foraging. Kūa foragers tend to expand their foraging activities and exchange their labor in order to generate income and subsistence resources. In the socioeconomic system of interdependence among foragers and agropastoralists in the Kalahari, the ultimate safety net is the productivity of wild resources.

In the past thirty years, the Kūa who suffered nutritional stress were caught in a crisis which was due as much to their society's internal responses as it was to changes in the overall environment. It must be stressed, however, that greater involvement with the farming economy had so far not significantly transformed Kūa society. No new leadership patterns had developed, nor were there any indications of lineality or the formation of corporate groups. What we witnessed was a society that seemed to tolerate a greater degree of property accumulation than had been the case previously. A certain amount of internal socioeconomic stratification was also seen among Kūa, due in part to hoarding behavior and differential access to sources of employment and income. Relatively few Kūa had been able to acquire enough livestock to become self-sufficient pastoralists. They continued to use a mixed economic system of farming, livestock production, wage labor, emigration, and foraging as a means of long-term survival.

In the contemporary political, economic, and environmental context, these strategies are not as effective as they once had been in preventing people from becoming impoverished. One way to deal with the changes was for the Kūa to diversify not only economically but culturally as well.

Some Kūa passed themselves off as Tswana so that they would not be discriminated against. Others militantly proclaimed their status as Basarwa in order to underscore their sentiments about denial of basic human rights and the ways that minority groups were treated in Botswana. Still others called themselves Kūa in the full knowledge that they were distinct from other groups and had traditions and customs of their own. Cultural diversity, therefore, is a variable response to problems faced by local people and is capable of being manipulated for specific purposes. There was not a uniform "Kūa culture" nor was there a "foraging culture" (Kent 1992:61). Rather, there were variations in ethnic and cultural identity that came about as a product of specific sociopolitical, economic, and environmental factors.

Acknowledgements

Support for the research upon which this paper is based was provided by the US National Science Foundation, Canada Council, the Social Science Research Council, and the Remote Area Development Program of the government of Botswana. Much of this work was done in conjunction with several colleagues, including Jim Ebert, Melinda Kelly, Aron Crowell, John Holm, and Alec Campbell. We would also like to acknowledge the contributions of Sue Kent, George Silberbauer, Nick Blurton-Jones, Mathias Guenther, Richard Lee, Dori Bixler, Rod Brandenburgh, Neil Parsons, and Margaret Deith, who provided information and suggestions on ways to improve the chapter. The material presented here would not have been obtained without the help of the Kūa of the eastern and southeastern Kalahari, to whom we are deeply grateful.

6   Hunting variability at a recently sedentary Kalahari village

Susan Kent

In a book devoted to examining and understanding diversity among foragers, it is appropriate to examine both diachronic and synchronic diversity in hunting behavior, skill, and success, within and between groups.
As I shall show below, the factors responsible for variability within
groups are different from those that are responsible for it between
groups. How, then, do these differences affect other facets of culture and
behavior? Investigators with dissimilar theoretical orientations posit
different explanations for hunting variability, both within single hunter-
gatherer groups through time and between groups. There is, for
example, considerable variation among different Basarwa (Bushman,
San) groups; it is therefore inappropriate to lump them together uncritically (see Barnard and Widlok, chapter 4, Guenther, chapter 3, this
volume; Kent 1992 and chapter 1, this volume). Flexibility, which
encourages cultural diversity, is a trait associated with highly egalitarian
and nomadic, or formerly nomadic, foragers (also see Joiris, chapter 10,
Guenther, chapter 3, this volume and Guenther 1992). In spite of the
diversity, however, it is both appropriate and useful to compare Basarwa
groups so as to discover similarities as well as differences.

In subsistence strategies and involvement with non-foragers, the
Kutse group described below is more similar to the Ju/'hoansi (!Kung)
in the 1960s and 1970s described by Lee (1979 and elsewhere) and
Yellen (1977 and elsewhere) than it is to groups living today at ≠xade
(Osaki 1984; Tanaka 1987) or at Dobe (Draper and Kranichfeld 1990).
However, its mobility patterns and health are more similar to the
Ju/'hoansi of the 1990s than to those of twenty to thirty years ago (Kent
and Lee 1992; Kent and Dunn in press). The sharing of meat by Kutse
residents is more similar to the G/wi than that described for the Nharo
(Guenther 1992; Barnard 1986a) or Ju/'hoansi (Lee 1979; Marshall
1976). Unless stated otherwise, this chapter about hunting variability
refers specifically to Central Kalahari Basarwa.

My interpretation of the causes and consequences of hunting variation is based on a non-ecological theoretical orientation and on my

observations of the strongly egalitarian nature of the particular Basarwa society I have been studying (Kent 1993a). By looking at the data from a perspective that is more social than is common for hunter-gatherer studies in general, and for hunting variation in particular, I am not implicitly criticizing other, more widely accepted orientations. I am merely presenting a view that, in my judgment, best accounts for the data I have collected. Other anthropologists have noted that social factors underlie hunting variation. Lee (1979), for example, recorded that successful Ju/'hoansi hunters during the 1960s periodically reduced their hunting time by stopping hunting completely or by hunting less intensely. Hunting variation was a sociopolitical leveling mechanism which created opportunities for less skillful hunters to supply meat. He stated that, as a consequence, skillful hunters who brought in more meat did not gain greater prestige or higher status over anyone else. Bailey (1985), working with different foraging populations, has observed that variation in time spent hunting among individual Efe Pygmies varied as a result of social relationships. He wrote (1985:240–1) that Efe hunters do not act purely on the basis of energy efficiency or calorie maximization; instead "social relationships amongst people and between themselves and neighboring peoples placed significant costs on subsistence behaviors" (1985:244). Bailey's observation is consistent with the view of hunting variation employed here. This chapter explores the concept that social relationships among Kutse foragers influence hunting behavior through the sharing of meat.

The data and their collection

Although one or two-year periods of observation are most common in anthropology, I wanted to obtain a more long-term view of hunting variation and facets of sedentarization in a Kalahari community than I could do within a more synchronic framework. I specifically tried to avoid the situation experienced by Tanaka (1980b), who was in the field for over a year during a particularly severe drought. Although he gave an excellent picture of adjustment to extreme drought, his figures were not representative of typical patterns of hunting according to Silberbauer, who had earlier spent almost a decade in and out of the same area of the Kalahari. To obtain a more long-term view of hunting variation, I decided to make an intensive study of hunting and gathering for short periods over a number of years.

This chapter is based on research gathered during the dry season (May–August) over a five-year period – 1987–91. During this time, one rainy season was also observed (December–January, 1989–90). Since the

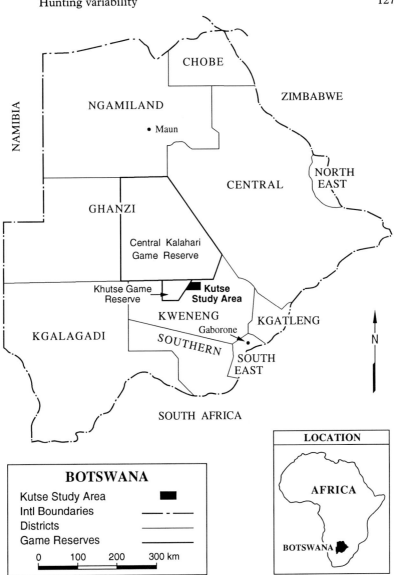

Figure 6.1   Map of study area

study project is still continuing, additional dry seasons have been observed during the publication of this book; the data from 1992 agree with the interpretations presented here but are not included in the quantitative figures since I wanted to view a five-year block of time.

During my visits to the Kalahari, I was able to observe severe drought conditions for several months during the last year in a five-year cycle of severe drought, in addition to a few months each of the four years following it (Draper and Kranichfeld 1990 characterized the 1980s drought as severe; also see Ringrose and Matheson 1991). Before my study, I assumed that hunting returns would be affected by the cycles of drought characteristic of the area, as has been suggested by Silberbauer (1981a) and others. I wanted to see if other less obvious factors also affect hunting variation and, if so, what their consequences are.

I observed the hunting activities of a group who were primarily, though not exclusively, hunter-gatherers located just outside the Khutse Game Reserve in the Kalahari of Botswana (Figure 6.1). The relatively recent community of Kutse (the alternative spelling of Khutse is used to differentiate the game reserve from the community) is dispersed and composed of camps with various styles of grass huts and windbreaks (see Kent 1989b, 1992, 1993a, b, for more complete descriptions). Depending on the year and season, the average population fluctuates between roughly 90 and 130 people. Of these, 70 to 80 percent are Basarwa (primarily G/wi and G//ana with some Kūa). The rest are Bakgalagadi or Bantu-speakers. Residents follow a semi-sedentary to sedentary settlement pattern. All residents originally occupied the Central Kalahari Game Reserve before coming to Kutse ten to twenty years ago (Kent 1995a, b).

Some Kutse Bakgalagadi have more in common with the Basarwa than with the better-known village Bakgalagadi described by Hitchcock and Campbell (1972), Kuper (1970, 1982), and Solway (1986). For example, only one full-time and one part-time Kutse Mokgalagadi (Mo is the singular of Ba) resident owns any cattle. A few Kutse Bakgalagadi do not even own goats. They do not consistently plant gardens and, in some cases, have never planted gardens at all. Many Kutse Bakgalagadi depend primarily on foraging, particularly for meat. Moreover, Kutse Bakgalagadi do not adhere to the sociopolitical stratification nor do they hold other cultural beliefs characteristic of village Bakgalagadi agropastoralists (Kent 1995a, n.d.).

Kutse is quite different from other contemporary communities in the Kalahari, including those discussed in chapters 3 through 5 in this volume. The most obvious difference is that Kutse is not a cattle-post or a developed village with store, school, or health clinic. A second difference is that horses are not available for hunting and no one owns or has access to a gun. Hunting at Kutse is solely based on traditional weapons: the primary weapons are the bow and poison arrows, spears, and clubs (the latter are usually digging sticks). Brush traps that funnel animals

Figure 6.2   A steenbok caught in a trap (Kutse, Botswana)

into snares are very popular during the dry season but not during the rainy season because they do not operate properly when wet (Figure 6.2). The traps are used to acquire steenbok, duiker, and springbok. Birds other than ostrich are obtained primarily by women, who use smaller versions of the antelope trap. Small animals, such as hare, ground squirrels, mongoose, wild cats, and jackals, are hunted with dogs. Most large game, such as gemsbok, are hunted with spears or poison arrows. Foxes are obtained with dogs, captured in traps baited with small pieces of bird meat, or snared with a long pole with a wooden hook on one end (Figure 6.3). Other burrowing animals, such as spring-hare, are acquired by dragging them out of their burrows with the long pole (Figure 6.3).

Kutse residents differ from those living in areas to the north and west, in that they do not use hunting blinds or practice nocturnal hunting (e.g., see Crowell and Hitchcock 1978), nor do they use game pits or stone fences (Guenther, chapter 3, this volume; 1992). Unlike hunters in the Nata River area (Hitchcock 1992: personal communication) and elsewhere (Guenther, chapter 3, this volume), Kutse residents do not use fire or communal drives in which animals are driven into pens. Moreover, the Nata River Tuya, who have been sedentary for centuries, hunt a wider range of species than do the recently sedentary Basarwa at

Figure 6.3   Wood point at the end of a long pole used to snare springhare and other burrowing animals such as fox (Kutse, Botswana)

Kutse today or than more mobile Basarwa did thirty years ago either at ≠xade or in Ngamiland. Hitchcock (1982a) believes that the sedentary Tuya first depleted the large prey locally, then resorted to hunting a wider range of species. Although no longer nomadic, Kutse hunters do acquire a limited inventory of species, similar to that of the more mobile Basarwa. This similarity may occur because none of the Kutse hunters has been sedentary for the whole of his life; most have become sedentary only in the past ten to twenty years. Moreover, unlike the Nata River area, depletion of local game has not become a problem at Kutse because, except for the drought years, many animals wander outside the game reserve boundaries and may, therefore, be hunted legally. Unlike elsewhere in the Kalahari, there is no meat trade at Kutse (i.e., all Kutse hunting is household subsistence-based).

Kutse men hunt by themselves, with male friends, or with their wives, and collect wild plants during foraging excursions. The hunters studied specifically in the quantitative portion of this chapter usually engaged in solitary hunting or in foraging with a spouse. They occasionally hunted with one or more men on overnight hunting trips.

I thought trapping would be more popular among modern sedentary Kutse hunters than among the nomadic Central Kalahari Basarwa of several decades ago. My reasoning was that a brush trap, which takes several hours to build, can be reused over a longer period now that Kutse residents are relatively stationary. However, traps appear to be as important today at Kutse as they were thirty years ago at ≠xade (Silberbauer 1993: personal communication). One difference in trapping methods between the two time periods is the use of plastic threads from mealie meal bags to weave snares at Kutse. These plastic bag thread snares have been popular since 1988; they are stronger and more likely to hold a springbok captive than snares constructed from wild plants.

If they have been unsuccessful for a while, most hunters (whether otherwise generally skillful or not) dismantle their traps in disgust or stop encounter-hunting for a time. Most also give up foraging in general until they have performed the hunting ritual described below or until they are in the mood to try again. This lack of motivation may last from days to weeks and even occasionally to months. The hunters are supported by their sharing partners during this period of inactivity. When ready to resume hunting, they usually place their traps in a new location or look for game in a new area.

Hunter 1 and his family belong to a sharing network, as do most people at Kutse, but he and his family are not related to anyone in his sharing network. In fact, Hunter 1 and his family speak a different dialect from those most commonly spoken at Kutse, although because of their universal kinship system, Hunter 1 and his family are considered to be vaguely related in some way by other Kutse residents. Depending on the year, the sharing network is composed of the families of Hunters 3, 5, and 6. Hunter 3, who is Hunter 5's brother-in-law, occupies a nearby camp with his family. Hunter 6, who is Hunter 5's spouse's uncle, lived in Hunter 5's camp for five months during 1991. Hunter 8 is a fictive brother of Hunter 5. Hunter 7, like Hunter 1, is not related to the others in the network. I do not have detailed time allocation data for Hunters 7 and 8, which is why they are not listed in Table 6.1, although I do have success rates, species procurement, and other information.

In contrast, Hunter 2 and his family are a sharing isolate in that they do not belong to a particular sharing network and do not formally share food outside camp (Kent 1993a), even though they have relatives living at other camps at Kutse. Nevertheless, Hunter 2's family still participates in community-wide meetings and other events, but they do not socialize as much as most families do. They are not ostracized in the community for their less social behavior; they simply are not visited as much as are residents of camps who belong to a sharing network. However, if people come by at an opportune time when meat is being consumed, they are given some to eat during their visit. Although Hunter 2 and his wife are therefore still part of the Kutse community, they do not formally exchange meat or objects regularly with any camp because of their less sociable nature.

The following quantitative analyses are based on 175 separate hunting trips made by six hunters over 290 days between 1987 and 1991. In addition, observations through spot checking of hunting at several other camps brings the total number of observation days to 368 and the total number of hunters observed to eight, which is 33.3 percent of all hunters who have lived at Kutse between 1987 and 1991 (not all live at the

Table 6.1. *Results from Kutse time allocation studies*

Observation	Hunter	Season	Year	Observation days	Hunting hours/week	Tending goats hours/week	Making traps[a] hours/week	Hunting success animal/success/attempt
1	1	Dry	1987	43	19.32	0.00	2.96	3/ 3/15
2	2	Dry	1987	14	14.76	3.79[b]	0.01	1/ 1/6
3	3	Dry	1988	40	14.52	0.00	0.01	9/ 7/14
4	2	Dry	1988	18	2.29	2.68[c]	0.00	1/ 1/2
5	4	Dry	1989	37	24.65[d]	1.74	0.67	6/ 6/18
6	2	Dry	1989	11	22.26	2.29	0.24	8/ 6/10
7	2	Wet	1989	15	22.53	3.46[e]	0.94	4/ 3/4
8	5	Dry	1990	50	19.19	1.95	2.34	19/15/41
9	2	Dry	1990	14	18.53	—[f]	1.57	7/ 5/14
10	1	Dry	1990	41	20.34	0.00	—[g]	3/ 3/16
11	2	Dry	1991	8	19.25	3.05	—	3/ 3/7
12	5	Dry	1991	40	12.31	1.91	—	7/ 7/23 (one was inedible)
13	6	Dry	1991	37	21.45	0.00	—	5/ 5/17

Total observation days: Hunter 1 = 84 days   Hunter 2 = 80 days (including 15 days during the wet season)   Hunter 3 = 40 days   Hunter 4 = 37 days   Hunter 5 = 90 days   Hunter 6 = 37 days

[a] Amount of time observed making traps; therefore represents the minimum amount of time spent in weaving traps in camps.
[b] Not including watering day when goats were taken to the borehole on the nearby game reserve = 1.98 hours/week.
[c] Not including watering day = 1.47 hours/week.
[d] This figure is an approximation of the actual number of hours hunting per week because it estimates one 9-day hunt conducted June 8–16, 1989, and one overnight hunt, June 30–July 1, 1989.
[e] Not including watering day = 2.08 hours/week.   [f] For a variety of reasons, this figure could not be calculated.
[g] I did not live in the camp of this individual in 1990 (I lived in the camp next to his) and therefore did not observe his in-camp activities, although I did record and monitor his hunting trips.

community at the same time). Hunting data are based on direct observations of when hunters left and returned to camp, what they acquired, with whom they shared, and so on. Interviews added details, such as whether an animal had been caught in a snare but subsequently escaped or was eaten by a predator.

It is important to note that the 368 observation days represent only the times when the quantitative data were collected; I spent additional observation days at different camps conducting more qualitative research, including participant-observation and interviews. During this time, hunters from different camps were compared (for example, to determine whether, in the drought or the rainy season, hunters with comparable skill were bringing in comparable numbers of animals). My spot checks of 24 hunters at other camps, interviews with 84 residents, and qualitative observational data all support the quantitative data presented below.

Foragers or agro-pastoralists: the impact of neighbors on Kutse hunter-gatherers

Because recent claims question the validity of studying any Basarwa population as legitimate foragers, it is germane to discuss first whether these people are twentieth-century hunter-gatherers or impoverished agro-pastoralists, as some anthropologists have claimed (e.g., Wilmsen 1989; Wilmsen and Denbow 1990; Schrire 1980; but see Harpending 1991 and Lee and Guenther 1993). While Kutse residents undoubtedly adopted goat herding/pastoralism and sedentism from their Bantu-speaking neighbors, it is important to determine precisely what influence these adoptions have had on people's beliefs and behavior. Interaction between two groups does not automatically result in the assimilation and loss of cultural autonomy of one of them (see Kent 1992).

Classification of the Kutse residents as full-time, part-time, supplemental, or secondary hunter-gatherers is necessary in order to interpret hunting variation for the reasons described by Eder (1988). He discusses differences between former foragers who hunt only to supplement domesticated staples in their diet, and those who are more full-time hunters. He notes (1984) that people who hunt recreationally, seasonally, or sporadically might have different patterns of hunting and more variability in skill than those who depend primarily on foraging and who therefore train and practice more. Silberbauer (1993: personal communication) likewise observed significant differences in the success rate of full-time and part-time hunters because "one very quickly loses that fine edge of judgment of time and distance and the relative motion problems, as one loses steadiness of eye and aim." To understand the context of Kutse hunting it is necessary to determine the impact of goat ownership on certain facets of hunting.

Some researchers claim that goat ownership affects hunting in such a way as to transform a hunting-gathering society into an agropastoral, or at least a non-foraging, society (Wilmsen 1989; Wilmsen and Denbow 1990, but also see Lee and Guenther 1991, 1993). How can we assess such claims? One way is to examine attitudes and beliefs (e.g., Kent 1993a and 1995a, b). Below, I examine behavior as it pertains to hunting variability, the subject of this chapter. The Kutse study population depends primarily on wild foods but not to the exclusion of domesticates. I therefore characterize them as twentieth-century foragers – that is, as culturally autonomous foraging people in contact with, but not assimilated by, their non-foraging neighbors.

At Kutse, an estimated 90 to 95 percent of all meat comes from wild animals that are hunted with arrows, spears, dogs, clubs, and/or traps. Of 53 Basarwa interviewed, 59 percent do not own any goats (in this study, Hunters 1 and 3 did not own goats and Hunter 6, who was visiting, did not have any goats at Kutse).[1] Those who own goats usually have small herds of less than 20 or 30 head.[2] Although goat milk is occasionally consumed by those who own goats, or begged by those who do not, it is not a prominent or even an important part of anyone's diet. Of 34 Basarwa who were asked in 1989 if they drank goat milk, 41 percent said they did not and 29 percent said they drank one cup or less occasionally (which I defined as once a week or less and it usually was less).

Goat ownership does not interfere with hunting.[3] Those individuals who own goats practice what I call opportunistic herding. That is, they let the goats out in the morning and hope they will make it back on their own at night. If some are missing, individuals look for them the next day, but no one stays with the herd (search time for lost goats is included in the herding figures in Table 6.1; otherwise the time spent caring for goats would be much less). People become annoyed when jackals kill a goat, but they still do not send anyone out with the herd to protect it

---

[1] It is interesting that the same percentage of Basarwa (59 percent) said their parents never owned any goats.

[2] For example, Hunters 2, 4, and 5 have 10 to 30 goats each, depending on the year and season.

[3] Goat meat is not a vital part of residents' diets. The vast majority of Basarwa, 78 percent of those interviewed in 1987, did not butcher any goats within a 12-month period. When asked why not, most individuals said they do not own enough goats to be able to kill one. Goats are commonly butchered when they are ill since it is presumed that they will die anyway.

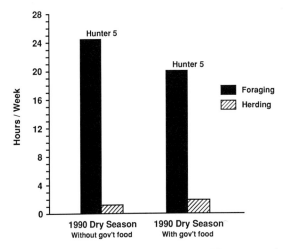

Figure 6.4 Time spent foraging by Hunter 5 when government-supplied food was and was not available

the next day. I do not mean to imply that the goats are completely unimportant; they are cared for, although minimally compared to most pastoralists' standards (i.e., many village Bakgalagadi and Batswana hire herd boys for their cattle and sometimes for their goats). Kutse residents state that they want goats because the animals provide a backup food resource should the men be unsuccessful in hunting; that is, goats represent a source of meat over which they have more control than they have over wild animals. In the past, they used mobility as a buffer against poor hunting; today they cannot and, instead, use goats as a buffer. Although many families own a few chickens, my observations suggest that dogs and wild animals eat chickens much more frequently than do people.

Some Kutse Basarwa sporadically and opportunistically plant small melon and bean gardens. However, during the past nine years, which includes five years of direct observations and four years reconstructed from interview data, harvests were bountiful only once, in 1988, the year after the drought broke. In other words, for most years during my observations (1987–92), gardening has not been an important subsistence endeavor in terms of time invested or resource yield.

The Botswana government distributes free maize meal, soy meal mixture, beans, and cooking oil approximately once every month or two. Since 1990, drought relief has been provided sporadically (for example, once every four to six months, after being available for two months in a row and then skipping two to four months). In spite of the presence of

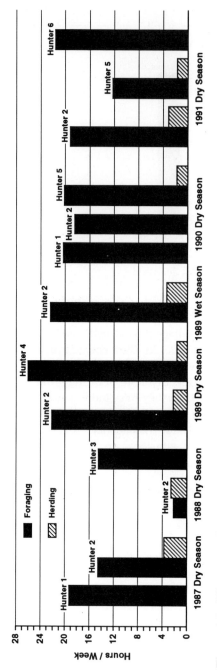

Figure 6.5   Time spent foraging and herding 1987–1991

drought-relief food, individuals within Hunter 5's household consumed wild plants – mostly various species of wild melons, berries, and tubers – on 85 percent of 48 days of continuous observation in 1990 and on 70 percent of 40 days in 1991. To view within-year variation, Hunter 5's household can be compared to Hunter 2's household, where wild plants were consumed on 39 percent of 14 days of observation in 1990 and 63 percent of 8 days in 1991.

When no drought-relief food is available, both women and men gather wild plants more intensively (Figure 6.4). Regardless of the repercussions that drought-relief provisions may have had on the collection or consumption of wild plants, the free food did not interfere much with hunting activities, the focus of this chapter (see Figure 6.5). Limited observations suggest that men tended to make slightly more numerous and longer foraging trips when there was no government-distributed food available. Without more data, it is difficult to determine conclusively whether the longer trips were due to increased gathering activities or to an increase in hunting activities. However, it seemed that men were collecting more plants rather than hunting more. I did *not* note an increase in the number of animals acquired during that period, but did note a significant increase in the quantity of wild plants gathered.

Thus we can see from the extensive time allocation studies that foraging is the dominant subsistence activity at Kutse even for those individuals who own goats (Table 6.1). Figure 6.5 illustrates the time spent hunting and herding over the past five years during thirteen observational periods. These periods varied in time from 7 to 49 consecutive days each.[4] Whereas the herding time in Figure 6.5 and in Table 6.1 includes all time spent in goat husbandry, the hunting figures include actual foraging time only. Time spent in gear maintenance, hunt preparation, and other activities that would increase the foraging time figures are excluded. In spite of that exclusion, examination of time spent only in subsistence activities, and not in other pursuits, reveals that an average of 91 percent of all subsistence time is spent foraging (with a range of 81 to 100 percent; Kent 1992).

Further indication of the importance of hunting at Kutse is the retention of rituals that are still commonly practiced to ensure hunting success. One ritual involves rubbing a mixture of meat and bone marrow

---

[4] It is difficult to separate trapping from encounter bow-and-arrow or spear hunting since a hunter always takes his bow and arrows and/or spear with him even when he just plans to check a trap. A hunter who plans to bow-and-arrow hunt will terminate his trip if he finds an animal in his trap. Likewise, a hunter who plans to check his traps may forgo them if he obtains an animal through encounter hunting on his way to the traps.

into cuts the hunter makes on his arms, chest, and face. The mixture is also used to paint his face, arms, and chest with lines and/or dots (I observed a woman with snares also perform this ritual to bring success to her traps; Kent 1993a, Figure 2). Meat taboos and rituals for the consumption of specific wild species are still practiced (for reasons suggested in Kent 1989a, there are no taboos or rituals concerning herding or the consumption of goats).

What can we conclude from the above? Basically, that a majority of Kutse residents do not own goats; those who do own goats tend to have small herds. Most important in terms of this chapter on hunting variation is the fact that goat owners do not hunt more or fewer hours than those who do not own goats. As shown below, goat owners also are not more or less successful, do not bring in more or less meat, and are not in any other way significantly distinguishable from their non-goat-owning neighbors. Similarly, gardens do not alter hunting patterns; nor does the availability of drought-relief food. Therefore, in my opinion, to call such a group anything but foragers would be inaccurate as well as misleading.

Goat ownership and hunting variation

In order to test multiple competing hypotheses, goat ownership is still included in the analyses because it is perhaps the most visible influence from Bantu-speaking neighbors. I wanted to test the validity of my contention that goats do not greatly impinge on the Kutse foraging way of life. If the political economists are correct in their assertion that Basarwa who own goats are "degraded" pastoralists who cannot be considered hunter-gatherers, then there should be a quantitative difference in certain aspects of hunting between those who own goats and those who do not. The difference would partly result from factors noted by Silberbauer (1993: personal communication) and Eder (1988), which show that part-time foragers are not as skilled at hunting as are full-time foragers. A t-test reveals that there is no significant difference between goat owners and those who do not own goats in the average number of hours spent hunting per week or in the number of animals acquired per day of observation. There is no significant difference in the number of animals acquired per hunting attempt, the frequency of success, or in hunting skill. Nor is there any significant difference in the number of hunting attempts per observation day. Moreover, there is no significant difference in the diversity of species acquired. In fact, the most significant difference between goat owners and those without is the number of hours spent caring for goats, not an unexpected finding!

Different kinds of data, including interviews, observations, and time allocation studies,[5] all support the view that the Kutse Basarwa can and should be considered twentieth-century foragers. While they are certainly not pristine relics from a bygone era in human prehistory, the impact of contact with neighboring people has not affected their hunting and gathering, nor, I suggest, has it affected more social and symbolic facets of their life, such as attitudes and beliefs (Kent 1993a, 1995a, b). In other words, the fact that some individuals own a few goats does not make them pastoralists any more than the occasional hunting and gathering practiced by many pastoralists makes them foragers.

Hunting variation and its source

If we accept that the Kutse Basarwa are, indeed, foragers, we can begin to examine the much more interesting questions of what causes hunting variation and its consequences. Monitored variables are:

1 the average number of hours spent hunting per week;
2 the average number of hours spent herding goats per week;
3 the number of animals obtained per day of observation;
4 the number of hunting attempts per observation day (or how often they went hunting);
5 the number of successful ventures; that is, the ratio of successes to attempts;
6 the number of animals acquired per hunting attempt (more than one animal can potentially be obtained per successful attempt);
7 the number of species acquired, i.e., the diversity (richness) of species;
8 the edible meat weight (using calculations from Silberbauer 1981a) acquired per hunting attempt;
9 the edible meat weight per number of animals caught (or size of animals acquired);
10 the edible meat weight procured per observation day.

Hunting variation and seasonality

Researchers who have worked in the Central Kalahari where the Kutse residents originated have noted marked seasonal variations in hunting

---

[5] Note that a study of the faunal remains located at various camps demonstrates a lack of association between goat versus non-goat owners and total number of bones per camp (NISP), dressed meat weight calculated from the faunal remains per camp, minimum number of individuals represented by the bones per camp (MNI), or number of species

activity and in hunting yields. For example, Silberbauer (1981a:219–20), who observed G/wi from 1958 to 1966, found that they consume almost four times the amount of meat during the rainy summer months, December and January, as they do during the dry-season months, August and September. He noted that hunting was easier during the summer. Kutse follows a similar pattern, which differs from that recorded by Lee (1979:104–5) in Ngamiland. The lowest level of hunting in the Central Kalahari occurs during the hot months of early summer before water accumulates in the pans and when it is difficult to obtain sufficient moisture from plants (both people and game are thirsty). According to Murray (1976:11), game densities are lower at this time because herds are fragmented and dispersed. Also during this period, arrow poison has either been exhausted or has lost its virulence and fresh poison is not available (Silberbauer 1965:29). Tanaka (1980b), working in the same area almost a decade later, similarly noted seasonal variation in the timing of hunts during the day.

The Kutse data reveal a few significant differences between dry and rainy season in the ten variables monitored. Variables affected by seasonality are the number of successful hunting attempts (or general success), the number of animals acquired per hunting attempt, and the number of different species acquired per hunting attempt (or species diversity, specifically richness). These statistics indicate that hunting is easier, or at least more successful, during the rainy season than the dry, particularly after the pans fill with water. Also during the rainy season, there is a greater diversity of species procured per hunting attempt (Table 6.2). The Kutse data agree with various researchers' observations of Central Kalahari hunting.

While the Kutse data do not contradict other anthropologists' descriptions of seasonal variability in Central Kalahari Basarwa hunting, they do differ from those for Bakgalagadi agro-pastoralists living elsewhere in the Kweneng District described by Solway (1986; 1990: personal communication). Village Bakgalagadi agro-pastoralists hunt mostly in the dry season for two reasons: during the rainy season, they are particularly busy planting gardens and caring for their cattle and goats and, as a consequence, they have no time to hunt. The second reason is that they hunt only to supplement their diet, unlike Kutse residents who forage year-round.

calculated from the faunal remains per camp (taxa diversity or richness; Kent 1993b discusses faunal remains at camps in more detail). This study further supports the ethnographic studies described here.

Table 6.2. *t-test analysis of hunting and herding subsistence activities (independent variables were converted to dummy variables and asterisks indicate statistical significance at the 0.05 level)*

Independent variable	t value	Prob. > t	Significant means
Dependent variable = number of hours spent hunting per week			
Season	−0.8223	0.4284	N.A.
Ethnic affiliation			
(Basarwa; Bakgalagadi)	−0.4430	0.6663	N.A.
Hunting skill	−1.7232	0.1128	N.A.
Drought	2.5243	*0.0283	Yes = 12.7; No = 20.1
Dependent variable = number of hours spent herding goats per week			
Season	−1.3034	0.2217	N.A.
Ethnic affiliation			
(Basarwa; Bakgalagadi)	0.9420	0.3684	N.A.
Hunting skill	−0.8219	0.4303	N.A.
Drought	0.2002	0.8453	N.A.
Dependent variable = number of animals caught per day of observation			
Season	−0.1151	0.9105	N.A.
Ethnic affiliation			
(Basarwa; Bakgalagadi)	0.4635	0.6521	N.A.
Hunting skill	−3.6894	*0.0088	Yes = 0.37; No = 0.09
Drought	1.7796	0.1027	N.A.
Dependent variable = number of animals acquired per hunting attempt			
Season	−2.9954	*0.0122	Dry = 0.40; Wet = 1.00
Ethnic affiliation			
(Basarwa; Bakgalagadi)	−0.2465	0.8089	N.A.
Hunting skill	−2.9547	0.0131	Yes = 0.59; No = 0.28
Drought	0.6552	0.5258	N.A.
Dependent variable = number of successful hunting trips per hunting attempt (percentage of successful attempts)			
Season	−2.8155	*0.0168	Dry = 35%; Wet = 75%
Ethnic affiliation			
(Basarwa; Bakgalagadi)	−0.2864	0.7799	N.A.
Hunting skill	−2.5731	*0.0259	Yes = 48%; No = 28%
Drought	0.5766	0.5758	N.A.
Dependent variable = number of hunting attempts per observation day			
Season	1.0146	0.3321	N.A.
Ethnic affiliation			
(Basarwa; Bakgalagadi)	0.7684	0.4584	N.A.
Hunting skill	−2.0460	0.0654	N.A.
Drought	2.2859	*0.0428	Yes = 0.31; No = 0.64

Hunting variation and drought

I expected hunting statistics from drought years, and the year immediately following before plants and animals had time to recover, to differ significantly from non-drought years. I thought that drought-associated years would severely reduce the availability of plants and the animals that consume them (and as suggested by Silberbauer 1981a). Indeed, people do hunt, on average, significantly fewer hours per week during a drought than during non-drought conditions (see Table 6.1). Related to this, there are fewer hunting attempts during drought conditions.

Furthermore, during drought years, there is a significantly higher number of species acquired – that is, higher species diversity (Table 6.2). The reasons for this are not readily apparent at this point, although proponents of optimal foraging theory may disagree. For example, it has been suggested by a number of these scholars that diet breadth increases as preferred species decline in number (e.g., Winterhalder 1990:82). This perspective would explain the focus on a variety of smaller-sized animals during the drought as a result of the dispersal of larger species, as suggested by Murray (1976) and others (animals were noticeably less numerous than during non-drought years). Hitchcock's (1982a) observation that a greater diversity of animals is procured by completely sedentary Tuya Basarwa along the Nata River, is relevant here. It also agrees with the diet breadth model. In the Tuya case, larger animals are not available because they have been overhunted. In contrast, during the drought at Kutse, although there were some larger animals, they were more dispersed and therefore more difficult to obtain. Even so, I am not convinced that diet breadth satisfactorily explains the Kutse variation, particularly since it does not explain why a wider variety of species per hunting attempt is *also* acquired during the rainy season, which is generally more favorable for hunting. Although this explanation is perhaps acceptable for drought conditions, it cannot also explain the same variability during non-drought rainy seasons.

There are no other significant differences in any other variables examined between drought and non-drought years (Tables 6.2, 6.3). The influence of hunting skill may be one reason why drought and non-drought years are not as significantly different as one would otherwise expect. Skillful hunters are defined as such on the basis of success rates of 30 percent or more and on the size of animals regularly acquired. One exception to this definition is Hunter 2, whose success rate during the drought year of 1987 dropped to only 17 percent. He compensated for it by hunting on 43 percent of the days during my 1987 observations.

Table 6.3. *t-test analysis of variation in dressed meat weight (i.e., the edible portions only) and species diversity (asterisks indicate statistical significance at the 0.05 level)*

Independent variable	t value	Prob. > t	Significant means
Dependent variable = dressed meat weight acquired per hunting attempt			
Season	−1.4072	0.1870	N.A.
Ethnic affiliation			
(Basarwa; Bakgalagadi)	−0.7354	0.5941	N.A.
Hunting skill	−3.1561	*0.0177	Yes = 3.55; No = 0.94
Drought	−3.0274	*0.0138	Yes = 0.80; No = 3.03
Dependent variable = dressed meat weight per number of animals caught			
Season	0.1456	0.8869	N.A.
Ethnic affiliation			
(Basarwa; Bakgalagadi)	−0.7287	0.5989	N.A.
Hunting skill	−1.0819	0.3150	N.A.
Drought	1.2743	0.2288	N.A.
Dependent variable = dressed meat weight per observation day			
Season	−0.2524	0.8054	N.A.
Ethnic affiliation			
(Basarwa; Bakgalagadi)	−0.4498	0.6616	N.A.
Hunting skill	−4.2885	*0.0038	Yes = 2.18; No = 0.42
Drought	4.0420	0.0030	Yes = 0.29; No = 1.85
Dependent variable = number of species per animal acquired (diversity of species)			
Season	−0.4044	0.6937	N.A.
Ethnic affiliation			
(Basarwa; Bakgalagadi)	−0.5078	0.6216	N.A.
Hunting skill	1.1515	0.2739	N.A.
Drought	−3.3713	*0.0062	Yes = 0.92; No = 0.52
Dependent variable = number of species per hunting attempt			
Season	−3.5190	*0.0048	Dry = 0.23; Wet = 0.75
Ethnic affiliation			
(Basarwa; Bakgalagadi)	−0.6035	0.5584	N.A.
Hunting skill	−1.5261	0.1552	N.A.
Drought	−0.1868	0.8552	N.A.

Consequently, and in spite of his low success rate, by hunting more often, he was able to provide an average of 0.36 kg of meat/day. Hunter 1, in contrast, hunted about the same number of times during drought and non-drought years – 32 percent of the days during the 1987 drought and 39 percent during the non-drought year of 1990.

Hunter 1 was successful 20 percent of the time during the drought

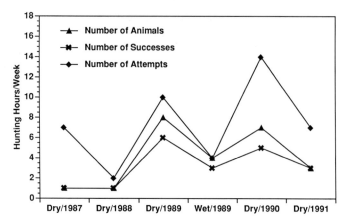

Figure 6.6   Time spent foraging by Hunter 2 from 1987 to 1991

year of 1987 and 19 percent of the time during the non-drought year of 1990.[6] However, he procured only steenbok or smaller game. He spent about the same amount of time per week hunting during drought and non-drought conditions – 18 hours during the drought and 20 hours during the same season of a non-drought year. In other words, despite hunting about as often as other hunters, Hunter 1 was not very success-ful, regardless of the hunting conditions. Hunter 2, in contrast, followed a different strategy during the drought – he simply did not hunt as much when conditions were poor (Figure 6.6). He hunted more often and was more successful during the non-drought years of 1989 through 1991. For example, he hunted 15 hours/week during the drought of 1987 and 2 hours/week in 1988. During the same season but in non-drought years, he hunted more – from 19 to 22 hours a week. He was successful 17 percent and 50 percent of the time during the two years of drought conditions, respectively, in contrast to 36 percent to 60 percent of the time during three non-drought years. Based on frequency and size of animals acquired, Hunter 2 is generally a skillful hunter who expends energy when there is a good chance of a return but hunts less when chances of success decline (e.g., during the 1988 dry season).

Hunting variation cannot be attributed to the number of dependents being supported. During 1987, Hunter 1 and Hunter 2 were both providing meat for six individuals within their immediate families, not including themselves (in each case, one was a dependent female adult

---

[6] Hunter 1 procured three animals on 15 hunting ventures during the drought of 1987 and three animals from 16 attempts during the post-drought of 1990. He went hunting approximately once every three days in both 1987 and 1990.

daughter or mother-in-law, one was a spouse, and the others were children or step-children). The amount of edible meat procured per observation day by Hunter 1 and Hunter 2 during 1987 was equivalent (0.36 kg of meat per day for each), but Hunter 2 was able to obtain it by hunting for fewer hours than Hunter 1.

In 1988 Hunter 2 procured less than 0.36 kg/observation day.[7] In other non-drought years, he hunted more often so that he could acquire more than the perceived minimum of meat required (meat is a favorite food).[8] However, Hunter 1 had to hunt regardless of conditions in order to acquire enough meat to feed his family *in addition to* contributing to families in his sharing network, while Hunter 2 had the option of hunting less when conditions were poor.

Why did Hunter 2 forage less during drought years than non-drought years when Hunter 1 foraged a similar amount regardless of the year? And why did Hunter 2 bring back less meat during the drought than after it? The difference between the two hunters' strategies reflects the fact that Hunter 1 belongs to a sharing network while Hunter 2 is a sharing isolate, who needed to worry only about the consumption requirements of his own household. Hunter 1, in contrast, had to forage enough to provide not only for his family, but for his sharing partners as well.

Hunting variation and hunting skill

As noted above, skillful hunters are defined here as those who are successful in at least 30 percent of their hunting attempts and who regularly bring in duiker and larger-sized animals.[9] Although on one

---

[7] In 1988 Hunter 2 procured only 0.02 kg per observation day; this was substantially lower than any other of the six periods of observation during which I recorded his hunting activities, including the drought year of 1987. No hunter at Kutse, regardless of skill, season, drought, animal availability, or other factors brought in less than 0.36 kg/meat per observation. I suggest that the amount of meat brought in by Hunter 2 in 1988 merely represents sampling error and is unduly low (based on 19 days of continuous observations). This interpretation is supported by the fact that during the drought period proper, Hunter 2 brought in 0.36 kg/meat per day. He brought in even more meat during periods of observations between 1989 and 1991. In 1992 Hunter 2 also brought in far more than 0.36 kg/observation day. This highlights the need for conducting longitudinal research when studying behavioral variability.

[8] Although meat is valued highly as a food, people complain after eating only meat for several days. They state that they will grow thin if they do not also eat plants (they also complain they are hungry for meat if they are able to eat only plants).

[9] Hunting attempts are defined as those times when a hunter left stating that he was going hunting/trapping (I always ask where people are going as they get ready to leave, although in most cases they volunteer the information in discussions with others or with me). People leave camp for specific purposes; therefore the number of hunting attempts

level people know that some hunters are more skillful than others, they usually do not discuss it or analyze why. They most often claim that success and failure are related to luck or the whim of a rather capricious god (a highly variable concept among residents). During an interview when Hunter 1 was absent, others within his sharing network were unwilling to speculate about his consistently poor success, beyond suggestions that maybe his traps or their locations were not good. In other words, they gave situational answers. Additionally they were not able to answer my follow-up question as to why Hunter 1 would not move his traps to a better location. In fact, they were uncomfortable acknowledging that Hunter 1 was significantly less skillful than others. This discomfort exists because recognition of differences in skill contradicts their highly egalitarian ethos (discussed in Kent 1993a). Hunter 1 blames his success rate of only 20 percent or lower on his poor eyesight.

As might be predicted, skillful hunters bring in significantly more edible meat weight per hunting attempt and per observation day than less skillful hunters (Table 6.2): it is not a consequence of increased individual hunting time (Tables 6.2, 6.3).[10] In general, only skillful hunters obtain animals larger than a duiker (duikers average 9 kg of edible meat per animal). Of those factors monitored, one of the most important variables influencing the amount of meat acquired is hunting skill.

Unlike the Aché, as described by Hill (1983 and elsewhere), better Kutse hunters do not necessarily have more or fewer children than poor hunters. For example, none of the best hunters is polygamous, a practice which would enable them to have more children. Generally skillful Hunter 5 has only one child because of fertility problems, and, because of personal preference (revealed in interviews), he has only one wife (nor does he have extramarital affairs, according to observations and local gossip). In contrast, Hunter 1, the least skillful hunter, has four children (Table 6.4; note that data on number of children are for 1990, when the quantitative data were collected, although there have been no new births since that date). Reproductive histories for each hunter reveal that the average number of live births for skillful hunters is 2.0–2.5 (the former value includes the unmarried Hunter 7 in the figure and the latter

per hunter is unambiguous, particularly since I interview people when they return to camp and ask about their activities off-camp.

[10] During non-drought years, good hunters hunt about as often as less skilled hunters but bring in more meat, over 0.36 kg/day. As one example during 1990, Hunter 1 acquired 0.36 kg/day while hunting for a similar length of time as Hunter 5, who brought in 1.94 kg/day, and Hunter 2, who brought in 2.99 kg/day (the latter is high because I observed the camp for a shorter period than I observed Hunter 5 and in that short time, Hunter 2 happened to obtain two springboks, an unusual occurrence for anyone).

Table 6.4. *Age and number of children by hunter and success rate for eight Kutse hunters*

	Age	Number of live births	Number of dead children	Number of abortions	Number of live children
Sharing network					
Hunter 1	40–50	1 F; 3 M	0 F; 0 M	0	1 F; 3 M
Hunter 3	30–35	1 F; 3 M	0 F; 1 M	0	1 F; 2 M
*Hunter 4	30–35	2 F; 2 M	0 F; 0 M	1	2 F; 2 M
*Hunter 5	30–35	1 F; 0 M	0 F; 0 M	1	1 F; 0 M
Hunter 6	40–50	4 F; 2 M	1 F; 0 M	0	3 F; 2 M
*Hunter 7	25–30	0 F; 0 M	0 F; 0 M	0	0 F; 0 M
*Hunter 8	35–45	3 F; 1 M	1 F; 1 M	0	2 F; 1 M
Sharing isolate					
*Hunter 2	40–50	1 F; 0 M	0 F; 0 M	0	1 F; 0 M

(also cares for spouse's two daughters and three grandchildren, for a total of five dependents)

* Skillful hunter

excludes him). In contrast to what Hill (1983) would predict from his model, the average number of live births for *un*successful hunters is almost double, 4.0. However, because of the large standard deviation, a t-test shows that the difference is not statistically significant (t = 1.793; $p = 0.1232$). Thus, the data show that successful hunters at Kutse do not have more children.

Furthermore, some individuals, such as Hunter 5, hunt less or stop hunting for varying periods of time, which certainly is not a practice that would increase fitness, unless one defines fitness to include social networks. Fitness, in the evolutionary sense, is usually defined as relative reproductive success. Individuals who have access to more meat are often assumed to be more fit (e.g., see Hawkes 1990; Hawkes *et al.* 1991; Hill 1983). However, this does not occur at Kutse. Periodic abstentions from hunting by more successful Kutse hunters promote equality in meat acquisition and encourage food sharing, which in turn encourages social bonds between friends and families.[11]

[11] A number of anthropologists whose theoretical orientations demand an economic explanation for sharing have suggested that the sharing relationship between Hunters 1 and 5 may serve as insurance against future accidents for Hunter 5 or against a natural reduction in hunting success with age. Hunter 1 is approximately ten years older than Hunter 5, so age-dependent skills will deteriorate for Hunter 1 before they do for Hunter 5. Moreover, when questioned, the people themselves deny an economic basis to sharing. When asked why they share with someone who they know cannot reciprocate, they explain that the individual has children or a wife who need food, and when

Success rates, and therefore skill, are not directly related to variation in hunting time (time engaged in hunting/trapping recorded from the moment a hunter leaves camp until he returns). Rather, such variation is a complex issue that is influenced by a number of variables. Most important is sharing, which influences hunting skill and success by motivating individuals who belong to a sharing network to provide not only their own family's needs, but those of their sharing partners as well (for example, as in the case of Hunters 1 or 3). Sharing itself is not economically motivated. Instead, sharing is a leveling mechanism that encourages egalitarianism because good hunters give away more meat than do poor hunters, and this evens out differences in skill and success rates (Kent 1993a, b).

Hunting variation and sharing

Variations in meat yield due to differences in hunting skill thus tend to be negated by sharing. Such sharing occurs formally through sharing networks and informally through sharing with whomever is at a hearth during a meal. Sharing networks are based on a combination of friendship and kinship (Kent 1993a; 1995b).

Sharing and the social networks it fosters within a milieu of egalitarianism explain more variation in hunting time and other facets of hunting than does skill. Hunter 5 reduced his hunting time in 1991 to a degree that superficially resembles the drop in hunting time for Hunter 2 in 1988. There was no environmental reason (i.e., seasonal differences, droughts, or the availability of animals) for Hunter 5, who belongs to a sharing network, to reduce the amount of time he spent hunting in 1991. In fact, Hunter 2, my control over the five-year period, maintained a similar success rate and time spent in hunting during the years of 1990 and 1991, the period when Hunter 5 experienced a substantial drop (Figure 6.5). Note that in 1992 Hunter 5 increased his hunting time to an amount that surpassed that of 1990, to 25 hours/week over 40 days of continuous observations in 1992.

I interpret the deliberate reduction in foraging by Hunter 5 in 1991 to the presence of Hunter 6, his wife's uncle, who was visiting his camp for

they are pressed for another reason they say, "That is the way we do things here at Kutse." They also say no when asked if they share so that when the other person has meat and they do not, the other person will want to reciprocate. Further, if observations over six years do not show an economic gain in a relationship, I think it is unfounded to claim that an economic explanation is still the primary motive, even if not visible for another 10 or 20 years, particularly among a people who are not as future-oriented as westerners are (the tyranny of theoretical orientations in Basarwa research is discussed in Kent 1992).

four to six months. Hunter 6 was not particularly successful at hunting. Upon request, he checked Hunter 5's traps on several occasions when Hunter 5, who had been very successful in 1990, did not feel like going out to check them himself (although Hunter 6 was a visitor from the Central Kalahari Game Reserve, he had traps set and regularly went hunting in the Kutse area because of the anticipated length of his visit). In one instance, Hunter 6 returned with a steenbok from Hunter 5's trap. Hunter 6 had killed it, brought it home after initial butchering and cooking at a temporary processing site, and performed secondary butchering activities back at his windbreak in Hunter 5's camp. The steenbok was technically Hunter 5's, and he and his wife told Hunter 6 which pieces to keep and which pieces to give to others within the sharing network (when questioned the next day, Hunter 5 said he gave Hunter 6 two thighs, and his father the chest of the animal; those pieces were further distributed in a tertiary wave of butchering and distribution). Everyone, including Hunters 5 and 6, attributed the steenbok to Hunter 5; his 1991 success rate was therefore only a little lower than it was in 1990. The single major difference between 1990 and 1991, then, was the amount of time Hunter 5 spent hunting. I suggest that Hunter 5 would have hunted more in 1991 if Hunter 6 had not been present. Although I occasionally observed Hunter 5 asking other hunters in camp to check his traps in 1990, he asked Hunter 6 to do so much more often in 1991. This gave Hunter 5 a break from hunting and gave Hunter 6 the opportunity to bring home and butcher meat. It allowed Hunter 6 to distribute meat that was indirectly, even if not technically, his when his own traps were empty. However minimally, the opportunity allowed Hunter 6 to participate in the sharing network more than he otherwise could have done. While other hunters will occasionally ask someone to check a trap, I never observed a less skillful hunter, such as 1 or 3, ask this of a more skillful hunter, such as Hunter 5.

Sharing is an important social mechanism which consolidates friendship and kinship bonds that unite separate camps. Hunter 5's behavior allowed Hunter 6 to reinforce his ties within the sharing network through supervised distribution of meat, and to maintain important social relationships. Moreover, it levels out the larger number of animals that skillful Hunter 5 obtained.

This explanation of hunting variation based on social relationships and sharing is consistent with other facets of Hunter 5's behavior. Hunter 5 consistently shared much more meat with friends and kin than he received. He gave large amounts of meat away to those within his sharing network. By so doing, individuals incapable of sharing meat, because of skill or age,[12] were then able to perpetuate social bonds through secondary and tertiary sharing. This allowed Hunter 5's sharing partners to share excess meat with others within their sharing network. In terms of hunting variation and intra-band sharing, the Kutse Basarwa seem very similar to the Ju/'hoansi (!Kung) in that social factors influence both (Lee 1979).[13] Note that *hxaro*, or formalized inter-band exchange practiced by the Ju/'hoansi and Nharo, does not occur among Central Kalahari Basarwa (see Kent 1993a, endnote 16, for a discussion on why *hxaro* does not exist in the Central Kalahari; Kent 1995b).[14]

There are two basic types of sharing – informal and formal. Informal sharing occurs when people come from their camps to the camp of the successful hunter to partake in the feast. Everyone at Kutse, even the few sharing isolates such as Hunter 2 and his family, participates in some informal sharing of meat and other food. Formal sharing occurs when meat and bones are taken by sharing partners to a different camp from that of the successful hunter (sharing of non-food items is discussed in Kent 1993a). In the latter case meat can be raw or cooked but it is almost always cooked in informal sharing.

Very small animals, the size of hares or less, are usually not shared, either formally or informally (they are only sometimes informally shared with young children who are visiting a hearth when the food is being

[12] Silberbauer (1993: personal communication) noted that hunting skill among G/wi during the 1950s and 1960s was heavily dependent on age. Only young men were truly successful hunters. Men reached and rapidly passed their peak in hunting success at about age thirty or earlier (ibid.). The situation at Kutse is a little different because of the popularity of traps that allow older men to be successful, more through their knowledge of animal behavior than their eyesight or endurance, as is more common with encounter hunting (some increased reliance on trapping may be a consequence of sedentism and construction investment time). For example, Hunters 1 and 2 are similar in age but their hunting skills differ significantly. In contrast, Hunters 2 and 5 are 10–15 years apart in age but are fairly similar in skill and success. A t-test of the hunters' ages and successes is insignificant ($p = 0.2997$; $t = 1.135$).

[13] While goat ownership and hunting skill do not influence the number of bones or number of species represented at a camp, belonging to a sharing network, rather than living as a sharing isolate, does influence the patterning of faunal remains (Kent 1993b). In fact, sharing patterns appear to be more critical than hunter skill in influencing the number of bones and species at a camp, which are a rough index of meat consumption. Sharing does this by equalizing hunting skill between hunters and between camps.

[14] Because goats are so rarely killed at Kutse, I have not observed many shared. The few goats I have observed butchered were usually shared within a sharing network, just as wild meat is. Goat milk, when it is consumed, also appears to be shared within the sharing network, although, as with the butchering of goats, I have not witnessed the behavior often enough to be able to make any definitive conclusions. Because the sharing axiom is so strong and goes far beyond subsistence items, it is not surprising that the occasional goat meat and milk are shared along the same lines as other items (plant food is also shared, particularly when large quantities are collected, such as berries during the rainy season).

eaten). There are notable exceptions related to hunters' skills because the less skilled hunters have little else to share with their more successful sharing partners. An example of this occurred in 1990 when Hunter 3 gave an entire squirrel to Hunter 5's family, who lived at a separate camp but belonged to his sharing network.[15] I suggest that less successful hunters, such as Hunter 3, who have less frequent access to larger animals, sometimes share small animals, like squirrels, in order to maintain the sharing bond.

Sharing takes place even when it is not economically necessary. For example, when Hunter 3 and Hunter 5 both killed a steenbok on the same day, they exchanged the shoulder area from the same side of each steenbok (Kent 1993a, b). There was no gain or loss in economic terms, but there was a gain in social terms. The lack of economic motivation to belong to a sharing network is further evident in that hunters do not schedule hunting with one another. Hunters within the same sharing network do not necessarily forage consecutively, even when there is no meat in camp (see Kent 1993a: Table 3). With the exception of the drought years, poor hunters do not hunt more than good hunters, they simply bring in less meat. However, the amount of meat available for consumption is evened out between good and poor hunters through participation in a sharing network. The nature and structure of sharing at Kutse is a complex subject (Kent 1993a). Here it is important because it indirectly influences hunting variation more than any other variable examined.

Sharing appears to be more important than skill in determining the actual amount of meat acquired and consumed at a camp. Hunter 1, for example, a relatively poor hunter, brings in more meat through sharing than he loses, while Hunter 5 loses more meat through sharing than he gains. Each is the male head of his household and camp. They live in adjacent camps but are not kin; they are unrelated friends who speak different linguistic dialects. It is obvious why Hunter 1 would want to belong to the more skillful Hunter 5's sharing network. It is less obvious why Hunter 5 would want Hunter 1 to participate since Hunter 1 cannot reciprocate economically, either in kind or in other products. That is, Hunter 1 and his wife have never planted a garden and do not own any livestock that they could give Hunter 5 and his family, nor do they perform chores for Hunter 5 and his family or otherwise contribute non-food-oriented labor (for example, they do not babysit or fetch firewood for Hunter 5). When asked why he continues to share with Hunter 1, Hunter 5 was confused by the question and claimed that

---

[15] The same applies to wild plants which are not always formally shared but often are.

economics do not structure sharing relationships. He then said that he provides Hunter 1 and his family with meat because they are friends. Sharing helps to consolidate their friendship and to maintain an atmosphere of egalitarianism. Hunter 5 found it difficult to imagine not sharing with Hunter 1. There are other camps with much better hunters with whom Hunter 5 potentially could share, such as Hunter 2, the sharing isolate. However, they are not as friendly and Hunter 5 does not consider sharing formally with Hunter 2. The same, I propose, is the case with Hunter 5 and his wife's uncle, Hunter 6, who lived at Hunter 5's camp during the dry season of 1991. Elsewhere I have detailed how and why egalitarianism is perpetuated by sharing, including its link to solidifying social relationships (Kent 1993a).

Intra-Central Kalahari Basarwa hunting yields

At Kutse, the average amount of edible meat acquired per hunter per day is 1.5 kg, excluding Hunter 2's anomalous 1988 figure (if that figure is included, meat per hunter per day is 1.4 kg). Calculated per capita on an annual basis, using the mean number of 5.7 persons per household (the average number of people in each household used in this study over five years), the figure is 96 kg per capita per year. This is surprisingly similar to Silberbauer's overall estimated annual per capita meat consumption of 93 kg for the G/wi almost thirty years earlier. Although I do not think Hunter 2's 1988 figure is representative of his hunting yield for that year or for his overall skill, including it still produces a figure (90 kg/capita/year) similar to Silberbauer's when the G/wi were still nomadic and without domesticates of any kind. Silberbauer's data (1981a:204) were based on eight years of observations, including drought and non-drought years.

Both my data and those of Silberbauer disagree with Tanaka's (1976:112) figure of only 55 kg/person/year or 0.15 kg/capita/day (Tanaka 1976:112).[16] As Silberbauer pointed out, the discrepancy is probably due to the fact that Tanaka's observations were made solely during a very severe drought. Tanaka's data, therefore, provide a good lower figure for the amount of meat obtained during very unfavorable hunting conditions in the Central Kalahari. Because Silberbauer's

[16] This figure was obtained by multiplying his estimate of edible meat/person/day by 365 days. Note that Tanaka (1980: 68) presents a slightly different figure for the amount of meat per person per year in a later publication (0.18 kg/person/day or 66 kg/person/year). Both figures are substantially lower than that obtained by either Silberbauer (1981a) or by myself.

findings are so close to mine, we can combine our two studies, and thereby have information on Central Kalahari hunting that spans a period of more than 35 years, and includes rainy and dry seasons, as well as those in between (i.e., his figures are within the same range of variation as are mine).

Diversity in cross-Basarwa hunting yields

Lee (1984) calculated that Ju/'hoansi (or !Kung) Basarwa consume an average of 85 kg/capita/year, which is less than the average for Kutse hunters today and less than the average for G/wi in the 1950s–1960s as reported by Silberbauer (1981a). Central Kalahari Basarwa tend to eat slightly more meat than the Ju/'hoansi even when drought years are included in the calculations, except for the particularly bad year observed by Tanaka. Why does a very small discrepancy exist between Central Kalahari and Northern Kalahari Basarwa groups? Is the reason related to local animal availability and other environmental differences within the Kalahari?

Lee's (1979) and Yellen's (1977) descriptions of hunting productivity indicate that Ju/'hoansi may regularly hunt larger animals than those hunted at Kutse today (and apparently also at ≠xade in the past; Silberbauer 1981a; Tanaka 1980b). According to Lee (1979:227), warthog, gemsbok, kudu, and wildebeest were most frequently obtained by the Ju/'hoansi in the 1960s, whereas at ≠xade in the 1950s–1960s and at Kutse in the 1980s–1990s, steenbok, duiker, springbok, and gemsbok were the most common. Although fewer large animals are caught, Kutse hunters acquire more small- to medium-sized animals. The end result is that Central Kalahari groups acquire and consume a little more meat than the Ju/'hoansi.

Animal depletion might account for the smaller quantity of meat consumed by Ju/'hoansi. Yellen (1977:27) noted that already by the 1960s–1970s, game had diminished in Ngamiland with springbok (an important and common food resource at Kutse and elsewhere in the Central Kalahari) having disappeared completely by the time he concluded his fieldwork (probably a consequence of overgrazing by Herero cattle). Moreover, Lee's (1979) systematic study on hunting returns was conducted over a brief period of time compared to either the multi-year Kutse or ≠xade studies (the latter conducted by Silberbauer). I think it probable that Ju/'hoansi consumed the same amount of meat as Central Kalahari Basarwa before the eradication of springbok in Ngamiland.

Conclusions

Although this longitudinal study of hunting variation includes only one rainy season, the interpretations and conclusions are based not only on the data I personally collected but on those collected by Silberbauer, who also worked with Central Kalahari peoples and who studied them during rainy and dry seasons over many years. Because of the generally strong agreement with Silberbauer's observations, quantitative figures, and interview data on hunting, in combination with my six-year span of research that includes both drought and non-drought periods, I believe that the Kutse data represent a valid and generalizable view of Central Kalahari hunting based on traditional techniques and methods (other Central Kalahari groups currently use horses and guns and/or are involved in meat trading that would make such generalizations more difficult).

Time spent herding goats at Kutse is fairly constant through the years; it does not appear to be influenced by drought, season, skill, or the ethnicity of the goat-owners. For most interviewees, goat herds are not viewed as sources of meat but as potential emergency rations if hunting should be unsuccessful; that is, goats provide a buffer against the insecurities of foraging. In the past, mobility served this purpose. With sedentism, mobility is no longer an option and people must find other sources of security.

Although not true for all hunters and gatherers, a hunter's skill among Kutse residents does not influence the number of hours spent hunting. Even though drought influences the amount of time spent hunting, it does not affect hunting variation as much as one might expect because hunting skill compensates for overall hunting yields. During drought conditions, poor hunters hunt as often as they do during more favorable conditions in order to procure an acceptable minimal amount of meat for their families and sharing partners.

Sharing networks are much more common than sharing isolates at Kutse today; this was probably the case in the past as well. Having both in the same community allows us to compare the two and elucidate the influence of sharing on various aspects of behavior. Also because of sharing, better hunting skills do not necessarily mean greater meat consumption or reproductive success.

A single hunter experiences hunting variation from year to year; there additionally is variation within years between hunters. In both cases, this variability is reduced by sharing. Social concerns, specifically as embodied in sharing behavior, motivate decisions concerning hunting (for example, Hunter 5 chose to under-achieve to maintain a perceived equality of contribution among sharing partners). During drought, concerns of sharing prompt hunters who participate in a sharing network to forage for approximately the same amount of time as they do when rainfall levels are normal, even though the returns are lower, while hunters who do not contribute to a sharing network hunt less. The unusual case of a family that is a sharing isolate allows us to see the extent to which sharing influences behaviors that have been attributed to other causes in the past. While I acknowledge the economic and environmental aspects of sharing, the Kutse data suggest that the establishment and perpetuation of social networks that parallel sharing networks are most important in influencing facets of hunting behavior among (primarily) full-time foragers, such as those at Kutse. In particular, hunting variability is encouraged by the inherent flexibility of Basarwa culture, as noted by other authors in this volume (e.g., Guenther, chapter 3; Barnard and Widlok, chapter 4; also see chapter 1). This flexibility allows hunters to modify their hunting patterns in order to maintain the all-important social bonds and an atmosphere of egalitarianism. Thus, even in an activity as materialistic and economic as hunting, variation among people and between years is explainable largely by the social relationships intertwined with the sharing networks (though not totally because droughts and seasonality also have some affect, but ones that are mediated through sharing).

How do people at Kutse create an atmosphere of egalitarianism and maintain social interaction and relationships? Social relationships are flexible, a consequence of the people's former mobility pattern which encouraged the formulation and dissolution of specific relationships. It is in this context of flexibility and strong egalitarianism that sharing becomes more social in nature than economic or political, as it perhaps is in other societies (also see Petersen 1993). This pattern, I suggest, is not a human universal, but one that is most pronounced in highly egalitarian societies. Sharing, social relationships, and hunting variation are fundamentally different in less egalitarian societies. Thus, it is more appropriate to *contrast* highly egalitarian hunter-gatherers with non-egalitarian hunter-gatherers, such as the Northwest Coast Indians, than it is to *equate* them because, except for an emphasis on wild resources, they have little in common, whereas they have much to contrast.

In the attempt to document and understand diversity, it is crucial not to dismiss the similarities between groups. In this case, sharing establishes and perpetuates social relationships that integrate Kutse residents in a manner similar to other Basarwa hunter-gatherers, such as the G/wi described by Silberbauer (1981a and chapter 2, this volume) and the Ju/'hoansi (!Kung) hunter-gatherers in the 1960s, though not necessarily the Ju/'hoansi of the 1990s. Such comparisons allow us to move on to cross-cultural studies of hunter-gatherers. By examining both the similarities and differences between groups we can begin to understand and to appreciate the complexity, flexibility, and diversity of human societies, past, present, and future.

Acknowledgements

I am most grateful to my Kutse friends who so generously shared with me their knowledge, experiences, and meat. I also thank Willy, my field assistant, translator, and friend, who has helped me in too many ways to recount since 1987. I still grieve his recent, premature death. I hope the memory of his brief life of less than 25 years will live on through the data he helped me collect.

I further am very grateful to the government of Botswana, including the Office of the President, Ministry of Local Government and Lands, Office of Rural Development, and National Museum and Art Gallery, for their continual permission of my research.

I would like to thank sincerely the following individuals for their extremely valuable discussions and comments on various drafts of the manuscript: Alan Barnard, Martha Graham, Mathias Guenther, Barry Hewlett, Bob Hitchcock, Mitsuo Ichikawa, Stuart Marks, and Jean Hudson. I also thank Ted Gragson for sharing pre-publication data. Any deficiencies in this chapter, however, are entirely my responsibility. The data upon which it is based were gathered as a result of the generous funding provided by the Wenner-Gren Foundation for Anthropological Research, Fulbright Foundation, and Old Dominion University College of Arts and Letters. Margaret Deith, Denise Elliott, and Marion Blue edited the grammer and Old Dominion University drafted the figures.

Part II

Eastern African foragers

7 The global process and local ecology: how should we explain differences between the Hadza and the !Kung?

Nicholas Blurton Jones, Kristen Hawkes and James F. O'Connell

Introduction

In this chapter we discuss explanations for the diversity of behavior of contemporary forager populations. Other contributors document variation among southern African savanna Bushman groups, and central African forest Pygmies. We confine ourselves to trying to explain some differences between two savanna groups who have been studied quantitatively, the Hadza and the !Kung. We further confine ourselves to discussing two kinds of explanation that are currently considered to be opposed to one another, behavioral ecology (Smith and Winterhalder 1992), and political economy/historical revisionism as presented to hunter-gatherer researchers by Wilmsen (1989). We believe that explaining variation in human behavior is a major aim of anthropology, and that success in this task is a good test of any anthropological theory.

We choose the Hadza foragers of northern Tanzania (Woodburn 1968a, 1988 and elsewhere) because we work with them (O'Connell *et al.* 1988a, b, 1990, 1991; Hawkes *et al.* 1989, 1991; Blurton Jones *et al.* 1989, 1992). We choose the !Kung of north-western Botswana because so much quantitative work on their behavior in the 1960s and early 1970s has been published (Lee and DeVore 1976; Lee 1979; Howell 1979). Both live in sub-Saharan African savanna, exploiting some of the same plant and animal genera, hunting with bow and poison arrows, and collecting with digging stick and kaross. While other authors attend to variation within a single culture, we generalize here, to compare two cultures. Except when reporting census data, when we write "Hadza" we mean those we have worked with between 1984 and 1992, living in the Tli'ika region of Hadza country.

We limit our main effort to explaining five points of difference between the Hadza and the !Kung:

1 Hadza children collect food for themselves while !Kung children seldom do (Blurton Jones *et al.* 1989; Obst 1912 and many others since; Draper 1976; Draper and Cashdan 1988).

159

2 Hadza women are more fertile than !Kung forager women (Blurton Jones *et al.* 1992; Howell 1979).
3 Hadza seem to be less responsive parents than !Kung.
4 !Kung men use various traps and acquire much small game; Hadza men rarely trap, they specialize in big game (Lee 1979; Hawkes *et al.* 1991).
5 Relations between men and women are described as segregated, or oppositional among the Hadza (particularly during the dry season) (Woodburn 1968a:52) but egalitarian among the !Kung (Kolata 1974; Draper 1975).

The previous accounts of the Hadza, some dozen reports of fieldwork from Bauman (1894) and Obst (1912) onward, show that throughout the past hundred years the Hadza have known and been known to their several neighboring tribes, and have traded with them. Much has changed in the surrounding countryside and the neighbors have moved ever closer, yet numerous aspects of Hadza behavior have not changed (Blurton Jones *et al.* in press; Woodburn 1979, 1988).

Political economy and evolutionary ecology

In *Land Filled with Flies*, Wilmsen (1989) presents his favored political economic explanations of contemporary forager behavior as directly opposed to ecological explanations. Furthermore, he criticizes any school of anthropology that perceives people as isolated and pristine, and that divides them into "tribes" to be understood without reference to their neighbors. He promotes the view that contemporary foragers should not be seen as inhabiting an unchanging and self-contained world in which people live in peaceful equilibrium with each other and their environment. He argues that contemporary hunters and gatherers are best regarded as "the rural proletariat," products of a global process of economic depredation. As such they are not "living fossils," and, he suggests, they have nothing to teach us about prehistoric hunting and gathering societies. He claims that anthropology has served merely to fuel the continuing deprivation of these peoples.

It is important for anthropology to respond to Wilmsen's challenges. Surprisingly, the debate (e.g., Solway and Lee 1990) has so far concentrated on local history and geography and included little discussion of the nature of the explanations given by political economists or comparison with the explanations given by other anthropologists, including ecologists. This issue is important because the debate between anthropologists and "revisionists/critical theorists" about contemporary foragers is a compact example of the wider debate in the social and behavioral disciplines, where the debate is also often seen as argument for or against science. As researchers who feel the study of human behavior has suffered from too little science, our aim here is to join the debate on the side of anthropology in general and one kind of ecological paradigm in particular, that derived from evolutionary ecology. Nonetheless, we are ambivalent about the task for two reasons. First, we too disagree with much in the earlier "ecological" presentations of the !Kung (see Hawkes and O'Connell 1981; Hawkes, O'Connell, Hill and Charnov 1985; and Blurton Jones *et al.* 1994a). Second, we hesitate lest we encourage a fallacious philosophy of science. We have in mind the common claim to have tested "the evolutionary explanation" of some piece of human behavior, disproved it, and thus shown that the evolutionary ecology enterprise should be abandoned. This claim neglects the distinctions between paradigm, theory, models, and hypotheses. Any particular "test" concerns one hypothesis, drawn by a certain model (explicit or intuitive), dependent on its particular starting assumptions and simplifications, employing the particular logic by which its predictions are derived from its assumptions. Many other tests are possible within the same paradigm and with the same overarching or unifying assumption. We illustrate such a case when we consider the Maynard-Smith models of mate desertion, and then the "show-off hypothesis." Both are used here to try to explain similar features of men's behavior. Both ultimately assume that people tend to behave in ways that maximize their reproductive success. But other starting assumptions differ, and the models attend to slightly different sets of observables. The two explanations usefully compete with each other. While one explanation can claim to account for more observations than the other, neither can claim to represent "*the* evolutionary explanation."

The same point could be made for Wilmsen's combination of political economy and critical theory. While we deal with some specific hypotheses close to his views, he can certainly develop others, which attend to other differences in the factors affecting the Hadza, and which suggest testable outcomes. No one should think that when we make a prediction by trying to take a political economy perspective, and find the prediction fails, we have "disproved political economy!" But the existence and competition of different hypotheses within a theory or family of explanations does not prevent us from comparing the performance of the two larger paradigms. Over the long term, which paradigm generates most rigorously testable hypotheses from its few basic assumptions, and by the most explicit logic? Over the long haul, which generates the greatest number of hypotheses that endure the test of real-life observations? (Those critical theorists who believe that the scientific method, and the guidance scientists take from philosophers of science, are merely instances of the devices by which the ruling class maintain their power, will disallow this contest.)

Thus in this chapter we begin to examine how each paradigm copes with the task of accounting for differences between the Hadza and the !Kung. We compare the ability of these paradigms to generate correct predictions. But this cannot be more than the first round of a longer term contest. As it happens, we conclude that the two paradigms have much in common, and either could easily be modified so as to become a component of the other.

Our effort is severely handicapped by the obscurantism with which authors such as Wilmsen write. We can only debate that which we understand. Perhaps we can provoke revisionists into being more explicit about their theory of human behavior, their methodology, and their criteria for distinguishing truth from falsehood. Fortunately other authors, such as Denbow (1990), have provided clear hints about their theory of human behavior. Their basic argument appears to be that all people respond opportunistically to the situations that confront them, and that primary among these are the opportunities presented by neighbors and their neighbors in turn. People seek to make the most of these opportunities, and in doing so change the opportunities available to each other. On the whole, people with more wealth and power are able to influence the interaction more than the poor and less powerful. A chain of interactions links the most powerful to the weakest in a global process of exploitation of the poor by the rich ("global process theory"). It seems to us that it takes little extension of this view to include the opportunities (costs and benefits) provided by the environment, or by members of the same "mother tongue group" (tribe!). Nor does it take much extension of ecological approaches to add neighbors and others as influences upon the costs and benefits of different courses of action. The combination of the two sets of factors is illustrated by several chapters in this book.

The version of ecology that we pursue (that based on evolutionary ecology: see Smith and Winterhalder 1992), and which we illustrate in the first half of the chapter, differs from the ecology that Wilmsen has in mind. His criticism, though expressed as generally "anti-ecology," seems specially targeted at an ecology he understands to view foragers as Rousseau-esque "originally affluent," primevally peaceful, unwilling to change, or incapable of it. We, and most of those who apply evolutionary ecology principles to the study of human behavior, see individuals as more restless, opportunistically (but often unconsciously) weighing costs and benefits of different behavior in their current circumstances, and behaving in a way that maximizes production of descendants – a "reproductive strategy." Our approach is like an economics in which descendants are seen as a more important currency than dollars. This perspective has guided much recent field work, especially on hunters and gatherers (reviewed by Smith and Winterhalder 1992; Smith 1992; Borgerhoff-Mulder 1991; Cronk 1991).

The settings

The !Kung and their social and material circumstances are so well known to anthropologists that we will not describe them here, except to make an initial contrast between "remoteness" and "isolation." Wilmsen has presented evidence against the view that the Dobe !Kung were isolated from the events of the world around them. If lack of isolation can be claimed for the geographically remote !Kung, we must expect it to be shown easily for the geographically accessible Hadza. Until the mid-1980s, the Botswana-based anthropologist visiting the !Kung had a two-day journey from Maun, the nearest market-town, where there was a small airfield, finally crossing a 100-km waterless stretch to reach the Dobe area. In complete contrast, the Hadza researcher has a drive of a mere six hours from an international airport, and only about two hours from either the district capital or a major tourist route to a point where he may find Hadza who gain much of their food by hunting and gathering. While this clearly shows that the Hadza cannot be described as either remote or isolated, it gives us little clue about their relationships with non-Hadza. Woodburn (1988) describes the remarkable extent to which the Hadza have kept themselves separate from others. We support his observation of Hadza inclinations. Even in those regions of Hadza country where non-Hadza have settled most densely, Hadza seem eager to keep to themselves.

Archaeological evidence suggests the periodic presence of farmers and herders in the Hadza area for several centuries, and of hunter-gatherers for far longer (Mehlman 1988). Among this evidence is the presence of rock construction irrigation channels at Endamagha (Sutton 1986). Rainfall in the rift valley floor inhabited by the Hadza is much lower than in the surrounding highlands. Most successful agriculture in the area today depends on irrigation. Written historical evidence, dating only from the memories of Obst's (1912) informants, is unclear about the presence of herders, although it does suggest that few, if any, farmers lived within the area Hadza describe as their country. Since then there has been an accelerating influx of herders, farmers, charcoal traders, and gemstone miners. The influx has been greatest in the Mangola and Siponga regions (Figure 7.1). Herders and farmers moved

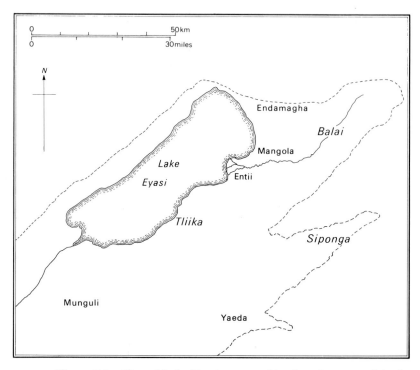

Figure 7.1   Map of Lake Eyasi area marking locations named in the text. Names by which Hazda refer to regions of their country are marked in italic script. The approximate line of the 1500-meter contour is marked by the partly double line. Sections of this line that run SW to NE approximately correspond to the rift escarpments

into both. Higher parts of Siponga have now been reduced to bare rock beneath thorn scrub. Charcoal traders have felled most of the Balai valley trees and berry groves. The Balai delta is the home of a thriving onion industry with trucks calling daily. A prison is sited nearby at Enti.

Hadza told Obst (1912) that they hunted and gathered as long ago as anyone had heard about. But Obst claimed that among the Hadza words for domestic animals, only that for goat was a loan, suggesting an agricultural past. Others (Dempwolff 1916–17; Berger 1943) claim most such words as loans from one or another of the representatives of the several major language families (Bantu, Cushitic, and Nilotic) in the surrounding countryside. The persistence of Hadzane as a language whose affinity to any other is still under debate means that Hadza have been distinct from all these neighbors for a very long time indeed. But their separateness does not tell us that they always lived only by hunting and gathering.

Few tourists come to Hadza country but it is a game-controlled area and commercial hunting outfits use it in some years for foreign clients. Since at least Bagshawe's day (1917–23, see Bagshawe 1923) game officials have not restricted Hadza hunting with traditional weapons, except to ask them not to kill giraffes and elephants, and not to trade meat. Poachers seem to visit the area from time to time, and Hadza sometimes get meat from the animals that the poachers kill. There may be more illegal hunting by non-Hadza than this suggests. We have met and heard tell of unknown trucks with armed people. Frequent hunting visits are made by non-Tanzanian residents. At the turn of the century, Obst's informants describe raids by Isanzu who came to hunt elephants, and who also captured women and children. Sukuma hunting parties were smaller and negotiated "permission" to hunt in exchange for iron goods. Hadza have made arrowheads and knives from iron obtained by barter as far back as we have written accounts (1910).

The Datoga herder neighbors of the Hadza seem to make little demand for Hadza labor and do not practice the mafisa system that allows !Kung a chance to acquire livestock. Hadza experiences with livestock and with the Datoga have been traumatic, as discussed later in this chapter. A few Hadza have one or two chickens; one elderly woman tried to keep some in remote bush camps for a while. Not many dogs are kept, but recently two survived in bush camps for several years. Although some Hadza at the south of their range have farmed for some decades, fewer currently do so. We know of no Hadza who owns a goat, a sheep, a cow, or a donkey.

The demand for Hadza labor from farmers and others seems small, and it is locally variable. Some Hadza take seasonal employment guarding maize fields from animals, for which they extract payment in maize as well as the marauding game. Some take occasional employment harvesting sweet potatoes. Over the past twenty years or so, two German farmers have been favored sources of temporary employment for Hadza, perhaps because they treat the Hadza with much more respect than do other non-Hadza. One of these employers has commented many times on the unusual honesty of his Hadza employees, an impression we can confirm by our totally unguarded bush camps. During the latest settlement scheme about five young educated Hadza men were appointed as Community Development Assistants, which involved some form of payment.

The most conspicuous "outside" influence upon the Hadza in recent decades has been the string of settlement schemes, listed by McDowell

(1981) and Ndagala (1986). The number of people involved in each of these, and the length of time they stayed at a settlement, may have been exaggerated. None of these interludes of imposed village life lasted long. No generation of Hadza has grown up unfamiliar with life in the bush and the techniques of hunting and gathering. But probably no Hadza has failed to experience some version of village life. Indeed, many Hadza seem able to switch instantly and quite easily between village and bush, and to have done so for many years. The Hadza ambivalence to settlement and their loose and fleeting economic ties to neighbors set up a striking contrast to the rapid change described among the !Kung since the early 1970s. Should this contrast be explained by differences in the alternatives to foraging that the modern world has offered, or by differences in the opportunities provided by life in the bush?

We have shown here that there are ample manifestations of the "global process" impinging upon the Hadza. Yet, as Woodburn (1988) describes, the Hadza had until late 1988 in no way been swallowed up by it. But can we account for their behavior as reactions to this process? How many of the differences between the Hadza and the !Kung (as described by Lee 1979, Howell 1979, the authors in Lee and DeVore 1976, and others) can be accounted for by the global process and the different forms it takes as it reaches down to each of these small rural populations? We will return to these questions after outlining the ecological explanations offered by our research.

An evolutionary ecology account

We claim that many differences between !Kung and Hadza behavior can be accounted for by the relatively simple idea of reproductive strategy. It should come as no surprise that fertility, child rearing, marriage, and sex roles should be intimately linked; their links to subsistence may be less obvious.

Children's foraging

Hadza children forage, both accompanied by adults (Figure 7.2), and unaccompanied. Children aged 5–10 are able to acquire 200–600 kcal/hr and seem to contribute from a third to a half of their RDA by their own efforts, and much more from age 12 onward (Figure 7.3). !Kung children did not forage at all (Draper 1976; Draper and Cashdan 1988). Blurton Jones *et al.* (1994a) report !Kung informants' confirmations of this observation and their explanation for it – children who try to forage without adults get lost in the flat and featureless landscape, and some

Figure 7.2   Hazda women and children digging roots. Just beyond the horizon, a main road crosses the plateau atop the rift wall, bearing tourists to view game, and trucks to and from Lake Victoria

have died this way. Children who go with adults get tired and thirsty and want to go home, they "spoil the work." Blurton Jones *et al.* (1994b) present data that show how little food !Kung children could acquire by foraging without adults, a strong contrast with the Hadza situation, which (like the risks of getting lost) arises from the botany and geomorphology of their habitats. Blurton Jones *et al.* present data and computations about children accompanying mothers on long trips to the nutgroves. The calculations show that, because nuts require lengthy processing (unlike the berries that Hadza children collect on equally long trips with adults), unless !Kung children can carry a hefty load of nuts (with the unlikely absence of significant costs due to intense heat

Figure 7.3   Some Hazda children processing baobab fruit in a camp

with no shade or water *en route*), they would be as much help to their mothers and siblings if they stayed home and spent some time cracking mongongo nuts, just as Lee reports that they do. Thus we claim to have presented evidence of an economic explanation for this difference, dependent on the distribution of food and water in the environment, and differences in the processing costs of the highest-return foods. We also suggest that this difference in children's dependence on adults for food has important consequences for adult reproductive strategies.

Fertility

Hadza women living to menopause bear an average of 6.2 children (Dyson 1977; Blurton Jones *et al.* 1992). This is a great deal higher than the 4.7 reported by Howell (1979) for !Kung women who completed their childbearing years before 1968. The Hadza figure resembles the mean of forager and farmer populations summarized by Campbell and Wood (1988). The Hadza have been increasing quite fast while the !Kung population was scarcely growing at the time of Howell's study.

Given limited resources, a fitness-maximizing parent is faced with a trade-off between number of offspring and the fitness of each offspring

(Smith and Fretwell 1974; McGinley and Charnov 1988; Lack 1966; Krebs and Davies 1987; Lessels 1991; Blurton Jones and Sibly 1978; Blurton Jones 1986, 1987; Pennington and Harpending 1988). Parental care enhances offspring fitness. Providing food keeps children alive, and enables them to grow larger and perhaps enhances their later reproductive success. But food given to one offspring is not available to another, nor is it available to the mother to supply her next pregnancy and lactation. We have argued (Blurton Jones *et al.* 1989) that Hadza children's opportunity to feed themselves affects the mother's trade-off between numbers and care of offspring. A Hadza mother who keeps more food for herself, or takes more rest, will threaten the growth and survival of her children over 5 years old much less than if she lived in the !Kung environment, where children do not have the same opportunities for making up the shortfall by their own efforts. We thus expected Hadza women to bear more babies than !Kung women, and our demographic studies show that they do. But there are other important biological explanations of variation in fertility, two of which involve influences from neighbors. Although these have long been discussed in anthropology, they are the kind of "external" influence to which "global process theory" makes us sensitive.

Does the average Hadza woman bear more children than the average !Kung woman because more Hadza women have spent more time in villages or settled around farmers? We showed that, on the contrary, age structure was younger among the most bush-living Hadza than in the population at large (Blurton Jones *et al.* 1992). Since age structure most readily reflects fertility, we conclude that "settlement" is not the explanation for Hadza having higher fertility than the !Kung.

Pennington (1992) suggested that !Kung fertility is low because of diseases of the reproductive tract. Bennett *et al.* (1973) reported a low incidence of treponemal antibodies in Hadza blood samples (but Hadza reported VD as a reason for having gone in search of outside medical help). Thus Hadza fertility might be higher because of less disease, or because of better access to medicine. The suggestion about the !Kung is based on the observation of low fertility, albeit expressed as the proportion of older women reporting that they had never borne a child (10 percent !Kung, 2.5 percent Hadza 1990), on secondary sterility (Harpending 1994; Blurton Jones *et al.* 1994), and on arguments about the low fertility of the Herero herders early this century, when the evidence of venereal disease is absent and there is good evidence of extreme hardship due to the "global process" (rinderpest, and fleeing into Botswana after losing a war with the Germans in South-West Africa).

Blurton Jones *et al.* (1994) concluded that TFR (Total Fertility Rate) of forager !Kung women seemed to be uninfluenced by disease of the reproductive tract but was just over 5, higher than Howell's 4.7 but still substantially lower than the Hadza 6.2. However, the VD explanation remains quite plausible, if relatively untested. While immunological tests of exposure to gonorrhea and syphilis are possible and might confirm the theory, there are other, less easily identified diseases for this theory to fall back upon. Its mirror image – availability of antibiotics – should be more testable, but in the case of the !Kung and Hadza, dating their arrival and availability in either location would be no mean feat of historical research (but a very interesting study of the global process).

Consequences for maternal behavior?

Parental care enhances offspring fitness. Blurton Jones (1993) suggested that it might help us to think about parental behavior if we discriminate mother's fertility, and two aspects of offspring fitness: survival, and later offspring reproductive success (ORS). Food is likely to enhance both (nutritionists believe that the effects of undernutrition on susceptibility to disease is a major factor in child mortality in the Third World; biological life history theory suggests that growth rate has important effects on length and fertility of reproductive career (Hill 1983)). Providing food for her children might thus be expected to take precedence over other forms of care. But local circumstances may determine the actual benefits to mother's fitness from different kinds of care (e.g., Ache women provide very little food but exert considerable effort to keep children from the dangers of the forest floor: Kaplan and Dove 1987). In populations with high mentality such as the Hadza and the !Kung we might expect care that enhances child survival to take precedence over care that enhances adult skills and competitive ability, such as teaching. Little direct teaching is seen in either society.

If the Hadza mother invests a larger portion of her resources, including time, in her own fertility we may expect her to invest less in each child's survival. If providing for offspring is less effective among the Hadza, then, other things being equal, we should also expect a little less time or energy to be spent in other forms of survival-enhancing care (Blurton Jones 1993; Rogers and Blurton Jones in prep.). Having a larger family, the Hadza mother may also invest more in care that affects all her offspring at once, care that needs no more effort for five children than for four. Thus we may be able to predict differences in child-rearing practices or styles of parent–child interaction between the Hadza and the !Kung. The Hadza do appear much less responsive, less vigilant, and more directive and punitive than the famously gentle !Kung parents described by Konner (1972, 1976), Bakeman *et al.* (1990), Barr *et al.* (1991), Draper (1976), and Draper and Cashdan (1988). Furthermore, Hadza parents allow, even command, children to take risks by fetching water, sometimes firewood, and even to approach and throw rocks at snakes. Alternative predictions can be derived from the trade-off between the low reproductive value of infants (who suffer high mortality and thus have less chance of reproducing) and the higher RV of children, and the smaller effect of parental care on the survival of older children. Among the !Kung, where children are so dependent upon adults for food, care directed to older children may have a relatively greater effect on mother's fitness than it would among the Hadza. This would suggest that the greatest difference between !Kung and Hadza parenting should be found in their behavior to older children.

Differences between behavior of !Kung and Hadza men

It has been traditional in much of anthropology (and psychology and other social sciences) to think of families as fully cooperating units, with men as providers and protectors of their wives and children. Indeed, among both !Kung and Hadza, men and women seem to think of men in this way. This assumption has also been particularly prevalent and mostly unquestioned in discussion of "evolutionary scenarios," e.g., Lovejoy (1981). It has been challenged by Hawkes (1990; 1991; Hawkes *et al.* 1991), particularly in respect to the inability of this view to offer a convincing adaptive advantage to big-game hunting – held to have been so formative in human evolution. Does the comparison of the !Kung and the Hadza, and the proposed difference in consequences of parental provisioning, shed any light on men's reproductive strategies?

Well-known models of mate desertion were set out for biologists by Maynard-Smith (1977). These models are mainly aimed at understanding why there are some animal species in which males desert, others in which females desert, some in which the deserted partner stays to rear the offspring, and others where the deserted partner also deserts. They also predict differences in time spent with each "brood," whether it is likely to be deserted earlier or later. One of these models attends to two parameters: (1) effects on offspring survivorship from desertion by father or mother; (2) opportunities for new matings or marriages by the deserting partner. Desertion depends on the trade-off between costs to the survival of offspring and the opportunities (and productivity, an important issue that may require a revised model for humans) of new matings. If there is no opportunity for increased reproduction by a new mating, there is no benefit to set against even a slight cost to the survival of existing offspring that may result from desertion. An anthropological example was presented by Hurtado and Hill (1992), who compared Ache and Hiwi men.

We have already suggested that reduced effort by either parent should have less effect on Hadza children's survival than on !Kung children. If we assume maternal care is more effective than paternal care, we will expect men to desert before women (unless this effect is overwhelmed by new matings promoting women's reproductive success more than men's). (This does not exclude other possibilities, such as a woman expelling her husband, which does not necessarily involve deserting her children.) Unless sex ratios are very different, or women are somehow taken out of circulation (e.g., by marriage to neighbors of richer tribes), the proposed weaker effect of Hadza parental care should lead us to expect Hadza men to invest less in their children with their current wife, desert more readily, and pursue alternative matings more energetically than !Kung men.

If we take a further small step, from investing less in their children to a wider range of parental and "husbandly" behavior, we may expect Hadza men to be less inclined to be "homebodies" than !Kung husbands (more like "Cads" and less like "Dads," Draper and Harpending 1982). Some observations seem to confirm this expectation. !Kung men make clothes, mortars and pestles, digging sticks, karosses (Lee 1979: table 9.1 and pp. 273–80), and also collect firewood. While we have seen Hadza men staking out and scraping skins, and occasionally picking up firewood as they return to camp, we have seldom seen a Hadza man sew more than a patch on his own clothes, and only rarely have men asked us for needles, often demanded of us by women. Hadza women make their own digging sticks and women regularly collect firewood. In any gathering of Hadza, men and women divide into separate groups. Hadza men who are in camp during the daytime stay at a separate place on the edge of or outside camp where women seldom go (quantitative account in O'Connell *et al.* 1991). Hadza have frequent ceremonies conducted by men, which women may not attend. While small children are sometimes handed to Hadza men to care for at "the men's place," such care does not seem to last more than a few minutes. Quantitative information may correct the impression, but Hadza men seem to have much less interaction with small children than do !Kung men. Hadza men do, however, make bows for their sons (aged 3 and up) and lend axes to older sons (10 and up) to get honey.

This is a nice story but how much of it can be substantiated with further quantitative data? Two assumptions of the model were that a

Hadza father has less effect on his children's survival than a Hadza mother, and less effect than a !Kung father has on his children. We have already suggested that Hadza children's foraging made them less dependent on parental care. We could furthermore point to the widespread sharing of meat in both societies. Little of the big-game meat that a child eats comes from its own father. If, as appears to be the case, small game are less widely shared in each society, and !Kung men bring in more small game and gather 19 percent of the plant food (Lee 1979), then the !Kung father might be expected to have more effect on his children's nutrition and survivorship. Is there any evidence of the effects of men upon their children's survival?

Evidence about the !Kung has already been published by Howell (1979) and Pennington and Harpending (1988), but it is very indirect and, although based on large samples, these samples include a mixture of subsistence types. Howell, arguing from meat sharing as we did above, suggests that the effect of father on child survival would be very small. She compared the observed population with the number of !Kung of each age predicted by the AMBUSH simulation to have a parent still living. The simulation used the assumption that the mortality of a child is independent of mortality of its parent. The predicted number of people with a living father was very slightly lower than observed. This suggests !Kung fathers do have a small effect upon the survival of their offspring.

Pennington and Harpending (1988) compared survivorship of children of women who had only one marriage (her husband survived and stayed) with those who had more than one marriage (at least one husband died or departed, and they show that most were cases in which the husband died). Child survivorship was significantly and substantially lower in the second group, from which these authors conclude that !Kung fathers have a significant and large effect upon child survivorship.

We can offer direct, longitudinal data from the Hadza but on a very small sample. We have conducted two censuses of the Hadza, one in 1985, another in 1991. We extracted the data on how many of the children who were aged less than 5 in the 1985 census survived until 1991 (Table 7.1). Among the eleven whose mothers died before 1991, only six survived. Despite the foraging success of the over-5s, mother seems very important to the survival of younger Hadza children. We next looked at the families in which father had died or left by 1991. There is no difference in the survivorship of under-5s between those whose father stayed and those whose father left or died; children of broken marriages always stayed with the mother if she was alive. Thus, if there is an effect of a

Table 7.1. *Survivorship of Hadza children aged 5 or less in 1985 until 1990*

	Parents together	Father died	Mother died	Divorced or single mother
Child died	13	1	6	5
Child lived	38	10	5	20

Table 7.2. *Ratios of males to females among !Kung (from Howell 1979) and Hadza (!Kung aged over 10 from Howell p. 247 and mean of three diagrams p. 40)*

	Men	Women
Hadza total	340	366
Hadza aged 15–45	145	149
!Kung aged over 10	91	100
!Kung aged 15–45	53	47

Hadza father on the survivorship of his young children, it looks as if it is small (but we might expect desertions to be timed so as to reduce their effect on offspring mortality). These results are a strong contrast with Pennington and Harpending's finding on the !Kung.

Let us conclude that desertion is less costly for Hadza men than for !Kung men. Now what about opportunities for remarriage? How many women are available? Personal tastes are likely to be as important among Hadza and !Kung as among anyone else, but just as with Americans or Europeans, some of the variance may be accounted for by etic generalizations, including mere opportunity.

Table 7.2 shows that sex ratios are similar in the two populations; neither is significantly far from the usual. There is no obvious shortage of men or women in either society. Other issues may be more important, such as hypergamy, an effect of neighbors. Bailey (1988) discusses the widespread tendency for hunter-gatherer women to marry richer men from other tribes, and reports extensively on this for the Efe. He reports Howell (pp. 233–4) as showing that fifteen out of 149 !Kung women aged over 19 were married to Bantu men (10.07 percent). Including the 15–19-year-old girls from Howell's Table 12.1 (!Kung girls commonly marry around 15) makes little difference (17/165 = 10.3 percent). Bailey reports that 13 percent of Efe women were married to villagers. The corresponding figure for Hadza in our 1985 census was 9/223 = 4 percent of Hadza women were married to villagers. This is a significant difference from the !Kung (chi-squared = 6.07, df = 1, p < 0.025 > 0.01).

Thus the opportunities for a new marriage may be lower for a !Kung man than for a Hadza man. The conditions under which the mate desertion models predict early desertion by males seem to hold more strongly among the Hadza than among the !Kung. Not only does the departure of the Hadza cost him no increased child mortality but his opportunities for new matings seem to be greater than for a !Kung man. (Since both cost to children and mating opportunity differ, we cannot attribute the difference between !Kung and Hadza men to either factor alone. In Hurtado and Hill's (1992) comparison of Ache and Hiwi men, it appeared that differences in mating opportunity overwhelmed the differences in cost to children.) It would indeed seem that we may expect Hadza men, more than !Kung men, to divert effort away from provisioning their offspring with their current wife and invest it in effort toward additional matings. In so far as this strategy characterizes the "Cad" more than the "Dad" and the "homebody," the conditions fit the differences summarized above.

We might use these models to predict when men will leave, and who initiates divorce. If the !Kung man has so much effect on his children's survival then "Women who lose mates either to death or divorce appear to lose a resource significant to their fitness" (Pennington and Harpending 1988:312). !Kung women might be expected to try harder to keep their husbands and to be less inclined to leave them than Hadza women. These considerations might be relevant to understanding the apparently great "power" of Hadza women.

The "show-off" model

The model proposes four strategies, two for women, two for men. Although Hawkes (1990) uses the word "married," we should emphasize that the model attends not to residence, nor to social labels, but to sources of food and sexual access. Some women ("wives" W) limit their matings so that only m percent of their children are fathered by men other than their "husband," an individual man whose strategy is that of provisioner; he acquires food to pass to his wife and her children and uses none of it to gain matings with other women. He tolerates the m percent of children to his "wife" fathered by other men (m can vary; in Hawkes' 1990 model the experimenter varies m, but a provisioner might be expected to try to limit m in relation to the benefit gained by his own children from his wife's lovers, the "show-offs").

These other men, show-offs, pursue big game to distribute the meat widely and increase their chances of matings with a variety of women. These men may be tolerated, and their children may receive special treatment, in order to keep the flow of meat bonanzas coming. Hawkes denotes the special treatment as i, another given variable. Again we should develop some suggestions about conditions that would be expected to increase or reduce i. The cost of i to each of its donors would not be expected to exceed the benefit from their share of the bonanzas. Hawkes (1990) shows that under quite a wide range of these parameters, showing off is a strategy that can invade a population and persist.

Since only provisioners provide for and confine their matings to one female, and since men are either provisioners or show-offs, there will be fewer provisioners when there are more show-offs; some women cannot capture a provisioner for themselves, so we will expect more "unmarried" women in a population with more show-off males. Thus if we expect more Hadza men to adopt a show-off strategy than !Kung men, we should expect to find more single Hadza women than !Kung women, in so far as marriage or co-residence represents the W strategy. We gave arguments for suggesting that Hadza men might be expected to direct more effort to matings and less to provisioning when compared to !Kung men. The show-off strategy, hunting big game which can be widely distributed (even at cost of very high variance in hunting returns, Hawkes *et al.* 1991), is one way of directing effort to increased matings. The amount of big game available may influence the frequency of a show-off strategy. If little is available and it is caught extremely seldom, one would expect the balance to tip away from show-off and toward provisioner. Hawkes *et al.* (1991) showed that trapping small animals can lead to an almost daily but small supply of meat, probably a good strategy for a provisioner. The ethnographies seem to show that !Kung catch many small animals that Hadza mostly ignore or eat in the bush rather than bring home.

Consequently, proposing that more Hadza men adopt a show-off strategy and more !Kung men play provisioner accounts for the observations reported above, and leads us to expect to find more unmarried Hadza women than !Kung women. In our 1985 census there were 27 unmarried Hadza women out of 110 women between the ages of 20 and 45. Thus 24.5 percent of Hadza women of reproductive age were unmarried, despite the equal sex ratio. Howell (1979:234, table 12.1) shows 7 unmarried !Kung women out of 87 aged 20–45, which is 8 percent. Chi-squared is 9.23, df = 1, which gives p < 0.005. We do not really know whether the methods used to arrive at the counts of married and single women are comparable but it appears that there are significantly more unmarried women of reproductive age among the Hadza than among the !Kung. As with any confirmed prediction, we should remember that it might be possible to generate the prediction from hypotheses other than the one we used.

At first sight, our claim that the show-off strategy is more frequent among Hadza is contradicted by the Woodburn (1968b) and Kohl-Larsen (1958) reports of homicide as a normal response to adultery among the Hadza. But Kohl-Larsen's discussion of adultery makes it clear that the response includes much flexibility. The matter is more easily settled if the husband has "a good heart," or if the offender pays some retribution. The Hadza view of big-game hunting as reported by Woodburn (1968b), emphasizing reciprocity much more strongly, also seems not to coincide with ours. We are only just beginning to investigate these issues among the Hadza. We hope to continue thinking, modeling, predicting, and testing. It should be evident that both sets of models suggest many issues to investigate.

The show-off model seems to account for the use of traps by !Kung and their absence among the Hadza. Not only do the Hadza seldom trap (even though they know how to do it, and sometimes do so as children), but Obst (1912) reports them as viewing trapping as "unmanly." Traps catch a reliable supply of small game (see also Kent's figures from Kutse in chapter 6), which is a good technique for a provisioner (Hawkes *et al.* 1991). Hunting acquires large game. Whether the theory will ever give us any insight into the wider range of hunting techniques and social arrangements such as Pygmy net hunting, or the extensive game drives and large pit traps described by Guenther in chapter 3, is at present quite unclear.

It should be evident by now that we have generated a picture of !Kung men's interests as being closer to those of their womenfolk (if, as Hawkes argues from the show-off game, women do better by capturing a provisioner than by manipulating show-offs) than are Hadza men's interests. We think it is a small step from this to the description Woodburn gives of a degree of separateness and almost opposition between the sexes in Hadza society. He seems to regard this as one of the key features of Hadza social organization. While some have stressed the equality and relatedness of men and women in !Kung society, no one has claimed unity or equality between the sexes for Hadza society. This is not to say that Hadza society is dominated by men. Hadza women vote with their feet quite effectively, and the obligations of son-in-law to mother-in-law that Woodburn describes seem to be very much in evidence. Older women (and some young women) have powerful and aggressive personalities, which anthropologists and male informants treat with awe!

Thus, although false confirmations may arise too easily in a comparison of just two populations, even though several of our predictions were genuine predictions to data awaiting analysis (e.g., effects of Hadza father's death, number of unmarried Hadza women), and some links in our argument are weak, some are quite strong, and we have been able, working in the evolutionary ecology framework, to link many features of Hadza and !Kung life, and offer explanations around the single idea of a trade-off between effort to promote survival of offspring and effort to generate more offspring. We are able to derive predictions from the framework, and find some support for them in the data.

"Global process theory": another family of explanations

What can thinking about the global process add to our account of differences between the Hadza and the !Kung? Does global process theory suggest we should attend to different costs and benefits? Does it offer alternative, competing explanations for the observations? Of course, however hard we try, we cannot generate hypotheses from global process theory as fruitfully as can its true proponents. Consequently, we restrict our discussion to a few ideas that can be found in the literature. The influence of neighbors was already implied in our discussions of settlements and venereal disease in connection with fertility, and hypergamy in connection with male strategies.

Men's response to "hypergamy," forager women marrying rich neighbors

Hypergamy has been suggested as a reason for hunters emphasizing hunting, and resisting settlement. The pressure of hypergamy might lead forager men, unable to compete in the village, to resist settlement and increase their emphasis on positive aspects of hunting and the forest life, such as the greater access to meat (Headland 1985; Bailey 1988). While the !Kung seem to show no reluctance to farm or herd (given the chance), the Hadza conform to Headland's pattern, showing lasting ambivalence to settlement schemes, and seldom staying in them for long. Thus we might attribute the Hadza emphasis on hunting big game and distributing its meat to the need to combat the attractions of village life and villager husbands. Yet these attractions seem weaker for Hadza women than for !Kung women. We observe that fewer Hadza women marry neighbors, and of those who do, many return to the bush with their children. But if we are stubborn, we might suggest that !Kung men compete (in a context of sparser big game) by performing more tasks about the house (building houses, making clothing, and spending more time with their wives), and that !Kung women are married so young because !Kung men try to marry them before the Bantu do!

But is a low level of hypergamy an indication of a less severe threat of it, or of a more successful adaptation to prevent it? Could we assess the threat to be greater among the Hadza? Is there demand for Hadza wives? One might expect the many immigrants to the Mangola area to be looking for wives, but few Hadza were married to them. As far as we can see, not many Datoga seek or take Hadza wives, unlike the Herero and Tswana neighbors of the !Kung.

Would a Hadza woman or a !Kung woman have more to gain by marrying a neighbor? Although Hadza women work longer hours than !Kung women, it appears that they usually get more calories per hour, and the climate is less demanding. Hadza men apparently bring in more meat than !Kung men. Thus Hadza women may eat more meat than !Kung women, and they have as many children as the average farmer, while !Kung women had fewer. Hadza women are as successful at keeping their children alive as are !Kung women. The bush is simply a better economic/reproductive alternative where the Hadza live than where the !Kung live. This would explain not only why fewer Hadza girls marry "Swahilis" but also why some of those who have done return with their children to resume life as Hadza. These points do not amount to evidence that hypergamy is a greater threat to Hadza men. Indeed Bagshawe (1923) reported that during a famine among farmers around 1917, several Isanzu girls married Hadza men.

Fertility and population increase

Wilmsen (1989) presents the argument that !Kung fertility is lowest among those with least access to resources. Motzafi-Haller (1990) implies the same. This view is easily reconciled with our own. There are other theories in the literature, some of them very well known such as the "wealth-flows theory"; others less well known but more in tune with global process theory.

Murdoch (1980) provides one of the more lucid summaries of the view that poverty increases fertility. He emphasizes the security provided by a large kin network under the unpredictable and uncontrollable environments of the very poor and exploited. This "people as security" idea resembles the argument of Draper (1989) about "people as resources." Raising many children, and promoting pro-natalist beliefs among one's kin and allies, may generate a usefully large network of exchange partners that better buffers hard times. While much has been made of the "reliability" of hunting and gathering, uncertainty of this type has been discussed extensively in work on the !Kung and other southern African foragers (e.g., Kent, chapter 1, this volume). Among the !Kung, spatial variation is dampened by the *xharo* exchange system (Weissner 1982). Temporal variation is sometimes localized, and so it can be translated into spatial variation, and solved by moving to another locality or calling on help from distant partners or kin. Among the Hadza, we observed in our 1985 census data that women with more living siblings had more living children, which we interpret to mean that there may be reproductive benefits that accrue from having more kin. But these kin tend to live together; thus they cannot buffer spatial-temporal variation in resources. We have seen no mass movement of people from one region to another, and like Woodburn (1968b) are impressed with the stability of these regional populations. There is no record of serious shortage among the Eastern Hadza (but Bleek's 1930 informants told her of famine in the area of the Western Hadza which people had moved to avoid: Bleek 1931). As Lee (1979) reports for the !Kung, there are accounts of farmer neighbors of the Hadza using bush foods in times of crop failure (Bagshawe 1923). On the other hand, some Hadza foods, particularly berries, seem very variable from year to year, especially in the time and size of the harvest.

By the standards used in accounts such as Murdoch's (1980), the Hadza and the !Kung are both dramatically poor, and perhaps indistinguishably so, but the theory would have to predict from the observed difference in fertility that the Hadza were poorer than the !Kung. We could view the Hadza as poorer than the !Kung because they work longer hours. But Hadza get more for their work, their women are fatter, their men more muscular, and their children survive as well.

In Blurton Jones *et al.* (1992) we showed that the Hadza population was increasing and might have been increasing for some time. We suggested that it might have been suppressed in pre-colonial (or pre-rinderpest) times by the raids described by Obst's informants. These may well have been associated with the slave trade, which continued until 1873 in east Africa (Sheriff 1979). Thus, even though we cannot muster support for the poverty theory of fertility, our favored explanation of population increase, another key demographic parameter derives directly from global process ideas.

Poverty and parental behavior

If contemporary foragers are the rural proletariat (as Wilmsen 1989 and others suggest), perhaps we should explain their parental behavior in the same way as we explain differences in parental behavior between socioeconomic groups in other contexts, such as in industrial societies. (a) Sociologists and psychologists have suggested that children of the lower classes may be trained in deference (Newson and Newson 1968, and references in Belsky 1984). Does this shape !Kung or Hadza child-rearing? Neither Draper nor Konner has described anything in !Kung child-rearing that they interpret as deference training. Draper (1975:92) in fact describes almost the opposite. Nor can we decide which population we should expect to show most training in deference: perhaps the !Kung, in so far as they more often work for more powerful neighbors. (b) There is an enormous literature on socioeconomic status differences in parental behavior in industrial societies. In so far as socioeconomic status differences in child-rearing reflect the kind of exploitation that global process theory holds to be so important, perhaps we should expect the !Kung and the Hadza to differ accordingly. Lower status and greater poverty in industrial societies are associated with less interaction between parents and children, and less response by parents to child behavior (most clearly in respect to response to speech), more physical punishment, and more verbal commands and prohibitions directed to the child (McLloyd 1990). Thus, very, very loosely, the Hadza more resemble parents of low socioeconomic status and the !Kung more resemble higher-status parents (although their actual frequency of response to infant vocalization was shown by Konner [1977] to be the same as that of Boston working-class parents). So again global process theory leads us to propose that the Hadza are more exploited and impoverished than the !Kung. We have yet to identify evidence that Hadza are poorer than !Kung.

Meat trade and men's subsistence strategies

Could we explain the Hadza concentration on big game and their neglect of trapping by a greater demand by neighbors for traded meat? Several contemporary descriptions of the !Kung and other San peoples indicate that they are often employed to hunt by their richer neighbors who own horses and guns (Osaki 1984; Kent, chapter 6, this volume). That the quarry of these hunts are large game may support the premise that commercial hunting would lead to concentration on large game. Very little meat was traded by the Hadza that we have observed, but they are the people who live furthest from villages. Less than 5 percent of their food was farm produce. This would have come from relatives in villages, trading honey, nagging, and possibly least of all in exchange for meat.

We imagine that the demand for meat from villagers is great. The

Hadza are surrounded by dense populations of farming people
(WaIraqw and WaIsanzu). Although these are mixed farmers (Iraqw
adding pigs to the usual chickens, cattle, goats, and sheep), we have no
reason to think that animal protein is in any less demand than elsewhere
in Africa. Meat is often discussed when non-Hadza (of any level in
society) meet Hadza. In 1992, several instances of trading meat were
observed and they seemed to be associated with and arise from the latest
settlement efforts (the "Hadza Centrement Scheme" and a newly initiated Pentecostal mission).

Another external influence is probably important. Trade in wild game
is illegal in Tanzania, and Hadza seem quite aware of this. The game
laws may be more effectively enforced on the Hadza than in the remote
areas of Ngamiland. But this would allow !Kung to conduct more trade,
and if larger game is better for trade, the meat-trade theory should lead
us to expect the !Kung and not the Hadza to specialize in large game.
However, the relative scarcity of large game in !Kung country might
offset this, an ecological factor lowering the trading opportunity.

Avoiding Datoga and other strangers

Hadza show some fear and distrust of their Datoga herder neighbors,
and of strangers of any sort. Some Hadza attribute their flight from the
sound of a vehicle to the fear that it is "the government" coming to settle
them (see also Woodburn 1979). But we should note that unfortunate
experiences at the hand of strangers go back beyond the turn of the
century. Obst (1912) was told of neighbors coming to hunt elephants
(apparently Isanzu and Sukuma, not Europeans); they also captured
women and children. He was told of the peace that followed the decline
in the elephant population.

Over the years there are said to have been some killings of Hadza by
Datoga, and some retaliation by Hadza. Bagshawe (1923) reports:

Once, according to tradition, some Kangeju [Hadza] killed an elephant and
obtained a few goats from a native stranger in exchange for the ivory. Next
morning the goats strayed into the bush and were lost, for all were eating
elephant meat and no one bothered to follow them. The feasting Kangeju were
attacked by Tatoga, who declared that the goats had been stolen from them, and
many were killed. Their first experiment as pastoralists ended in disaster and
they have never repeated it.

For the Hadza, such incidents may have been repeated sufficiently often
to create a persistent fear that has efficiently cut off herding as a possible
way of life or direction for "development."

Datoga traditions by which the killer of an "enemy of the people" (most often a lion) is lavishly rewarded may have led young Datoga once in a while to classify Hadza as such. Hadza say that their fear of Datoga is the reason why Hadza women forage as a group, and demand the company of at least one male with poison arrows (even if a young teenager). Datoga are used by adults as "bogeymen" to persuade children. Datoga have been known to capture children to raise as herders (Sellen, pers. comm.). A Hadza informant told us of one Hadza child held temporarily by Datoga, and of a vigorous raid on a Hadza camp some 25 years ago from which all the children escaped. Despite this, Hadza children are often the only daytime occupants of the camp, or are in the bush as a small group of mixed ages. In complete contrast, Datoga are the main customers for Hadza honey, which they need to make mead for frequent and important ceremonial and political occasions.

In O'Connell *et al.* (1990) we suggested that models of the economics of bone transport might need to take account of the Hadza wish not to linger at lowland kill sites where encounters with Datoga might be likely. It remains to be seen whether doing this enables us to account for any more of the variance in which skeletal parts are transported from kill site to home site.

National politics

Global process theory claims that even the "remotest and most isolated" locations are influenced by the global process, by the state, and by its relation to other states. Thus the different political systems of Botswana and Tanzania might affect the !Kung and the Hadza differently. Socialism claims to promote equality between individuals, sexes, parents and children, and neighbors. This could be a reason for the apparently weaker impact of neighbors on the Hadza, although it has not stopped substantial parts of their land being taken or devastated. Furthermore, the direct or indirect impact of the state (e.g., threat of state power by those who would settle the Hadza, in the last decade with no authority from the state) has been conspicuous from time to time (Woodburn 1979, 1988; Kaare 1988). We observe that the foragers in the socialist state show greater separation between men and women, and less attention by parents to children's interests. This is the opposite of the intuitive "global process" expectation.

Encapsulation: Is Woodburn describing an influence of the global process?

Woodburn (1988) describes the way Hadza maintain their independence from their neighbors. He argues that their "immediate return" system allows them to avoid lasting trade or work arrangements, and thus to resist absorption by agricultural neighbors. He suggests that this may be why so many of the forager populations that survived into this century were immediate-return societies. Nonetheless, he argues that the Hadza were not changed into an immediate-return society by the need to stay separate from neighbors.

But given that Hadza wish to preserve their identity, and given the nature of the outside forces that have impinged on them ("farm or else stay backward!"), then their endurance, their presence as foragers in the twentieth century, is partly explained by global process theory. The global process demands that they farm or perish, and trying to farm in the land that is now left to them also means to perish, leaving occasional labor for farmers as their only obvious livelihood. Because they refuse, the process leaves them little alternative but to cut themselves off and to avoid lasting entanglements with the outside world. Having done that, there is little left for them to adapt to but each other, and the natural environment. Thus global process theory becomes a part of the ecological explanation of Hadza behavior.

We are of course obliged to try to explain why Hadza wish to preserve their identity! In his hypergamy paper, Bailey (1988) implies that it would be mainly men who are concerned about this. If Hadza get too close to neighbors, Hadza men will not get wives and will not leave descendants. But we have no evidence of gender differences in the tendency to move away from "Swahilis."

The issue is complicated additionally because a further consequence of the immediate-return habit seems to be loss of land. Welcoming outsiders into their land, Hadza ask only gifts of small amounts of maize from time to time. When in due course the presence of the outsiders becomes problematic, the Hadza simply move away. As is now evident to a few educated younger Hadza, they thus sacrifice land and habitat and their long-term security (the habitat quickly becomes almost desert under the destructive farming practices of their neighbors) for tiny short-term gains.

Conclusions

We have suggested that influences of neighbors and the global economy can easily be incorporated within the behavioral ecology approach. Neighbors modify the costs and benefits of alternative courses of action just as do flora, fauna, climate, geomorphology, and friends and relatives. We suggested that the lower cost of Hadza children, determined by the greater opportunities for children to acquire food for themselves, allows women to invest in higher fertility and devote less effort to their children's survival, and allows Hadza men to invest less in child-care and more in affairs or new marriages. Since the opportunity for men to make new marriages depends upon women being available, the incidence of marriage to men of neighboring tribes enters into the issue. More !Kung women marry men of other tribes. Thus neighbors, and the higher costs of desertion, work in favor of !Kung men staying with their spouses and investing in them and their children. Data support the implication that fathers have more effect on survival of children among the !Kung than among the Hadza.

But when we looked at some other influences of neighbors suggested in the literature, things did not go so smoothly. Much literature suggests that poverty increases fertility, and makes for harsher child rearing, which would imply that Hadza are poorer or more exploited than !Kung. Yet Hadza get more food for their work, and are heavier. Large game may be better for trade, yet Hadza, who specialize in big game, seem to be not heavily involved in meat trading. While the strongly socialist government of Tanzania aims for equality between tribes and sexes, and continued Hadza autonomy may be partly an outcome of this ideology, the sexes are described as opposed among Hadza and equal among the !Kung. On the other hand, the apparently steady increase in Hadza population is probably best explained by the cessation of raids by neighbors during the last century. Clearly one cannot assume that potential influences of neighbors and the wider world are either inevitably effective, or inevitably detrimental. Therefore, the global process as a cause of behavior becomes one of the many ecological and economic influences affecting people and their strategies.

Our evolutionary ecology framework drew attention to a series of interdependent differences in behavior and reproduction between the Hadza and the !Kung. The apparent ease with which Hadza children can help provide their own food lowers the reproductive penalties of more frequent births and harsher treatment by mother, and lowers the penalties of desertion by father. We claim this explains the higher fertility, less attentive child rearing, and greater separation between the sexes among the Hadza. Evolutionary ecology generates testable predictions about a variety of aspects of behavior from a small number of premises. Although many think it unwise to expect models based on natural selection to apply to people, the attraction of logically consistent models that make testable predictions about differences may outweigh these reservations.

These differences may follow from small (but we believe crucial) differences in the environment: the spatial separation of water and food in most of !Kung country and their intermingling in most of Hadza country, and the resource type and possible return rates. It is important to realize that we do not claim to have created a general rule, such as that wherever water and food are intermingled there will be sexist societies! We think this aspect of geography only shows up as important because many other costs and benefits of behavior have been so similar in the Hadza and !Kung environments and lifeways. The rule that we espouse is much more general: behavior will be that which combines costs and benefits in such a way that more descendants are left than are left by behaving in another way. The actual costs and benefits, and thus the optimal behavior, will depend on local circumstances (and the behavior of other individuals) and it would be difficult to generalize about how they will play out. Thus we often see ourselves as "evolutionary particularists!" Note that this formulation excludes no kind of material influence upon costs or benefits.

Although we are likely to pursue our comparisons between the Hadza and the !Kung, it is important to compare other groups, or larger samples, and, as the reader of other chapters in this volume will readily agree, it is likely to be chastening. We expect it will strengthen the "evolutionary particularist" view, reducing emphasis on the importance of any single environmental factor (such as ease of foraging by children), and increasing emphasis on cost-benefit analyses that pay attention to more variables. For instance, if we begin to think about the fertility of Hadza and Ache, we immediately see that Ache high fertility does not entail specially successful foraging by children. Details about the effects of children on women's subsistence seem unlikely to explain much about Ache fertility, or about the differences of Ache from !Kung and Hadza. The greater proportion of food acquired by Ache men must be a much more significant factor for this comparison.

The arguments outlined here are unfinished. Within our presentation of evolutionary ecology we have used provisional results or impressions from investigations that are still incomplete. Our answer to the critique of ecological approaches by writers such as Wilmsen must also be regarded as incomplete because global process theorists should be able to generate more competing explanations for the phenomena than we have discussed here. But if global process theory is taken to imply "change based upon opportunistic responses to new economic, social, and market possibilities" (Denbow 1990:126), then it can draw attention to costs and benefits of behavior that we might otherwise have ignored. Some are, once noticed (like "hypergamy," and opportunities to trade meat), easily incorporated into the evolutionary ecology approach. Others simply failed, or are more difficult to test, including some that more obviously compete with evolutionary ecology explanations, such as the implication from child rearing and from high fertility that Hadza are poorer or more downtrodden than !Kung. The difficulty arises merely because we cannot pin down the concept of poverty (it may refer to many variables – from food intake to control or extent of options available, all of which need further definition but can be usefully translated into costs and benefits accruing to the key participants from alternative actions).

Elsewhere we (Blurton Jones *et al.* 1992) and others (e.g., Schrire 1990) have suggested that the global process of interaction between peoples tends to produce similarities between contemporary hunters and gatherers. But in principle, as we and other contributors to this volume have made quite evident, global process theory should also be able to account for differences, because the global process may act in different ways in different localities. Not only are there differences in the behavior of the herder neighbors of the Hadza and the !Kung but the demands of the larger world system have shown differences in the two localities during the past century or so. Ivory has been extracted from both localities. But while cattle were extracted from Namibia, slaves were extracted from east Africa. People have migrated from the remotest corners of Botswana to work in the mines in South Africa. Little or no long-range demand for labor seems to have impinged on the Hadza since the end of slave export from east Africa in 1873. Displacement of people was a major event in Namibia and Botswana in 1904–6. Herders were displaced into and expanded into Hadza country much more recently, but historical and archaeological evidence suggests that some have been there from time to time during the past several hundred years.

The assault on anthropology from global process theory is of course much wider than a call to attend to more factors influencing cost-benefit equations. Revisionists claim that anthropologists err in their concept of separable cultures, err in writing only of a "time slice" assumed to represent a lasting and stable condition, and err in selectively perceiving constancy and contentment where there is neither. (Both evolutionary ecologists and revisionists criticize anthropology for neglecting conflicts of interest.) Revisionists argue that anthropologists ignore, or "peel away," crucial events and lasting pressures of "history" or the "social relations of production." But anthropologists are likely to continue these habits as long as none of the revisionist concepts is explained clearly or dissected very usefully. So long as global process theory offers neither a clear, explicit theory of human behavior, nor a criterion for the truth of its own claims, it cannot claim to be a serious theory, at least not a serious scientific theory. But its vigorous challenges may continue to stimulate reexaminations of many issues in anthropology.

8 Fission, fusion, and foragers in East Africa: micro- and macroprocesses of diversity and integration among Okiek groups

Roderic H. Blackburn

Introduction

The Okiek, a hunter-gatherer society consisting of two dozen groups in Kenya (Fig. 8.1),[1] reveal considerable cultural and social diversity,[2] as do many other hunter-gatherer peoples in eastern Africa.[3] This widespread diversity suggested to me that it might be possible to find general explanations for how and why the many different hunter-gatherer peoples throughout East Africa developed (eighty, by a recent count, have existed during the past hundred years), by examining the explanations the Okiek give for their own fragmentation into many groups and the resulting diversity in social and cultural characteristics.

Members of several Okiek groups in and near the Mau Forest have described how and why they have been divided by migration during the past century and dispersed from one forest to another in response to a wide range of stimuli. Most of these changes of residence by individuals, families, lineages, or whole groups have *not* occurred mainly to find new food sources. Rather, as evidenced from cases dating primarily from the first half of this century, most Okiek made long-term or permanent changes of residence in response to non-subsistence personal needs and social events.

This chapter addresses diversity by demonstrating how interpersonal conflicts, usually not related to subsistence, have arisen, how these conflicts have often resulted in residence changes, and how these changes in turn resulted in other social and cultural changes, thus contributing to Okiek diversity. I shall also use this occasion to demon-

---

[1] Fieldwork was carried out in 1968–70 and for shorter periods in 1990–2 among several Okiek and Dorobo groups in the Narok and Nakuru Districts of Kenya.

[2] In and around the Mau Forest are about a dozen Kalenjin-speaking Okiek and Maa-speaking Dorobo groups who believe they are all essentially the same people, though basic cultural similarities may actually mask different origins (see note 6).

[3] The [East] African Hunter-Gatherer Survey, initiated in 1985, is an ongoing assessment of past and present forager peoples based on data provided by informed professionals. Since 1990 it has been extended to all of Sub-Saharan Africa.

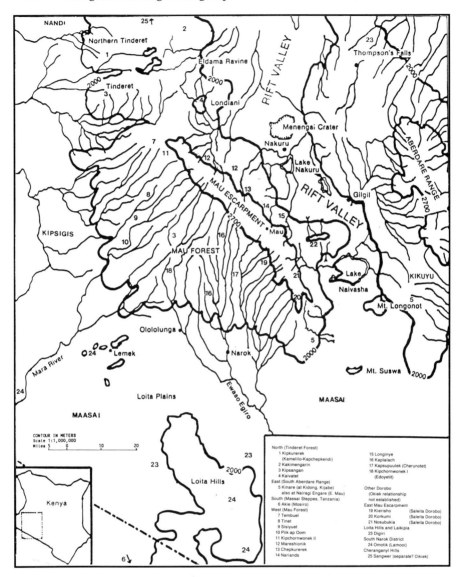

Figure 8.1   Map of the Central Kenya Highlands showing location of
Okiek and other Dorobo groups

Figure 8.2 "Wandorobo near Molo" was the caption naturalist Carl Ackley put on his 1905 (about March 5) photo. This Okiek family were living in the high elevation mixed bamboo forest (their house is made entirely from bamboo) of the western end of the Mau forest. This was likely a temporary honey season camp after the rainy season, affording an opportunity to collect honey and make or repair hives. Okiek use of the forest has changed little since then, though forest trips are less frequent as cultivating and herding become more prominent food sources. Photo courtesy of the Department of Library Services, American Museum of Natural History (Neg. no. 212176. Photo: Carl E. Ackley)

strate the application of a broader theoretical framework than has been considered in some of the others chapters in this book, and a different method of analysis, both of which I believe could be used with profit in the study of other hunter-gatherers.

In this chapter I have chosen to concentrate on the processes of Okiek migration (including any form of resettlement, residence change, etc.). Relocation has often exposed Okiek to other Okiek or to people of other beliefs and practices. In the course of these contact situations there is a continual process of mutual social and cultural adaptation taking place, the outcome in each case influenced by a variety of existing conditions,

Figure 8.3   Deep in the Mau Forest, killing a giant forest hog affords Kaplelach men a midday break to cook and eat the ribs. Such "sweat meat" is relished while lesser cuts are tossed to the dogs which brought the animal to bay. The bread and butter of Okiek forest life are honey and giant forest hog meat. This large pig is plentiful and more frequently taken – if you have hunting dogs – than any other animal. Cut in strips and dried, it is easily transported to permanent camps on the edge of the forest to share with each man's family. Author's photo, 1969

motivations, and events. By concentrating on this type of microprocess, we may be able to postulate macroprocesses of diversity among other hunter-gatherers. There are, of course, other conditions or events which lead to change and diversity. These I intend to address at another time.

Okiek diversity

Most Okiek groups speak a dialect of Kalenjin, some now speak Maasai, and at least one speaks a Proto-Datoga language, distantly related to Kalenjin. Dialect or language diversity has generally resulted from linguistic borrowings from the more populous non-Okiek peoples with whom each Okiek group trades, sometimes intermarries, or fights.

Figure 8.4   High in a forest tree this Okiek man is "milking his cow",
a reference to honey hives being analogous in Okiek eyes to Maasai
cows. Golden combs of *setiot* (*Mimulopsis solmsii*) honey sparkle in the
sunlight as they fall to companions below eager for a snack. *Setiot* is a
plant that blooms every seven years in great profusion throughout the
forest rewarding the Okiek with a bumper harvest so plentiful that they
can supply the Maasai with honey for mead necessary to conduct their
large ceremonies held, not just coincidentally, about every seven years.
Author's photo, 1992

Okiek subsistence has become increasingly diverse as each group has
incorporated additional sources of food by trade, cultivation, and animal
husbandry during this century. Since the 1960s all groups have had
some gardens and/or domestic animals, yet all continue to hunt wild
game and to gather (especially honey).

Cultural diversity is also evident in variations in their beliefs (such as
conceptions of the supernatural) and material culture (both function and
style). Differences in social organization are evident, such as the varying
occurrence of clans or lineages, kinship terminology and associated
roles, ceremonies (most obvious in initiation and subsequent age-set
ceremonies), and settlement patterns (permanent and temporary).

Some groups live mainly on the plains and are mostly herders,
although they hunt and collect honey within adjacent forests. Other

groups are primarily forest-adapted: their lineage territories extend over a wide range of forest types, depending on elevation, with a consequent variation in fauna and flora.[4] Overlying this diversity are seasonal climatic changes (rains and dry periods) and multi-year cycles of occasionally severe rains or droughts. While the Okiek forest environment is comparable to the Pygmy's forest adaptation (chapters 9, 10, and 11), Okiek use of the plains and open bush is comparable to that of the Hadza (chapter 7), who hunt many of the same species.

While the Okiek have not been studied by as many researchers[5] as the Basarwa, even brief encounters with some of their groups indicate that diversity among the Okiek may be as great as or greater than that among the Basarwa. Indeed some "Okiek" groups are so different from others in at least some features that their common origin is questionable. They may have "become" Okiek by adaptation, adoption, or assimilation.[6]

Diversity among Okiek groups can usually be accounted for by reference to differences in subsistence base, ecosystem, and/or the length of time and closeness of relationship to neighboring non-Okiek peoples.[7]

[4] This dichotomy of subsistence pattern has contributed to other people's use of the term "Dorobo" to refer to the Okiek. Those Okiek who have adopted herding are also in close proximity to the Maasai, speak Maa, and outwardly appear to be like Maasai. In Maa they call themselves "Dorobo" which has about the same meaning as "Okiek" does to Kalenjin speakers – people who live by hunting and gathering (see also note 6 for further discussion).

[5] The first substantial study of Okiek was by G. W. B. Huntingford, who studied the Kipkurerek of Tinderet Forest, north of the Mau Forest, in 1938–9. The author's 1968–70 field work was primarily with the Kaplelach, Kapsupuulek, Marishioni, and Kipchornwonek Okiek groups in the Mau Forest, and in 1990–2 with the Kaplelach and Marishioni Okiek, and the Saleita, Digiri, and La Moot (Omotik) Dorobo, the latter two in the Loita Hills south of the Mau Forest. Corinne Kratz has undertaken extensive periods of fieldwork primarily with the Kipchornwonek and Kaplelach beginning in 1974, which is ongoing. Her most recent publication (1994) addresses some issues related to this chapter. Thomas Evans did an economic survey of all Kenya Okiek groups in 1977–9.

[6] Some groups exhibit differences that I once thought were relatively insignificant (Blackburn 1974, 1976). Closer examination has recently led me to believe that some groups, such as the Saleita and related Digiri, may not be Okiek in origin. Their similarities to Okiek may be a result of recent adaptation. This may also be true of the La Moot (Omotik), who, while knowing a distantly related Kalenjin language, speak Maa. The Okiek of Cherenganyi, who called themselves Sangewer and assert, in their Kalenjin dialect, that they are "Okiek," but "not the same" as other Okiek, may have a different origin from that of Okiek but have "become like" other Okiek because of a similar highland forest hunting and gathering adaptation. The question of whether some Okiek and Dorobo groups are genetically, linguistically, and/or historically related continues to be difficult to establish to all researchers' satisfaction. Data are incomplete and often contradictory, leaving me to draw changing opinions more than factual conclusions.

[7] The relationship of the Okiek to neighboring ethnic groups has been discussed elsewhere (especially Blackburn 1982). Like the Okiek, both Pygmies (see chapter 9) and Basarwa (see especially chapter 5) have long-standing social relations with dissimilar

Likewise, similarities between one Okiek group and its neighbors can be accounted for largely by the degree of shared subsistence, the similarity of ecosystems, and the closeness of relationship in terms of marriage and descent. But these factors alone do not explain why Okiek groups settled in different kinds of places nor why they came to live near certain other peoples and were thereby influenced in particular ways. The following case studies demonstrate processes which help account for how and why these changes have occurred.

Okiek history

One of the characteristics of Okiek history has been the migration of groups to other forests, sometimes in search of more adequate supplies of food, but an analysis of case studies reveals that it is more often for other reasons. For example, quarrels often provide the motivation for migration; it has been most dramatically evident when two Okiek lineages, often within the same group and interrelated by marriage, have not effectively controlled individual arguments or fighting. A series of fights, killings, and further killings in retribution have led to a general and often long-term feud, resulting in the deaths or flight of many lineage members. Recorded cases report the extermination of entire lineages – men, women, and children.

Okiek lineage feuds have been a major cause of individuals and families moving to other groups, even other societies. Ironically, what is at first disruptive to a lineage becomes a mechanism for cross-group cultural integration as men and women, who have fled to other lineages or groups for safety, marry into them, and each adopts some of the ways of the other. This phenomenon has also occurred when individuals or groups of other peoples join an Okiek group: when the Purko Maasai defeated the Laikipia Maasai in the Rift Valley about 1876, the few remaining Laikipia men fled to other Maasai or to the Okiek to seek shelter and to be adopted. In this case ethnic elements were incorporated into some Okiek groups, thus adding to diversity between Okiek groups.

With a history of diverging experiences caused by families, lineages,

neighbors characterized in the literature as dependence, submission, serf, subclan, and other pejorative descriptions, usually derived from non-forager informants. It is clear to those of us who have studied these foragers that the relationship is far more complex, subtle, reciprocal, interdependent, and far-reaching than others have described. Foragers often have access to resources non-foragers need and can get nowhere else. The Maasai are dependent on the Okiek for honey for ceremonies and drink, for forest medicines, and (formerly) craft production and ivory. The Maasai need the Okiek more than vice versa, and this may prove to be true with other forager–non-forager relations.

or groups leaving one area for another over so long a period of time, one might more reasonably ask how Okiek groups can continue to share and assert a common identity. What are the countervailing influences that have resulted in the Okiek still being the Okiek? What are the processes of fusion which have counteracted the more obvious stimuli for fission? How have fission and fusion worked in Okiek society and culture to create wide diversity, yet not disintegration?

An analysis of case studies drawn from some Okiek groups will show underlying mechanisms or processes of change that account for a surprising amount of diversity within just a few of the Okiek groups. If these same processes later prove to be operative in other Okiek groups, it may then be possible to make generalizations about the history of the Okiek as a whole over a longer period of time. I have chosen to investigate why certain individuals, families, or lineages have moved permanently from one forest to another. How did the original stimulus, such as drought, famine, feud, or outside hostility, play itself out in subsequent resettlement, lineage relations, subsistence types, cross-societal relations, and territoriality? From an examination of several cases it is possible to see some long-term trends (over a hundred years) as well as to make some generalizations about this microprocess.

The microprocess of recent Okiek history

If "all politics is local," so ultimately all large social actions come down to individuals making personal decisions and acting on them. All behavior is motivated and the locus of motivation is in the individual. Through an examination of cases involving the decisions made by individuals in their dealings with others, one should be able to identify the cultural, social, and psychological bases for their actions. Further, one should be able to identify those actions that ultimately change individuals, society, and culture.

Among the Okiek, cases of theft, witchcraft, cursing, wife-beating, incest, fighting, murder, and many other infractions of norms of self-control, many of which the Okiek generally call *igenon* (cheating), as well as unusual events, such as famine or injury, lead to individual choices that have altered Okiek relations among themselves and with other peoples, and have changed beliefs and practices.

To bring some order out of the plethora of behavior found in many different cases, it is useful to introduce some analytical concepts which have proved helpful in this study, specifically *micro-* and *macroprocesses*, and *transactions*. Microprocesses consist of a series of transactions, which are actions and reactions caused by a *presenting event* (such as a famine or a theft). Each step in a series of transactions consists of a choice of options based on certain underlying *principles* in Okiek culture. From a presenting event the chosen option leads to an *initiating action* by one party (which may be an individual or group such as a lineage or even a tribe), followed by a response by a second party, and so forth through one or more transactions. Based on an analysis of each different type of microprocess, one could hypothetically develop a set of interconnected propositions to form a *theory of action*. If it is applied to Okiek events over a long period of time, that theory of action could become a tool for explaining the macroprocesses of Okiek history and, by extension, could also explain the degree to which the micro- and macroprocesses of Okiek life fit the experiences of other hunter-gatherer societies in eastern Africa.

I have recorded several dozen cases or case-like events among the Mau Forest Okiek. Each demonstrates the processes underlying Okiek life during the past century. From these I have selected twenty-seven cases that consist of one or more transactions leading to a change of residence and the establishment of new relationships with different individuals, groups, or tribes. Those changes usually have resulted in some modifications of behavior or beliefs that help to explain the diversity that now characterizes Okiek groups. Not surprisingly, there are far more cases in which the outcome was resolved in such a way that a change in residence did not take place. Were this not the case, the Okiek probably would not have survived as a distinct people.

The following three cases describe a variety of conditions, events, participants, transactions, and principles.

Case 1: intergroup hostility

Here, briefly, is an informant's account of a case, followed by an analysis of its social actions and underlying cultural assumptions.

Naiponoi was a girl of about eight when the following events took place during the age-set of Il Twati, that is when the Il Twati age-set were *muranik* (warriors, ca. 1900–5). She was born to the *kap* (lineage) of Kimengish in the 1890s, near Lake Nakuru, where her people, the Marishioni Okiek, then lived. Her account is paraphrased here:

Our lineage used to put our hives in the trees near where the Tinet lived [a neighboring Okiek group she termed "the enemy"], so when the Tinet came there, they dropped the hives out of the trees. Our lineage became annoyed. We were brave so we wanted to fight the Tinet. The Tinet said, "We must attack first or they will come and finish us." There was a Tinet lady who was married to a Marishioni in our village and she was told by the Tinet to go hide in the forest so that if they attacked she would not be killed accidentally. Within a few days the Tinet came. They brought Kipsigis and Nandi warriors with them, too, as they knew the Marishioni were very brave. They attacked before dawn and they killed all the men of my lineage. In those times girls were not killed. I was allowed to pass through [leave] these Tinet. I wanted to be killed because my whole lineage was dead, but I wasn't killed. So I went with other Marashioni women and girls. I went to the Kipsigis and they took care of me until they had initiated me and I was married to a Kipsigis.

In this account the presenting event is not stated, but doubtless included an earlier dispute between the Tinet and this Marishioni lineage over who had rights to use a contiguous part of the forest for putting hives in trees, an important resource coveted by any Okiek lineage (Blackburn 1986). The Tinet anticipated that the Marishioni would attack them for "dropping their hives." Defeat was likely as the Marishioni were reputed to be the bravest Okiek in the region. In this transaction the Tinet preempted the attack with their own attack, which was successful because they brought greater numbers of warriors by enlisting the help of Kipsigis and Nandi (non-Okiek tribes).

The outcome of interest here is that the surviving women and girls were apparently dispersed to whomever would take them in. Naiponoi was taken in by the Kipsigis, either by those who captured her or others who were sympathetic to her plight. The Tinet woman who betrayed her husband's relations and was no longer welcome among the Marishioni left to live with the nearby Purko Maasai. While there were other consequences to this case, the point here is that some Okiek were dispersed to other groups and tribes by an intergroup conflict based on competition over a scarce resource (forest areas for honey collecting). In this event a dramatic dispersion of people from one group, whose social identity was extinguished, resulted in a dissemination of some of their ways among other groups. The extinction of a people may not mean the extinction of their entire culture.

This case is only one of several in which common principles and processes are evident. A principle evident here is the high value Okiek place on the exclusive possession of forest areas for placing hives. A second principle is that a dispute over a serious matter – places to put hives – cannot be settled by negotiation if the sides culturally define each other as "enemies." The presenting event (which may not be the original cause of the event) was the destruction of others' hives. This led to a transaction in which there are apparently only two alternatives: fight to the death or withdraw to another forest area if there is one available. The deciding factors inspiring both sides' willingness to attack were the Marishioni confidence in their braver warriors and the Tinet's superior numbers.

A third principle has to do with the value of human life, which is defined by kinship. Obliterating all male members of an enemy lineage so as to suffer no future revenge appears to be inconsistent with saving and adopting all the enemy's females. Not so. Male enemies are defined for life by their kin affiliation in this patrilineal society, but the wives and daughters of an enemy are seen as members of whatever kin group "owns" them by marriage, or by capture and the subsequent marriage or adoption.[8]

In similar cases involving interlineage or intergroup hostility, a series of transactions led to feuds in which the deaths of several people on both sides resulted in group migration or, through fear of complete annihilation, in peace and compensation. Even with an established equilibrium, residual anger over the kin who were killed persisted, threatening the safety of the survivors and thus the survival of their lineage.

A fourth principle, therefore, is that men strive to have as many descendants as possible. In a country where police protection is either distant, capricious, or (formerly) non-existent, an Okiot (singular of Okiek) looks to his adult male relations for his security.

Case 2: intralineage hostility

The second case involves the lineage of Leboo among the Kaplelach local group on the south side of the Mau Forest. To paraphrase informants' accounts:

In those days there were many people in the lineage of Leboo who were dying. My father was dead, only my father's brother was left alive, all the others had died. They were being killed, not by others but within the lineage. They were killing each other. This fighting began long ago when two parts of the lineage of Leboo fought a great deal. Two brothers argued over who had the right to put hives in and get honey from one small territory [*kotungo*, smaller than a *koret*, is a family territory; many of both compose a *konoito*, a lineage territory] where they were living. It was, and still is, a place the bees especially like and you can get a lot of honey there. In an argument in one of their houses, one brother speared the other, and the other, before he died, speared his brother in return. They both died and that is how the feud started. Later their families made up and stopped fighting during the time when the Lemek age-set were warriors [ca. 1910]. That is when they had a ceremony to make peace as they saw too many people were dying. Because they were related, nothing was paid in compensation for those killed . . .

---

[8] The offspring of Okiek and non-Okiek unions will be regarded as Okiek in this patrilineal society if the father is an Okiot.

The lineage of Leboo was large once, but many died from fighting and even now it is getting smaller as people frequently die young. I think it can be from *oiik* [ancestors who have power to affect – usually adversely – the living] . . .

Even today these two branches of Leboo don't get along so well. If they meet and bad words are said, they can remember and fight. Or when drinking someone can say a bad word and the others not like it. I don't know what they might say, but they know.

The presenting event in this case derives from what an Okiot holds most dear: next to life itself, he covets his own or his family's exclusive right to collect honey in his own territory. The fact that a fight could break out within a lineage is clear evidence of how strongly individualistic this covetousness can be. There have been other such cases of fights and extended fights (feuds) between families within a lineage, with various outcomes. Here the outcome was an extended period of feuding until so many had died that both parties realized that further fighting would be more likely to end in yet more deaths than the vanquishing of the other party. The result was an agreement to stop the feud. This decision was given outward and public recognition in a ceremony of peace (*tumdo ap ngaungisto*, literally ceremony for cutting off [the fighting]).

When such a ceremony is held to end a feud between lineages, it is mediated by elders of a neutral lineage, compensation (formerly in ivory tusks, honey, and/or rights to one or more family territories) is paid by each side for those they have killed, and normal relations are usually reestablished. Since the Okiek hold that a lineage is responsible for paying compensation for deaths caused by any of its members, compensation was not paid in the Leboo case because it would only mean the lineage paid itself; no material benefit would result.

Peace without compensation, however, was apparently only partly satisfying to the Leboo lineage, leaving unresolved a sense of hostility which could break into fighting at any time unless the parties were physically separated. In contrast, a feud settled about the same time between the Mengwari and Nagul lineages resulted in compensation and a resumption of normal relations and, after a decent interval, intermarriage.

For the lineage of Leboo, however, a breach of a jural rule – you don't fight with affines – led to an inadequate resolution and to the migration of one family to another lineage. This case illustrates the process by which other lineages have also split and new residences have been established for some of them adjacent to other Okiek groups or with the Maasai or Kipsigis.

Case 3: intralineage hostility

This case, like the previous one, involved intralineage hostility brought
on by the fatal fight between brothers, the dispersal of one branch who
sought refuge among the Kipsigis (food and marriage), and the attempt
by a third branch of the lineage, aided by Il Damaat Maasai, to take
advantage of this weakness to defeat the remaining branch and take its
territory.

Apparently the drunken murder was only that, signifying no greater
issue that could have caused a feud like that experienced by the Leboo.
Two generations later this lineage, which came near to extinction
because all but two men were killed, has recovered so well that it is now
three lineages. The lineage could recover because the survivors were
males. If they had been only females, regardless of their number, the
patrilineage would have died (as with the lineage in the first case), the
name would have been lost to posterity, and the lineage territory taken
by other relations (a likely motivation for the Kip Kwonyo attack).

Perpetuation of the lineage is a strong motivation, a basic principle of
Okiek life. An Okiot aspires to have his lineage named after him, to
preserve his name and his reputation, especially for bravery in attack on
both humans and animals. To ensure immortality beyond memory, the
Okiek say one must name offspring after *oiik* (dead ancestors) lest the
latter become annoyed and cause sickness and death among one's children or grandchildren. Such curses – by elders, ancestors, witches, and
the *urgoiyot* (ritual expert, medicine man) – encourage moral behavior in
a society where social controls are inadequate.

The microprocesses of these cases overlap. Examining the variations
among them, however, reveals subtle factors which tend to determine
the outcome of transactions. The social outcome of a feud or massacre
depends more on who (younger males) survived, not how many survived. This was true for the two intralineage fights and the two intergroup (or tribe) massacres. In each case this had a direct bearing on the
"cultural distance" experienced as a result of residence change and thus
the likely increase in resulting diversity.

From the above cases plus twenty-four more, I have identified so far
eleven types of case in which microprocesses involving changes in Okiek
culture or society are usually triggered by a change of residence among
the Okiek. They are: (1) feuds, (2) avoidance of the dispute by fleeing,
(3) government coercion, (4) enemies fleeing to Okiek for protection, (5)
capture of other Okiek or other peoples, (6) Okiek seeking protection
from enemies or starvation by living with others, (7) moves to other

forests in search of food, (8) leaving the forest to seek new subsistence sources (cultivation, pastoralism), (9) the seizure of Okiek territory by an enemy tribe, (10) the establishment of equal relations between Okiek and other tribes, and (11) lineages of one group becoming lineages of another.

There are undoubtedly several more types of case if one were to collect data from additional Okiek groups. These cases are sufficient, however, for demonstrating the utility of the analytical procedure presented here.

Analytical categories of microprocesses

Each case can be subjected to a transactional analysis whereby actions of individuals are recorded and then explained by reference to the causes and consequences of those actions. There are certain underlying assumptions in this type of analysis which include the following: the basis for individual decisions on what action to take in any situation is derived from shared cultural goals, individual needs and motivations, and certain existing conditions. Underlying these individual and group goals are several principles of Okiek life, some of which have been mentioned above. The conditions include certain psychological, social, cultural, and naturally occurring factors which inhibit or facilitate a decision to act. For example, the presence of kin may inhibit a man's decision to perform a hostile act while his own inebriated state may have the opposite effect. The curse of an elder or the fear of an ancestor's retribution may be part of the existing conditions of a situation.

A microprocess begins with an issue, usually a presenting event (such as a theft of honey) or circumstance (e.g. a severe drought) that precipitates action on the part of an aggrieved party. A presenting event may have as its ultimate cause an internal conflict among the Okiek, or an external conflict with another people, or an environmental failure or problem such as famine or disease. The immediate cause of a presenting event is usually an individual action which can be categorized as a breach of a jural rule, an agreement, an obligation, or of normal conduct. In the case of a presenting event, such as theft, a complaint may lead to a response by the second party who may disagree, deny, insult, threaten to utter a curse against the complainant or to fight him, or who may even carry out his threats. This reaction completes the first transaction in the microprocess. Ensuing transactions may escalate the disagreement, leading to more threats, and physical or supernatural aggression. More often, however, it results in an agreement to settle the transaction through discussion, mediation, an interlineage meeting, or appeals to the government.

One or more further transactions may take place. Greater numbers of transactions decrease the likelihood of a quick settlement and make continued disagreement more likely, with possible fighting and killing. At each step in a transaction or series of transactions, there are usually several choices of action open to each party based on appropriate goals, principles, needs, motivations, as well as on a wide range of existing conditions. These conditions can be natural (drought or heavy rains, failure of honey) or supernatural (curses by an ancestor [*oiik*], witch [*ponindet*], medicine man [*urgoiyot*], or god [*tororo*]).

Transactions lead to an outcome, either an initial or a final one, or both. An initial outcome may consist of a compromise and payment of compensation. Failing this, the result may be long-term continuation of the dispute: withdrawal of one party from the arena of action, escalation to a more aggressive level (feud); or escalation to a win/lose outcome (massacre of all or most of a group). Final outcomes include: the reestablishment of normal relations; permanent withdrawal and change of residence; temporary withdrawal followed by a settlement; capture and incorporation into the other group; or extermination of one group. Outcomes affect all levels of social organization, from the individual to the tribe as a whole, and may be seen as changes in residence, behavior, values, and beliefs.

An analysis of a microprocess makes it possible to identify motivations. For example, Okiek individual goals that have been identified from this analysis include a desire to be trusted and to trust others, to be healthy and strong, to live a long life, to have a wife or wives and many children, to have many hives, enough food and drink, and a large lineage and family. Okiek lineage goals are identified in the same way. They include: to perpetuate its existence, to increase its size so as to ensure its strength and thus its survival against others, and to provide a network of relations for assistance in the case of need. These goals are sometimes clearly articulated in action and words, either during transactions or in other contexts (ceremonies, singing, folk tales, discussions). They can also be inferred indirectly in similar situations or in a wider range of social actions and cultural beliefs. Underlying them are a number of the principles of Okiek life mentioned above, including: (1) relationships are defined by kinship; (2) "enemies" are defined by (non)relationship, or by social and geographical distance, and/or by conflict; (3) there is safety against enemies only in numbers (of relations and friends); and (4) possession of forests and forest resources is essential to life and is often the basis for conflict, and therefore the origin of enemies. For other principles and goals of Okiek life underlying other types of case see Blackburn (1971).

Figure 8.5   The traditional Okiek house is covered juniper bark (or bamboo if in that forest) just like a hive and for the same reason – it is long lasting, weather tight, and keeps the denizens warm inside. The maize garden is an innovation to this Kaplelach family in the last generation, giving this wife a secure supply of food for her children when her husband is away for weeks hunting and collecting honey. Author's photo, 1992

Trends in Mau Okiek recent history

A discussion of microprocess can be expanded to macroprocess when we examine aspects of Okiek history, especially diversity, over a longer period of time. If we look at those Okiek groups who have lived in the region of the Mau Forest during the past hundred years, we can see from an analysis of the present cases and from other discussions (Blackburn 1974, 1982, 1986) that certain long-term processes have been at work which relate to the issue of diversity. For example, over the past century Okiek groups at different periods shifted their subsistence base from foraging to mixed cultivation and pastoralism while retaining hunting and honey-gathering. This was primarily stimulated by a desire for more reliable food sources. Trading with other tribes for domestic foods during droughts has been a tradition that made the shift to the production of domestic foods easier.

Throughout this same period there was another trend in the arena of conflict resolution. While the Okiek exercised choices in their means of achieving their major life goals, some of their actions resulted in conflicts. These conflicts, as the above cases show, varied in scale from individual disagreements which resulted in separation by changing residence, to long-term interlineage and intergroup hostilities resulting in widespread killings and even the extinction of entire lineages. Major feuds continued up to about the 1920s and to a lesser degree until about the 1940s. Thereafter there have been and continue to be sporadic individual disagreements, a few of which have resulted in one, sometimes two deaths. Though this period coincided with the imposition of government authority, the Okiek do not see this as the cause of more peaceful times.

As one Okiot (of the Marishioni group living at Nesuiit) put it:

Before, the Okiek had only one child after five years, and did not have more than two or three sons because then there were enemies, and the Okiek waited a long time between children so that each would be old enough to run and hide from enemies. This, and a lack of food, are the two reasons for their small population. Everyone were enemies, they [Okiek] would kill [other] Okiek if they caught one. Maasai and Kalenjin tribes too did this. Even our own groups were enemies. If you came to the Kaplelach and were not known, you would be killed. Even if you were just going through some other lineage's land they would suspect you and kill you. Always people were at war.

Now they know one another, [there is] only an occasional case of fighting and killing without realizing [unintentional]. Before, like eighty or a hundred years ago, people were completely wild. Even in those times people did not know those living ten miles away. In your own group [Marishioni], if you did wrong in another's land [take honey] they could kill you. If you went into Chepkurerek [an Okiek group] land and were not recognized, you could be shot.

Another man (Kipchornwonek group) reflected this same conclusion:

When Lomperai's brother was killed [in the 1940s] there was a lot of killing then . . . People you don't live near are people you don't know and can be enemies. But nowadays they live together [both on the east side of the river] so they make friendship and are not enemies. So no killings. Less killing now is because of this, not the government.

Government records do not contradict this assertion.

This process of increased social integration between Okiek groups and between the Okiek and neighboring tribes continues today and is evident in the changes which have taken place within groups since I first visited them in the late 1960s. As each group has developed friendlier relations with neighboring groups and tribes, it has more readily adopted the characteristics of those neighbors and thereby become increasingly different from how each group was in the past or from its previous neighbors.

The Okiek see this process of adaptation as primarily facilitated by proximity and friendship – the two are seen as usually going together – which provide opportunity for individuals to see how another group or tribe is living, observing what their neighbors do that would be useful in meeting their own needs, and then trying to do the same themselves. This process of adaptation is facilitated by an Okiek willingness and ability to adapt to changing situations. The Okiek are well aware of their numerical inferiority and their consequent vulnerability to annihilation. While they have vigorously defended their rights where practicable, they have accommodated to others where it has been necessary or to their advantage. In this sense one can say that the Okiek are flexible, a term often used to describe other hunter-gatherers.

A Kipchornwonek man, observing the more traditional Kaplelach, commented:

These Kaplelach, their fathers' fathers from long ago stayed in the forest and their boys learned their ways. When each was eight or nine years old he would learn by going to the forest every time until he knew the work of the forest. Now others [Kipchornwonek], who have mixed with the Nandi or Kipsigis, they see them digging, then they learn to make small gardens. They learn to have gardens by living with people who have them.

A Kaplelach man observed the same process, but for a different purpose:

We did not have clans before the Kipsigis and Maasai came. We called ourselves after the name of our fathers [lineages]. We mixed with the Maasai and Kipsigis . . . We made friendships, so then you got a very good friend and you would "be" his clan. You can live with a person [Maasai or Kipsigis] in the same place until you make friends and then take his clan. So if a Maasai comes to an Okiot's house he can have honey. So an Okiot goes to a Maasai house, the Maasai will say "This man fed me so I will feed him."

In both examples, each man is seeing the process as one of meeting needs for food in a more reliable manner, either by borrowing techniques for growing it or by becoming "related" to a friend from another tribe and "borrowing" the food more directly when he needs it, just as a member of his own lineage would be expected to do. Either way, proximity has resulted in friendship, friendship leads to sharing, sharing results in more reliable food sources and also leads to relationship through marriage, and this results in progressive assimilation through generations.

This process has been well advanced with some Okiek groups for generations, while others show evidence of close intertribal assimilation only in more recent years. In the future the more interesting question will be not how or why Okiek assimilate, but how and why they retain and maintain their separate identity as Okiek.

The major difference for the Okiek in this century, and presumably for other peoples, is that previously the tendency to fission was more likely to result in wide dispersion to uninhabited areas, while in this century it has led to greater fusion with other peoples. Dramatically increased population has eliminated the safety valve of virgin territory but has increased the awareness of and relationship with neighboring peoples. The resultant tendency toward peaceable assimilation is encouraged by the imposition of central government control.

This is not to say that the push and pull of intergroup hostilities or the threat of starvation are the only stimuli to past migrations and assimilation. There is a multiplicity of ways in which the Okiek have come to relate to other peoples (see Blackburn 1982) and which therefore help to account for the diversity we see among Okiek today. However, the apparent prominence of inter-family, -lineage, -group, and -tribal hostilities among the Okiek argues for this process being the most important in accounting for migrations and thus for a substantial part of the diversity we see among Okiek groups today.

Microprocess and its relation to macroprocess

It is thus apparent that the Okiek have experienced a fundamental contradiction in their relationship to each other and to other peoples. Informants quite objectively state that their system of territoriality (which is more correctly a system of resource tenure: see Blackburn 1986) is their way of keeping families, lineages, and groups separated in space so as to reduce the frequency of contact and thereby reduce the potential for disputes caused by transgressions such as honey theft. If you don't live near others you are less likely to be tempted into stealing from them, becoming involved with their women, or drinking to excess with them and starting a fight. Yet we have seen in the above cases that physical distance is also a major cause of social distance, and results in the lack of the kind of relationships that motivate people to get along amicably. If another lineage is not related to you by blood or marriage, and you do not have friends among them, and do not socialize or trade with them, then it does not take much suspicion or unfriendly action for them to be regarded as "enemies" who can be harassed, intimidated, stolen from, captured from, defeated, or killed. If a lineage fears that the "enemy" may attack them, this will encourage them to attack first, hoping to annihilate the other group, the only really permanent solution to dealing with an enemy.

This structural contradiction in Okiek society is independent of recent historical events or the presence of other tribes or the government and, therefore, is likely to have had a very long-term effect on Okiek life – a macroprocess. The consequence of this macroprocess is to reduce the rate of potential conflict caused by trespass (primarily honey theft), but to increase the potential for conflict resulting from other causes not related to space, such as substantiated or even unsubstantiated "fear of enemies." The Okiek have a generalized fear of others who are not kin or with whom relations are not established. This is recognized not only by outsiders (other tribes, the government, anthropologists) but by the Okiek themselves. It is certainly a well-founded fear, given the confrontations the Okiek have repeatedly had with more populous tribes around them, as well as the feuds they have had among themselves. It is also reinforced by the nature of their own methods of socializing aggression which, I have argued elsewhere (Blackburn 1971:192), are causally related to the development of fear of others, in turn related to such projective areas as the fear of *oiik* (ancestor spirits), *ponindet* (witch), *urgoiyot* or *loibon* (ritual expert), and of certain relations, especially affines.

This contradiction between fearing and relating to others is given physical expression when Okiek sit down to share their favorite drink, honey wine. *Rotik* is the most commonly used and most highly valued vehicle for facilitating Okiek communication. It draws people together in friendship, hospitality, and respect; however, excessive drinking can cause the opposite reaction – outbursts of anger, rejection, and contempt. Okiek, wishing to overcome their usual sense of self-preserving mistrust and fear of others, are drawn together by the elixir of *rotik* to share a tentative feeling of trust, of communitas – the essence of real social life and the religious experience. It works most of the time. In the home, at *kook* (the men's campfire), and at the big ceremonies, the Okiek reinforce their affection for others and their way of life when they sit, talk, sing, and drink together. For those long-remembered moments, when "everyone is happy here," each Okiek feels secure with others. But the tension between trust and mistrust is a universal one and long-repressed fears and angers may break through under the uninhibiting influence of alcohol. Mild insults escalate into "bad words," then into "shouting," shoving, fighting, and sometimes into hitting and killing. The veil of culture lies but lightly upon our primal self.

This psychological dilemma of trust versus mistrust – self-preservation verses community interest – underlies the micro- and macro-processes of Okiek life discussed in this chapter. It is fundamental to understanding the basic goals, the motivations to achieving those goals, and the structural contradiction of social distance versus familiarity discussed above. This dilemma, of course, is universal in all societies to a greater or lesser degree. As it has been significant in inspiring migrations over a long period of time, and has thus contributed to diversity among the Okiek, it is likely to have had some effect upon diversity among other hunter-gatherers, at least in eastern Africa.

The Okiek and other African hunter-gatherers

While comparing and contrasting one ethnic group with another becomes increasingly problematical in proportion to the methodological and theoretical differences of the researchers, and the ethnic and geographical distance involved, there are nevertheless some remarkable differences that I and others (e.g., Woodburn 1982) have remarked on between the Okiek and other hunter-gatherers in Africa. I would like to address the issue of individual and group conflict, which has been characteristic of Okiek life to a degree rarely heard of among other African hunter-gatherers. Why is there so much hostility and violence among the Okiek?

On a day-to-day basis, individual aggression is rarely evident. The Okiek are quite careful about avoiding conflict – even just disagreements – by resolving disputes peacefully and avoiding situations that might lead to disputes. Hostility exists but is usually repressed, sublimated, or denied. There have been no feuds for nearly two generations, although older men and women remember well the feuds of the past. On the other hand, accusations, disputes, and sometimes fights and murders, do take place today and for basically the same reasons as those mentioned in the cases discussed here, often rights to resources.

The issues of rights over resources is probably the most important distinction between the Okiek and most other hunter-gatherers in Africa. I believe this is at the heart of the issue of conflict. The Okiek way of life, their forest adaptation, their complex system of territoriality (a resource tenure system: see Blackburn 1986), are explicable primarily in terms of the pervasive importance of honey and its derivatives. If the Okiek had not elaborated the central role of honey in their society and culture (Blackburn 1971), their adaptation, customs, and beliefs would be more akin to those of other hunter-gatherers in Africa – more egalitarian (see Kent, chapter 1), with more delayed gratification (Woodburn 1982), and less "asset-consciousness."[9]

The Okiek are keenly interested in accumulating certain types of assets, but the value they place on assets is not characteristic of most other hunter-gatherers. The latter have often been characterized by researchers as "egalitarian," as can be seen in the other chapters of this book. Formerly Okiek interest in assets was only in terms of honey and hives. The latter they quite explicitly compare to Maasai cattle, calling hives the "cows for Okiek." Today they also avidly accumulate domestic stock. As with the Maasai, the desire for assets leads to their acquiring more of them. For the Okiek that means making more hives and collecting more honey (one man is renowned for owning as many as 1,000 hives, though most men own between 50 and 200, which incidentally is a range of numbers familiar to Maasai cattle-owners).

For the Maasai, who apparently cannot acquire cows quickly enough by natural procreation, rustling has been the accepted institutionalized method for increasing wealth. Taking cows from other Maasai or from other ethnic groups is equally acceptable and socially approved, though not by the government. For the Okiek, stealing honey, let alone hives, from anyone is totally unacceptable and relatively rare. Next to homicide and warfare, it is conceived as about the most threatening event in their society. Even the suspicion of theft of honey has led to conflict and killing. While killing animals in another lineage's territory is quite acceptable ("How can I say it is mine when tomorrow that animal may wander into his territory?"), even taking wood or bark from another's territory to make a hive is cause for accusation, an interlineage meeting, a collective decision of guilt, and a fine.

Okiek asset-consciousness is also evident in the disparity in the rights accorded each sex. A woman is born to a lineage, is "given" to another lineage in exchange for a substantial bride price, and is "owned" by that lineage. Her husband has the right to beat her at will, though excessive and unjustified beating will bring a verbal rebuke from her parents and lineage. If he should kill his wife, it is unlikely that he would have to pay compensation to his wife's lineage, though I have heard of no case to test this.

[9] The Okiek, however, can be fairly characterized as sharing a similar adaptive flexibility with other hunter-gatherers. In terms of traditional subsistence, for instance, they exploit successfully both highland forests and lowland plains. Their adoption of domestic stock and cultivation is an example of this flexible ability to exploit resources as needed or desired. Their ability to ingratiate themselves by friendship, intermarriage, and trade with neighboring peoples is another example. On an individual level their ability to manipulate relationships to their social and economic advantage is well developed, though I think other fieldworkers have experienced this same talent with their own groups.

It may appear inconsistent but Okiek concern for possession of assets does not extend to private ownership of land. Recently the Kenya government has been allowing private ownership of plots and issuing title deeds to families. Okiek who have received plots have, with rare exceptions, not husbanded this resource with anywhere near the zeal with which they have husbanded other resources. They often sell off parts of their plot for transient profits, primarily to cultivating tribes such as the Kikuyu who have a long tradition of land acquisition. For the Okiek, however, this trend will have dire consequences for their future as a people. In fact, this attitude is entirely consistent with Okiek traditional beliefs. Lineages do not "own" land, they only own the rights to certain products found on the land – trees to make hives from and place hives in, and the honey that comes from them. While lineages do not own land, the Okiek do conceive of the forest and the land on which it grows as their own, which other peoples cannot inhabit without permission. It is a subtle distinction but an important principle of Okiek life, from which much of the drama of their lives and future emanates.

Asset-consciousness as a defining ethnic concept

On the matter of assets, it is interesting to point out here a contrast between the three neighboring peoples: pastoral Maasai, foraging Okiek, and cultivating Kikuyu (although these days each shares some of the subsistence techniques of the others, the main distinctions still hold). The Okiek partly share with the Maasai a similar mode of subsistence in the sense that both depend heavily on animals. Both peoples must adapt to the needs of these animals to move from place to place for forage by moving themselves. Yet the Maasai own their animals; the Okiek do not.

On the other hand, the Okiek share with the Kikuyu a stationary food source (honey-collecting from hives and crops from gardens) which ties families in both tribes to specific places for long periods of time. While the Kikuyu see land as their chief possession, the Okiek do not. For the latter it is the uncultivated vegetation on the land that is possessed – certain trees and the products that can be made from them.

What is important to notice here is that the type of subsistence – pastoral, foraging, and cultivating – is less important in defining these three groups than are their distinctive differences and similarities in relationship to land, mobility, and ownership of assets. This approach contrasts with the traditional anthropological focus on defining people by their subsistence. But should not people be defined according to those issues over which they define themselves, that is, those over which they will fight and which they most desire to pass on to their progeny? If so, then these (and perhaps other issues) may prove more appropriate bases for categorizing societies than the subsistence categories western-ers traditionally use.

Such identification can be established through analyzing behavior in individual cases, i.e. the microprocesses. By these criteria, the Kikuyu are land-holders, the Maasai stock-holders, and the Okiek tool-holders. From these three types of possession or asset each group derives its principal sustenance and wealth. In their own eyes, Maasai without their stock are not Maasai, Kikuyu without their land are not Kikuyu, and Okiek without their hives, spears, arrows, traps, and the like, are not Okiek. These are stock cultures, land cultures, and tool cultures. Evans-Pritchard long ago defined for us a stock culture among the Nuer; Herskowitz characterized this culture as a "cattle complex." Okiek culture has been described in terms of a "honey complex" (Blackburn 1971), and numerous monographs have demonstrated the central role of land among cultivating societies.

Conclusion

Although anthropology is the study of human beings and therefore ought to be as comprehensive in its theories and methods as in its data, it is an obvious fact that most ethnographers have adopted their own more limited approach (theory and method) to recording and interpreting the people they study. This book is a good example of just how diverse approaches can be, even within a single subfield of ethnology, the study of African hunter-gatherers. That diversity has the advantage of opening up new ways of understanding behavior, while having the disadvantage of making comparisons and contrasts among ethnic groups, as interpreted by each ethnographer, more difficult. One contri-bution to this issue is to demonstrate, as I have attempted here, a method for analyzing transactions and micro- and macroprocesses com-bined with a broad theory of action which integrates social, cultural, and psychological systems (see Blackburn 1971). This analytical approach can help bridge the often quite different types of data and issues presented by other ethnographers.

On the other hand, given the fact that all behavior is motivated, and each of us tends to be motivated to interpret the world around us with a theory (or theories) which best matches our personal world view as well as our professional training, I reluctantly conclude that within our field the fission of approaches will continue to outpace the fusion of theories, making professional diversity more interesting but less productive;

stimulating more ideas but less understanding; and producing more arguments but less consensus. Progressive diversity, and the dynamics of fission and fusion characteristic of the Okiek, would appear to be evident in even the most informed arenas of social action.

Part III

Central African foragers

Barry Hewlett

Turnbull's work provides exceptionally lucid, sensitive, and rich ethnographic accounts of Mbuti Pygmies. His book, *The Forest People* (1961), and the more detailed ethnographic monograph, *Wayward Servants* (1965b), have been so popular that no comparable ethnography has come along to replace them. As a result, most individuals, including anthropologists, view Mbuti culture as synonymous with African Pygmy culture, just as !Kung culture has become synonymous with "Bushman" culture. Several monographs on other African Pygmy populations (e.g., Bailey 1991; Bahuchet 1985; Hewlett 1991) have recently been published but they are more problem-oriented and specialized. However, the recent work has contributed significantly to our understanding of African Pygmy populations and therefore enables us to place the Mbuti within a comparative perspective. This chapter utilizes the recent research to describe some of the differences and similarities between four African Pygmy populations (Figure 9.1), and offers preliminary hypotheses to explain the diversity and commonalities.

Unfortunately, no term has emerged to replace "Pygmy," a derogatory term that emphasizes short stature. For the remainder of this chapter, "forest forager" is utilized rather than "Pygmy." African tropical forest foragers generally have the following characteristics: (1) they spend at least four months of the year in the tropical forest hunting and gathering; (2) they have a strong identity with and preference for forest life; (3) they maintain many-stranded social and economic relations with neighboring farming populations; and (4) they practice important ritual activities associated with elephant hunting. There are at least ten ethnolinguistically distinct populations of forest foragers in central Africa and they are unevenly distributed throughout the Congo–Zaire basin: the Efe, Mbuti, Aka, and Tswa are found in northeastern Zaire (see Ichikawa and Terashima, chapter 11, this volume, for discussion of Mbuti and Efe); the Aka, Bofi, and Benzele live in northern Congo and southwestern Central African Republic; the Baka are in southeastern

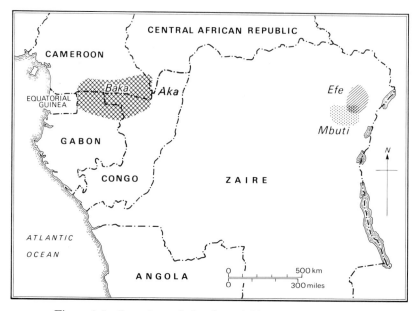

Figure 9.1 Location of the four African tropical forest foraging populations discussed in chapter 9

Cameroon, northern Gabon and northern Congo (see Joiris, chapter 10, this volume, for discussion of this group); the Gyelli and Tikar are smaller groups in western Cameroon; and the Bongo are in southeastern Gabon and central Congo.

While there are cultural commonalities between these foraging populations, the cultural differences are dramatic and striking. I have selected the Aka, Baka, Mbuti, and Efe for comparison because they are some of the largest and best documented populations of forest foragers. They also provide equal representation of the eastern and western Congo–Zaire basin: the Baka and Aka are from the western Congo–Zaire basin while the Efe and Mbuti are from the Ituri Forest in the eastern Congo–Zaire basin.

There are methodological problems with most comparative studies and this one is no different (see Silberbauer, chapter 2, this volume, and Bird-David, chapter 12, this volume, for excellent discussions of problems with comparative research). First, the ethnographic data for the four groups were collected at different times in history. Turnbull collected the Mbuti data in the late 1950s and early 1960s, whereas Bailey, Peacock and other members of the Ituri Project collected the Efe data in the mid-1980s. Most of the Baka data reported in this chapter were collected by Vallois and Marquer in the mid-1940s while the Aka data were collected by myself and Bahuchet in the late 1970s and early 1980s. All of the above-mentioned studies took place before the forest foragers adopted farming to any great extent. Second, comparative studies emphasize general or the most frequent cultural patterns of an ethnic group rather than the variability in cultural patterns found within an ethnic group. This can be problematic as there may be just as much variability within an ethnic group as there is between groups. For instance, Table 9.2 lists the Aka as having forest camps more than one day's walk from the village, while Efe camps are listed as within a four-hour walk of the village. These refer to general patterns, but it is of course true that some Aka groups like to live near villages and some Efe groups live deep in the forest. This intracultural variability is just as interesting as the study of intercultural variability, but given the page limitations of this chapter, emphasis is placed upon cross-cultural diversity and only a few pages in the final section are devoted to intracultural variation (see Joiris, chapter 10, this volume, and Barnard and Widlok, chapter 4, this volume, for discussions of intracultural variability). Finally, the anthropologists who conducted the research on the four foraging groups collected most of their data with a limited subpopulation (generally 200–400 individuals). The study of one subpopulation is utilized to make generalizations about the whole ethnic group. This is problematic as there are over 20,000 individuals in three of the ethnic groups and over 6,000 individuals among the Efe (see Table 9.1). Although there are problems with comparative studies, this does not mean that they should be abandoned: rather, it implies that one should be aware of the limitations of these studies and interpret the results cautiously. Examining diversity is vital to prevent stereotyping; my own field experiences with each of the four groups and the ethnographic descriptions of others indicate that dramatic differences between these groups do exist.

Linguistic diversity

Table 9.1 summarizes the linguistic distinctions between the four foraging groups and their farming neighbors. The Efe are the most distinct linguistically as their language comes from a language phylum totally different from that of the other three. The Aka and Mbuti are the most similar, even though they are hundreds of miles apart, in that they both speak Bantu languages. Conventional practice in ethnography is to drop a Bantu prefix when writing about the population. Consequently, BaAka are called Aka and BaMbuti are called Mbuti in the literature. The

Table 9.1. *Linguistic affiliations*

	Forager group			
	Efe	Mbuti	Baka	Aka
Phylum	Nilo-Saharan	Niger-Kord	Niger-Kord	Niger-Kord
Family	Chari-Nile	Benue-Congo	Adamawa-Oubanguian	Benue-Congo
Number of principal farming groups living in association	3	4	15	19
Linguistic families of these groups	Chari-Nile	Benue-Congo	Benue-Congo (13) Adamawa-Oubanguian (2)	Benue-Congo (11) Adamawa-Oubanguian (8)
Closest farming ethno-linguistic group	Lese	Bira	Ngbaka	Ngando
Estimated population	6,000	27,000	25,000	30,000

Baka, who live just across the Sangha River from the Bantu-speaking Aka, speak a language from a completely different linguistic family (i.e., Oubanguian). Some people tend to group Aka and Baka altogether as their ethnic designations sound so similar and their territories are contiguous. For instance, anthropologists who have read my book on the Aka have said that they show the National Geographic film *Baka: People of the Forest* to illustrate Aka parent–child relations. While the intimate parent–child relations implicit in the film are reasonable representations of Aka parent–child relations, the Baka are linguistically and culturally (see following sections) very different. For instance, Bantu languages require singular and plural prefixes for nouns (e.g., BaAka or BiAka are plural and MouAka is singular), whereas the Baka's Oubanguian language does not require singular and plural prefixes for nouns.

There is some evidence for an original forest forager language (Bahuchet 1989), yet all forest foragers who are known to the ethnographic record have adopted languages of their current or previous farming neighbors. The Efe usually live in association with Lese, Mamvu, and Mangbetu, all of whom speak languages from the same linguistic family as the Efe; the Mbuti usually live in association with the Ndaka, Bila, and Budu farmers, all of whom speak languages from the same language family as the Mbuti. In the western Congo–Zaire basin, a very different pattern exists. Baka are unique by comparison to the three other forager groups as only two of the fifteen ethnic groups with whom Baka have social and economic relations speak languages from the same linguistic family. This, of course, does not limit Baka communication since they are fluent in the language of their farming neighbors. Yet the reverse is seldom true in that their farming neighbors infrequently speak the Baka language. Consequently, the Baka and Aka are often described as speaking their own language, which is unintelligible to their farming neighbors, while the Mbuti and Efe are often said not to have a language of their own, which means they speak the same language as their farming neighbors, or one similar to it.

Explaining the linguistic diversity among forest foragers is beyond the scope of this chapter. Bahuchet's (1993) recent three-volume study of this topic is a significant contribution, but several questions remain.

Diversity in subsistence and settlement patterns

Table 9.2 summarizes differences and similarities in selected features of subsistence and settlement (see Vierich and Hitchcock, chapter 5, this volume, and Barnard and Widlok, chapter 4, this volume, for discussions of cultural diversity in Basarwa subsistence and settlement). The

Table 9.2. *Subsistence and settlement*

	Efe[a]	Mbuti[b]	Baka[c]	Aka[d]
Subsistence				
Primary hunting technique	bow	net	spear	net
Net hunters only – males or females as beaters?		females		males
% daily calories provided by meat	13.3–27.0	35.0–86.0	ND	36.0
Time allocation – men only				
% of time hunting-gathering while in forest camp	44.6	ND	ND	67.2
% of time hunting-gathering while in village camp	23.4	ND	ND	0.0
% of time working for villagers while in village camp	7.8	ND	ND	17.8
% of diet from cultivated foods/% of diet from wild foods	63.5/36.5		ND	55.0/45.0
% of calories from females	6.5	50	ND	4.5
Collection of fish and shellfish by women	important	not important	important	not important
Settlement				
Distance to most forest camps	4–5 km	5–15 km	4–8 km	15–40 km
No. of months/year in forest	5	8	4–5	7–8
Mean camp size	17.8	37.4	31.7	25.5

References:
[a] Bailey 1985; Peacock 1985; Bailey and Peacock 1988; Hill 1982; Harako 1976.
[b] Turnbull 1965a, 1965b; Hart 1978; Ichikawa 1978; Hill 1982.
[c] Vallois and Marquer 1976.
[d] Bahuchet 1985, 1988; Hewlett 1989, 1991.

Figure 9.2 Aka and Mbuti use nets that are about 1 m tall and anywhere from 10 to 150 m long. This Aka boy is checking the net for tears before the net hunt begins

primary hunting techniques reflect important distinctions in the sexual division of labor between the foraging groups: men, women, and children participate in the Mbuti and Aka net hunts (Figures 9.2, 9.3), whereas generally only men participate in the Efe bow and Baka spear hunts. Efe and Baka women seldom hunt and spend much of their time working in the fields for village women. The differences in the sexual division of labor appear to be associated with other features of subsistence and settlement. For instance, net-hunting Mbuti and Aka acquire a greater percentage of their calories from meat and wild foods and go somewhat farther into the forest for longer periods of time. Aka men seldom hunt while they are in the village and Aka and Mbuti women

Figure 9.3   Net hunts involve both men and women. This Aka woman
is collecting the net after a cast of the nets

seldom collect fish or shellfish. Efe and Baka, on the other hand, who
have separate male and female subsistence activities, tend to stay closer
to the village for longer periods of time and acquire fewer calories from
meat and wild foods. Efe men hunt from their village camps and Efe and
Baka women frequently collect fish and shellfish, an important supplemental source of protein for those who acquire less meat through
hunting.

The interests of men and women in these two patterns (i.e., male–
female cooperating vs. male–female separate) are quite distinct. Bailey
and Peacock (1988) indicate that the "village world" versus "forest
world" dichotomy that Turnbull (1965b) uses to distinguish Bila
farmers and Mbuti foragers is useful in describing the different interests

of Efe men and women: Efe men prefer to go hunting in the "forest world" whereas Efe women prefer the subsistence regularity and certainty of the "village world." The different preferences of Efe men and women are one reason why Efe spend less time in the forest than Mbuti and Aka, usually establish camps within a four-hour walk of the village, and have less meat in their diet. Camps a short distance from the village allow Efe women to return to the village to acquire village foods. Efe men also go hunting in the forest while residing in a village camp because the family stays in the village camp for most of the year. The Baka gender task dichotomy today may not be as pronounced as the Efe dichotomy (Joiris, personal communication), yet Vallois and Marquer (1976) and Dodd (1979) indicate that men's and women's activities in the recent past were separate (e.g., men spear-hunting and collecting honey; women fishing and collecting fruits and tubers), as they are today, and in contrast to the Aka and Mbuti patterns where male and female subsistence interests are relatively more similar.

Other features of net hunting also contrast with archers and spear hunters. The average net hunt lasts 6–8 hours and covers 8–15 kilometers (Tanno 1976; Hewlett, personal observation); the average bow hunt lasts three hours and covers 7–8 kilometers (Bailey 1991). Net hunters tend to hunt 5 or 6 days per week (Hart 1978; Hewlett 1991); archers tend to hunt 2 or 3 days per week (Bailey 1991) while they are in forest camps. Comparable data for Baka spear hunters who hunt for medium-size game do not exist. Spear hunting for elephant is practiced by all the groups and usually involves very long hours and great distances. The differences between net hunting and bow hunting suggest that net hunters are the more intensive foragers, as might be expected, because they acquire more of their village foods (e.g., manioc, corn, etc.) through trading game meat rather than by labor exchange. Efe archers acquire their carbohydrates in exchange for the labor of Efe women. The nature of Baka spear hunting is presumably similar to Efe bow hunting because the sexual division of labor is separate rather than cooperative and forest camps are close to villages.

Are the Efe and Baka more dependent upon villagers than Aka and Mbuti?

Efe and Baka camp closer to villages (Figure 9.4), spend more time in the village, and eat more village food than Mbuti and Aka, but does this mean that they are more "dependent" on villagers? This question has been raised by several Ituri ethnographers. Turnbull (1965b) and Putnam (1948) indicate that Efe archers are more dependent on villagers

Figure 9.4   Baka spend much of the year in semi-permanent village camps. This is a small Baka village camp in southern Cameroon

because bow hunting is less efficient than net hunting, therefore they stay close to the village to acquire regular and sufficient amounts of food. This propinquity and "dependence" has led to similarities between the social-political organization of the villagers and the Efe; a lineage system, greater hierarchy, less egalitarianism, and more formalized exchange relations. Harako (1976), on the other hand, suggests that net hunters are more dependent on farmers than are archers because women participate in the net hunt. Harako assumes that before women started net hunting they gathered vegetable foods, which contributed the majority of the calories to the diet. When women participate in the net hunt they have to give up the collection of wild foods, which means the group becomes more reliant on farmers for their carbohydrates. The supposed result is that net hunters have less flexibility because they must trade with farmers to acquire carbohydrates while archers are not as strictly tied to villages because women still collect wild foods. Harako also indicates that net hunters' closer economic ties with farmers leads to increased social and religious ties (i.e., acculturation and dependence).

Harako's field data were reanalyzed by Abruzzi (1979) and Milton (1985) to examine differences in Efe and Mbuti hunting techniques and dependence on villagers. These researchers came up with completely opposite results! Abruzzi believes Efe rely more heavily on villagers while Milton believes the reverse. Their hypotheses will be discussed in greater detail in the next section.

The Mbuti–Efe dependence debate assumes that the foraging group that lives closer to villagers and eats more village foods is more acculturated and less traditional. In fact, all of the forest foragers depend rather heavily on the domestic crops of the villagers. However, the number, diversity, and nature of religious, ritual, and social activities that foragers and farmers have in common are more often related to the length of time foragers and farmers have been living in association with one another than with the foragers' dependence on village food. In this regard, the relations of the bow-hunting Efe and the net-hunting Mbuti with farmers appears more similar than those between Aka and Baka foragers and their neighboring farmers. The Efe and Mbuti speak languages that are very similar, if not identical, to the language of their long-time Lese and Bila neighbors. They also share many ritual activities with their village neighbors (e.g., male initiation ceremonies, marriage). The Aka and Baka, who have most lived near village farmers for about 100 years, tend to speak their own languages and retain more separate traditions.

However, outward appearances of similarity can be misleading and some confusion may have been compounded by a lack of data; long-term studies did not exist when Turnbull and Harako made their arguments. For instance, Harako assumed Efe acquired a good percentage of their diet from collected wild foods, which we now know is not true (Bailey and Peacock 1988). Actually, there is currently no evidence to suggest that Efe or Baka social life (e.g., egalitarianism, autonomy, leadership, dispute resolution, child rearing), forest life, or ethnic identity is closer to that of farmers than that of Mbuti or Aka. Efe and Baka have simply developed different strategies for dealing with their farming neighbors.

Why are there different subsistence technologies among African tropical forest foragers?

This question reflects another lively debate that has emerged from research in the Ituri – why are there archers and net hunters in the same forest? The basic assumption has been that net hunting is more efficient and productive than bow hunting; consequently, researchers, such as Turnbull (1965b) and Harako (1976), explained Efe's persistent use of the bow as related to concerns other than immediate hunting returns. Turnbull indicated that Efe developed closer relations with farmers in order to compensate for the lowered efficiency. He (1968) also suggested that forest game was plentiful and thus it did not matter which hunting technique was utilized. Harako suggested nets were introduced by Bantu-speakers and only those foragers who associated with Bantu-speakers adopted the use of nets. The Efe continued their relations with Lese and other Sudanic speakers who used bows rather than nets.

Turnbull's and Harako's hypotheses and data have generated several analyses and more detailed research by ecological anthropologists. Abruzzi's (1979) reanalysis suggested that an increase in population density created by farming groups moving into the Ituri reduced the forest areas available for hunting, which in turn led to intensification of hunting effort and consequent adoption of net hunting by Mbuti; Efe did not adopt nets because they received more foods from villagers and relied less on forest resources. Milton (1985) also reanalyzed Harako's data but suggests instead that distinctive hunting techniques existed because the forests of the Mbuti and Efe were different. Net hunting was adopted in less diverse, relatively unproductive and resource-poor forest areas where *Gilbertiodentron dewevrei* species dominated. In forested areas with greater species diversity (*Cynometra-Brachysteagis* forest) game was more plentiful and therefore it was not necessary to adopt nets; bow hunting would be sufficient.

As stated above, these hypotheses assume that net hunting is more efficient than bow hunting. Ichikawa (1982), Terashima (1983), and Bailey and Aunger (1989) have examined this assumption by comparing how many kilograms of game meat are acquired per person/hour with net and bow hunting. After summarizing several systematic and quantitative studies from the Ituri they have indicated that there are no differences in hunting efficiency. More game is captured on net hunts, but there are generally twice as many people involved as on the bow hunts because women and children participate in the former. Thus, there are no statistical differences in the amount of game captured per person/hour.

Because some of their findings differed from earlier hypotheses, Bailey and Aunger (1989) recently field tested Abruzzi's and Milton's ideas. They found no difference in the composition or diversity of forest areas, and generally no difference in population densities in net- and bow-hunting areas. This contradiction may be partly due to the fact that Abruzzi and Milton never conducted fieldwork in the areas, but developed their hypothesis on the basis of knowledge of other areas.

Bailey and Aunger offer an alternative hypothesis based upon their findings that Mbuti net-hunting women bring in more calories by participating on the net hunt than by working in the villagers' fields, whereas Efe women bring in more calories by working for villagers. The authors demonstrate that Lese and Mamvu fields are larger than Bila and Budu fields, so Efe women who work for Lese and Mamvu get more in return (i.e., more calories) for their labor than do Mbuti women.

The value of Efe women's labor in villagers' fields is greater than that of Mbuti in large part because the Lese and Mamvu fields worked in by Efe are larger. Lese and Mamvu can give more because they have more. But why are Lese and Mamvu fields larger? Bailey and Aunger argue that Lese and Mamvu live in more remote areas and therefore have fewer opportunities for a cash income. They therefore have to grow more of their food than do Budu and Bila, who live along frequently traveled roads. However, in one of their tables (ibid.: 228), they show that Mamvu have coffee plantations twice the size of all groups investigated, which suggests Mamvu do have cash incomes.

An alternative hypothesis is that Lese and Mamvu fields are larger because they have regular, almost daily, help from Efe women and can therefore cultivate larger areas. This coincides with the fact that net hunters capture more game than bow hunters because there are more people on the hunt. Wrangham and Ross (1987) have demonstrated that a prime factor in determining the size of a Lese family's field is the number of relatives it has to depend upon. Efe women are relatives to Lese. Bila and Budu fields are smaller because they do not have Mbuti women to help them out on a regular basis.

If the return of calories is similar, then the development of net hunting versus bow hunting has less to do with subsistence efficiency than with cultural history. That is, Efe women work in villages because it is part of an evolved cultural pattern established with villagers. There are several ways to adapt to a particular environment; again, net hunters have established relations with farmers in one way while bow or spear hunters have established relations with farmers in another way.

The local economy may well play a role in the development of those relations. Bailey and Aunger found that meat in net-hunting areas had a greater currency value and greater exchange value than in bow-hunting areas. This assumes that the increased demand for meat comes from larger towns and good roads in the area, both of which encourage meat marketing. Bailey and Aunger hypothesize that if the value of meat increased in bow-hunting areas, women would participate in bow hunting or possibly adopt net hunting.

The most recent paper in this debate (Wilkie and Curran 1991) reconfirms Ichikawa's and Terashima's findings that net hunting is not more efficient than bow hunting and also complements Bailey and Aunger's hypothesis of bushmeat market economy affecting hunting methods. The authors indicate that net hunting focuses almost exclusively on small to medium-sized ungulates (e.g., duikers, antelopes, chevrotain) and further indicate that bow hunting is better utilized for a greater diversity of animal species. Although the authors believe net hunters target medium-sized ungulates for bushmeat trade they do not provide evidence to support their contention that ungulates are preferred or have a greater monetary value per unit effort at the market than do monkeys or other game that are hunted with bows.

Wilkie and Curran do not provide historical evidence to support their bow- to net-hunting hypothesis. It is necessary to ascertain when bushmeat markets were established and then try to determine from ethnohistorical data if net hunting happened in the area previous to the development of these markets. Wilkie and Curran, and Bailey and Aunger, indicate that the frequently traveled Kisangani–eastern Zaire road that passes through the Ituri has contributed greatly to the development of a lucrative meat market. Truck drivers and other travelers purchase bushmeat relatively cheaply in the Ituri and transport it to market in population centers in eastern Zaire or Kisangani. Indeed, most of the groups along this road are net hunters. The implication of the meat-market hypothesis is that the construction of this road increased market capabilities and contributed to the shift to net hunting.

There is no question that bushmeat markets have dramatically influenced the social, economic, and religious life of forest foragers (Bahuchet 1985; Hart 1978; Ichikawa 1991), but to suggest that bushmeat markets were a prime mover in the shift from bow hunting to net hunting is questionable.

The Kisangani–eastern Zaire road was the first road to be constructed in the Ituri and was opened in the early 1930s (Harako 1976; Ichikawa 1991). The meat-market hypothesis suggests Mbuti should have been bow hunting before this road contributed to the development of meat markets. Ethohistoric data suggest that this was not the case; thirty or more years before construction of the road, several early travelers to the Epulu area describe Mbuti net hunts as they are known today (i.e., with male and female participation). Schebesta does not mention the meat trade and Turnbull, who did his work in the late 1950s, does not mention meat-market trade among the Mbuti in Epulu, which is a regular and important rest stop for most travelers. Hart (1978) and Ichikawa (1991) indicate Ituri meat-markets developed in the late 1950s and early 1960s as Nande peoples moved into the Ituri from eastern Zaire. While there has probably always been some meat-marketing on this road, it appears that the frequency and intensity of meat trading increased dramatically just after independence.

Comparative data from the Baka and Aka also question the validity of Wilkie's and Curran's hypothesis. The Aka in the Central African Republic are generally involved in meat-markets because roads are relatively good and there are several large towns to market the meat. The Aka in the interior regions of northeastern Congo, on the other hand, are not actively involved in meat-markets because roads and large villages are rare. Aka in both areas use nets most of the year.

Data from the Baka of southeastern Cameroon are more instructive because they do not use nets and have more subsistence and settlement patterns in common with the Efe. Regular public transport is available on most SE Cameroon roads. By comparison, this service seldom exists in the Mbuti, Aka, and Efe areas. SE Cameroon is more "developed" than the other areas because it is closer to the populated areas of West Africa and it is near the Douala seaport. People have moved into the forest from populated coastal areas of West Africa and it is relatively easy and inexpensive to export forest hardwoods, such as mahogany, and cash crops, such as coffee and cacao. Consequently, there are more people with more money to purchase highly valued game meat. There are extensive meat-marketing systems and the monetary and exchange value of game meat is at least twice as high in Cameroon than it is in the Central African Republic or Congo. The Baka have responded to all of the changes in several ways, but they have not taken up net hunting even though farmers in the area (e.g., Fang) have nets. Baka continue to spear hunt for medium-sized game, but now also rely heavily on trap lines. Baka women do not participate in hunting nor do they adopt the use of nets in spite of the above-mentioned high monetary and exchange value of game meat.

Finally, as noted above, linguistic data suggest language affiliation may be a useful factor for understanding the distribution of net hunting in the Ituri (see Ichikawa and Terashima, chapter 11, this volume, on how language influences plant use in the Ituri). A strong, but far from perfect, relationship exists between speaking a Bantu language and net hunting. The Aka and Mbuti speak Bantu languages and both net hunt; in fact, there are several differences between Mbuti and Aka in the organization of net hunts, but only one is listed in Table 9.2: Mbuti women chase the game into the net and the men usually stay near the net and kill the game after it is trapped, while among the Aka it is just the reverse. This is listed simply to illustrate the diversity and flexibility in the types of net hunting. Efe and Baka do not speak Bantu languages and do not net hunt even though other foragers or farmers in their area use nets. The Bongo foragers of Gabon and the Gyeli foragers of Cameroon are both Bantu-speaking foragers and both utilize nets. The Bantu-speaking Bila and Budu neighbors of the Mbuti use nets, but the Sudanic-speaking Lese and Mamvu neighbors of the Efe do not use nets. The Mangbetu, who are also Sudanic speakers in northeastern Zaire, use nets and say they learned to do so from the Azande. Of the thirteen Human Relations Area Files societies located in Central Africa, five are described as actively using large nets for cooperative (men only) hunting. Four of the five societies are Bantu speakers (Fang, Ganda, Mongo, and Bemba). The Azande are the only Central African non-Bantu-speaking group in the HRAF that uses nets.

The point is that language and the socialization process associated with the acquisition of language and culture dramatically influence cultural preferences – in this case the preference to use one hunting technique rather than another. Boas pointed out long ago that emotions are intricately bound to habits or customs. For instance, individuals generally have strong emotions about what foods are edible. When I ask undergraduates if they could eat caterpillars or termites, I generally get a rather strong emotional negative response. Individuals often cannot tell you why they do or do not like things one way rather than another, but they often have strong feelings about which is better. Cultural transmission mechanisms among forest foragers are also rather conservative (Hewlett and Cavalli-Sforza 1986), which means the adoption of new hunting technologies would be difficult, especially given the recent research which shows no difference in efficiency between nets and bows. If cultural traits are not under selective pressures, then they persist. Boyd and Richerson (1985) also point out that individuals usually adopt new traits from other individuals for one of two reasons: the individual with the new trait is similar (i.e., speaks the same language, looks the same) to the individual without the trait, or the individual with the new trait is more successful. Efe children learn to bow hunt from their family members who speak the same language and Efe adults do not adopt nets because the foragers they see using them are not more successful at acquiring calories.

Ecologists have expended tremendous amounts of time and energy in attempting to understand and demonstrate how different hunting techniques are adaptive to different environments (see Vierich and Hitchcock, chapter 5, this volume). Their research is useful and significant – for instance, it has shown that net and bow hunting are equally efficient – but more consideration and systematic research is needed on the roles that cultural history, cultural transmission, and symbolic systems play in patterning people's preferences in hunting techniques (see Kent, Silberbauer, Joiris, Ichikawa and Terashima, and Barnard and Widlok, all in this volume, on the importance of symbolic systems).

Table 9.3. *Marriage, kinship, and descent*

	Efe[a]	Mbuti[b]	Baka[c]	Aka[d]
Kinship	Hawaiian	Hawaiian	Hawaiian	Hawaiian
Descent	patrilineal	patrilineal	patrilineal	patrilineal
Marriage payment	sister exchange	sister exchange	bride service	bride service
	small gifts	small gifts	small gifts	small gifts
Post-marital residence	patrilocal	patrilocal	patrilocal	patrilocal
	flexible	flexible	flexible	flexible
Polygyny rate	3.0	14.0	19.5	17.5
% Pygmy females that marry village males	common (13%)	rare	rare	rare

References:
[a] Bailey 1985; Peacock and Grinker, personal communication.
[b] Turnbull 1965b; Harako 1976; Ichikawa 1978.
[c] Vallois and Marquer 1976; Bahuchet 1992.
[d] Hewlett 1989, 1991.

The different subsistence technologies among African tropical forest foragers today may have little to do with contemporary ecological and economic conditions. Nets were adopted by foragers who associated with Bantu speakers, possibly, as Bailey and Aunger (1989) suggest, because Bantu farmers often gave and continue to give their nets to foragers to use in exchange for part of the catch. The foragers often end up keeping the nets because farmers do not net hunt much any more. Other foragers may like the nets simply as an optional hunting method, but do not want to invest the time and energy to make the large nets.

Kinship, marriage, and descent

Table 9.3 summarizes the similarities and differences between the Mbuti, Efe, Aka, and Baka in kinship, marriage, and descent patterns. These four groups are remarkably similar; all have Hawaiian kin terms, patrilineal descent, and patrilocal post-marital residence. These characteristics resemble the patterns of most farmers with whom foragers associate, so it is unclear whether the patterns existed before relations were established with farmers or whether foragers adopted these patterns from farmers and modified them in their own ways. However, beyond the surface patterns the differences between foragers and farmers are striking. Foragers' versions of Hawaiian kinship terminologies are more classificatory or generalized than are farmers'; adult foragers' ideology about patrilineages is not strong and utilization of

Figure 9.5   Aka and Baka men live in the camp of their wife for several
years before moving back to the camp of their patriclan. This Aka man
will carry the net of his in-laws as part of his bride service

patrilineages is more flexible (e.g., mother's relatives are important and
are often recognized with a specific term) and less precise than that of
farmers (e.g., adult farmers often identify 5–6 generations of patrilineal
links while foragers generally identify only 2–3 generations of patrilineal
links); post-marital residence is more flexible among foragers than
farmers as foragers frequently visit in-laws and distant relatives for long
periods. The comparative data also indicate that several of the earlier
characterizations (Turnbull 1965b) of forest forager descent as bilateral
and post-marital pattern as bilocal are incorrect. The African forest
forager bands are not organized for warfare nor do they have a strong
patrilineal ideology as Service suggests. Nonetheless, though patterns

are flexible, they do tend to practice patrilocal residence where related men hunt together.

Form of marriage payment is interesting because there are distinct western versus eastern Congo–Zaire basin patterns: in the east, Efe and Mbuti prefer sister exchange, while in the west, Aka and Baka prefer bride service (Figure 9.5). The similarities between each of the two neighboring groups suggest the following possibilities: (1) similar marriage rules between the two proximate groups (Baka and Aka or Efe and Mbuti) exist to facilitate easy intermarriage today or in the past; or, (2) in the past, before bride wealth became common, farmers and foragers in the east practiced sister exchange and farmers and foragers in the west practiced bride service. The first hypothesis suggests forest forager marriage patterns remained relatively distinct from farmers' marriage patterns. This seems reasonable in today's context because most forest farmers' marriage practices are distinct from those of foragers – i.e., farmers practice bride wealth while foragers practice bride service or sister exchange. Intermarriage between Aka and Baka or Efe and Mbuti occurs today, but it is relatively infrequent (see Ichikawa and Terashima, chapter 11, this volume).

The second hypothesis suggests foragers and farmers shared marriage patterns in the past, possibly to facilitate easier intermarriage between foragers and farmers. There is some support for this hypothesis. In the east, Lese, Mamvu, Mangbetu, and Bila say that they practiced sister exchange before colonial times and some Lese continue to use this type of marriage today (Bailey, personal communication). In the west, the Kwele, Konabembe, and Bangandou with whom the Baka associate say that bride service was a common practice in the past and that some families practice it today (Joiris, personal communication). While foragers and farmers may have shared marriage patterns in the past, there is no evidence to suggest that foragers adopted farmers' patterns rather than the reverse. The proposition that forest foragers and farmers had much closer relations in the past is consistent with Bahuchet's (1992) recent ethnolinguistic analysis of forest foragers.

There are also differences in polygyny rates and the frequency with which foragers intermarry with farmers. The Efe polygyny rate is substantially lower than that of the Mbuti, Aka, and Baka. This is apparently due in large part to the relatively high frequency with which Efe females marry Lese farmers (Bailey 1988) (see also Blackburn, Vierich and Hitchcock, and Blurton Jones *et al.*, this volume, for greater discussion of hypergyny and marriage between foragers and farmers/pastoralists). Such intermarriage always involves Efe women and Lese men, therefore there are simply fewer Efe women for Efe men to marry.

Table 9.4. *Infant care and demography*

	Efe[a]	Mbuti[b]	Baka[c]	Aka[d]
Infant care				
Women other than mother nurse infant	common	rare	rare	rare
Multiple caregiving in early infancy	very common	common	common	common
Father's role in infancy	distant	very close	close	very close
Secondary caregiver	other female	father	older sibling	father
Demography				
adult male/adult female ratio	110	88	89	80
percentage of adults	76.0	47.1	46.3	52.0
percentage of children (<15 years of age)	24.0	52.9	53.7	48.0
TFR (Total Fertility Rate)	2.6	5.5	ND	6.2
infant mortality	12.0	33.0	ND	20.0

References:
[a] Bailey 1985, 1988; Morelli 1987; Tronick *et al.* 1987; Winn *et al.* 1990.
[b] Turnbull 1965b, 1986; Ichikawa 1978.
[c] Vallois and Marquer 1976; Leonhardt, personal communication.
[d] Hewlett 1989, 1991.

Why is there more intermarriage among the Efe and Lese than between other forager and farmer groups? There are at least two possible explanations. First, Efe and Lese both have remarkably low fertility (see Table 9.4). Village men are generally not very interested in marrying forager women, but under low fertility conditions where a woman may have only one child, a village man may be willing to marry a forager woman, especially as a second wife, in order to increase his chances of having children. Also, bride price for forager women is substantially lower than that for village women. Second, Lese are the poorest farmers in the Ituri region and it is difficult for Lese men to attract women from their own or other ethnic groups; finally, Lese women often marry wealthier men from other ethnic groups, so there is a shortage of Lese women. Since Lese are marginal farmers in the area, they frequently go into the forest to trap game. Consequently the Efe and Lese share not only language and ritual, but utilization of the forest as well.

The frequency of forager–farmer intermarriage also seems to increase where foragers adopt farming and where farmers experience low fertility. In 1979 Dodd states that "in Lomie . . . 4.5% of married Baka women are married to Bantu, in Abong Mbang area the figure is 8.6% and in the Bessamena region the figure is even higher." Bessamena is about 300 km from Yaoundé, the capital of Cameroon, while Abong Mbang is 350 km and Lomie 380 km from Yaoundé. The Baka in these more densely populated areas relatively close to the capital are more likely to have started farming; most Baka live to the south and east of Lomie where intermarriage is less common. Vallois and Marquer (1976) indicate that Baka–Bantu marriage in the late 1940s was very rare. Dodd indicates that Bantu men in these areas near Yaoundé marry Baka women for their high fertility; many Bantu women are infertile because of venereal disease. Again, it is always Bantu men marrying Baka women rather than the reverse. It would be interesting to know if it is the poorer Bantu men in these towns who are marrying the Baka women.

In summary, the Efe and Baka data suggest forager–farmer marriages are most likely to occur when the following conditions exist: (a) female farmers have relatively low fertility, and (b) either farmers are very similar to foragers or foragers are very similar to farmers.

Infant care and demography

This section explores two distinguishing features of infant caregiving among African tropical forest foragers: father's involvement with infants, and multiple caregiving. These two features of infant care have recently been described by two independent research projects on two different groups of African forest foragers. As part of the Ituri Project, Edward Tronick, Gilda Morelli, and Steve Winn have worked with the Efe archers of the Ituri Forest in northeast Zaire and have identified multiple caregiving of infants as a distinguishing feature. I have worked with the Aka net hunters of the Central African Republic and have indicated that Aka fathers do more infant caregiving than fathers in any known culture. Each research project has offered explanations for the infant caregiving practices in their particular foraging population. This section examines the following question: Do all African forest foragers have these features of infant care or are they unique to these populations? Forager demography is considered in this section because I believe these factors are important for answering this question·(see Blurton Jones *et al.*, chapter 7, this volume, for an excellent discussion of relations between childcare and demography).

Multiple caregiving

Tronick, Morelli, and Winn have identified multiple caregiving as a distinguishing feature of Efe infancy (1987). The bases for this characterization of Efe include: (1) the Efe mother was often not the first to nurse her infant, and during early infancy women other than the mother nursed the infant; (2) Efe 4-month-old infants spent only 40 percent of their time with their mother; (3) Efe infants were transferred frequently – 8.3 times per hour on average for 4-month-olds; and (4) many individuals contributed to the Efe infant's care – an average of 14.2 different people cared for an infant during eight hours of observation.

Qualitative data for the three other forager groups are given in Table 9.4, but comparable quantitative data exist only for the Aka. The following Aka–Efe comparisons on multiple caregiving apply only to 4-month-olds. The Efe study included 3- and 7-week-olds as well, but comparable data for Aka do not exist.

First, consistent with the Efe data, Aka mothers receive a substantial amount of assistance with infant care while they are *in camp*: mothers provide 34–45 percent of the infants' care while individuals other than mother provide the major portion of care. Unfortunately, all observations were conducted in camp so it is not known if Efe multiple caregiving exists outside that context. Aka data on infant caregiving outside camp (i.e., on the net hunt) indicate that multiple care does not occur very frequently; almost 90 percent of the infants' care is provided by mother. Thus, extensive multiple caregiving occurs in particular contexts. Turnbull has also described extensive multiple care in camp among the Mbuti (1978:172), and recent ethnographers among the Baka have indicated a similar pattern.

Second, also consistent with the Efe study, Aka infants are frequently transferred *in the camp*. Four-month-old Aka infants are transferred 7.3 times per hour, while Efe 4-month-olds are transferred 8.3 times. But again, the context or setting substantially influences the transfer rate. While on the net hunt, which lasts six to seven hours per day while in the forest, Aka infants are transferred only twice per hour on average.

Third, somewhat like Efe, Aka are cared for by a number of different individuals during observational periods. On average, 7.0 different individuals held the Aka infant during 12-hour observation periods. This is substantially lower than the 14.2 different individuals for the Efe.

Fourth, unlike the Efe, Aka mothers are always the first to nurse their infants. Seventeen of 18 mothers who were interviewed within six months of giving birth indicated that they were the first to nurse their infant and that no other woman had ever nursed their infant. A number of them said it took a day for their milk to come in so they gave their infant water until they were able to nurse. Aka mothers did not give their infant colostrum – all the mothers reported expressing their colostrum into the fire. The women indicated they would not let another woman nurse their infant because she might pass along *ekila* through her milk. The illness is characterized by convulsions and is attributed to eating taboo foods. The one mother who did report letting another woman nurse her newborn indicated that she did so because it took one week for her milk to come in. The interview data are consistent with the observation data: at no time did a woman other than the mother nurse an infant. In contrast, Efe mothers were never the first to touch or hold their infants. Usually an older female-in-law cleaned the infant and took it to the hut until the mother arrived (Aka women give birth outside of camp). Ethnographic descriptions of Baka and Mbuti are consistent with the Aka pattern in that only mothers are reported nursing their infants.

Why do the Efe appear to have an especially pervasive multiple caregiving pattern, as is demonstrated by the frequent occurrence of women other than mother nursing infants and the number of different caregivers per infant? Tronick *et al.* indicate that Efe multiple caregiving functions to meet the infant's biological demands for fluids and energy supplies as well as the cultural demands to develop cooperation, sharing, and group identification. Some of the problems with their hypothesis have been discussed elsewhere (Hewlett 1989). Only a few points will be mentioned here: (1) Aka birthweights are similar to Efe birthweights so the biological demands are similar, but multiple caregiving is different; (2) cooperation is especially important for Aka because women, men, and children regularly participate together on the net hunt, but the pervasiveness of Aka multiple care is less than that of the Efe; and (3) mothers in other foraging groups (e.g., !Kung) do not receive as much assistance with infant care as do Efe mothers, yet they are equally cooperative, or more so.

An alternative hypothesis may be that Efe multiple caregiving is more of a response to unique demographic patterns: 47 percent of postmenopausal women have had either no live births or only one (Peacock 1985) and children constitute only one-fourth to one-third of the population (Bailey and Peacock 1988). Peacock (1985) indicates that women without dependent children spend about 6 percent of their time in child care (compared to 16 percent of time for mothers with dependent children). This means that nearly half of the Efe adult females in camp are available and active in child care. In contrast, all of the other forest foragers have relatively high fertility, which means that most females in camp usually have a nursing infant and would have a difficult time helping out another woman regardless of the cultural values of sharing and cooperation. Table 9.4 summarizes some infant care and demographic features of the Efe.

While Efe multiple care is distinctive in some ways, multiple caregiving does appear to be a common feature of tropical forest forager socialization. Another demographic factor may contribute to this tendency: the density or compactness of settlement. Forager settlements are very compact and usually have three to nine households living within a 10–15-meter radius; by comparison only one or two farmer households would occupy the same area. As a result, forager camps are essentially open public places, and the infant and mother are exposed to all camp members, while village farmers' homes are relatively private. Thus, alternative caregivers are more available to and familiar with the forager infants than are the alternative caregivers in farmers' houses.

But why is multiple caregiving among forest foragers most likely to happen in the camp setting and why are there differences in who usually provides the assistance to mothers? While in camp, a woman's workload increases dramatically – women are responsible for food preparation, cleaning and repairing the hut, and the collection of firewood and water – while the workload of men and children usually decreases. Women need help with infant care while they do tasks; the camp's men and older children are sitting around or playing outside the huts and are generally available to help out. Table 9.4 indicates that, among the Mbuti and Aka, father is most likely to help out mother, while among the Efe and

Baka the older daughter or another female usually assists mother. Several factors are important for understanding who assists a mother. First, cultural precedents tend to be established during subsistence activity (see Blackburn, chapter 8, this volume, for a discussion of a similar concept – cultural assumption). Among the Efe and Baka, an adult or juvenile female often assists the mother with infant care while she works in villager fields (the primary subsistence activity of Efe and Baka women), and consequently a cultural precedent is established for infant care in other contexts or settings – i.e., the older female is likely to assist mother with infant care in camps, at dances, ceremonies, etc. Among the Aka and Mbuti, the father assists the mother with infant care on the net hunt because an older sibling cannot carry infants for long distances. Consequently, among the Aka and Mbuti, a cultural precedent is established for fathers' assistance, so they are more likely to help out with infant care in camp or other settings. I have also described elsewhere (Hewlett 1991) how extraordinarily close are husband–wife relations among the Aka, due in large part to the cooperative nature of the net hunt, and that closeness contributes to the increased role of father with infants. A biological factor should also be considered in understanding multiple care among forest foragers – the mother generally receives assistance from individuals who are genetically related to the infant – be it father, older sibling, grandmother, mother's sister, etc.

Intracultural variation in multiple care

In a separate paper, the Ituri researchers examined intracultural variability in Efe infant caretaking practices (Winn *et al.* 1989). They found that:
1 Fussier infants spent more time with mother.
2 Fussier infants had fewer caretakers.
3 Efe infants in larger groups were likely to spend less time with their mothers, were transferred more often, and encountered a greater number of different caretakers.
The researchers use (1) and (2) above to support Brazelton's (1972) contentions that a culture's practices and beliefs are partly shaped by the behavior of its infants, while (3) is given as an example of how variability within a culture can influence infant caregiving.

Aka data tend to support (1) and (2), but not (3). Fussy (more than five fusses per hour) infants spent about 15 percent more of their time with mother and averaged 1.6 fewer caregivers (4.0 versus 5.6) than those who are not fussy (63.4 percent versus 49.2 percent). These data seem reasonable since both Efe and Aka mothers are the primary caretakers and mothers know their infants better than anyone else. Also, non-mothers may not want to hold fussy infants. But why do some infants fuss more than others? Aka infants often fuss to nurse, so those who are fussy may simply be hungrier or prefer to nurse more frequently. Also, they often fussed because they were under the care of another child or adolescent who played roughly with them. Fussier infants may simply be those who have less experienced alternative caretakers.

Group size among the Aka was not significantly related to multiple caregiving. Again, this may be a consequence of differences between Aka and Efe demographic patterns. It does not make a difference if Aka group size is 15 or 40, as most Aka women have an infant or small child to care for and are often unable to help out other women. Also, Aka fathers are usually helping out with their own infants or children. Among the Efe an increase in camp size means there are more women without infants to help out.

Fathers' role in infant care

In a recent study of Aka Pygmies of the Central African Republic, I found that Aka fathers provided an extraordinary (by cross-cultural standards) amount of direct care for young infants (Hewlett 1991). Specifically, Aka fathers: (1) were holding or were within an arm's reach of their infant 51 percent of a 24-hour period; (2) did 22 percent of the caregiving of 4-month-old infants in the camp setting; (3) were the second most active care givers (mother being the primary care giver); (4) provided most of their caregiving in the camp context and the least during the net hunt; and (5) were characterized by their intimate, affectionate, and helping-out style of caretaking, rather than by its playfulness.

Is intimate fathering a characteristic of all forest foragers or is it specific to Aka? The only comparable quantitative data come from Steve Winn's behavioral observations of Efe 4-month-olds in the camp setting. His data indicate that Efe fathers do significantly less caregiving than Aka fathers; Efe fathers hold their infants 2.6 percent of the time in the camp setting by comparison to 22 percent of the time for the Aka fathers (Winn, personal communication). Efe fathers are also not the secondary or even tertiary caregivers of their infants; several other females (older siblings, grandmother, mother's sister) provide more care (Peacock 1985). Winn subjectively describes Efe fathers as inactive, passively engaged in care-giving, and generally uncomfortable with infants; also, they seldom solicit infants. Efe fathers do not appear to be intimately familiar or affectionate with their infants or to be especially attached to them.

Winn's descriptions of Efe fathers are consistent with those provided by Bailey (1985) and Turnbull (1965b). Bailey found that men actively engaged in child care only 0.7 percent (about five minutes per day) of the daylight hours, but explained the low percentage as a consequence of only two of his 16 focal males having a child under the age of 4. Efe low fertility influenced this average childcare percentage. Bailey also indicated that "strong father–child attachments among Efe were uncommon. While fathers took on the responsibility of disciplining their children, they were no more likely to take care of their children than most other men in camp." This points to another distinction between Aka and Efe. Aka fathers seldom discipline the child – it is usually the mother who does the disciplining – while among the Efe the father contributes substantially.

Turnbull first identified net hunter–archer distinctions in father's role over twenty years ago. He states: "There is not only greater parity between the sexes among the net hunters, but the father enters more fully into family life than among the archers . . . The [net hunting] men are good fathers and, contrary to Schebesta's assertion for the archers, take pleasure in looking after their children" (1965b:232, 245).

While Efe fathers are not as involved in infant care as the Aka, Efe infants receive considerable care from several different males (Morelli 1987). Aka male care comes almost exclusively from fathers.

If one considers existing hypotheses for predicting the level of father involvement in human populations (Katz and Konner 1981), one would expect Efe fathers to be more involved with infant care than Aka fathers. Efe women contribute more calories to the diet than do Aka females (see Table 9.2), the polygyny rate is much lower among Efe, and the adult sex ratio indicates there are many more Efe adult males available to help out with child care than there are Aka males (see Table 9.4). The first two characteristics have been identified as critical variables in predicting high father proximity (Katz and Kooner 1981). Existing models for understanding the degree of father involvement would predict that Efe fathers should provide more caregiving than Aka fathers. Just the reverse is true because Aka practice a subsistence activity where men, women, and children participate together on a regular basis. This subsistence pattern has implications for husband–wife relations and consequent parent–infant relations – women with infants have to walk far and need the help of another adult caretaker, and since fathers are often selected to help out, they become intimately familiar with and attached to their infants (Hewlett 1991).

Table 9.5. *Efe intracultural variability in father holding (after Winn, personal communication)*

Variable	n	Mean % time father holding
Number of father's brothers		
none or one	5	1.3
two or more	2	6.7
Infant birth order		
Firstborn	4	5.4
Later born	3	4.0
Age of father		
Under 30	4	5.4
Over 30	4	4.0
Sex of infant		
Female	3	7.1
Male	4	3.3

Intracultural variability in father's role

In comparison of Aka fathers who held their infant frequently with fathers who seldom held their infant, a generalized pattern of traits emerged. High-investment Aka fathers tended to have the following traits: no brothers, few relatives in general, wife from a distant clan, married relatively late in life, monogamous, a small hunting net, more reliance on individual hunting techniques (i.e., small traps), a close relationship with Ngandu villagers, and a family with no particular status (neither he nor his father held a position as leader, great elephant hunter, or healer). Aka fathers who seldom held their infant tended to have the opposite characteristics (Hewlett 1988). When a number of variables for predicting intracultural variability are considered, the data suggested that the higher-status fathers, that is those with more "kinship resources" (brothers), invested the least time in the direct care of their infants; a high-status male is one who has many brothers, two wives, and a father who was a leader, elephant hunter, or healer.

Steven Winn was very generous in sharing some unpublished preliminary data on Efe fathers so that I might examine Efe intracultural variability. As Table 9.5 indicates, the number of brothers a father has is also very useful for predicting the level of Efe father investment. One Efe father was especially active – he held his infant 19 percent of the time. Steve Winn indicates that the reason this father was so involved was that he had no living relatives in camp and his wife was not known to the group (i.e., he had few "kinship resources"). Winn's preliminary data indicate another distinction between Aka and Efe – the little time Efe fathers do spend with infants is preferentially biased toward daughters.

Summarizing, Aka fathers do significantly more infant caretaking than Efe fathers because of differences in subsistence activity. Also, like multiple caretaking, the setting dramatically influences the degree of father involvement – fathers are more likely to help out in the camp than in the forest.

Also, both Efe and Aka intracultural variation in father's role is related to resources – men will spend more time with their infant when they have fewer resources to offer. In another paper that examines father's role cross-culturally (Hewlett 1988), I find that this variable is useful in predicting intercultural variation as well. Men in societies in which men accumulate essential resources (e.g., land or cattle), or contribute the majority of calories to the diet, spend significantly less time in the direct care of infants and children than do men in societies where the reverse is true.

Conclusions

This chapter has described some of the diversity and commonalities among African forest foragers and has offered preliminary hypotheses to explain the diversity. The chapter focused on the following aspects of culture: language; subsistence and settlement; kinship and marriage; and infancy and demography. Three general patterns of similarities and differences emerge.

First, there is an eastern (Efe and Mbuti) versus western (Baka and Aka) pattern. Western groups associate with a greater diversity of ethnolinguistic groups of farmers, generally speak a language not familiar to their farming neighbors, and practice similar marriage patterns (i.e., bride service or sister exchange). The eastern groups associate with fewer horticulturalist ethnolinguistic groups, generally speak the same language as their neighbors, or one that is similar, and practice sister exchange rather than bride service. The eastern groups are also genetically distinct from the western groups, which suggests eastern and western groups have been independent groups for at least thousands of years (Cavalli-Sforza 1986).

Second, there is a subsistence-linguistic pattern. Eastern and western groups are over 500 miles apart and have been separate groups for a long time, but there are more similarities between some groups from the east and west than there are within the eastern and western groups as a whole. Aka (western group) and Mbuti (eastern group) are both net hunters and speak Bantu languages, while the Efe (eastern group) are archers and the Baka (western group) are spear hunters; both speak non-Bantu languages. Aka and Mbuti net hunting is distinct from Efe and Baka bow or spear hunting in several ways: net hunting takes them further into the forest for longer periods of time and involves the participation of women and children; it lasts more hours each day and occurs more days of the week; it involves making as much noise as possible rather than being quiet and stalking animals. The differences in subsistence activities reflect differences in several other aspects of culture: Mbuti and Aka eat more game meat, spend less time in the village, establish camps further in the forest, rely less on women for getting starch for caloric intake, eat less fish and shellfish collected by women, have fathers more involved in infant and child care, and have closer husband–wife relations and greater sexual equality (i.e., less violence against women).

Finally, the Efe are unique in several ways. Efe (1) speak a language from a totally different language phylum, (2) have markedly lower fertility and mortality, (3) intermarry with farmers more frequently, (4) have substantially more adults in camp than children, (5) have more extensive multiple caregiving, and (6) have relatively low father involvement.

While there are commonalities between African tropical forest foragers, this chapter has emphasized the patterns of diversity. In doing so, it has perhaps contributed to a better understanding of those diversities and also made it clear that it is difficult if not impossible to refer to an African "Pygmy" culture.

Acknowledgments

I would like to acknowledge gratefully the useful comments and suggestions made by Robert Bailey, Serge Bahuchet, Nick Blurton Jones, Daou Veronique Joiris, Mitsuo Ichikawa, Robert Moise, Robert Aunger, and Sue Kent on earlier drafts of this chapter.

10   A comparative approach to hunting rituals among Baka Pygmies (southeastern Cameroon)

Daou V. Joiris

1   Introduction

Integrating research on ritual practices in Pygmy societies within the larger debate about hunter-gatherer diversity is no easy task. While environmental and economic studies make it possible to compare modes of adaptation of the many groups of forest foragers, information is limited in all other areas of study. Those publications that mention the ritual aspect of social life are generally monographs or contributions to dictionaries and encyclopedias, whose sources are most often legends and song-story collections. Currently, studies of cosmogony and ritual practices are limited to three ethnic groups: the Zairian Mbuti (Schebesta 1952; Turnbull 1961, 1965a), the Aka from the Central African Republic (Bahuchet 1985; Motte 1980, 1982) and the Cameroonian Baka (Brisson and Boursier 1979; Brisson 1981–4, 1988; Higgins n.d. a, b, c; Dodd 1979, 1980; and Kilian Hatz 1989). The problems are compounded by the fact that the studies that do exist are often designed around particular anthropological theories. Thus, within the evolutionist, functionalist, and cultural ecological perspectives, available ethnographic data reveal more about the proponents' preoccupations than about similarities and diversity among Pygmies.

A second kind of problem arises from intracultural variability, which complicates the research process. Research data from one group tend to be taken as a standard for all groups until proved invalid. Sometimes such diversity can go unnoticed for a long time. For instance, my interest in the following comparative study developed when it became obvious that an important cynegetic ceremony, the *yeli*, as described in literature on the Baka (notably by Higgins and Dodd), was not observed in the Baka camps where I conducted my investigations. My observations further indicated that aspects of the hunt ceremony were prepared differently, and that the diverse rituals I observed were longstanding. Because data for comparison are limited, it is difficult to make definitive comments about such diversity. However, my hypothesis is that there is pronounced intracultural variability among the Baka. Past research on the Aka, who populate an extremely large area in the Central African Republic and Northern Congo, indicates that their ritual practices also vary from one region to another (Bahuchet 1985:428–9; 1989). This diversity is linked to the fact that each of these societies is regularly exposed to non-Pygmy societies. The Baka and Aka alone are in contact with about thirty non-Pygmy ethnic groups (Bahuchet 1989:50). Considering the frequency of such contact, behavioral osmosis has undoubtedly occurred. The diversity among non-Pygmy groups would naturally produce further intracultural diversity among the Aka and the Baka.

A third problem for comprehensive research is that these are acephalous forest societies, characterized by organizational mobility and fluidity. Practices within groups consequently evolve continually and independently of other groups. Indeed, entire ritual practices may die out with a generation. Thus it becomes vital to understand the similarities and the differences in order to discover what cultural impetus lies behind behavior, rather than simply noting the behavior itself or assuming that all groups are basically the same.

These three factors – intracultural variability, inter-ethnic contacts and exchange, and organizational fluidity – are certainly not limited to religion. Nonetheless, they seem to present greater difficulties for researching aspects of religion because rituals are not easily observed in hunter-gatherer societies. For instance, hereditary ritual figures are often missing and there is no ancestor worship. In addition, there exists a plethora of private rites, which are both difficult to observe and difficult to categorize. There is also no regular schedule for ceremonies; one not performed for years may suddenly be organized repeatedly in a short period of time.

In spite of the problems, the best way to establish a foundation for further study is by focusing on a single aspect of a society at a time and building up a more comprehensive picture gradually. Thus this study begins with the specifics of a small part of the ritual life of the Baka groups of southern Cameroon.

The following intracultural comparative analysis of hunting rites finds its inspiration in Barnard's (1988, 1992a, 1992b) writings about Khoisan religion. The working hypothesis aims at underlying common factors in the religious system that are not apparent in regional variants. The analysis attempts to take into account intracultural variability as well as organizational fluidity. My objective is to reveal that certain ritual associations between individuals underpin social organization and perpetuate it, thereby contributing to the evolution of certain funda-

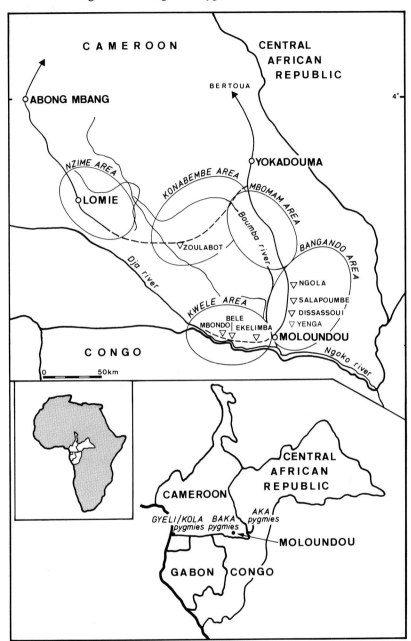

Figure 10.1   The Baka land and designated sub-cultural areas

mental philosophical Baka concepts that, in turn, reflect the diversity and similarities in this Pygmy culture.

After describing the ritual associations and the leaders, I shall present a comparative description of hunting ceremonies practiced in different parts of the region; these include the methods of determining in which direction hunters should look for game and who will make the kill (before the hunt), the attraction of game (during the hunt), and the thank-offerings to the spirits (after the hunt).

The environment and social context

Baka Pygmies from southern Cameroon constitute a linguistic and cultural entity that is distinct from other Pygmy ethnic groups in western parts of the Congo basin. They speak an Oubanguian language. The other Pygmy groups of this area speak varieties of Bantu language.[1]

In spite of language differences, Baka Pygmy cultural, economic, and social patterns do resemble those of the Aka Pygmies (Central African Republic, northern Congo) and they share common origins as attested by recent ethnolinguistic research (Bahuchet 1989). The rites of the Aka therefore make an interesting contrast to the hunting practices described below.

The Baka population totals between 30,000 and 40,000 persons according to surveys (Ndii 1968; Oko Mengue 1977). After a process of sedentarization began in the 1950s (Althabe 1965), the Baka settled near non-Pygmy populations with whom they have since maintained economic and ritual relationships. Baka permanent camps of between thirty and a hundred people (Althabe 1965; Vallois and Marquer 1976; Joiris, personal observations) are located close to trails in the vicinity of villages inhabited principally by the Nzime and Konabembe in the north, the Mbomam and Bangando in the east, and the Kwele in the far south near the Congolese border (see Figure 10.1). My investigations took place among groups in permanent settlements in contact with the Kwele, the Konabembe, the Bangando, and the Mbomam (1986–91). "Regional areas" and "cultural sub-areas" correspond here to what the Baka consider the boundaries between non-Pygmy groups.

[1] The Gyeli from southwestern Cameroon speak an A80 Bantu language, the Bongo from Gabon a B70 Bantu language while the Aka from the Central African Republic and the Popular Republic of Congo employ a C10 Bantu language.

2   Organizational principles of hunt ceremonies

Ritual associations

Public ceremonies are organized by groups of people or "ritual associations," who share a link with certain spirits. The ceremonies, or "dances," that these groups organize are known by the name of the "dances." Thus *yeli* refers to the ritual association, the ceremonies it organizes, and the spirits with whom it is associated. When a member of a ritual association dies, that person's spirit remains connected with the group. For the purposes of this chapter, "ritual association" will apply only to a group that organizes ceremonies. "Ceremony" will apply to the entire organized events, which may be subdivided into several sections, here called "dances." The leaders of ritual associations and of ceremonies will, unless otherwise stated, be *nganga* (or main/specialized initiates), while all other members of the ritual association will be known as "initiates."

The Baka have a total of some twenty ritual associations;[2] there are up to half a dozen in every Baka camp. It is possible within one or two generations for new ritual associations to be created or for others to disappear. Consequently, at any one time, the groups include some very old ritual associations and some that have been introduced recently. The ceremony leader may use his own expertise to give a personal touch to the rites he performs.

Each camp may focus on different rituals at different times. For example, the Bele and Mbondo camp people (in the Kwele region, see Figure 10.1) included four ritual associations: *abale*, *ebuma*, *yenga poto*, and *jengi*. The Salapoumbe camp (in the Bangando region) included at least five ritual associations: *abale*, *ebuma*, *sonjo*, *yeli*, and *jengi*. These two groups comprise the focus of the following discussion.

The female *yeli* ritual association is the only one primarily associated with large-game hunting, especially elephant. Other ritual associations are generally multifunctional. For instance, the *abale* ritual association framework involves the use of ritual substances to cure illnesses or to initiate a divining-medium session to identify sources of evil or to locate game. This ritual association is old and includes both male and female initiates in the Baka group I studied. The *yenga poto* ritual association fulfills similar functions; including only female initiates, it has been

---

[2] The list of associations, which comes mainly from Brisson's and Boursier's dictionary (1979), is of great interest and merits being updated following future investigations into regional variants.

observed only in the Kwele region camps, where it apparently began
around 1970. *Ebuma* ceremonies are very widespread as mourning
dances (Brisson and Boursier 1979; Higgins 1981; Joiris, personal observations),[3] but they also include ritual manipulations of a hunting char-
acter in which male and female initiates participate. The old and very
widespread masculine *jengi* ritual association is indirectly concerned
with hunting, although its main function is to establish protection
towards the forest and to contribute to the preservation of peace and
harmony in the community.[4] It does so by acting against witchcraft and
social conflict. The sixth ritual association, called *sonjo*, was remembered by only a few elderly initiates. It is closely associated with
witchcraft. Last, *nabula* is a secret ritual restricted to master-hunter
initiates (who have visionary power) as a secret ritual institution.

Hunting ceremonies are not identical from one subcultural area to the
next, and can differ from one camp to the next. At the Bele-Mbondo
camps (Kwele area), the ritual associations involved with hunting ceremonies are *yenga poto*, *abale* (or *nganga*), and *ebuma*; in the other sample
camp, Salapoumbe-Ndongo from the Bangando-Mbomam region,
hunting preparation involves *yeli* and *abale* (or *nganga*) ritual associations. Hunting rites, which constitute a major dimension of these four
ritual associations, are part of other ritual systems. For instance, the
jengi ritual association and the *nabula* master-hunter initiates do not
organize hunting ceremonies as such, but their ritual powers contribute
to the success of the organized hunting ceremonies and therefore of the
hunt itself.

There is a great diversity in the performance of "dances" and the
general organization of these ceremonies by ritual associations. Generally, however, they all include activities before, during, and after the
hunt. Some rites may be practiced simultaneously or in sequence within
the space of a few days. Four or five complementary or sequential ritual
systems coexist in this manner; each is regarded as a part of a harmonious whole and is not in competition to establish authority over the hunt.

Among the ritual associations mentioned above, the following categories can be established (see table 10.1):

---

[3] From the data I have gathered thus far it appears that it is not exactly a mourning dance
but rather the overall organization of a dance to honor the initiates after they have passed
away. A number of dances (*abale*, *yenga poto*, etc.) are performed in succession during
the mourning ceremonies. It can be hypothesized that there are many *ebuma* initiates
because the *ebuma* dance is often performed in these mourning ceremonies.

[4] The *jengi* ritual association corresponds to the *ezengi* Aka dance. *Ezengi* seems to be less
sacralized in the Aka framework. According to Bahuchet (1989:459), this spirit must
have been a part of the ritual and symbolic corpus of an old civilization to which
ancestors of the present Baka and Aka belonged.

Table 10.1. *Gender and ritual association categories surrounding the hunt in the Bangando-Mbomam region and Kwele-Konabembe region*

Ritual association quite similar in every camp	Bangando-Mbomam region	Kwele-Konabembe region
Abale	Male/female	Male/female
Jengi	Only male	Only male
Nabula (?)	Only male	Only male

Ritual association only performed in certain camps	Bangando-Mbomam region	Kwele-Konabembe region
Yeli	Only female	—
Yenga poto	—	Only female
Ebuma	—	Male/female

(a) those that are quite similar in every camp (same name, same kind of ritual practice, same function). This is the case for the *jengi* and *abale* ritual associations and may be the case for *nabula*;

(b) those that are performed only in certain camps. This second category includes intrinsically original and regional ritual associations.

During a public ceremony, all camp members may participate minimally by observing and singing. Those who manifest natural tendencies towards ritual substances or the interpretation of dreams (or other related spiritual awareness) undergo an apprenticeship to become specialized ritual agents. Children as young as 12 or 14 years who demonstrate singing and dancing aptitudes may be integrated into a ritual association after an informal rite, and thus become initiates. Generally, the initiation-apprenticeship[5] is informal; however, the Baka practice more formal initiation rites as well. For example, there is the masculine ritual association of the *jengi* that involves a rite of passage for a group of prospective initiates.

The main initiates, or nganga

Camp members participate in rituals at several levels but those who become skillful may become *nganga*. The main initiates, or *nganga*, are ritual agents whose responsibilities are broader than those of the diviner-healers presented in literature on the Baka (Brisson and Bour-

---

[5] According to the expression "initiation-apprentissage" used by Bahuchet (1985:442) for the Aka Pygmies.

sier 1979:335). They have a variety of functions besides those associated with healing and the hunt, including practicing various methods of divination such as interpreting smoke and reading fire. They also practice oneiromancy.

Nganga may be individuals of either gender; marriage partners frequently practice their skills together, although they perform different roles. The percentage of *nganga* to population varies but is important to the residents' well-being. Hence, a camp with a population of one hundred may have up to a dozen *nganga*.[6]

The term *nganga*, used by the Baka, is also common in Bantu languages.[7] However, in the Baka Oubanguian language, the word resembles that for ritual associations in that it designates several different things. Thus *nganga* refers to the ritual agent (main/specialized initiate or leader), ritual power, ritual association (the *nganga* ritual association being equivalent to the *abale* one), as well as the dancing performance (in the *nganga* ritual association framework).

Nganga are the beneficial agents who may also act as sorcerers and witches (*wa-mbu*). This concept of the *nganga* is similar to that found throughout the Bantu world. The Baka distinguish those *nganga* who have become witches willingly and those who have done so unwillingly. An inadvertent misuse of a ritual substance could result in someone becoming an unwilling witch by spilling human blood instead of animal blood. Willing witches may perform witchcraft for a long period of time. On the other hand, *nganga* who are sorcerers are affiliated to *wa-mbu* sorcerer ritual associations such as that of the *sonjo*.[8]

Through their connections to the spirit world, *nganga* acquire a wealth of personal secrets. The most competent are called old initiates (*di-nganga*) and the least experienced are young initiates (*le-nganga*). Main initiates develop a network of privileged relationships with the

[6] This subject is being developed in my dissertation.
[7] The *n-*gàngà* proto-Bantu radical designates the magic protective agent (de Heusch 1971:180).
[8] According to Evans-Pritchard's classification (1937), Baka "willing *wa-mbu*" seems to be a witch even if he/she willingly performs witchcraft for a long period of time; see also Sevy (1960) and Motte (1980). In his article on Baka conflict resolution, Dodd (1980) makes reference to factors other than that of dispersion (meaning a "process of flux as conflict resolution"), which is often mentioned in literature about Pygmy societies, particularly by Turnbull (1968:135). Dodd underscores most notably the religious factor. It appears, however, that he opts to ignore the practices of witchcraft and sorcery because such practices might be regarded as a recent borrowing from farmer/villager ethnicities. While the confines of this chapter do not allow a more detailed analysis of these questions, it is important to emphasize that the increasing sedentarization dates only from the 1950s and that the ambiguity surrounding the *nganga* personality attests to a very widespread practice of witchcraft and sorcery within the Baka religious system.

game spirits who, as in many other hunting societies,[9] are said to walk side by side with the game and thereby guide the hunters.

The power of the *nganga* and the respect accorded to them confer a political status which allows them to act as informal leaders (headmen and headwomen), maintaining harmony. They also give access to the forest world.

The guardianship of spirits

In most cases, Baka initiates or *nganga* share with their spouses the privileged relationship they enjoy with particular spirits; relationships are determined by membership in a particular ritual association. If the original ritual association is masculine, the husband will be the holder of the most important secrets (ritual substances or medicines), while sharing some with his wife; conversely, if the original association is feminine, the wife retains most of the secrets.

The *nganga* couple designated by the ritual status of spirit (*me*) guardians (*mo-me*), lead ceremonies organized by their ritual association. The wife leads the polyphonic "yodels" and the husband performs the rites (dancing, fire-divining, or other performances according to which ceremony is being performed) in the center of the camp. Many ritual associations are composed of at least one couple of *nganga* "specialists" initiates and a number of "minor" initiates. The "real" *nganga* are spirit guardians while the "minor" initiates are not spirit guardians. The real *nganga* progressively initiate followers, some of whom will in turn become real *nganga*, either through inheriting the guardianship of the spirits or through exchanging it for a close relative's life.[10]

Nganga spirit guardians are divided into different categories of ritual agents who maintain relationships with corresponding classes of spirits, as defined by ritual association. For instance, the lineage chief, or *kobo*, is often a former elephant hunter and is always the guardian of spirits from the *jengi* class. The *kobo* is therefore a *nganga* spirit guardian. He is less of a "chief" or headman than a camp (*bala*) guardian (*mo-bala*) (Dodd 1980) and uses his *nganga* or his master-hunter influence to act as a peacemaker. He keeps peace amongst the living as well as between the living and the spirits of the deceased, all within the general framework of maintaining harmony with the forest.

---

[9] The South American Ashuars are an example (Descola 1986).

[10] This type of widespread transaction is similar to that practiced by, for example, the Mbolia (de Heusch 1971:174), which is a clear example of sorcery. This recalls the ambiguity surrounding the *nganga* personality and highlights the relevance of considering the two categories of "witchcraft" and "sorcery" in Baka society.

Within a single camp there are sometimes several *nganga* presiding over one and the same ritual association, but in such cases only one couple officiates at a time. The absence of *nganga*, who often leave for extended visits like any other camp member, is no hindrance to the performance of rituals. Able initiates are always available to perform a ceremony.

Moreover, there is so much overlapping within the ritual and political spheres that it results in a selective sharing of responsibilities, a multiplicity of male and female actors, and an organization that is most notable for being flexible and fluid. Much of this is no doubt an extended expression of the individual mobility evident in the common practice of visiting; some visits between members of different camps are lengthy, a practice which modifies the sedentarization of the population.

Supralocal co-guardianship networks

Each permanent camp established along the track maintains special relationships with other permanent camps. Like the Aka who "travel great distances to visit relatives" (Hewlett *et al.* 1982:427), the Baka maintain regular contacts with others who may be very far away in a different subcultural area. These relationships, which exist within the framework of what could be called the regional band, are established through matrimonial links; they generally share economic, social, and religious structures. Large gatherings of such far-flung families are common. The result is a similar flexibility to that of the Efe Pygmies (Harako 1976:47–8): the band is gathered together while settled near the villages and is fragmented during the forest trips. This type of mobility offsets the isolation that can be associated with sedentary life.

The regional band of the Baka consists, then, of a set of permanent camps situated near different villages, but without any formal structure of relationships. Rather, various visits frequently take place between families. While visitors are in another camp, they become completely integrated into its social structure. No doubt behavior patterns are often introduced from one camp to another in this way, then are modified to suit the new system.

Camps of a regional band are often linked not only by family ties but also through co-guardianship of the tutelary spirits of the dead. This is a strong cohesive factor that stems from the familial ties, since families often share a ritual association membership linked to particular spirits. For example, the Bele camp share the guardianship of the *jengi* category of spirits with the Mbondo, Ekelimba (Kwele area), Yenga (Bangando area), and Zoulabot (Konabembe area) camps (Figure 10.2). In each

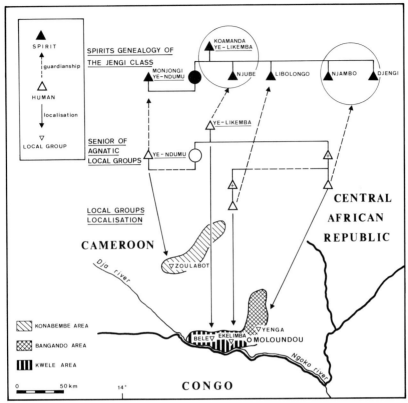

Figure 10.2   Sample of a regional band (set of Bele, Ekelimba, Yenga
and Zoulabot permanent camps or local bands) sharing the guardianship of a genealogy of the *jengi* class spirits

camp, the *jengi* spirits are guarded by the lineage headman or camp
guardian *kobo*. As shown in Figure 10.2, the *kobo* lineage chiefs are
related to each other and usually belong to the same patrilinear group or
ye-.[11] They perform rites together. Ritual relationships are usually
maintained with spirits of the same patrilinear group.

[11] The Baka kinship system is patrilinear, at least in the way Baka transmit their clan
identity, which is a kind of exogamous emblematic group called *ye-*. The nucleus of
each camp consists of the descendants of one lineage or segment of a lineage and
belongs mainly to a given *ye-*, whereas the wives and husbands of the nucleus and most
camp initiates are attached to other *ye-*. About ten *ye-* are thus represented in the camps
(Vallois and Marquer 1976:120–1; and Joiris, personal observations), they bear the
names of animals, plants, or objects to which dietary or behavioral prohibition is often
related. The composition of the local group is independent of the clan and we can find
people belonging to different clans. The residence rule is either virolocal or uxorilocal

Thus Figure 10.2 should be read on three levels: the first represents the geographical location of permanent camps for local bands which make up the regional band; the second reveals the family links which exist between *kobo* lineage chiefs and the permanent camps; the third level depicts the spirits with whom lineage chiefs maintain special ritual relations.

The permanence of the very old ritual associations of *jengi* has facilitated investigation into how the exchange network of ideas and behavior functions between camps that are very far apart. The data referring to more ephemeral ritual associations, varying from one camp to the next, are less complete,[12] but are sufficient to put forward the hypothesis that bonds between camps are founded upon the co-guardianship of spirits. The genealogy of these spirits spreads geographically in accordance with the places where their ritual guardians live and travel. It seems that certain camps become part of different regional bands, depending on the class of spirits they guard.

The game spirits

The tutelary spirits called *me* (generic term) are anthropomorphic figures. They are of human, not animal, origin and therefore are not animal spirits. Animal spirits, as such, do not exist. Game do have a *molili* 'shadow" similar to that of humans but, at the time of death, no spirits emanate from the animal. Only initiates and members of their family metamorphose into game spirits. Contrary to what Dodd wrote on the subject (in Woodburn 1982), the concept of metamorphosis into

and every marital combination is possible with monogamous and polygamous families. The Baka kinship system needs to be analyzed further and is being addressed in my dissertation.

[12] The *nganga* are more difficult to identify than the *kobo*, not only because of the ephemeral quality of these ritual associations but also because they are very discreet in everyday life, and because the initiatory power somehow protects them. It is necessary to have the opportunity of witnessing the ritual performances of every dance in order to start investigation. For such opportunities to arise, given the abundance and mobility of *nganga*, the observer needs to be present over long periods of time. In a given camp, there may be ritual associations which do not organize ceremonies for months or even years. Ceremonies seem to come in waves: one ceremony which takes place may stimulate the organization of another. In 1987, a *nganga* and his wife traveled 100 kilometers from their camp in Zoulabot to Bele, where they stayed for several months. The *nganga* organized a number of fire-"divining" ceremonies (*abale*) at which all the Bele and Mbondo inhabitants were present. It seems the *nganga* transmitted the guardianship of one of his *me* to the Bele *kobo*'s sister's husband. When the *nganga* and his wife left, no ceremony was organized for the next two years (or perhaps I never had the opportunity of witnessing it), although the camp's ritual activity was intense and dances took place at least every third day.

spirits at the time of death is widespread, although it chiefly concerns very specific initiates and some of their relatives.

The element being metamorphosed is primarily the initiate's *molili* or "shadow." While "shadow" is used in the literature on the Baka, the term "reflection" seems more appropriate. *Molili* corresponds to a miniature "shadow" residing in the eye, like the reflection of a person in the pupil of another. Dodd (in Woodburn 1982:195) defines it as "the light in . . . [the person's] eye . . . perhaps best translated as his vitality or his essence." The word *molili*, which has an Oubanguian root, means "dream" (Bahuchet 1990:459); it alludes to the appearance of spirits in dreams. This visual experience shared by game spirits and a specialized initiate is reminiscent of some Amerindian, Siberian, or !Kung Bushman societies (Marshall 1969; Rouget 1990; de la fête à l'extase 1986; de Heusch 1971).

The *jengi* and *nabula* initiates are different in some respects from other initiates in that their power, *ndambu* (located in a person's intestines), and not their *molili* "shadow," is transformed into spirit. According-ing to the Brisson and Boursier dictionary (1979:314), *ndambu* is also a ritual substance which helps in the struggle against sorcerers.

Thus, at the time of death, the *yeli, abale, ebuma, yenga poto, jengi* (and *nabula*) ritual association initiates (and their relatives) are transformed into spirits belonging to the particular classes of spirits that are involved in those ritual associations. These various categories of *me* spirits (*yeli, abale, ebuma, yenga poto, jengi*, and *nabula* spirits) are guarded by the ritual association to which they belonged when they were alive.[13]

Game spirits can be seen in the forest only by initiates but in camp they sometimes appear to non-initiates, wearing different types of mask (see Joiris, 1993a, 1993b). They are organized into families and the initiates, having contacts with the spirits, "guard" them, as the Baka put it, within the ritual association for the benefit of the whole community.

Most new "dances" or ceremonies are created in camp following the meeting of a spirit of a deceased Baka with a main initiate in the forest. The initiate offers a present, such as honey, to the spirit as an entice-ment to come back to camp. Often, the spirit presents the initiate with specific medicinal plants, dance costumes, songs, and dance steps in a dream. The initiate then organizes the first ceremony of the newly created ritual (or new version of a ritual), during which he uses his experience for therapeutic and cynegetic purposes.

[13] *Abale* initiates will therefore be metamorphosed into *abale me* spirits called *mokondi* (in the Kwele-Konabembe area) and *kose* (in the Bangando region), *ebuma* initiates into *ebuma me* spirits, *yeli* initiates and their relatives into *yeli me* spirits, *yenga poto* initiates into *yenga poto me* spirits, *jengi* initiates into *jengi me* spirits.

Initiates have no trouble in identifying spirits of their own family; they belong to the same patrilineal descent group, *ye-*, as the deceased Baka from whom the spirits originated. Each spirit class consists of lines of ancestors linked to the living within their particular ritual association. The Baka know the spirits' names associated with their own camp and sometimes those of other camps within their regional band. The number of individuals in each family is much greater than the number of initiates in any ritual association, but initiates make contact with only a small number of spirits.

While there is no real ancestor worship within this Baka culture, it is clear through the ritual association tradition that the notion of ancestrality–spirit links is well established. It is manifested by the special relationship that exists between initiates and the spirits of the deceased; all of these relationships are linked closely with the forest.

3   Intracultural variability in hunting ritual

In this section, I shall focus on the ritual activities of two sets of camps, one in the Bangando-Mbomam region and the other in the Kwele-Konabembe region.[14] The hunt, and particularly the big-game hunt, is surrounded by rituals. Because the elephant is considered the acme of game animals, there is a rich symbolism associated with, as the Baka say, this "really enormous beast."[15] The spear-hunt ceremony frequently refers to elephants and implies that long distances will be covered in the forest.

Even though rites differ from one ritual association to another, the ceremonies include activities with identical functions. Some rites are designed to locate and to attract game; others designate the hunters who will make the kill; others facilitate tracking and/or thank game spirits. Generally a hunt ceremony can be divided into three phases: the first takes place prior to the hunt; the second in the forest during the hunting of the beast; the last phase occurs after the kill.

Two ceremonies occur as ritual preparation for a hunt. Each involves divination by a main initiate, along with singing and dancing. The singing and dancing can occur simultaneously in different locations or in either order within a few days of one another.

The ceremonies may be prepared by the combination of two or three

[14] A more detailed ethnography of the principal characteristics of these ritual activities (including the history of some ritual associations from their original "region" to their present area) may be found in Joiris 1993a.
[15] The symbolic elements surrounding the elephant are developed in Joiris 1993b.

ritual associations. At Salapoumbe (Bangando region), these are the *yeli* and *abale*. At Bele-Mbondo in the Kwele region, they include the *yenga poto*, *abale*, and *ebuma*.

Ceremonies are usually performed in public, in the center of camp, although the *yenga poto* and *yeli* (exclusively female ceremonies) partly occur in private rituals reserved for main initiates. Individual rituals, such as the application of ritual substances to make hunters invisible, strong, brave, etc., apparently take place (Brisson and Bouriser 1979; Brisson 1988).

Rites preceding the hunt (table 10.2)

In the Bangando region, preparatory rituals in *yeli* and *abale* ritual associations occur in different places but at the same time. These rites are directed at locating and attracting game.

For divination,[16] the *yeli* female initiate (who is a *nganga*) gathers ritual substances such as bark or leaves and rubs them until her palms stick together. The direction in which her hands point indicates where game is to be found (the other initiates repeat the same operation, each with her own ritual substances). The second ritual reinforces the first: the *nganga* burns young tree shoots and the direction in which smoke curves points to where hunters should aim.

The *abale* ritual reinforces the *yeli* by means of a mystical relationship between the *nganga* and spirits of the deceased.[17] A *loko* ritual substance linked to clairvoyance is placed, drop by drop, into the *nganga*'s eyes.

---

[16] If we accept the definition of Singzingre (in Bonte and Izard 1991), divination corresponds to a "culturally codified system of interpreting past, present, and future events" (my translation).

[17] The ancient *abale* framework, called *mbomba* in both subcultural areas, seems to have involved divining techniques like hand rubbing and hearing the sound of the divining rattle (*ligbegbe*) until 1960.

The *abale* dance is the same as *nganga*, *mokondi*, and *kose*. They are said to have different names "because everybody has his own way." The dictionary, which includes vocabulary from the Salapoumbe and Lomié areas, confirms the nexus between *mokondi*, *abale*, and *kose*. According to Brisson and Boursier (1979:153–253), *mokondi* is a fire spirit (*me na wa*) whose dance is similar to *kose*'s dance. *Kose* is a spirit who presides over divining sessions (*me na nganga*) to cure people and prepare the hunt. *Kose* dances *abale*. The importance of the part played by these spirits to divining powers is attested on the one hand in oral literature, particularly in the *mokondi* song-fable which involves *sese*, the divining bird (Brisson: personal communication), and in the origin of the term *kose* on the other hand. The original **kose* was a kind of "trouble-making evil." In the old Baka society, the diviner looked for **kose* in fire. Bahuchet (1989:465) points to the meaning of the original **kose* which may explain the fact that the present Baka *kose* is a spirit who helps the diviner in his introspection.

Table 10.2. *Regional variations of the rites prior to the hunt and during yeli, ebuma, abale, and yenga poto ceremonies organized in their respective yeli, ebuma, abale, and yenga poto ritual association framework*

A1 = Bangando-Mbomam area
A2 = Kwele-Konabembe area

Rites prior to the hunt	*yeli* A1	*ebuma* A2	*abale* A1–A2	*yenga poto* A2
Rites to locate game				
Divining techniques (based on the interpretation of phenomena)	Hand rubbing Observation of smoke direction	Hand rubbing	Hand rubbing, in the ancient *mbomba* framework (A1, until 1960) Hearing the sound of divining rattle (*ligbegbe*) in the ancient *mbomba* framework (A1)	N.A.
Clairvoyance/mediumistic techniques (a visionary experience during which the agent enters into a trance)	—	—	Fire reading Reading in a civet skin *Divining* rattle (*ligbegbe*) associated with fire (ancient *Mbomba* ceremony A2)	—
Application of clairvoyance *medicine*	—	—	*loko* ritual substance put in eyes to look into fire (and to interpret dreams in which initiates and spirits also pass by)	Prepare a ritual substance for the reading in a civet skin by an *abale* initiate

Absorption of medicine producing powers enabling the initiates to locate wild animals	yeli pot liquor (kind of hydromel)	—	Abangama liquid (kind of hydromel) in the ancient mbomba ceremony (A1), borrowed by the yeli women initiates by 1960	—
Rites to attract game				
Yodel songs (and dance)	yeli songs (ndando)	ebuma yeli	—	yenga poto yeli
Medicine in order to improve song-dance and hunt	—	ndambu ritual substance	N.A.	N.A.
Absorption of medicine in order to reinforce the attraction effect of yodel songs	yeli pot liquor (kind of hydromel)	njambu liquid (kind of hydromel)	Abangama liquid (kind of hydromel) in the ancient mbomba ceremony (A1), borrowed by the yeli women initiates by 1960	N.A.
Rites to designate the hunter(s)				
Mediumistic rite to designate the master-hunter	Gift of the mojuma stick	—	—	—
Rite to designate all the hunters	—	Gift of the mokobaka ritual substance to be tied to hunt charms (simbo)	—	—
Rites facilitating the approach to game				
Application of medicines . . .	invisibility medicine, luck blessing	N.A.	N.A.	Luck blessing applied by the wife initiate to her husband (if no public ceremony is organized)

Table 10.2. (*cont.*)   A1 = Bangando-Mbomam area   A2 = Kwele-Konabembe area

	yeli A1	*ebuma* A2	*abale* A1–A2	*yenga poto* A2
Rites prior to the hunt				
Absorption of *medicines* including trance in the master-hunter or *nganga* when the game is nearby	*yeli pot liquor* (kind of hydromel)	—	*ndambu* ritual substance (also a master-hunter's vision power received by initiation)	—
Game spirits (*me*) *intervention*	*yeli me*	*ebuma me*	*abale me* (also called *mokondi* A1 or *kose* A2)	*yenga poto me*
Masked spirits	—	—	Couple of noisy masks. Chest covered up with a cloth, arms folded on the torso, long raffia fiber skirt under a short one	Two or three silent masks, dancing backward, bending forward. Chest covered up with a cloth, arms folded on the torso, short raffia fiber skirt worn over trousers, feet covered with cloth or banana leaves
Unmasked spirits	Said to dance around the camps when the *yeli* women initiates sing	Said to be present in the square dance while the ceremony has reached its climax	Said to be present but invisible, close to the *abale* initiate who reads in the fire The spirit ancient *mbomba* form in the framework (A2) called *ala* did not have a mask, did not come to the camp to dance	

Subsequently he can "read" a fire or civet skins[18] or interpret dreams in which the spirit appears. The *nganga* goes into a light trance, when his gaze crosses that of a spirit or when he sees his *molili* "shadow" or that belonging to an animal. The initiate then indicates the direction hunters should follow either by speaking or by falling down in such a way that his body points in the right direction.

Two ritual techniques can be thus identified: the first, that of the *yeli*, implies divining techniques based on interpreting phenomena; the second, that of the *abale*, implies mediumistic techniques of vision (i.e. "inner vision"). However, in the ceremony to determine the master-hunter who will kill the game, the *yeli* uses a mediumistic technique and trance.

The *yeli* initiate takes a stick (called *mojuma*) with leaves tied to one end. It supposedly symbolizes the *molili* "shadow" of the game. The master-hunter crushes the leaves attached to the stick; if the *nganga* is thrown into convulsions and collapses, this indicates that this particular master-hunter will make the kill. The notion of vision is implied. The sequence utilizes the same *molili* "shadow" concept as the *abale* rite of reading fire or in civet skin.

Rites performed in order to attract game are very elaborate in the *yeli* ceremony. Powerful hunting prowess is attributed to the "yodel" poly-phonies performed by the principal *yeli* initiate soloists. Some of the *yeli* songs, called *ndando*, refer to the first hunt as it is described in the *tibola* song-fable;[19] that story explains the origin of this hunting power, by virtue of which *nganga* women then cooperate with the *me* spirits to locate and to call animals. These songs may also invoke the name of a renowned master-hunter recently deceased. The *yeli* spirits, according to the Baka, stay in the bush and start dancing when they hear women singing *yeli*. Meanwhile, the entire community partakes of a ritual substance called *yeli* "pot liquid" (a kind of hydromel made from water and a sweet honey-like substance); this community activity reinforces the "yodel" songs' capacity to attract game. There is some evidence that in the past (until approximately 1960), a similar ritual liquid called *abangama* was used during the *mbomba* ceremony – an old form of *abale* in certain camps in the Bangando-Mbomam area. Although the *yeli* songs represent a very different ritual from the *abale*, there is some

---

[18] Fire divining has been progressively abandoned in favor of civet-skin divining, which the Baka learned from the Bangando. According to the Baka, the Bangando use it in the sorcerer's dance *bidi*, a "villagers" equivalent to the *nganga* dance.

[19] I wish to express my sincere thanks to Robert Brisson who translated this song-fable which we recorded in Bele in 1990. This version corresponds to a variant told in Salapoumbe (Brisson: 1981–4) and to that of Kaloma in the vicinity of Lomié (Kilian-Hatz 1989:152–69).

Figure 10.3   *Abale* mask at a funeral dance (Mbondo camp, Kwele area, 1990)

indication that *yeli* initiates adopted *abangama* and incorporated it in their *yeli* pot liquid.

The *yeli* pot liquid also plays a role in attracting game. During a *yeli* ceremony, the initiate applies substances that make the hunters' bodies invisible and bring them luck. For the Baka, a state of balance is located on the forehead and is determined by the harmonious quality of relationships between people, as well as between people and forest spirits.

During the *abale* game-attracting ritual, the initiate drinks a ritual substance called *ndambu*, which causes convulsions when game is nearby. It seems that, following initiation, most hunters (or perhaps only master-hunters) receive a "visionary power" which bears the same name of *ndambu*. This power enables the hunters to have a close association with spirits who appear in camp. They dance in couples, shouting or uttering certain sounds. Their chests are covered with cloth, their arms are folded on their torsos; and they wear long raffia fiber skirts under shorter ones (see Figure 10.3).

In the Kwele-Konabembe region, hunting ceremonies follow different rites organized by representatives from the *ebuma*, *yenga poto*, and *abale* ritual associations. In spite of the differences, there are some

Figure 10.4 *Ebuma* dancers at a funeral dance (Bele camp, Kwele area, 1990)

Figure 10.5 *Yeli* initiation (Dissassoui camp, Bangando area, 1989)

Table 10.3. *Rites performed during the hunt*

Rites during the hunt	yeli A1	ebuma A2	abale A1–A2	yenga poto A2	jengi A1–2	nabula A1–2
Rites to locate game						
Divining rites (based on the interpretation of phenomena)	—	—	Hand rubbing (ritual substance given by *yeli* women initiate)	—	—	—
Mediumistic rites ... clairvoyance/ mediumistic techniques (a visionary experience during which the agent enters into a trance)	—		Fire and civet-skin reading	—		—
Game spirits (me) intervention	*yeli me*	*ebuma me*	*abale me* (also called *mokondi* A1 or *kose* A2)	*yenga poto me*	*jengi*	*nabula* (A1) or *pembe* (Konabembe area)
Announcing the fruitful beat (in the morning before the start of the hunt)	—	—	—	—	—	Shouts from the edge of the forest

Guidance on game and protection of the hunters	Anthropomorphous dwarf similar to traditional master-hunter (walks side by side with all kind of game)	Anthropomorphous dwarf similar to traditional master-hunter backward-forward motion in walk (points to all kinds of game, honey, and yams) Kwele area	*shadow molili* (only seen by *abale* initiate in fire or civet skin)	Anthropomorphous dwarf similar to traditional master-hunter	Anthropomorphous dwarf similar to traditional master-hunter (walks side by side with elephant, only seen by master-hunter *jengi* initiates)	Anthropomorphous dwarf similar to traditional master-hunter (walks side by side with elephant, only seen by hunters who have *ndambu* visionary power)

similarities to rites found in the Bangando-Mbomam region. According to the Baka of the Kwele area, the techniques used to locate games in the past included using of a divining rattle and fire reading. Otherwise, much of the ceremony is the same, with vision central to the activities and with the initiate thrown into a trance when his eyes meet those of spirits.

Although the *yeli* ritual has no adherents in the Kwele area, the *ebuma* rites have much in common with *yeli*. The divining technique for locating game is identical: *ebuma* initiates use the same palm-rubbing divining technique. The power of the *ebuma* songs to attract (called *ebuma yeli*) is as strong as that attributed to *yeli* songs, but here the dance comes into play as well. The song sung by the whole group in harmony with dance steps and tambourines, is necessary if the ceremony is to be successful (see Figures 10.4, 10.5). The *ebuma* women also make a ritual liquid, *njambu* described as a mixture of leaves, honey, and water (Brisson and Boursier 1979:355). They drink this liquid to assist with the performance of the *ebuma yeli* song. Even though it is prepared differently, the Baka say that *njambu* is the same as *yeli* pot medicine.

The *ebuma* designation of the hunter who will make the kill follows the same ceremonial lines as the *yeli*, but here the process is less personalized and does not require a mediumistic technique. The *ebuma* initiate distributes ritual hunting substances to all the hunters, who put them with their hunting charms (*simbo*). Finally, the *ebuma* spirits are present in the dance area during the ceremony but are visible only to the main initiates.

As noted, the powers of attraction of music are common to all the rites: *yeli*, *ebuma*, *abale*, and *yenga poto*. The importance of the song is stressed through the use of ritual substances (*yeli* pot, *njambu*, and *abangama* liquid; the *ndambu* ritual substance), all of which are supposed to improve both song and hunt.

Rites during the hunt (table 10.3)

In both regional areas, *jengi* and *nabula* master-hunter initiates intervene during the hunt, although they do not exactly organize ceremonies. Rather, they maintain privileged relations with those spirit classes that are intimately associated with the elephant. They also possess special powers such as the *ndambu* visionary power which guides and protects them.

Initiates of other ritual associations are similarly categorized according to their respective spirit classes, or, as in the case of the *yeli* which has only female initiates, according to the spirits who are visible follow-

ing the consumption of ritual substances during the preparatory ceremony. These spirits appear as anthropomorphic dwarfs similar to traditional elephant hunters – with loin-cloths, elephant spears, and *simbo*
hunting charms. *Abale* spirits alone remain distant: only an *abale* initiate
sees their shadow when repeating mediumistic rites of fire or civet-skin
reading. In the Bangando-Mbomam region, this initiate guides the
hunting procession with the help of the palm-rubbing divining rite and
yeli ritual substances. He or she also selects places to camp by the same
rite. Certain women thus participate indirectly in the grand hunt
process, which is otherwise reserved to men.[20]

Rites closing the elephant hunt (table 10.4)

Rites closing the hunt are generally of an expiatory nature, based upon
relations with spirits. Generally, initiates offer raw or cooked food as
gifts to the spirits for their protection and assistance. The symbolic
treatment of the *jengi* spirit class, which is identical in both regional
areas, is the most complex: the eldest spirit of the *jengi* spirit family
attached to the local group of initiates is said to come close to the
elephant's head. He belongs to the same patrilinear clan as the old
lineage chief for whom the master-hunter directed the hunt. The building of sacred enclosures in the direction of the elephant's head marks the
inauguration of a long process of initiation to the *jengi* ritual association.

4   Aka–Baka comparison

Similarities and differences in Baka and Aka hunting rituals are
revealed, most notably, in Bahuchet and Thomas (1991), Motte-Florac
(1980, 1982, 1992). This literature emphasizes a diachronic perspective.
The authors each note a gradual disappearance of big-game spear-
hunting, reduced human mobility, and an increased recourse to collective net hunting. These elements contribute to the erosion of rites
formerly associated with the hunt. Nonetheless, present-day rituals
occur prior to, during, and after the hunt for both Aka and Baka. An
unchanging succession of rites – propitiation–purification–propitiation–
expiation–giving (Bahuchet and Thomas 1991:189) – are also elements
that are observable in both groups.
    The master hunter (*tuma*) and the lineage elder (*mbai*) are responsible
for the organization of the hunt. Given the decrease in large-game

---

[20] See Joiris: 1990.

Table 10.4. Rites practiced after the elephant hunt

Rites after the hunt	*yeli* A1	*ebuma* A2	*abale* A1–A2	*yenga poto me* A2	*jengi* A1–2	*nabula* A1–2
Game spirits (me) intervention	*yeli me*	*ebuma me*	*abale me* (also called *mokondi* A1 or *kose* A2)	*yenga poto me*	jengi	*nabula* (A1) or *pembe* (Konabembe area)
Signals the elephant's death	Present but silent and invisible	N.A.	Present by silent and invisible during the day; shouts and turns around the cadavre at night)	N.A.	—	Utters thundering tones similar to those of the tusk elephant (close to the animal and around the camp)
Get close to the elephant's head	—	—	—	—	The eldest spirit of the *jengi* spirit family attached to the initiates gets close to the elephant head, he belongs to the same clan as the lineage chief	
Expiatory rites	*yeli* A1	ebuma A2	abale A1–2	*yengo poto* A2	*jengi* A1–2	nabula A1–2

Building of sacred enclosures	—	—	—	—	In the direction of the elephant's head
Songs	*yeli* (*ndando*) song performed by women initiates	N.A.	—	N.A.	—	—
Trance	Performed by a woman initiate while an *abale* spirit turns around the camp at night	N.A.	—	N.A.	—	—
Offering (*likabo*) *to thank spirits for their protection and assistance*	Raw pieces of heart fat, heart, and ribs; *dandu* honey	Pieces of the game heart and ribs	Cooked sometimes seasoned and salted, ribs and heart pieces; *dandu* honey. Ancient form called *ala* in the *mbomba* framework (A2) did not eat anything special	Pieces of the game heart	Cooked unseasoned ribs and heart pieces; *dandu* honey	Nothing, do not like to eat

hunting, however, the diviner (*nganga*) plays a more important organizational role.

Aka ceremony prior to the hunt (*nzoli*) takes place within the camp. Initiated men and women as well as non-initiates take part. The ceremony is led by the master-hunter, who appeals to the elephant spirit (*bomo* or *zoboko*) (ibid.:125, 127, 167) and to ancestor spirits (*dio*). Like the Baka, Aka believe that these friendly spirits "govern animal populations" (ibid.:172). The master-hunter is assisted by personal protective spirits, or protective powers (*kulu*), which are transmitted from father to son and from master to apprentice (ibid.:127, 188).

Unlike the Baka, the Aka seem to distinguish between spirits of human and animal origin, especially when it comes to prestigious animals such as elephants, gorillas or bongo antelopes (ibid.:127). Moreover, the existence of personal protective spirits underscores the privileged relation between a spirit category and some categories of initiates, usually elder sons. However, this is a symbolic system different from that of the Baka. Their (*dio*) ancestor spirits are not categorized in the same manner and these spirits do not emanate from particular initiates – the only exception here is that of a (*mbimbo*) deceased diviner's spirit (Motte-Florac 1991:215).

Dio do not have specific names, nor do they belong to the clan of the deceased. But, just as with the Baka, these spirits manifest themselves wearing masks. The spirits wear raffia costumes (similar to the Baka *jengi* mask) (Figure 10.6) in the case of superior ancestor *dio* spirits (*zengi*); short leafy headdresses for other *dio* spirits, and leafy masks with elephant tusks for the elephant spirits (*bomo* or *zoboko*) (ibid.:167).

If it becomes difficult to locate game, the *nganga* diviner practices a divining rite (*bondo*) to complement the one preceding the hunt. He reads in fire while conversing with *dio* spirits. As for Baka, this contact may lead to a state of trance. A second ceremony (*zoboko*) takes place in the forest, away from the main camp. This rite is open to hunters only and is directed by the master-hunter, who appeals to ancestor spirits (*dio*). He causes the (*bomo*) elephant spirit mask to dance.

The close of the hunt is marked by the intervention of the *mbai* elder who offers the game's blood and internal organs to the game spirits as a thank-offering. The master-hunter also makes an offering to his *kulu* which can be interpreted as a protective spirit or power.

There are four principal similarities between Aka and Baka hunting rites. First, spear-hunting rites, which are common to many ceremonies, including a major fecundity rite (*kondi*), are similar to the Baka *jengi* rite.

Figure 10.6   *Jengi* mask (Salapoumbe, Bangando area, 1989)

Such ceremonies involve the reestablishment of social harmony, male initiation, transmission of hunting power, and the privileged relations between the elder, the *zengi* spirit, and the *dio* ancestor spirits (ibid.:181).

Second, Aka ritual actors such as the master-hunter, diviner, elder, wife of the diviner, and the elder's wife correspond to those of the Baka even though the role of Baka women seems to be more developed than that of the Aka. However, certain elements of the Aka women's ceremonies are powerful. These include the female musical bow (*ngbiti*) with which women charm spirits in order to make them direct animals toward hunters; the *sapa* ritual, whereby women call back their men and thereby enable them to slay game quickly; the *zau* rite in cases of an unsuccessful hunt (ibid.:199); as well as the crucial role played by women during rites of passage (ibid.:202).

Third, ritual techniques used in spear hunting share some identical elements, such as *simbo* hunting charms or *loko* clairvoyance ritual substances (ibid.:203, 205). There is also comparable importance attributed to music for establishing contacts with spirits. Even in similarity, however, their lies diversity. Although the diviner enters into a state of trance, the Aka's spirit travels throughout the spirit world (ibid.:222), which makes him more of a shaman than a Baka *nganga*.

Finally, the supralocal network of relations developed with spirits is equally important in both ethnic groups, but the observation is academic with respect to the Aka. According to the seasonality of Aka rituals (ibid.:131, 132), the major fecundity rite (*kondi*), for example, takes place during large camp meetings when net hunting is also taking place – in January and February (ibid.:131, 132, 189). At other times, however, when the camps are dispersed (due to the well-established visiting custom among both Aka and Baka), local groups intermingle.

5   Conclusion

Baka identity is partly linked to ritual associations in which initiated individuals are involved. Ritual practices vary from one local group to another, and, at a different level, from one regional area to another. This variability depends on specific combinations of ritual elements. Such composite variability may be connected with what Pederson and Waehle (1991:79) claim in respect of the Bamgombi Pygmies: the Bamgombi "identify their local groups in relation to a name and to a number of rituals particular to each local group . . . [which] . . . has its own unique names for the *Edjengi* (spirits) father, mother and son." Data on the Baka, however, indicate that their identity is based on a much wider ritual perspective that, characterized by fluidity and mobility, reaches as far as the regional band.

That regional band level is vital to Baka identity. It has been established that the guardianship of the same genealogical spirits of the deceased constitutes a very strong cohesive factor linking integrated local groups. These spirits, which are both socialized and naturalized, guide the Baka in the exploration of their regional band range. This facilitates, thanks to ritual procedures, access to the forest's resources. Because the Baka camps are linked according to the class of spirits they guard, their relationships do not depend solely on economic and ecological adaptation, but also on social and religious structures. Consequently, religion extends well into the structure of entire social connections within the Baka culture, perhaps to a greater degree than subsistence or economic concerns. Certainly, then, this is an area that warrants additional research.

Acknowledgments

Field work and research (1986–91) for this chapter received financial support from the CNRS (Lacito), from the Université Libre de Bruxelles (ULB), and from the Fondation Belge de la Vocation. I would like to thank Serge Bahuchet, Pierre Van Leynseele, Susan Kent, and Barry Hewlett for their invaluable advice; Catherine Daems and Theodore Trefon for the translation. This analysis is the subject of a doctoral dissertation being completed at ULB.

11 Cultural diversity in the use of plants by Mbuti hunter-gatherers in northeastern Zaire: an ethnobotanical approach

Mitsuo Ichikawa and Hideaki Terashima

Introduction

Hunter-gatherers have adapted to nature by accumulating extensive information about their environments. They name thousands of animals and plants, and learn specific details about each species, including its habitat, ecology, behavior, and utility. Walking with them in the bush for several hours provides insight into their profound sensibilities to the natural world.

Although their accumulation of specifics about their world is detailed and remarkably useful, their peculiar explanations for some natural phenomena rise from a mixture of observation and cultural perception that we find unscientific. For instance, Mbuti hunter-gatherers in the central Ituri Forest say, 'Termites transform into honeybees,'' as an explanation for the cyclical appearance of two insects that resemble one another. Mbuti regard the large termites (*Macrotermis* spp.) as a delicacy during the time that the insects have wings for their mating flight, usually late in the rainy season (Ichikawa 1982).

Mbuti carefully observe the termite behavior and mound, weather conditions, and the behavior of other smaller termite species. In the late rainy season, the outer wall of the termite mound becomes thin in several places; this is where termites build platforms for flight. Mbuti often visit the mound and sometimes break the walls to check the inside. Worker termites immediately repair the broken walls since it is still too early for the winged termites to fly. Mbuti say, "When the weather clears after a heavy rainfall, and the smaller type of termite, *amatapa-tapa*, are seen flying in the forest, the larger *bandonge* will fly at dawn the next day." The Mbuti move to the termite mound the evening before they expect the mass flight to occur. They clear the site and prepare a bonfire of *eta* (*Polyalthia suaveolens*) wood to attract the termites. They dig a pit to hold captured termites, then make a series of fences to prevent their escape. The fences are 30 cm in height and made of the large leaves of Marantaceae plants. The women usually build a hut in which to wait for dawn.

276

After capturing some termites, Mbuti become less diligent; a considerable number of winged termites escape for their mating flight. The Mbuti say, "These termites will drop their large wings and transform into honeybees. These same honeybees store honey high in the tree hollows in the honey season half a year later." Without large wings, the termites resemble honeybees in both size and shape. In our entomology, these insects belong to different taxonomic orders, Isoptera and Hymenoptera, and are in no way connected. However, Mbuti have noted that both species live in colonies and that they emerge successively, after half a year, in abundance. These facts may provide the Mbuti with the basis for relating these two insect species within the concept of metamorphosis. Certainly Mbuti have witnessed metamorphosis; they may extrapolate from what they know to explain what they suspect is a relationship between different species or even different phyla, such as insects and plants.

Explanations for natural phenomena vary according to culture. The Efe hunter-gatherers in the northern part of the Ituri Forest have a different termite story, one that associates them with plant life. The Efe say, "The termite will transform into the termite mushroom, *ikimaku*."

Both explanations, though they vary slightly, are influenced by a kind of "totemic" thought characterized by analogy, producing different stories of termite metamorphosis. This example illustrates well the characteristics of folk knowledge derived from mixing objective and empirical observations with subjective and cultural impositions. It also demonstrates how intergroup diversity appears in connection with the zoological and botanical world that they share.

This chapter focuses on "natural" (objective) and "cultural" (subjective) factors in folk knowledge concerning plants collected by hunter-gatherers for food, medicine, and rituals. In particular, it aims to analyze cultural diversity in plant use through specific references to different groups of hunter-gatherers in the tropical rain forest of central Africa.

Plant use deserves special attention in discussions of cultural diversity. Individuals' knowledge about plant use is not so formalized or consistent as ritual knowledge is often required to be. Nor is it totally bound to proven, practical techniques, such as that used to make tools or build structures. Thus plant use will vary more readily than many other facets of a society and will therefore provide the basis for analyzing intergroup cultural diversity. Although we cannot accept folk explanations as scientific, we can accept them as windows into culture.

In any kind of comparison, we must provide constants. By taking plants as the constants, we can fairly establish similarities and diversity in the uses of those plants among different cultures, when the cultures share a botanical environment. By taking people as a constant, we can compare how different environmental settings influence plant use by people who share cultural values and views.

We shall first compare how different hunter-gatherer groups use plants within the same environment. The comparison of plant use by different language groups will provide us with a clue to understanding cultural diversity and general variation in cultural practices. Narrowing that comparison to groups of similar linguistic (ethnic) and environmental backgrounds will reveal intergroup variations not attributable to either environmental or ethno-cultural factors. Conversely, expanding comparisons to groups in similar environments but very distant from one another will give us insight into how regional groups may have been more closely linked in the past.

Material and method

The hunter-gatherers in the Ituri Forest are generally called Mbuti. However, they are divided into two subgroups according to their language. The "true" Mbuti (hereafter "Mbuti") speak a Bantu language. The Efe are Sudanic speakers.

Mbuti are primarily net hunters, although they also use bows and spears. They live in a close relationship with the Bantu-speaking farmers, such as the Bira, Ndaka, and Budu peoples in the southern and western parts of the forest (Ichikawa 1978).

Efe are predominantly archers who also use spears but no nets. They are associated with the Sudanic-speaking Lese or Mamvu farmers in the northeastern Ituri Forest (Harako 1976; Terashima 1983; Bailey 1985). This study compares data collected in four residential groups (hereafter "bands"); two are Mbuti (TTR and MWB) and two are Efe (NDY and ADR). For the location of these four bands, see Figure 11.1.

Intermarriage between Mbuti and Efe is rare, except in areas where the two groups live adjacent to one another. Between neighboring Mbuti bands, however, there are several cases of intermarriage. By contrast, there is no intermarriage between the two Efe bands, ADR and NDY, living some 20 km apart, although these bands know each other. Efe of the ADR band occasionally visit the village of Nduye (with which the NDY band is associated), where the traditional Lese chief, *chef de collectivité*, lives. However, there is little direct communication between these distant bands since Lese villagers usually act as mediators between them.

Mbuti net-hunter bands have been involved in commercial meat trading since the early 1950s (Hart 1978). They obtain farmed produce

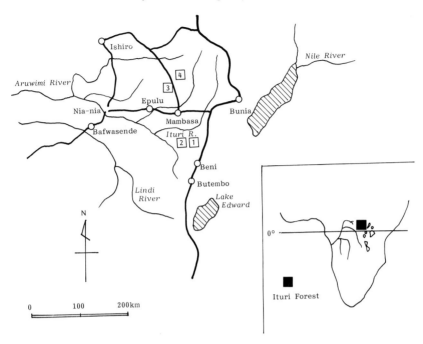

Figure 11.1   The Ituri Forest and the study area. 1: TTR (Bantu-speaking); 2: MWB (Bantu-speaking); 3: NDY (Sudanic-speaking); 4: ADR (Sudanic-speaking)

either in exchange for meat with traders or villagers, or in exchange for agricultural and related manual labor in the village. Mbuti and villagers have long formed an interdependent relationship based on pseudo-kinship, in which exchanges are made mainly in the form of gift-giving. The importance of this traditional relationship has been declining in these areas (Ichikawa 1991). The Efe have not systematically traded meat, but they do traditionally maintain a closer relationship with villagers than the Mbuti do; Efe still depend heavily on agricultural food obtained from their patron villagers (Terashima 1986; Bailey 1985; Hewlett chapter 9, this volume).

In the present study, the data for the Mbuti TTR come from Tanno (1981), with our corrections and modifications added. For the Efe ADR, data from Terashima et al. (1989) are used. For the remaining two bands, the Mbuti MWB and the Efe NDY, we used data collected by Ichikawa (Terashima et al. 1991). For each band, we collected ethno-botanical data on vernacular names and usages from hunter-gatherer informants on site while collecting plant specimens. Information was later supplemented by questioning informants about dried botanical specimens. Specimens were further identified at the herbaria of the Center of Natural Sciences Research in the Kivu Region, the University of Kinshasa, Kinshasa, Zaire, and also at the National Botanic Garden of Belgium. The more than 1,100 specimens included at least 450 distinct botanical species.

As in all fieldwork, errors can occur. Informants may mistake one plant for another and/or supply the wrong vernacular name, which can lead to inaccurate information about plant use. In addition, scientific identification becomes increasingly difficult when fertile specimens (with flowers or fruit) are not available. Consequently, some specimens of the same species may have been identified as different species, or those of different species as the same species. Although we excluded questionable samples from the analysis as much as possible some errors might be present. For this study, we compared the use of individual plant species only when their identification seemed assured at both folk and scientific levels.

As the basic unit for our quantitative comparison, we define "record" of information as equivalent to the "record" used in a database program. Therefore, one "record" is a set of data obtained from one residential group on one scientific species (see AFLORA Committee 1988). The information on the same scientific species from two different groups is thus counted as two records.

Vernacular names and usages in different groups

Record/species ratio in different use categories

We collected a total of 1,119 plant specimens in the Ituri Forest. Excluding those records that were unidentified or dubious, there are 720 records. Table 11.1 lists the number of specimens and records collected in each band.

To determine which plants are used most often among the Mbuti and Efe bands, we establish a record/species ratio (the number of records divided by the number of scientific species) in four major use categories – food, material culture, medicine, and ritual. By definition, if the ratio is high, similar use of the plant among the bands is also high. The ratio is 1.93 for food, which indicates that an average of 1.93 bands use the same plant species for food. The ratios for medicine, material culture, and ritual are 1.31, 1.24, and 1.16, respectively (Table 11.2). Although the food ratio is highest of the major categories, it is important to note that only 49 species out of 106 are used by more than one band (Table 11.3).

Table 11.1. *Numbers of specimens and records collected in each band*

	TTR	MWB	NDY	ADR	Total
No. of specimens	241	282	315	281	1,119
No. of records*	188	217	189	126	720
Estimated no. of records**	200	263	246	154	863

* Number of records on the species identified at species level. The number of records in each group is the same as the number of different species collected in each band.
** Including the number of records of the species identified only at the genus level, but clearly of different species.

Table 11.2. *Numbers of species* and records for each use category*

	Species	Records	Record/species ratio
Food	106	205	1.93
Material culture	295	385	1.31
Medicine	140	174	1.24
Ritual	155	180	1.16

* Estimated number of species (see Table 11.1).

Table 11.3. *Numbers of species used by one to four groups*

No. of groups*	4	3	2	1	No. of species**
Use categories					
Food	20	10	19	57	106
Material culture	11	14	31	237	295
Medicine	2	6	16	116	140
Ritual	1	5	12	137	155

* Number of groups using the same species for the same purpose.
** Total number of botanical species for each use category recorded among the Mbuti–Efe.

Those used for medicine or ritual show the lowest ratio, with only a few species found in all four bands.

Similar use patterns

We compared the number of plant species used for the major four use categories (food, medicine, material culture, and rituals) among the four bands (Figure 11.2). There are differences in the total number of plant

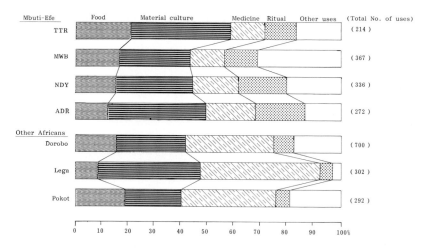

Figure 11.2   Comparison of the proportion (%) of plant species used for each use category among the four bands of the Mbuti and Efe, and among different ethnic groups in Africa. For the comparison among the ethnic groups, the intermediate NDY data are taken as the Mbuti–Efe representative. The Dorobo are hunter-beekeepers in the mountain region of northern Kenya (Ichikawa, 1987); the Lega are forest cultivators in Zaire (Ndunbo 1980); the Pokot are savanna pastoralists in western Kenya (Tanaka 1980)

species recorded (154–263; Table 11.1) and the total number of uses of these plants (214–367). At the same time, however, the proportion of plant species used for each category is quite similar (chi-square = 16.2, d.f. = 9, non-significant). Of all the uses recorded for each band, 14–23 percent are for food, 26–37 percent for material culture, and 13–18 percent for medicine.

The four bands demonstrate remarkable diversity in their selection of plants for use in each of the four categories, as we will see in more detail. However, the percentages of plants used in each category are similar. Such similarity could be related to the four bands having a shared cultural heritage in the Ituri Forest. This supposition is supported by the fact that their use pattern (the proportion of plants used in each category to the total number of plant uses) differs from that of ethnic groups in other areas of Africa (the data for the NDY taken as the Mbuti-Efe representative, chi-square = 114.2, d.f. = 9, P < 0.0001). The number of plants used for medicine varies considerably even between hunter-gatherer groups in the rain forest. The Mbuti and Efe groups use a total of 140 species for medicine, while the Aka in central Africa are reported to use more than 400 species (Motte 1980).

Table 11.4. *Numbers of common plant species collected and similarity indices* between the four bands*

	MWB	NDY	ADR
TTR	91 (0.245)	68 (0.180)	51 (0.168)
MWB		89 (0.212)	61 (0.171)
NDY			60 (0.176)

* Figures in parentheses show the similarity indices (S). $S = N(a, b)/(N(a) + N(b) - N(a, b))$, where $N(a)$ and $N(b)$ represent the number of species collected in bands a and b, and $N(a, b)$ the number of species collected in both bands.

Vernacular names

In order to understand diversity in actual plant use, we must investigate individual species of plants collected. Table 11.4 gives the numbers of common species collected and the similarity indices of the plant species collected in the four bands.

The similarity indices between the plants collected in the four bands are not high, ranging from 0.16 to 0.25. There is also little variation in similarity indices between the four bands. The slightly higher index between the TTR and MWB is not significant. These facts probably reflect the high floral diversity in the tropical rain forest, which gives each band a wide selection from which to choose. Each band lives in the same forest environment and has access to the same range of plants.

The four bands share an environment and they all name plant species, whether or not they use them in similar ways. Some of the vernacular names used by two groups may be exactly the same, or clearly derived from a common origin, whether borrowed or not. Such shared vernacular names are expected to reflect the common linguistic background of the groups. Our Ituri data confirmed this. The two Bantu-speaking Mbuti bands, TTR and MWB, share vernacular names of as many as 86 species (95 percent) out of the common 91 species. Between the ADR and NDY, the Sudanic Efe bands, common names account for 77 percent of the common species recorded, although these bands live about 20 km away from each other (Table 11.5).

As would be expected, the plant names vary considerably between the Mbuti and Efe: shared names range from 15 to 25 percent (Table 11.5). However, the relationship between a plant and its name is arbitrary in that the name may describe neither its use nor its appearance. Therefore, even this relatively low coincidence of shared names between different language groups is noteworthy. These common names are also

Table 11.5. *Coincidence* of vernacular names*

	MWB	NDY	ADR
TTR	0.945	0.250	0.196
MWB		0.236	0.148
NDY			0.767

* Coincidence (C) is calculated as the number of plant species with common vernacular names (Nv) divided by the number of common species collected (Ns), C = Nv/Ns.

used by the Bantu and Sudanic villagers (farmers); this may illustrate one of the examples of cultural convergence among different groups of people in the Ituri Forest.

Common usage ratio for each use category

As the numbers of common species between the four bands are known, we can use these as a basis for comparison. We here use the common usage ratio (the number of species with common usage divided by the number of common species) to compare plant use among the four. We can point out three tendencies. (1) The common usage ratios for food plants are comparatively high, ranging from 0.338 to 0.450. No significant difference was found between the same and different linguistic groups (Table 11.6). (2) The common usage ratios for medicinal plants are very low, ranging from 0.074 to 0.148, with little difference between the language groups (Table 11.7). (3) For material culture, the ratios are intermediate between food and medicinal uses, ranging from 0.275 to 0.400 (Table 11.8).

The common usage ratios agreed with the general tendencies found in the above record/species ratios.

Comparison of the Mbuti-Efe with the Aka

We can better understand the range of diversity in plant use by extending our discussion to other areas of African forest. Another large branch of forest hunter-gatherers, the Aka, resides in the western part of the Congo Basin almost 1,500 km away from the Ituri Forest (for a general comparison between the Mbuti-Efe and the Aka, see Hewlett, chapter 9). Initially, the Aka appear to use plants in ways that are similar to that of the Ituri Forest bands. In fact, many commonly found wild plant foods of the Mbuti and Efe are also common among the Aka. These include the nuts of *Irvingia, Treculia, Telfairia, Antrocaryon, Ricinodendron,*

Table 11.6. *Common usage ratios* for food plants*

	MWB	NDY	ADR
TTR	0.396	0.338	0.392
MWB		0.360	0.393
NDY			0.450

* The number of plants with common use divided by the number of common species collected.

Table 11.7. *Common usage ratios for medical plants*

	MWB	NDY	ADR
TTR	0.121	0.074	0.098
MWB		0.079	0.148
NDY			0.100

Table 11.8. *Common usage ratios for material culture*

	MWB	NDY	ADR
TTR	0.275	0.279	0.333
MWB		0.337	0.361
NDY			0.400

Tetracarpidium, *Chytranthus*, and the fruit of *Landolphia*, *Anonidium*, *Myrianthus*, and *Gambeya*.

However, a closer examination of all the food plants reveals a considerable difference. Of the 62 food plant species used by the two Aka groups (Bahuchet 1985; Ichikawa in prep.) and the 106 species used by the four bands of Ituri, only 22 species are common. The similarity index between the Aka and the Mbuti and Efe combined is as low as 0.151, while the average similarity index between the four Mbuti and Efe bands is 0.384. Although the tropical rain forest environment in the Ituri seems similar to that of the Aka, the difference in plant use may reflect a difference in the species composition of the forest. For example, there are important plants, such as *Canarium schweinfurthii*, used as a major food source by both Mbuti and Efe, but not by Aka. In this case, the plant is not available in the Aka area. In other cases, diversity of use may be related to the general cultural differences described by Hewlett (chapter 9). Clearly, more detailed study of this diversity would provide additional insight into hunter-gatherer cultures.

Characteristics of the commonly used plants

On first impression, similarity is more striking than difference in plant use among the four bands in the Ituri Forest. This may result primarily from common use of some of the important plant species, particularly of utilitarian plants. By examining the characteristics of these commonly used plants, we can hope to determine whether their common use is a result of shared culture or of shared environment.

Of the food plants, all four bands use the following: nuts of high lipid composition, such as *Irvingia, Treculia, Antrocaryon, Tetracarpidium*; fruit or roots as energy sources, such as *Canarium* and *Dioscorea*; tasty fruit and vitamin sources, such as *Anonidium, Landolphia,* and other Apocynaceae fruits; stimulants and condiments, such as Cola nuts and wild pepper (*Piper guineense*). Most of them, except Cola and *Piper*, comprise a major source of wild plant food in their seasons. Of the several dozens of plant species used as food by the Mbuti and Efe, about ten species provide 70 to 80 percent of all the wild plant food consumed at a forest camp (Ichikawa 1993). Most of those major food plants are common to all four bands. It is therefore not surprising that the similarities are more conspicuous than the differences in the food plants.

Besides the food plants, several other plant species are used similarly among the four bands. *Aidia micrantha* is used for making bows. *Rothmannia whitfieldii* provides fruit that is used for a black dye (Figure 11.3). *Eremospatha haullevilleana* is used for binding and construction. *Parquetina nigrescens* is used for arrow poison, and *Tephrosia vogelii* for fish poison. *Manniophyton fulvum* is used for strings and hunting nets (Figure 11.4). Various species of large Marantaceae leaves are used for thatching, wrapping, scooping, and other household purposes. Common use of these plants is based on their natural attributes. This premise is supported by the fact that those such as *P. nigrescens* and *M. fulvum* are also found and used similarly by the Aka. Other commonly used plants include *Musanga cecropioides, Croton haumaniana, Cynometra alexandri,* and *Julbernardia seretii*. All these plants have some special characteristics in their wood or importance as nectar sources, and are abundant in the forest.

At least one non-utilitarian plant receives common, outstanding treatment within the Ituri Forest. All four bands participate in the ritual protection of *Uvariopsis congolana* of the Annonaceae family. This small tree is called *akobishi* by the Mbuti and is regarded by them as a

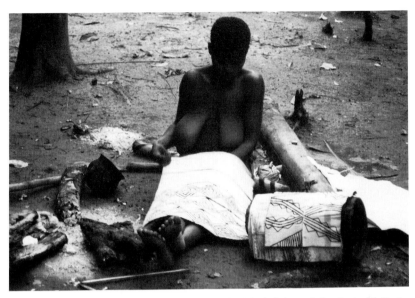

Figure 11.3 Mbuti women use the black juice of the fruit of *Rothmannia whitfieldii* for painting their faces. The same fruit is also used for decorating a barkcloth

Figure 11.4 An Mbuti woman making a hunting net from the inner bark of the *Manniophyton fulvum* liana

visible agent of the supernatural being called *apakumandura* (literally meaning "father of the forest"). It is strictly prohibited to cut or damage this tree. The Efe, who call the tree by the same name, also protect it ritually as a representative of the supernatural being. An outsider finds this small tree nothing extraordinary, except for the elongated cauriflory on its stem and its distribution, which is confined to the dense closed forest. Moreover, no similar ritual protection of this tree has been reported among the Aka, or among the Baka in the western Congo Basin (see, for example, Bahuchet 1985; Joiris, chapter 10). Its ritual value, therefore, derives mainly from cultural beliefs. This clearly shows the existence of a common cultural practice in the Ituri Forest, whether it is derived from a common origin or through cultural convergence.

Discussion

Most of the plant species with usages common among the bands have important roles in the Mbuti and Efe cultures. They are either major food resources, or raw material from which essential objects are made, or are important for religious reasons. These plants and their uses represent the basic plant culture of the Mbuti and Efe groups in the Ituri Forest. However, considerable differences do exist in plant use.

In part, cultural diversity in plant use reflects characteristics of the botanical environment, which itself exhibits great diversity. The flora of African tropical rain forests is less diversified than that of Southeast Asia or South America, but it still contains several dozen to a hundred woody plant species per hectare, or 2,000 to 3,000 plant species in a large region (see, for example, Richards 1964; Jacobs 1981). Certainly such diversity in the plant world is reflected in the diversity of plant use among the four bands. In addition, the numbers of individual plants of each species are limited. This leads to a biased sampling of plant specimens in a limited area. In other words, species composition in a small area is likely to differ from place to place, even if the general environment is similar throughout the forest.

However, such diversity of species and the limitations of individual plant populations fail to account for all diversity in plant use among the Ituri Forest bands. The four bands often use the same plants in different ways. Table 11.6–11.8 clarify this.

Despite such differences, the general use pattern, i.e., the proportion of species allocated to each use category, remains consistent. This suggests a common cultural practice, a common focus, within the Ituri Forest, if we suppose that the number of plants allocated to each use category reflects the degree of interest in, or importance of, that category. This supposition is quite reasonable. Our results therefore suggest that the four bands show a similar degree of interest in each of the major use categories.

Two factors are generally involved in the use of any plant. One is the natural attributes of the plant, including nutritional value, chemical substances, and the texture of the wood. For instance, any individual would eat tasty fruit that was high in calories. Likewise, anyone would think of using trees with strong, straight stems for making bows. In such cases, the use is largely dependent on natural attributes, and intergroup difference is usually small.

The other factor involves culture. Culture selection of plants is arbitrary in that it does not depend on the physical attributes of the plant. Of course, some conspicuous natural attributes of plants, such as shape, color, and smell, often attract human attention and are incorporated into cultural meanings. This occurs, in particular, in plant use based on metaphoric association. For example, the Efe use *Citropsis articulata*, which has sharp spines on the stem, for curing the disease caused by eating catfish, because these spines resemble those of catfish.

Any actual plant use is influenced by both these factors. The use generally varies according to which factor plays the more important role in determining the use of the given plant.

Among the four bands of the Ituri, the food plants show the highest rates of species similarity and common usage. The plants used for ritual and medicine vary more from band to band. This supports the idea that natural factors are more important for food plants than for other uses.

Medicinal plants show unexpected low rates of common use between the bands. This category may be more culture-dependent than is usually assumed. Such a possibility would help explain why neither the Mbuti nor the Efe in the Ituri use medicinal plants as frequently as do the Aka in central Africa. The exception, the Efe ADR band, has been least influenced by the economy of the outside world and retains a more traditional symbiotic relationship with the Lese villagers. The Lese show strong interest in medicine for controlling diseases and supernatural powers. (Incidentally, there are medicinal plants widely used in the Ituri, such as *ekeke* or *menje* [*Picralima nitida*, Apocynaceae] and *ekima* or *aima* [*Alstonia congensis*, Apocynaceae]. Mbuti use these plants because, according to them, "they were once intensively collected for selling to the white people.")

There are also common species even in the plants used for ritual purposes. *Uvariopsis congolana*, *akobisi* mentioned above, is regarded as the agent of a supernatural being in the forest. However, the same plant has no such ritual value among the Aka and Baka in the western Congo

Basin. Its common use and naming in the Ituri Forest, therefore, strongly suggest the same cultural impetus. It is probably related to a cultural identity that is linked to the forest.

We have seen, then, that the common use of plant species differs between bands most conspicuously in cases where the usage is least dependent on either natural or cultural constraints. The natural constraint is the adaptability of the plant's material attributes to its use. The cultural constraint is the social need to maintain ethnic integrity and uniformity through common cultural practices in which plants are involved. Use varies most with plants that can readily be replaced by other plant species. Cultural diversity is most prominent in the use of plants which have few natural or cultural constraints.

In this case, the relationship between a plant and its use seems analogous to that of the signifying (*signifiant*) to the signified (*signifié*) in human languages. Both relationships are arbitrary. The resemblance is, however, superficial. In a language system, communication is a necessity. Once the relationship of the signifying with the signified is formed, it must be fixed to serve as a common code for people within the same language group. People correct errors and inappropriate uses. Otherwise, the language would not serve as a communication medium. In other words, a language is strictly controlled by strong cultural forces which enable people to share the language code. Such cultural forces are also obvious in the vernacular names of plants: there is greater similarity between the vernacular names among bands of the same language group than there is between the uses of plants for food or medicine. Naming is part of the language system, which is originally of an arbitrary nature; it is highly subject to cultural factors.

In contrast, people are not always required to agree about how to use a given plant. They may not communicate with each other about the plants; likewise, they may not use plants as a communication medium. Intergroup or interindividual differences in plant use are often left as they are. No such attempt is made to unify them into a single system of knowledge as is made for language. The basis for intracultural variation in plant use lies, therefore, in the different nature of transmission of the knowledge of plants.

As in most hunter-gatherer societies, Mbuti and Efe learn about plants mostly from their parents and a few senior members of the band, usually while walking together in small groups in the forest. Boys learn from their fathers and elder brothers, and girls from their mothers and elder sisters. Children early acquire an extensive awareness of plants. However, as they seldom have opportunities to visit other distant bands, they do not exchange much information. Information about plants, then, is most often transmitted "vertically," from generation to generation, within a small group of people. As a result, diversity between groups is likely to be maintained and often increased (see Hewlett and Cavalli-Sforza 1986).

A similar intergroup (and intracultural) diversity exists concerning how and when certain animals should be eaten. Mbuti and Efe both regard nearly sixty mammal species as edible, but many of them are avoided by both Mbuti and Efe at certain periods in their lives, such as during or immediately after pregnancy. They believe the animals to be avoided have "dangerous powers" that cause diseases and other misfortunes to the person who eats them or to his or her dependent children. Although the fear of dangerous animals, *kuweri* (Mbuti) or *eke* (Efe), is common throughout the Ituri Forest, the animal species and the diseases they may cause vary from one area to another (Ichikawa 1987a). It is meaningless here to ask why specific animals are avoided in one area but not in other areas. As in some cases of plant uses, it is a "stochastically (naturally) occurring variation" in human practices.

Interestingly, similar intracultural variations between bands and between regional groups are found in the ritual practices of the Baka Pygmies (see Joiris, chapter 10). However, their rituals establish their identity on both local and regional group levels; variations are incorporated into the dynamics of relationships between bands and regional groups. On the other hand, it is unlikely that each band of Mbuti or Efe establishes its identity through maintaining intergroup differences in plant use; the variations do not seem to be incorporated into a social sphere.

Conclusions

When first encountering a plant, a person examines its structure, fruits, and seeds to determine how it might be used. Even a plant that is eventually used for rituals must first acquire importance on a personal, individual level. However, at this initial, individual stage, the knowledge of plants is not consistent, and shows a degree of variation. Individual knowledge will be incorporated later into the common knowledge of the society and then transmitted from generation to generation as shared knowledge. Thus ethno-science is established, but only within the group. Shared knowledge between groups requires communication and/or structure. In a loosely organized society, such as those of the Mbuti and Efe, it is not easy to extend such knowledge, as a standard system, to a social level larger than the band.

Mbuti and Efe societies have a non-centralized social organization and a low level of social integration (Ichikawa 1978). There is no strong motivation for reinforcing cultural homogeneity. The experiences of individuals are of course talked about. For example, people talk in the evening around the central hearth of their camp, and share their experiences with other members of the band. In particular, practical information on the use of a material is quickly transmitted. On the other hand, some knowledge remains more or less at an individual level. For example, individuals often have different knowledge of the plants that are used for hunting luck.

Even when band members share knowledge, they are unlikely to transmit it to other bands in distant places. Plant use, therefore, remains diverse as long as the various bands maintain their non-centralized social structure. There is no intellectual authority, no rigid ritual procedure, no strong cultural or social impetus toward unification. Their society lacks those structures that would otherwise have worked to establish a consistent system of knowledge.

Such lack of "structure" might be inherent to their hunting-and-gathering way of life. Alternatively, it might have been formed through social fragmentation caused by the intervention of a more organized society. In order to know which case is more likely, we need detailed historical analysis.

Plant use, especially for medicine and ritual, is not standardized and is, therefore, useful in the study of cultural diversity because it remains freer from outside contamination than many other aspects of life. This is especially true in a rich botanical environment, such as the Ituri rain forest, where the people have a wide variety of resources to choose from to meet all their needs, whether they be ritual, medical, material, or nutritional. Through examining diversity of plant use, we can gain insight into individual group belief systems which are not subject to authoritative standardization. These beliefs tend to be associated with vivid impressions of the people who originally discovered the plants. Thus we gain access to the personal and lively relationship of the hunter-gatherers with their environments.

Acknowledgments

We express our sincere thanks to Dr. Zana Ndontoni, the Director of the Center of Natural Sciences Research (CRSN), Zaire, who kindly accepted us as research collaborators. We are also grateful to Dr. R. Deschamps of the Royal Museum of Central Africa in Tervuren, Belgium, Dr. Paul Bamps of the National Botanic Garden at Meise, Belgium, Dr. Annette Hladik of the Institute of Ecology at Brunoy,

France, Dr. Breyne of University of Kinshasa, Mrs. Nseya Kalala and Mr. Ndumbo Kirundo of CRSN who kindly identified our specimens.

This study was financially supported in part by the Nippon Life Insurance Foundation.

Part IV

Commentary

12 Hunter-gatherer research and cultural diversity[1]

Nurit Bird-David

Introduction

Hunter-gatherer research was instituted by two seminal conferences. The first one, "Band Societies" (see Damas 1969), was inspired by Julian Steward's premise that band organization constitutes the lowest level of sociocultural integration (1936, 1955).[2] The conference initiated comparative study of contemporary band peoples (pursuing hunting and gathering), hoping to reveal patterns of residential and work grouping that would help us understand the origin of human *society*. The second conference, "Man the Hunter" (see Lee and DeVore 1968), was based on the premise that "the hunting and gathering mode of subsistence" had shaped the evolution of *Homo sapiens*. This conference changed the direction of research: the comparative study of contemporary hunting and gathering peoples (whether organized in bands or not) would, it was hoped, reveal common economic and cultural patterns that would help us understand early human *behavior*. In both cases, the objective was to reach high-level generalities, far above the ethnographic particulars. Toward this objective, research traditionally focused not on variations but on regularities within and between the groups in question.

---

[1] My thanks go to Sue Kent and Tamar El-Or for helpful comments, and to Tim Ingold for many instructive comments in the past and, in this chapter, specifically note 2. Thanks, as well as apologies, go to the authors of this volume; thanks – because their contributions made mine possible and helped me to view my own work from a new perspective; apologies – for possibly not keeping up with all the changes they introduced into their chapters, as they all continued to rewrite and improve their respective contributions.

[2] In his Theory of Culture Change (1955), Steward set at the bottom of his scheme the "family level of sociocultural integration," in which people associate together on the basis of immediate kinship but without forming groups with permanent membership. He described the latter kind of groups as bands. As it turned out, most of the societies that Steward thought were of this band type, in fact, had something more closely resembling the family level of sociocultural integration. But at the same time, ethnographers went on talking about these societies as band societies. The result was that the

Ensuing ethnographic work, however, showed manifold variations
within and between hunter-gatherer groups, so much so that the project
had to be rethought. During the late 1970s and the 1980s, solutions were
looked for in subclassifications. Arguments were made for two, four, or
even eight subtypes of hunter-gatherer societies (e.g., Woodburn 1980;
Testart 1981; Watanabe 1978). Then, during the 1980s, a call for
abandoning the project altogether gathered momentum (e.g., Schrire
1980; Wilmsen 1983). And by the late 1980s, it was even argued that
such populations are nothing but dispossessed poor peoples, whose way
of life had been shaped not by hunting and gathering but by regional and
global political-economic systems (Wilmsen 1989; Wilmsen and
Denbow 1991). They had simply been "invented," Wilmsen argued
(going over the top), by their ethnographers as "hunter-gatherers."

Against this background, the present book – a product of the 1990s –
modifies yet *continues* the project. It turns the focus directly on to
variations, concerning itself with those within single hunter-gatherer
groups, between culturally close as well as culturally distant groups,
diachronically and synchronically. The authors are concerned with
African groups, including: central African Mbuti, Efe, Baka, and Aka;
eastern African Okiek and Hadza; and southern African Bushmen –
!Kung, Nharo, Hai//om, G/wi, G//ana, and Kũa. However, the implications of their cumulative effort go beyond Africa: they are relevant to
the study of hunter-gatherers generally.

Intracultural diversity

The first general implication of *Cultural diversity among twentieth-
century foragers* is to raise intracultural diversity as a research topic in
its own right. The authors detail variations in settlement patterns,
mobility and hostility, hunting success and effort, plant use, children's
participation in food-collection, women's fertility, gender segregation,
marriage and kinship patterns, hunting ceremonies, and belief and ritual
systems. Their collective effort shows that intracultural diversity is
associated with a number of features that are inherent to the band
organization.

First, it is connected with the distribution of bands: bands of any
given group may come to occupy diverse ecological niches, and this in
itself may lead to emergent variations, as Blackburn points out for the
Okiek (chapter 8). Furthermore, since none of these peoples are
"without history" (Wolf 1982), their niches may be differently affected

criterion of permanent membership was simply dropped. Bands by 1965 came to be seen
as flexible associations without permanent membership.

by regional processes, for example water-drilling programs and pan-regional migratory patterns, as Vierich and Hitchcock show for Kalahari Bushmen (chapter 5). Moreover, each band may be in contact with neighbors of diverse cultures.

Secondly, intracultural diversity appears to be associated with the autonomy of bands. The lack of centralized organization may itself lead to dispersal, because conflicts are resolved by "voting with the feet" (see Blackburn, chapter 8). Furthermore, band autonomy goes in tandem with lack of uniformity between bands, including the use of natural resources by bands living within a similar environment, as Ichikawa and Terashima show with respect to plant use among Pygmy groups (chapter 11). Moreover, bands themselves may cultivate their own individual variations, in order to establish and maintain their separate identities, as Joiris shows in respect to hunting rituals among the Baka (chapter 10).

Thirdly, within each band itself, diversity is affected by sharing practices. Kent, for example, shows how sharing networks affect the amount of time individuals devote to hunting activities at Kutse (chapter 6).

Since all these features – distribution in space, the autonomy of bands, and sharing – are common to band populations (see Bird-David 1994), it may well be that intracultural diversity is conspicuous among not only African but all band populations. Indications to that effect – if not always overt – already appear in the ethnography of many Asian groups, including South Indian Nayaka (Bird 1983, Bird-David 1992b), Paliyans (Gardner 1966, 1985), and Hill Pandarm (Morris 1976, 1982), Philippine Agta (Griffin 1984; Headland 1987; Hoffman 1984), and Malaysian Batek (Endicott 1984; Eder 1987).[3] The issue should be pursued further, for it may well be that intracultural diversity is itself *inherent* in the band way of life, as Guenther argues for Bushmen (chapter 3), and Kent for hunter-gatherers generally (Introduction).[4]

Diversity of comparative strategies

The second general implication of the book is to promote diversification of comparative strategies, for any comparison involves choice on questions such as: What to compare? To what end? By whose yardstick? By

[3] As early as 1966, on the basis of his Paliyan study, Gardner noted intracultural diversity. He tried to explain it in psychological terms of intercultural pressure.
[4] Optimal foraging theory concerns itself with variations from a different angle. It premises that variations reflect individuals' choices between alternatives so as to maximize their respective gains, and demands a meticulous documentation of such variations, in order to learn about human choices.

which conceptual template? And from which point of view? In the current intellectual climate, when anthropologists are concerned to give local "voices" space in written texts, such questions are not at all trivial.

The book illustrates four comparative strategies. The first, regional comparison, is employed by Barnard and Widlok (chapter 4), following a strategy outlined in Barnard's recent book *Hunters and herders of Southern Africa* (1992a). In this book (see pp. 3–7), Barnard argues against global comparisons, where material is lifted out of diverse local and historical contexts. This global comparison, he argues, is "not controlled," because contexts that are not being considered may explain some of the differences in question. By contrast, the regional comparison employs the regional framework as a common prism through which to inspect the cultural spectrum of regional groups, avoiding, however, groups that are too closely related, for such comparisons would reveal only shallow differences, easily accountable by circumstances. Its focus on distinct groups – *within* the same region – invites more abstract comparisons and reveals differences which can, and should, be explained by reference to the "social milieu" of the groups compared.

While this regional comparison gives some voice to local conceptualizations (see also Kent and Vierich 1989), these local conceptualizations themselves are subordinated to the researchers' comparative template. It is that which determines the parameters of the research. For example, Barnard and Widlok examine the distance of settlements from commercial farms. This parameter is important to researchers, given their interest (still!) in the extent of local isolation from intrusive agencies. However, this detail is not necessarily important to the local people themselves, a point Silberbauer (chapter 2) makes, and to which I shall return later. In addition, this strategy is necessarily restricted to regions which, like the Kalahari, are large and ethnically diverse.

A second strategy, the grand comparison, is employed by Hewlett (chapter 9); its analytical procedures, and assumptions and aims as well, are almost opposite to Barnard's regional comparison, despite surface similarities. Though Hewlett compares groups within the same region, the choice of a single region is not necessary but convenient. The strategy is to begin with one group, regarded as a manifestation of "human society," and generate hypotheses in terms of independent factors (demographic, ecological, biological, economic), then turn to other groups, seen as other manifestations of "human society," to test and refine these materially oriented hypotheses. The aim of this approach is not to study diversity *per se*, as in the regional comparison, but, instead, to put diversity to use in the study of human universals.

While this comparison – traditionally employed in hunter-gatherer research – helps in pursuing grand questions, it is quite blind to local conceptualizations.

The third strategy, ethno-comparison, is pursued by Silberbauer (chapter 2), and gives pride of place to local conceptualizations. Silberbauer points out the relativity of the concept "cultural diversity": what would count as diversity within one frame of comparison would be regarded as uniformity within another frame, at a higher level of abstraction. Furthermore, diversity that attracts the observer, and may seem meaningful to him or her, may be irrelevant in the local context (diversity is in the eye of the beholder!). For example, he shows how the visible differences in lifestyle between G/wi who live in ranches, G/wi who sporadically visit ranches in search of water during drought, and G/wi who have no direct contact with ranches and continue to live entirely on sustenance gained by gathering and hunting – these differences, which are important to some anthropologists, have no relevance to the way G/wi feel towards each other. As a remedy, Silberbauer proposes the use of comparative templates based on emic "social distinctions," that is, on comparisons which local people themselves make.

While Silberbauer's strategy directly addresses local conceptualizations, there is (as always) a price to pay. This strategy restricts considerably the thematic scope of the comparison to what the local peoples themselves discern and compare. Furthermore, it advocates a kind of ethno-comparison, which, if its logic is followed through, totally sacrifices any comparison of peoples who do not come in contact with each other. It contrasts in that with the strategies of both Barnard and Widlok, and Blurton Jones *et al.*, to which I now turn.

The fourth strategy, evolutionary-ecological comparison, is pursued by Blurton Jones *et al.* (chapter 7). It employs a powerful comparative template, simplified and universalized to the extent that a great deal of data can be cast to fit. Derived from evolutionary ecological theory, the conceptual template is that, in any given circumstance, individuals weigh costs and benefits of different behavioral options – opportunistically, though often unconsciously – and opt for whatever maximizes their fitness. Any circumstance is meat for the grinding analytic device which is embodied in this conceptual template. Among other things, it can "parameterize" contact with neighboring populations and colonial world systems.

This comparative approach has merits – the template is sharp and clear, and calls for wide and systematic application. At the same time, and inevitably, it sacrifices the ethnographic flesh in order to show some of the bones clearly; local conceptualizations disappear completely. This should not be *a priori* held against it, as many "humanistic" anthropologists believe; there is a fair trade-off here, acceptable and even desired for certain purposes. However, its instrumental success should not be mistaken for a validation of its superior theoretical value. Its success only validates its heuristic value, as Winterhalder and Smith themselves point out (1981) but adopters of this strategy only too often forget. Moreover, this comparative approach should not be applied to comparison strategies themselves, that is, such strategies should not be compared in terms of "reproductive success" and "optimal performance," on the premise of a "struggle of survival" between them. To do so – and Blurton Jones *et al.* are close to doing it – is to mince the meat-grinder itself.

I think this book, rather, makes a case for a plurality and a complementarity of comparison strategies, in hunter-gatherer research, and beyond. For each strategy has its own strengths and weaknesses; each would suit certain needs and purposes and not others.

Directions for further research

Cumulatively, the authors make a case for studying intracultural diversity in relation not to the physical but to the social ecology of the peoples under study. This move away from the deterministic style of analysis, propagated by "Man the Hunter," should be followed by another one. Traditional anthropological analysis rests on the premise that individuals think and act according to scripts, and, in the face of diversity, the question being posed is why individuals depart from the scripts. After recent work (see Carrithers 1992, but also Wagner 1981), the premise should be reversed: each moment (we now presume) is historically and biographically unique. Individuals' lives are continuous streams of "inventions"; the "inventions" sometimes repeat themselves and constitute "conventions" (Wagner 1981). If intracultural diversity proves to be a common characteristic of band peoples, as I think it will, the question should be why the process of "conventionalization" is weak. Put differently, what preempts or mitigates "conventionalization" in these cases?

This question first calls for examining in earnest the day-to-day dynamics of making and sustaining social relationships. Some research in this direction has already been begun by, among others, Fred Myers in relation to Australian Pintupi (1986), Guemple (1988) for Belcher Island Inuit, and Bird-David (1994) for Nayaka (compared in this work with the other two cases). These studies suggest, among other things, that a sense of band togetherness rests on a fine balance of personal relatedness and autonomy, not on people being, as Sahlins once put it, "so many potatoes in a sack." This implies that conformity is not sought; rather, the band social environment tolerates naturally occurring diversity. Such research should be continued among African and non-African band peoples, including not only inter-band relationships but relationships with a whole gamut of other people with whom band-peoples – all *with* history – interact. Secondly, more attention should be given to the symbolic worlds and world-views of these peoples. Attesting to the resilience of the agenda generated by "Man the Hunter," studies of these aspects lag behind, partly, no doubt, also because of the comparative nature of the hunter-gatherer project. The ecology and means of adaptation of hunter-gatherers can be compared easily: these are western categories amenable to comparison (if not, even, co-constituted with the idea of comparison in mind). By contrast, the comparison of non-western world-views is problematic: the study of each involves analytic movement from western parameters to locally meaningful ones, and so a loss of common western parameters for comparisons.

While the "grand comparison" depends on western parameters, the "regional comparison" and the "ethno-comparison" (see above) to an extent are appropriate for this purpose, and where they fall short – for example, in cases of cross-regional comparisons – a fifth strategy can be pursued. It is not illustrated in this volume, but has been employed in hunter-gatherer research elsewhere (see Bird-David 1993; cf. Turner 1978). This type of comparison, cultural comparison, starts from the realization that any ethnographic work involves a kind of comparison; in a world of relativities we can only see something in relation to something else. The "straight" ethnographic work *differentiates* the ethnographic mass in "other" cultures by templates taken from our own – we "imagine" (in Strathern's idiom, 1988) other cultures through western categories; we "invent" them (in Wagner's idiom, 1981) under the "control" of western images. By contrast, the cultural comparison *differentiates* the ethnographic mass of other cultures in relation to *each other* – simultaneously and dialectically, (conceptually) moving back and forth between them, noticing similarity at a certain level, then looking for differences within it, then similarities, then differences, and so on. Of course, we are forever imprisoned within our own native (i.e., western) images – which themselves are constantly shifting – but this strategy at least undermines their hegemony.

Compared with the other four comparative strategies (above), the objective of this strategy is not to generate universals but, as in Barnard's regional approach, to gain richer understanding of each of these cultures. The comparison concerns itself not with isolated aspects, such as dances, hunting taboos, or sharing but, on the contrary, with central cultural images that commonly underlie and link such details in each culture. (For some examples, see Bird-David 1990, 1992a, 1993, where a start has been made in this direction.) It makes local conceptualizations "appear" by directing attention to their embodiment in local cultural matter.

Conclusions

Cultural diversity among twentieth-century foragers confines itself to African cases, yet suggests a new direction to the comparative project begun by "Band Societies" and "Man the Hunter." It is to shift the analytical focus from regularities to diversity, while retaining the commitment to comparison, and furthermore to a *diversity* of comparisons. Refocused in this way, changes undergone by these populations (just like those undergone by any other populations) do not make this field of research obsolete but, rather, enrich its scope. This field of research itself, no doubt, will continue to change (like any other field of research), for researchers themselves, no less than the communities they research, constantly undergo change.

References

Abruzzi, W. S. 1979. Population pressure and subsistence strategies among Mbuti pygmies. *Human Ecology* 7:183–9.

AFLORA Committee. 1988. Introduction to AFLORA: an on-line database for plant utilization information of Africa. *African Study Monographs* 9(1):55–64.

Alexander, J. 1967 [1838]. *An expedition of discovery into the interior of Africa through the hitherto undiscovered countries of the Great Namaquas, Boschmans, and the Hill Damaras*, 2 vols. Cape Town: Struik.

Alexandre, P., and J. Binet. 1958. *Le groupe dit Pahouin (Fang, Boulou, Beti)*. Paris: PUF.

Almeida, A. de. 1965. *Bushmen and other non-Bantu peoples of Angola: three lectures*. Johannesburg: Witwatersrand University Press.

Althabe, G. 1965. Changements sociaux chez les pygmées Baka de l'est Cameroun. *Cahiers d'Etudes Africaines* 5–20:561–92.

Andersson, C. 1856. *Lake Ngami*. London: Hurst and Blackett, Publishers.

Anthing, L. 1863. *Cape parliamentary papers: report A 39*. Cape Town: Government House.

Archives de L'Evêché de Bertoua. n.d. Komba et les origines. Unpublished manuscript.

Arom, S. 1978. *Anthologie de la musique des pygmées aka (Empire Centrafrican)*. 3 disques 33 t./30 cm., OCORA (Paris) n° 558526/7/8.

Arom, S., and J. M. C. Thomas. 1974. Les mimbo génies du piégeage et le monde surnaturel des Ngbaka-m'abo (République Centrafricaine). *SELAF*: 44–5.

Bagshawe, F. J. 1923. The peoples of Happy Valley (East Africa). The aboriginal races of Kondoa Irangi. Part II, The Kangeju. *Journal of the African Society* 24:117–30.

Bahuchet, Serge. 1985. *Les pygmées Aka et la forêt centrafricaine, ethnologie écologique*. "Ethnosciences 1." Paris: SELAF.

1988. Food supply and uncertainty among Aka pygmies (Loybaye, Central African Republic). In *Coping with uncertainty in food supply*, edited by I. de Garine and G. A. Harrison. Oxford: Oxford University Press.

1989. Les pygmées Aka et Baka: contribution de l'ethnolinguistique à l'histoire des populations forestières d'Afrique central. Thèse de doctorat d'etat ès Lettres et Sciences Humaines, Université René Descartes, Paris.

1990. Food sharing among the Pygmies of Central Africa. Kyoto: *African Study Monographs* 11:27–53.

1992. Spatial mobility and access to resources among the African pygmies. In *Mobility and territoriality: social and spatial boundaries among foragers, fishers, pastoralists and peripatetics*, edited by M. J. Casimir and A. Rao, pp. 205–37. New York: Berg Publishers.

1993. *Dans la Fôret d'Afrique Centrale: Les Pygmées Aka et Baka*. Paris: Peeters–SEFAF,

Bahuchet, Serge, Doyle McKey, and Igor de Garine. 1991. Wild yams revisited: is independence from agriculture possible for rain forest hunter-gatherers? *Human Ecology* 19(2):213–43.

Bahuchet, Serge, and J. M. C. Thomas. 1987. Pygmy religions. In *The encyclopedia of religions*, vol. 12, edited by M. Eliade, pp. 107–10. New York: McMillan.

Bahuchet, Serge, and J. M. C. Thomas (eds.). 1991. *Encyclopédie des Pygmées Aka*, I (2). Paris: SELAF.

Bailey, Robert C. 1985. The socioecology of Efe pygmy men in the Ituri forest, Zaire. Ph.D. dissertation, Harvard University, Department of Anthropology. Ann Arbor: University Microfilms.

1988. The significance of hypergyny for understanding the subsistence behavior of contemporary hunters and gatherers. In *Diet and subsistence: current archaeological perspectives*, edited by B. V. Kennedy and G. M. LeMoine. Calgary: University of Calgary Press.

1989. The demography of foragers and farmers in the Ituri forest. Paper presented at the AAA meetings. Washington, D.C.

1991. *The socioecology of Efe pygmy men in the Ituri forest, Zaire*. Ann Arbor: Museum of Anthropology, University of Michigan.

Bailey, Robert C., and Robert Aunger, Jr. 1986. Time allocation and association patterns among Efe men in northeast Zaire. Paper presented at the 55th Annual Meeting of the American Association for Physical Anthropology, Albuquerque, New Mexico.

1989. Subsistence strategies among BaMbuti pygmies: net-hunters and archers. *Human Ecology* 17:273–97.

Bailey, Robert C., G. Head, M. Jenike, B. Owen, R. Rechtman, and E. Zechenter. 1989. Hunting and gathering in tropical rain forest: is it possible? *American Anthropologist* 91(1):59–82.

Bailey, Robert C., and N. A. Peacock. 1988. Efe pygmies of northeast Zaire: subsistence strategies in the Ituri forest. In *Coping with uncertainty in the food supply*, edited by G. A. Harrison and I. deGarire, pp. 88–117. Oxford: Clarendon Press.

Bakeman, R., L. B. Adamson, M. J. Konner, and R. G. Barr. 1990. !Kung infancy: the social context of object exploration. *Child Development* 61:794–809.

Barkow, Jerome, Leda Cosmides, and John Tooby. 1992. Introduction: Evolutionary psychology and conceptual integration. In *The Adapted Mind: evolutionary psychology and the generation of culture*, edited by Jerome Barkow, Leda Cosmides, and John Tooby, pp. 3–15. Oxford: Oxford University Press.

Barnard, Alan. 1978. Universal systems of kin categorization. *African Studies* 37:69–81.

1979. Kalahari bushman settlement patterns. In *Social and ecological systems,* edited by Philip C. Burnham and Roy F. Ellen, pp. 131–44. ASA Monographs 18. London: Academic Press.

1980a. Basarwa settlement patterns in the Ghanzi ranching area. *Botswana Notes and Records* 12:137–48.

1980b. Sex roles among the Nharo bushmen of Botswana. *Africa* 50:115–24.

1983. Contemporary hunter-gatherers: current theoretical issues in ecology and social organization. *Annual Reviews of Anthropology* 12:193–214.

1986a. *The present condition of Bushmen groups.* Occasional Papers No. 12. Edinburgh: Edinburgh University, Centre for African Studies.

1986b. Rethinking bushman settlement patterns and territoriality. *Sprache und Geschichte in Afrika* 7(1):41–60.

1987. Khoisan kinship: regional comparison and underlying structures. In *Comparative anthropology,* edited by L. Holy, pp. 189–209. Oxford: Blackwell.

1988. Structure and fluidity in Khoisan religious ideas. *Journal of Religion in Africa* 18(3):216–36.

1992a. *Hunters and herders of southern Africa: a comparative ethnography of the Khoisan peoples.* Cambridge: Cambridge University Press.

1992b. The Kalahari debate: a bibliographical essay. *Occasional Papers* No. 35. Edinburgh: Edinburgh University, Centre for African Studies.

1992c. Social and spatial boundary maintenance among southern African hunter-gatherers. In *Mobility and territoriality: social and spatial boundaries among foragers, fishers, pastoralists and peripatetics,* edited by Michael J. Casimir and Aparna Rao, pp. 137–51. New York: Berg Publishers.

1993. Primitive communism and mutual aid: Kropotkin visits the bushman. In *Socialism: ideals, ideologies, and local practice,* edited by C. M. Hann, pp. 27–42. ASA Monographs 31. London: Routledge.

Barr, R. G., M. J. Konner, R. Bakeman, and L. Adamson. 1991. Crying in !Kung infants: a test of the cultural specificity hypothesis. *Developmental Medicine and Child Neurology* 33:601–10.

Bartram, Laurence Eugene, Jr. 1993. An ethnoarchaeological analysis of Kūa San (Botswana) bone food refuse. Unpublished Ph.D. dissertation, University of Wisconsin, Madison, Wisconsins.

Baumann, O. 1894. *Durch Masailand zur Nilquelle.* Dietrich Reimer, Berlin (Johnson Reprint Corp., New York, 1968).

Belsky, J. 1984. The determinants of parenting: a process model. *Child Development* 55:83–96.

Bennett, F. J., N. A. Barnicot, J. C. Woodburn, M. S. Pereira, and B. E. Henderson. 1973. Studies on viral, bacterial, Rickettsial, and Treponemal diseases of the Hadza of Tanzania, and a note on injuries. *Human Biology* 45:243–72.

Berger, P. 1943. Uberlieferungen der Kindiga. Mit einem anhang: ein jagdbericht. *Studien zur Auslandsk: Afrika* 2:97–122.

Biesele, Megan. 1976. Aspects of !Kung folklore. In *Kalahari hunter-gatherers: studies of the !Kung San and their neighbors,* edited by R. B. Lee and I. DeVore, pp. 302–25. Cambridge, MA: Harvard University Press.

1992. *Shaken roots: the bushmen of Namibia*. Johannesburg: Environmental Development Agency.

1993. *Woman like meat: the folklore and foraging ideology of the Kalahari Ju/'hoansi*. Bloomington: University of Indiana Press.

Biesele, Megan, Mathias Guenther, Robert Hitchcock, Richard Lee, and Jean MacGregor. 1989. Hunters, clients, and squatters: the contemporary socio-economic status of Botswana Basarwa. *African Study Monographs* 9(3):109–51.

Binford, Lewis R. 1978. Dimensional analysis of behavior and site structure: learning from an Eskimo hunting stand. *American Antiquity* 43(3):330–61.

1980. Willow smoke and dogs' tails: hunter-gatherer settlement systems and archaeological site formation. *American Antiquity* 45(1):4–20.

1982. The archaeology of place. *Journal of Anthropological Archaeology* 1(1):5–31.

1983. *In pursuit of the past: decoding the archaeological record*. New York: Thames and Hudson.

1987. Researching ambiguity: frames of reference and site structure. In *Method and theory for activity area research*, edited by Susan Kent, pp. 449–512. New York: Columbia University Press.

Bird, Nurit. 1983. Conjugal families and single persons: an analysis of the Naiken social system. Ph.D. dissertation, University of Cambridge, United Kingdom.

Bird-David, Nurit. 1990. The giving environment: another perspective on the economic system of gatherer-hunters. *Current Anthropology* 31(2):183–96.

1992a. Beyond "the original affluent society." *Current Anthropology* 33(1):25–47.

1992b. Beyond the hunting and gathering mode of subsistence: observations on Nayaka and other modern hunter-gatherers. *Man* 27(1):19–44.

1993. Tribal metaphorization of human-nature relatedness: a comparative analysis. In *Environmentalism: the view from anthropology*, edited by K. Milton. ASA Monograph Series. London: Routledge.

forthcoming. Sociality and immediacy: or, past and present conversations on bands. *Man*.

Blackburn, R. 1971. *The honey complex in Okiek society, culture and personality*. Ph.D. dissertation, Michigan State University, Department of Anthropology. University of Michigan Microfilm offprint.

1973a. Okiek ceramics: evidence for central Kenya prehistory. *Azania*, Journal of the British Institute in Eastern Africa.

1973b. Okiek history. *Azania*, Journal of the British Institute in Eastern Africa.

1976. Okiek history. Revised and expanded edition of (1974, above). In *Kenya before 1900, eight regional studies*, edited by B. A. Ogot. Nairobi: East African Publishing House.

1982. In the land of milk and honey, Okiek adaptations to their forest and neighbors. In *Politics and history in band societies*, edited by E. Leacock and R. Lee, pp. 283–305. Cambridge: Cambridge University Press.

1986. Okiek resource tenure and territoriality as mechanisms for social control and allocation of resources. *Sprache und Geschichte in Africa (SUGIA)*,

Band 7.1, pp. 61–82. Herausgegaben an den Universitaten Koln und Bayreuth. Hamburg: Helmut Buske Verlag.

Bleek, D. 1928. *The Naron*. Cambridge: Cambridge University Press.

1931. The Hadzapi or Witindiga of Tanganyika territory. *Africa* 4:273–86.

Blurton Jones, N. G. 1986. Bushman birth spacing: a test for optimal interbirth intervals. *Ethnology & Sociobiology* 7:91–105.

1987. Bushman birth spacing: direct tests of some simple predictions. *Ethnology & Sociobiology* 8:183–204.

1993. The lives of hunter-gatherer children: effects of parental behavior and parental reproductive strategy. In *Juveniles: comparative socioecology*, edited by M. E. Pereira and L. A. Fairbanks. Oxford: Oxford University Press.

1994. A reply to Dr Harpending. *American Journal of Physical Anthropology* 93:391–7.

in prep. !Kung optimal interbirth intervals re-examined.

Blurton Jones, N. G., K. Hawkes, and P. Draper. 1994a. Differences between Hadza and !Kung children's work: original affluence or practical reason? In *Key issues in hunter gatherer research*, edited by E. S. Burch, pp. 189–215. Oxford: Berg.

1994b. Foraging returns of !Kung adults and children: why didn't !Kung children forage? *Journal of Anthropological Research* 50:217–48.

Blurton Jones, N. G., K. Hawkes, and J. F. O'Connell. 1989. Modelling and measuring costs of children in two foraging societies. In *Comparative sociology*, edited by V. Standen and R. Foley. Oxford: Blackwell.

Blurton Jones, N. G., and R. M. Sibly. 1978. Testing adaptiveness of culturally determined behaviour: do bushman women maximise their reproductive success by spacing births widely and foraging seldom? In *Human behaviour and adaptation*, edited by N. Blurton Jones and V. Reynolds, pp. 135–58. Society for Study of Human Biology Symposium, No. 18. London: Taylor and Francis.

Blurton Jones, N. G., L. C. Smith, J. F. O'Connell, K. Hawkes, and C. L. Kamuzora. 1992. Demography of the Hadza, an increasing and high density population of savanna foragers. *American Journal of Physical Anthropology* 89:159–81.

Bodley, John H. 1990. *Victims of progress*. 3rd edition. Mountain View, CA: Mayfield Publishing Company.

Bonte, P., and M. Izard. 1991. *Dictionnaire de l'ethnologie et de l'anthropologie*. Paris: PUF.

Borgerhof-Mulder, M. 1991. Human behavioural ecology. In *Behavioral ecology*, 3rd edition, edited by J. R. Krebs and N. B. Davies. Oxford: Blackwell Scientific Publications.

Bourdieu, Pierre. 1977 [1972]. *Outline of a theory of practice*. Cambridge: Cambridge University Press.

Boursier, D. 1984. Enquête sur l'anthropologie Baka. Unpublished manuscript.

Boyd, Robert, and Peter Richerson. 1985. *Culture and the evolutionary process*. Chicago: University of Chicago Press.

Brandenburgh, Rodney L. 1991. An assessment of pastoral impacts on Basarwa subsistence: an evolutionary ecological analysis in the Kalahari. M.A. Thesis, University of Nebraska, Lincoln, Nebraska.

Brazelton, T. B. 1972. Implications of infant development among the Mayan Indians of Mexico. *Human Development* 15:90–111.

Brisson, R. 1981–84. *Contes des pygmées Baka du Sud-Cameroun*: vols. I and II, *Histoires et contes d'enfants*; vols. III and IV, *Contes des anciens*. Douala: BP 5351.

   1984. *Lexique français–baka*. Douala: BP 5351.

   1988. *Utilisation des plantes par les pygmées Baka*. Douala: BP 1855.

Brisson, R., and D. Boursier. 1979. *Petit dictionnaire baka–français*. Douala: BP 1855.

Brosius, J. Peter. 1991. Foraging in tropical rain forests: the case of the Penan of Sarawak, East Malaysia (Borneo). *Human Ecology* 19(2):123–50.

Budack, K. 1980. Die Völker Südwestafrikas. *Windoeker Zeitung* 23.4.1980.

Burch, Ernest S., Jr. and Linda J. Ellanna (eds.). 1994. *Key issues in hunter-gatherer research*. Oxford and Providence: Berg Publishers.

Campbell, K. L., and J. W. Wood. 1988. Fertility in traditional societies: social and biological determinants. In *Natural human fertility*, edited by P. Diggory, M. Potts, and S. Teper, pp. 39–69. London: MacMillan.

Carrithers, Michael. 1992. *Why humans have culture: explaining anthropology and social diversity*. Oxford: Oxford University Press.

Cashdan, Elizabeth. 1983. Territoriality among human foragers: ecological models and an application to four bushman groups. *Current Anthropology* 24(1):47–66.

   1984a. The effects of food production on mobility in the central Kalahari. In *From hunters to farmers: the causes and consequences of food production in Africa*, edited by J. D. Clark and S. A. Brandt, pp. 311–27. Berkeley: University of California Press.

   1984b. G//ana territorial organization. *Human ecology* 2(4):443–63.

   1986. Hunter-gatherers of the northern Kalahari. In *Contemporary studies on Hoisan*, I, edited by R. Vossen and K. Keuthmann, pp. 145–80. Hamburg: Helmut Buski Verlag.

   1987. Trade and its origins on the Botleti River, Botswana. *Journal of Anthropological Research* 43(2):121–38.

Cavalli-Sforza, L. L. 1986. *African Pygmies*. Orlando, FL: Academic Press.

Childers, Gary W. 1976. *Report on the survey/investigation of the Ghanzi farm Basarwa situation*. Gaborone: Government Printer.

Cillié, Burger. 1987. *Mammals of southern Africa*. Fourways, South Africa: Frandsen Publishers.

Colless, D. H., and D. K. McAlpine. 1970. Diptera (flies). In *The insects of Australia* (anon. ed.), 1st edition. Melbourne: C.S.I.R.O. and Melbourne University Press.

Cooke, C. K. 1969. *Rock art of southern Africa*. Cape Town: Books of Africa.

Cooper, B. 1949. The Kindiga. *Tanganyika Notes and Records* 27:8–15.

Cosmides, Leda and John Tooby. 1992. Cognitive adaptations for social exchange. In *The adapted mind: evolutionary psychology and the generation of culture*, edited by Jerome Barkow, Leda Cosmides, and John Tooby, pp. 163–228. Oxford: Oxford University Press.

Cowley, C. 1968. *Fabled tribe: a journey to discover the river bushmen of the Okavango swamps*. London: Longmans.

Cronk, L. 1991. Human behavioral ecology. *Annual Reviews of Anthropology* 20:25–53.

Crowell, A., and Robert Hitchcock. 1978. Basarwa ambush hunting in Botswana. *Botswana Notes and Records* 10:37–51.

Curran, Bryan, and David Wilkie. 1989. Foraging efficiency of pygmy bow and net hunters as a function of forest composition. Paper delivered at the 88th Annual Meeting of the American Anthropological Association, Washington, D.C.

Dahlberg, Frances (ed.). 1981. *Woman the gatherer*. New Haven: Yale University Press.

Damas, D. 1969. *Band societies: proceedings of the conference on band organization*. National Museum of Ottawa N.228.

Dansereau, P. 1957. *Biogeography – an ecological perspective*. New York: Ronald Press.

De la fête à l'extase. Transe, chamanisme et possession. 1986. *Actes des deuxièmes rencontres internationales de Nice, 24–28 Avril 1985*. Nice: Editions Serre and Nice Animation.

Demesse, L. 1978. *Changements techno-économiques et sociaux chez les pygmées Babinga (nord Congo et sud Centrafrique)*. Paris: SELAF.

Dempwolff, O. 1916–17. Beitrage zur Kenntnis der Sprachen in Deutsch-Ostafrika. 12. Worter der Hatzasprache. *Zeitschrift für Kolonialsprachen* 7:319–25.

Denbow, J. 1990. Comment on Solway and Lee.*Current Anthropology* 31:124–6.

Denbow, James. 1984. Prehistoric herders and foragers of the Kalahari: the evidence for 1500 years of interaction. In *Past and present in hunter-gatherer studies*, edited by Carmel Schrire, pp. 175–93. New York: Academic Press.

   1986. A new look at the later prehistory of the Kalahari. *Journal of African History* 27:1–25.

Denbow, James, and Edwin Wilmsen. 1986. Advent and course of pastoralism in the Kalahari. *Science* 234:1509–15.

Descola, P. 1986. *La nature domestique. Symbolisme et praxis dans l'écologie des Achuar*. Paris: edn de la Maison des Sciences de l'Homme.

Dodd, R. 1979. Notes in the sociology of Baka religious thought. Unpublished paper.

   1980. Ritual and maintenance of internal cooperation among Baka hunters and gatherers. Paper presented at 2nd International Conference, Hun. Gath. Societies, Quebec.

   1986. The politics of neighbourliness. Paper presented at the 4th International Conference, Hun. Gath. Societies, London.

Donald, Merlin. 1991. *Origins of the modern mind*. Cambridge, MA: Harvard University Press.

Dornan, S. S. 1917. The Tati bushmen (Masarwas) and their language. *Journal of the Royal Anthropological Institute* 47:37–112.

   1925. *Pygmies and Bushmen of the Kalahari*. London: Seeley, Service and Co.

Draper, Patricia. 1975. !Kung women: contrasts in sexual egalitarianism in foraging and sedentary contexts. In *Toward an anthropology of women*, edited by Rayna R. Reiter. New York: Monthly Review Press.

1976. Social and economic constraints on child life among the !Kung. In *Kalahari hunter gatherers*, edited by R. B. Lee and I. DeVore, pp. 200–17. Cambridge, MA: Harvard University Press.

1978. The learning environment for aggression and anti-social behavior among the !Kung. In *Learning non-aggression*, edited by A. Montagu, pp. 31–53. New York: Oxford Univerity Press.

1989. African marriage systems: perspectives from evolutionary ecology. *Ethnology and Sociobiology* 10:145–70.

Draper, Patricia, and E. Cashdan. 1988. Technological change and child behavior among the !Kung. *Ethnology* 27:339–65.

Draper, Patricia, and H. C. Harpending. 1982. Father absence and reproductive strategy: an evolutionary perspective. *Journal of Anthropological Research* 38:255–73.

Draper, Patricia, and M. Kranichfeld. 1990. Coming in from the bush: settled life by the !Kung and their accommodation to Bantu neighbors. *Human Ecology* 18(4):363–84.

Dunn, E. J. 1978 [1872/73]. Through bushmanland. *Cape Monthly Magazine* 30:374–84; 31:31–42. Reprinted in A. M. Lewis (ed.), *Selected articles from the Cape Monthly Magazine (New Series 1870–76)*. Cape Town: Van Riebeck Society.

Durham, William. 1991. *Coevolution: genes, culture, and human diversity*. Stanford: Stanford University Press.

Dwyer, Peter. 1974. The price of protein: five hundred hours of hunting in the New Guinea highlands. *Oceania* 44:278–93.

Dwyer, Peter, and Monica Minnegal. 1991. Hunting lowland, tropical rain forest: towards a model of non-agricultural subsistence. *Human Ecology* 19(2):187–212.

Dyson, T. 1977. The demography of the Hadza in historical perspective. In *African Historical Demography*. Edinburgh: Centre for African Studies, University of Edinburgh.

Eder, James F. 1984. The impact of subsistence change on mobility and settlement pattern in a tropical forest foraging economy: some implications of archaeology. *American Anthropologist* 86:837–53.

1987. *On the road to tribal extinction: depopulation, deculturation, and adaptive well being among the Batak of the Philippines*. Berkeley: University of California Press.

1988. Batak foraging camps today: A window to the history of a hunting-gathering economy. *Human Ecology* 16(1):35–56.

Ellanna, Linda J. (ed.). 1993. *Hunters and gatherers in the modern context*. Papers presented at the Seventh International Conference on Hunting and Gathering Societies (CHAGS 7). Vols. I and II. Moscow: Institute of Ethnology and Anthropology, Russian Academy of Sciences.

Ellenberger, V. 1953. *La fin tragique des bushmen*. Paris: Amiot, Dumont.

Elphick, Richard. 1977. *Kraal and castle: Khoikhoi and the founding of white South Africa*. New Haven: Yale University Press.

Endicott, K. 1979. *Batek negrito religion*. Oxford: Clarendon Press.

1984. The economy of the Batek of Malaysia: annual and historical perspectives. In *Research in Economic Anthropology* 6:29–52.

Endicott, Karen. 1979. Batek negrito sex roles. Unpublished M.A. thesis. Australian National University, Department of Anthropology.

Endicott, Kirk. 1988. Property, power and conflict among the Batek of Malaysia. In *Hunters and gatherers: property, power, and ideology*, edited by Tim Ingold, David Riches, and James Woodburn, pp. 110–27. Oxford: Berg Publishers.

Endicott, Kirk, and Peter Bellwood. 1991. The possibility of independent foraging in the rain forest of peninsular Malaysia. *Human Ecology* 19(2):151–85.

Evans-Pritchard, E. E. 1937. *Witchcraft, oracles and magic among the Azande*. London: Oxford University Press.

1972. *Sorcellerie, oracles et magies chez les Azandé*. Paris: Edn Gallimard.

Fischer, H. 1990. *Völkerkunde im nationalsozialismus*. Berlin: Dietrich Reimer Verlag.

Foley, Robert. 1988. Hominids, humans and hunter-gatherers: an evolutionary perspective. In *Hunters and gatherers: history, evolution, and social change*, edited by Tim Ingold, David Riches, and James Woodburn, pp. 207–21. Oxford: Berg Publishers.

Fourie, Louis. 1926. Preliminary notes on certain customs of the Hei//om bushmen. *Journal of the South West African Scientific Society* 1:49–63.

1928. The bushmen of south west Africa. In *The native tribes of south west Africa*, edited by C. H. L. Hahn, H. Vedder, and L. Fourie, pp. 79–105. Cape Town: Cape Times.

Fried, M. H. 1967. *The evolution of political society*. New York: Random House.

Galaty, John G. n.d. In the pastoral image: the dialectic of Maasai identity. Unpublished Ph.D. dissertation, University of Chicago.

Galton, F. 1889 [1851]. *Narrative of an explorer in tropical South Africa*. London: Ward, Lock and Co.

Gamble, Clive. 1992. Comment on dense forests, cold steppes, and the Palaeolithic settlement of northern Europe by Wil Roebroeks, Nicholas Conard, and Thijs van Kolfschoten. *Current Anthropology* 33(5):569–73.

Gardener, P. 1991. Foragers' pursuit of individual autonomy. *Current Anthropology* 32:543–72.

Gardner, P. 1966. Symmetric respect and memorate knowledge: the structure and ecology of individualistic culture. *Southwestern Journal of Anthropology* 22:389–415.

1985. Bicultural oscillations as a long-term adaptation to cultural frontiers: cases and questions. *Human Ecology* 13:411–32.

Good, Kenneth. 1989. Yanomami hunting patterns: trekking and garden relocation as an adaptation to game availability in Amazonia, Venezuela. Ph.D. dissertation, University of Florida, Department of Anthropology. Ann Arbor: University Microfilms International.

Goody, J. R. (ed.). 1958. *The developmental cycle in domestic groups*. Cambridge: Cambridge University Press.

Gordon, Robert. 1984. The !Kung in the Kalahari exchange: an ethnohistorical perspective. In *Past and present in hunter-gatherer studies*, edited by C. Schrire, pp. 195–224. New York: Academic Press.

1992. *The bushman myth: the making of a Namibian underclass.* Boulder, CO: Westview Press.

Gould, R. A., and J. Yellen. 1987. Man the haunted: determinants of household spacing in desert and tropical foraging societies. *Journal of Anthropological Archaeology* 6:77–103.

Gould, Steven. 1977a. The nonscience of human nature. In *Ever since Darwin: reflections in natural history,* edited by Steven Jay Gould, pp. 237–42. New York: Norton Publishers.

1977b. Biological potentiality vs. biological determinism. In *Ever since Darwin: reflections in natural history,* edited by Steven Jay Gould, pp. 251–9. New York: Norton Publishers.

1977c. So cleverly kind an animal. In *Ever since Darwin: reflections in natural history,* edited by Steven Jay Gould, pp. 260–7. New York: Norton Publishers.

Grafen, A., and R. M. Sibly. 1978. A model of mate desertion. *Animal Behavior* 26:645–52.

Griffin, Agnes Estioko. n.d. The ethnography of southeastern Cagayan Agta hunting. Unpublished M.A. thesis, University of Philippines, Department of Anthropology.

Griffin, P. B. 1984. Forager resource and land use in the humid tropics: the Agta of northeastern Luzon, the Philippines. In *Past and present in hunter-gatherer studies,* edited by C. Schrire. Orlando: Academic Press.

Gudeman, S. 1986. *Economics as culture: models and metaphors of livelihood.* London: Routledge and Kegan Paul.

Gudeman, S., and A. Rivera. 1990. *Conversations in Columbia: the domestic economy in life and text.* Cambridge: Cambridge University Press.

Guemple, L. 1988. Teaching social relations to Inuit children. In *Hunters and gatherers 2,* edited by T. Ingold, D. Riches, and J. Woodburn. Oxford: Berg.

Guenther, M. 1988. Animals in bushmen thought, myth and art. In *Hunters and gatherers 2: property, power and ideology,* edited by T. Ingold, D. Riches, and J. Woodburn, pp. 192–203. Oxford: Berg.

Guenther, Mathias G. 1975. The trance dancer as an agent of social change among the farm bushmen of the Ghanzi District. *Botswana Notes and Records* 7:161–6.

1976. From hunters to squatters: social and cultural change among the Ghanzi farm bushmen. In *Kalahari hunter-gatherers,* edited by R. B. Lee and I. DeVore, pp. 120–33. Cambridge, MA: Harvard University Press.

1977. Bushman hunters as farm labourers. *Canadian Journal of African Studies* 11:195–203.

1979a. Bushman religion and the (non)sense of anthropological theory of religion. *Sociologus* 29:102–32.

1979b. *The farm bushmen of the Ghanzi District, Botswana.* Stuttgart: Hochschul Verlag, Hochschul Sammlung Philosophie, Ethnologie, Band 1.

1981a. Bushman and hunter-gatherer territoriality. *Zeitschrift für Ethnologie* 106:109–20.

1981b. From "brutal savages" to "harmless people": notes on the changing western image of the bushmen. *Paideuma* 26:123–40.

1983. Bushwomen: the position of women in bushman society and ideology. *Journal of Comparative Society and Religion* 10:12–31.

1986a. Acculturation and assimilation of the bushmen of Botswana and Namibia. In *Contemporary Studies on Khoisan I*, edited by R. Vossen and K. Keuthmann. Hamburg: Helmut Buske Verlag.

1986b. From foragers to miners and bands to bandits: on the flexibility and adaptability of bushman band societies. *Sprache und Geschichte in Afrika* 7(1):133–59.

1986c. *The Nharo bushmen of Botswana: tradition and change*. Hamburg: Helmut Buske Verlag, Quellen zur Khoisan-Forschung 3.

1986d. "San" or "Bushman"? In *The past and future of !Kung ethnography: critical reflections and symbolic perspectives*, edited by Megan Biesele, with Robert Gordon and Richard Lee, pp. 27–51. Hamburg: Helmut Buske Verlag.

1989. *Bushman folktales: oral traditions of the Nharo of Botswana and the /Xam of the Cape*. Stuttgart: Franz Steiner Verlag Wiesbaden.

1991. "Independent, fearless, and rather bold": a historical narrative on the Ghanzi bushmen of Botswana. Paper presented at the 18th Annual Meeting of the Canadian Anthropological Society, London, Ontario.

1992. "Not a bushman thing": witchcraft among the bushmen and hunter-gatherers. *Anthropos* 87:83–107.

Gulbrandsen, Ornulf, Marit Karlsen, and Janne Lexow. 1986. *Remote area development programme*. Gaborone, Botswana: Government Printer.

Gusinde, M. 1966. *Von gelben und schwarzen Buschmännern*. Graz: Akademische Druck- und Verlagsanstalt.

Hahn, C. H. 1985. *Carl Hugo Hahn Tagebücher 1837–1860 diaries*, part 4, 1856–1860, edited by B. Lau. Windhoek: State Archives.

Hahn, T. 1870. Die Buschmänner. *Globus* 18:65–8, 81–5, 102–5, 120–3, 140–3, 153–5.

Hallpike, C. R. 1986. *The principles of social evolution*. Oxford: Clarendon Press.

Harako, R. 1976. The Mbuti as hunters: a study of ecological anthropology of the Mbuti pygmies. *Kyoto University African Studies* 10:37–99.

Harako, Reizo. 1981. The cultural ecology of hunting behavior among Mbuti pygmies in the Ituri forest, Zaire. In *Omnivorous primates*, edited by Robert Harding and Geza Teleki, pp. 499–555. New York: Columbia University Press.

Harpending, H., and T. Jenkins. 1973. Genetic distance among southern African populations. In *Method and theory in anthropological genetics*, edited by M. Crawford and P. Workman. Albuquerque: University of New Mexico Press.

Harpending, H., and L. Wansnider. 1982. Population structure of Ghanzi and Ngamiland !Kung. In *Current developments in anthropological genetics*, edited by M. Crawford and J. Mielke. New York: Plenum.

Harpending, Henry. 1991. Review of *Land filled with flies* by Edwin Wilmsen. *Anthropos* 86:313–15.

1994. Infertility and forager demography. *American Journal of Physical Anthropology* 93:385–90.

Harris, Capt. W. C. 1852. *The wild sports of southern Africa*. London: Henry G. Bohn.

Hart, J. 1978. From subsistence to market: a case study of the Mbuti net hunters. *Human Ecology* 6:325–53.

Hart, T. B., and J. A. Hart. 1986. The ecological basis of hunter-gatherer subsistence in African rain forests: the Mbuti of eastern Zaire. *Human Ecology* 14(1):29–55.

Hawkes, Kristen. 1987. How much food do foragers need? In *Food and evolution: toward a theory of human food habits*, edited by M. Harris and E. Ross, pp. 341–55. Philadelphia: Temple University Press.

　　1990. Why do men hunt? Benefits for risky choices. In *Risk and uncertainty in tribal and peasant economies*, edited by E. Cashdan, pp. 145–66. Boulder, CO: Westview Press.

　　1991. Showing off: tests of an hypothesis about men's foraging goals. *Ethnology and Sociobiology* 12:29–54.

　　1993. Why hunter-gatherers work: an ancient version of the problem of public good. *Current Anthropology* 34:341–61.

Hawkes, Kristen, Kim Hill, and James O'Connell. 1982. Why hunters gather: optimal foraging and the Aché of eastern Paraguay. *American Ethnologist* 9(2):379–98.

Hawkes, Kristen, Hillard Kaplan, Kim Hill, and Ana M. Hurtado. 1987. Ache at the settlement: contrasts between farming and foraging. *Human Ecology* 15(2):133–61.

Hawkes, Kristen, and James F. O'Connell. 1981. Affluent hunters? Some comments in light of the Alyawara case. *American Anthropologist* 83:622–6.

Hawkes, Kristen, James F. O'Connell, and Nicholas G. Blurton Jones. 1989. Hardworking Hadza grandmothers. In *Comparative socioecology: the behavioural ecology of humans and other mammals*, edited by V. Standen and R. A. Foley, pp. 341–66. Oxford: Blackwell Scientific Publications.

　　1991. Hunting income patterns among the Hadza: big game, common goods, foraging goals and the evolution of the human diet. *Philosophical Transactions of the Royal Society of London* 344(1270):243–51.

　　in press. Hadza children's foraging: juvenile dependency, social arrangements and mobility among hunter-gatherers. *Current Anthropology*.

Hawkes, Kristen, James F. O'Connell, Kim Hill, and Eric Charnov. 1985. How much is enough? Hunters and limited needs. *Ethnology and Sociobiology* 6:3–15.

Headland, T. N. 1985. Why foragers do not become farmers: a historical study of a changing ecosystem and its effects on a Negrito hunter-gatherer group in the Philippines. Unpublished Ph.D. dissertation, University of Hawaii, Honolulu, Department of Anthropology.

　　1987. The wild yam question: how well could independent anthropologists live in a tropical rain forest ecosystem? *Human Ecology* 15(4):463–91.

Headland, Thomas, and Robert Bailey. 1991. Introduction: have hunter-gatherers ever lived in tropical rain forest independently of agriculture? *Human Ecology* 19(2):115–22.

Headland, Thomas, and Lawrence Reid. 1989. Hunter-gatherers and their neighbors from prehistory to the present. *Current Anthropology* 30(1):43–66.

Heinz, H. J. 1972. Territoriality among the bushmen in general and the !Kō in particular. *Anthropos* 67:405–16.

1978. The male initiation of the !Kō bushmen and its acculturative changes. Paper presented at the 1st International Conference on Hunting and Gathering Societies, Paris.

1979. The Nexus complex among the !Xo bushmen of Botswana. *Anthropos* 79(3/4):465–80.

1994. *The social organization of the !Kō bushmen.* Cologne: Rüdiger Köppe Verlag.

n.d. The people of the Okavango delta. Unpublished manuscript.

Helm, J. 1968. The nature of Dogrib socio-territorial groups. In *Man the hunter*, edited by R. B. Lee and I. DeVore, pp. 118–25. Chicago: Aldine.

Heusch, L. de. 1971. *Pourquoi l'épouser? et autres essais.* Paris: Edn Gallimard.

Hewitt, R. 1986. *Structure, meaning and ritual in the narratives of the Southern San.* Hamburg: Helmut Buske Verlag.

Hewlett, Barry S. 1988. Sexual selection and paternal investment among Aka pygmies. In *Human reproductive behavior*, edited by L. Betzig, M. Borgerhoff Mulder, and P. Turke. Cambridge, England: Cambridge University Press.

1989. Multiple caretaking among African pygmies. *American Anthropologist* 91:186–91.

1991. *Intimate fathers: the nature and context of Aka pygmy paternal infant care.* Ann Arbor, MI: University of Michigan Press.

Hewlett, Barry S., and L. L. Cavalli-Sforza. 1986. Cultural transmission among Aka pygmies. *American Anthropologist* 88:922–34.

Hewlett, Barry S., J. M. H. van de Koppel and L. L. Cavalli-Sforza. 1982. Exploration ranges of Aka pygmies of Central African Republic. *Man* 17:418–30.

Hiernaux, J., and C. B. Hartono. 1980. Physical measurements of the adult Hadza of Tanzania. *Annals of Human Biology* 7:339–46.

Higgins, K. 1981. Narrative folklore discourse of the Baka language (preliminary analysis). Unpublished report. Yaoundé: SIL.

n.d.a. Religious ritual among the Baka people of southern Cameroon. Unpublished report. Yaoundé: SIL.

n.d.b. Ritual and symbol in Baka life history. Unpublished report. Yaoundé: SIL.

n.d.c. A purification ceremony. Some funeral rites among Baka pygmies in Cameroon. Unpublished paper.

Hill, K. 1982. Hunting and human evolution. *Journal of Human Evolution* 11:521–44.

Hill, Kim. 1983. Adult male subsistence strategies among Ache hunter-gatherers of eastern Paraguay. Ph.D. dissertation, University of Utah. Ann Arbor: University Microfilms International

Hill, Kim, and Kristen Hawkes. 1983. Neotropical hunting among the Ache of eastern Paraguay. In *Adaptations of native Amazonians*, edited by Raymond Hames and William Vickers, pp. 139–88. New York: Academic Press.

Hitchcock, Robert K. 1978. Kalahari cattle posts – a regional study of hunter-gatherers, pastoralists, and agriculturalists in the western Sandveid region, Central District, Botswana. Volume I. Report to the Ministry of Local Government and Lands, Botswana.

1980. Tradition, social justice, and land reform in central Botswana. *Journal of African Law* 24(1):1–34.

1982a. The ethnoarchaeology of sedentism: mobility strategies and site structure among foraging and food producing populations in the eastern Kalahari desert, Botswana. Ph.D. dissertation, University of New Mexico. Ann Arbor: University Microfilms.

1982b. Patterns of sedentism among the Basarwa of Botswana. In *Politics and history in band societies*, edited by Eleanor Leacock and Richard Lee, pp. 223–67. Cambridge: Cambridge University Press.

1982c. Tradition, social justice and land reform in central Botswana. In *Land reform in the making: tradition, public policy and ideology in Botswana*, edited by R. P. Werbner. London: Rex Colling.

1985. Foragers on the move: San survival strategies in Botswana parks and reserves. *Cultural Survival Quarterly* 9:31–6.

1987a. Botswana: fisherman of the Two Way River. *Cultural Survival Quarterly* 11:35–8.

1987b. Hunters and herders: local level livestock development among Kalahari San. *Cultural Survival Quarterly* 11:27–30.

1987c. Socio-economic change among the Basarwa of Botswana: an ethnohistorical analysis. *Ethnohistory* 34:220–55.

1987d. Sedentism and site structure: organizational changes in Kalahari Basarwa residential locations. In *Method and theory for activity area research: an ethnoarchaeological approach*, edited by Susan Kent, pp. 374–423. New York: Columbia University Press.

1988. *Monitoring, research, and development in the remote areas of Botswana.* Gaborone, Botswana: Government Printer.

1991. *Traditional and modern systems of land use and management and user rights to resources in rural Botswana.* Part II: *Community-based resource management.* Gaborone, Botswana: Department of Wildlife and National Parks and U.S. Agency for International Development.

1993. *Kalahari communities: indigenous peoples, politics, and the environment in southern Africa.* Copenhagen, Denmark: International Work Group for Indigenous Affairs.

Hitchcock, Robert K., and Alec Campbell. 1972. Settlement patterns of the Bakgalagadi. *Botswana Notes and Records* 4:148–60.

1982. Settlement patterns of the Bakgalagari. In *Settlement in Botswana: the historical development of a human landscape*, edited by R. Renee Hitchcock and Mary R. Smith, pp. 148–60. Marshalltown: Heinemann.

Hitchcock, Robert K., and James I. Ebert. 1984. Foraging and food production among Kalahari hunter/gatherers. In *From hunter to farmers: the causes and consequences of food production in Africa*, edited by J. D. Clark and S. A. Brandt, pp. 328–48. Berkeley: University of California Press.

1989. Modeling Kalahari hunter-gatherer subsistence and settlement systems: implications for development policy and land use planning in Botswana. *Anthropos* 84(1):47–62.

Hitchcock, Robert K., and John D. Holm. 1985. Political development among the Basarwa of Botswana. *Cultural Survival Quarterly* 9(3):7–11.

1993. Bureaucratic domination of hunter-gatherer societies: a study of the San in Botswana. *Development and change* 24(2):305–38.

Hoffman, C. 1984. Punan foragers in the trading networks of southeast Asia. In *Past and present in hunter-gatherer studies*, edited by C. Schrire, pp. 123–51. London: Academic Press.

Howell, N. 1979. *Demography of the Dobe area !Kung*. New York: Academic Press.

Hudelson, J. 1993. One hundred years among the San. Paper presented at the 13th International Congress of Anthropological/Ethnological Sciences, Mexico City.

Hurlich, S., and R. B. Lee. 1979. Colonialism, apartheid and liberation: a Namibian example. In *Challenging anthropology*, edited by D. H. Turner and G. A. Smith, pp. 353–71. Toronto: McGraw-Hill Ryerson Ltd.

Hurtado, A. M., and K. Hill. 1992. Paternal effect on offspring survivorship among Ache and Hiwi hunter-gatherers: implications for modelling pair-bond stability. In *Father–child relations: cultural and biosocial contexts*, edited B. Hewlett. Hawthorne, NY: Aldine de Gruyter.

Ichikawa, Mitsuo. 1978. The residential groups of the Mbuti pygmies. *Senri Ethnological Studies* 1:131–88.

 1982. *The forest hunters*. Kyoto: Jinbun-shoin (in Japanese).

 1987a. A preliminary report of the ethnobotany of the Suiei Dorobo in northern Kenya. *African Study Monographs*, Supplementary Issue 7:1–52.

 1987b. Food restrictions of the Mbuti pygmies, eastern Zaire. *African Study Monographs*, Supplementary Issue 6:97–121.

 1991. The impact of commoditisation on the Mbuti of eastern Zaire. *Senri Ethnological Studies* 30:135–62.

 1993. Diversity and selectivity in the food of Mbuti hunter-gatherers in Zaire. In *Tropical forest: people and food*, edited by M. Hladik, H. Pagezy, O. F. Linares, A. Hladik, and M. Hadley, pp. 387–96. Paris: UNESCO.

Ingold, Tim. 1987. *The appropriation of nature*. Iowa City: University of Iowa Press.

Ingold, Tim, David Riches, and James Woodburn (eds.). 1988. *Hunters and gatherers*, vol. I: *History, evolution, and social change*. London: Berg.

Jacobs, M. 1981. *The tropical rain forest: a first encounter*. Berlin: Springer-Verlag.

Joiris, D. V. 1990. Ritual participation of Baka women of southern Cameroon in activities considered exclusively masculine. Written communication presented at Sixtieth International Conference, Hun. Gath. Societies, Alaska.

 1993a. How to walk side by side with the elephant: Baka pygmy hunting rituals in southern Cameroon. In *Civilisations* 31 (1–2), *Mélanges Pierre Salmon*, vol. II: *Histoire et ethnologie africaine*. Bruxelles: Institut de Sociologie de l'Université Libre de Bruxelles.

 1993b. The jengi mask hungry for yam. Ethno-ecological elements of Dioscorea mangenotiana and associated ritual in the Baka pygmies group of southern Cameroon. In *Food and nutrition in the tropical forest: biocultural interactions*, edited by C. M. Hladik, H. Pagezy, O. F. Linares, A. Hladick, and M. Hadley. Paris: Parthenon/UNESCO.

Kaare, B. T. 1988. In *Hunters and gatherers* edited by T. Ingold, D. Riches, and J. Woodburn. Oxford: Berg.

 1994. The impact of modernization policies on the hunter-gatherer Hadzabe: the case of education and language policies of post-independence Tanzania.

In *Key issues of hunter-gather research methodology for behavioral science*, edited by T. M. Bwire, pp. 315–31. Oxford: Berg.

Kaplan, A. 1964. *The conduct of inquiry*. San Francisco: Chandler.

Kaplan, H., and H. Dove. 1987. Infant development among the Ache of eastern Paraguay. *Development Psychology* 23:190–8.

Kaplan, Hillard, Kim Hill, and A. Magdalena Hurtado. 1990. Risk, foraging and food sharing among the Ache. In *Risk and uncertainty in tribal and peasant economies*, edited by Elizabeth Cashdan, pp. 107–43. Boulder, CO: Westview Press.

Katz, M. M., and M. J. Konner. 1981. The role of father: an anthropological perspective. In *The role of the father in child development*, edited by M. E. Lamb. New York: John Wiley & Sons.

Katz, Richard. 1982. *Boiling energy: community healing among the Kalahari Kung* [sic]. Cambridge, MA: Harvard University Press.

Kaufmann, H. 1910. Aid = Auin. Ein Beitrag zur Buschmannforschung. *Mitteilungen aus den deutschen Schutzgebieten* 23:135–60.

Kelly, Robert L. 1983. Hunter-gatherer mobility strategies. *Journal of Anthropological Research* 39(3):277–306.

  1995. *The foraging spectrum: diversity in hunter-gatherer lifeways*. Washington, DC: Smithsonian Institution Press.

Kent, Susan. 1984. *Analyzing activity areas*. Albuquerque: University of New Mexico Press.

  1987. Parts as wholes – a critique of theory in archaeology. In *Method and theory for activity area research – an ethnoarchaeological approach*, edited by Susan Kent, pp. 513–47. New York: Columbia University Press.

  1989a. Cross-cultural perceptions of farmers as hunters and the value of meat. In *Farmers as hunters – the implications of sedentism*, edited by Susan Kent, pp. 1–17. Cambridge: Cambridge University Press.

  1989b. And justice for all: the development of political centralization among newly sedentary foragers. *American Anthropologist* 91(3):703–11.

  1990a. A cross-cultural study of segmentation, architecture, and the use of space. In *Domestic architecture and the use of space – an interdisciplinary cross-cultural study*, edited by Susan Kent, pp. 127–52. Cambridge: Cambridge University Press (reprinted 1993).

  1990b. Kalahari violence in perspective. *American Anthropologist* 92:1015–17.

  1991a. Partitioning space: cross-cultural factors influencing domestic spatial configuration. *Environment and Behavior* 23(4):438–73.

  1991b. The relationship between mobility strategies and site structure. In *The interpretation of spatial patterning within Stone Age archaeological sites*, edited by T. Douglas Price and Ellen Kroll, pp. 33–59. New York: Plenum Publishing Corporation.

  1992. The current forager controversy: real versus ideal views of hunter-gatherers. *Man* (N.S.) 27:45–70.

  1993a. Sharing in an egalitarian Kalahari village. *Man* (NS) 28(3):479–514.

  1993b. The influence of hunting skill, sharing, and mode of cooking on faunal remains at a sedentary Kalahari community. *Journal of Anthropological Archaeology* 12:323–385.

1995a. Does sedentism promote gender inequality? A case study from the Kalahari. *Journal of the Royal Anthropological Institute* (NS) 1:1–24.

1995b. Unstable households in a stable community: the organization of a recently sedentary Kalahari community. *American Anthropologist* 97(2):1–16.

n.d. Bakgalagadi: the other inhabitants of the Kalahari. Manuscript submitted for publication.

Kent, Susan (ed.). 1990. *Domestic architecture and the use of space – an interdisciplinary cross-cultural study*. Cambridge: Cambridge University Press.

Kent, Susan, and David Dunn. 1993. The etiology of hypoferremia in a recently sedentary Kalahari village. *The American Journal of Tropical Medicine and Hygiene* 48(4):554–67.

in press. Health and disease in a recently sedentary hunter-gatherer community: A follow up study. *American Journal of Physical Anthropology*.

Kent, Susan, and Richard Lee. 1992. A hematological study of !Kung Kalahari foragers: an eighteen year comparison. In *Diet, demography, and disease: changing views of anemia*, edited by P. Stuart-Macadam and S. Kent, pp. 173–99. New York: Aldine de Gruyter.

Kent, Susan, and Helga Vierich. 1989. The myth of ecological determinism: anticipated mobility and site spatial organization. In *Farmers as hunters: the implications of sedentism*, edited by Susan Kent, pp. 96–134. Cambridge: Cambridge University Press.

Khazanov, A. 1984. *Nomads and the outside world*. Cambridge: Cambridge University Press.

Kilian-Hatz, C. 1989. *Contes et proverbes des pygmées Baka*. Paris: ACCT.

Knauft, Bruce. 1990. Violence among newly sedentary foragers. *American Anthropologist* 92:1013–15.

Kohl-Larsen, L. 1958. *Wildbeuter in Ost-Afrika: die Tindiga, ein Jager- und Sammlervolk*. Berlin: Dietrich Reimer.

Köhler, O. 1989. *Die welt der Kxoe-buschleute; bd. 1: Die Kxoe-buschleute und ihre ethnische Umgebung*. Berlin: Dietrich Reimer Verlag.

Kolata, G. 1974. !Kung hunter-gatherers: feminism, diet and birth control. *Science* 185:932–4.

Konner, M. J. 1972. Aspects of the developmental ethology of a foraging people. In *Ethological studies of child behavior*, edited by N. G. Blurton Jones. London: Cambridge University Press.

1976. Maternal care, infant behavior and development among the !Kung. In *Kalahari hunter-gatherers*, edited by R. B. Lee and I. DeVore. Cambridge, MA: Harvard University Press.

1977. Infancy among the Kalahari desert San. In *Culture and infancy: variation in the human experience*, edited by P. H. Leiderman, S. Tulkin, and A. Rosenfield, pp. 287–328. New York: Academic Press.

Konner, M., and M. Shostak. 1986. Ethnographic romanticism and the idea of human nature: parallels between Samoa and !Kung San. In *The past and future of !Kung ethnography: critical reflections and symbolic perspectives, essays in honor of Lorna Marshall*, edited by M. Biesele. Hamburg: Helmut Buske Verlag.

Kranichfeld, M., and Patricia Draper. 1990. Types of households and villages among settled !Kung: measures of accommodation to Bantu. Paper presented at the 89th Annual Meeting of the American Anthropological Association, New Orleans, Louisiana.

Kratz, Corinne. 1988. The unending ceremony and a warm house: representation of a patriarchal ideal and the silent complementarity in Okiek blessings. In *Hunters and gatherers: property, power, and ideology*, edited by Tim Ingold, David Riches, and James Woodburn, pp. 215–48. Oxford: Berg Publishers.

 1994. *Affecting performance, meaning, movement and experience in Okiek women's initiation*. Smithsonian Institution Press.

Krebs, J. R., and N. B. Davies. 1987. *An introduction to behavioral ecology*. Oxford: Blackwell, Sinauer.

Kuper, Adam. 1970. *Kalahari village politics – an African democracy*. Cambridge: Cambridge University Press.

 1982. *Wives for cattle: bridewealth and marriage in southern Africa*. London: Routledge & Kegan Paul.

Lack, D. 1966. *Population studies of birds*. Oxford: Clarendon Press.

Laden, Gregory. 1992. Ethnoarchaeology and land use ecology of the Efe (pygmies) of the Ituri rain forest, Zaire. Ph.D. dissertation, Harvard University, Department of Anthropology. Ann Arbor: University Microfilms International.

Lakatos, I., and E. Zahar. 1975. Why did Copernicus' research program supersede Ptolemy's? In *The Copernican achievement*, edited by R. S. Westman. Berkeley: University of California Press.

Lau, B. 1987. *Namibia in Jonker Afrikaner's time*. Windhoek: State Archives.

Leacock, Eleanor, and Richard Lee (eds.). 1982. *Politics and history in band societies*. Cambridge and New York: Cambridge University Press.

Lebzelter, Viktor. 1934. *Eingeborenenkulturen in Südwest- und Südafrika*. Leipzig: Karl W. Hiersemann.

Lee, Richard B. 1965. Subsistence ecology of !Kung bushmen. Unpublished Ph.D. dissertation, University of California, Berkeley, California.

 1968. What hunters do for a living, or, how to make out on scarce resources. In *Man the hunter*, edited by Richard B. Lee and Irven DeVore, pp. 30–48. Chicago: Aldine.

 1969. !Kung bushmen subsistence: an input–output analysis. In *Environment and cultural behavior*, edited by Andrew P. Vayda, pp. 47–79. New York: Natural History Press.

 1972a. !Kung spatial organization: an ecological and historical perspective. *Human Ecology* 1(2):125–47.

 1972b. Population growth and the beginnings of sedentary life among the !Kung bushmen. In *Population growth: anthropological implications*, edited by B. Spooner. Cambridge, MA: MIT Press.

 1976a. Hunter-gatherers in process: the Kalahari research project, 1963–1976. In *Long-term field research in social anthropology*, edited by G. M. Foster, T. Scudder, E. Colson, and R. V. Kemper, pp. 303–21. New York: Academic Press.

 1976b. !Kung spatial organization: an ecological and historical perspective. In *Kalahari hunter-gatherers*, edited by R. B. Lee and I. DeVore, pp. 73–97. Cambridge, MA: Harvard University Press.

1979. *The !Kung San: men, women, and work in a foraging society*. Cambridge: Cambridge University Press.

1981. Is there a foraging mode of production? *Canadian Journal of Anthropology/Revue canadienne d'anthropologie* 2:13–19.

1982. Politics, sexual and non-sexual in egalitarian societies. In *Politics and history in band societies*, edited by E. Leacock and R. B. Lee, pp. 83–102. Cambridge and New York: Cambridge University Press.

1984. *The Dobe !Kung*. New York: Holt, Rinehart and Winston.

1988. Reflections on primitive communism. In *Hunters and gatherers: history, evolution, and social change*, edited by Tim Ingold, David Riches, and James Woodburn, pp. 252–85. Oxford: Berg Publishers.

1992a. Art, science or politics? The crisis in hunter-gatherer studies. *American Anthropologist* 94:31–54.

1992b. The Ju/'hoansi and us: 1951–1991. *Symbols* (September 1992): 5–14.

1993. *The Dobe Ju/'hoansi*. 2nd edition. New York: Harcourt, Brace.

Lee, Richard B., and Megan A. Biesele. 1991. Dependency or self-reliance? The !Kung San forty years on. Paper presented at the 90th annual meeting of the American Anthropological Association, Chicago, Illinois.

Lee, Richard B., and Irven DeVore. 1968. Problems in the study of hunters and gatherers. In *Man the hunter*, edited by Richard B. Lee and Irven DeVore, pp. 3–20. Chicago: Aldine.

Lee, Richard B., and Irven DeVore (eds.). 1988. *Man the hunter*. Chicago: Aldine Publishing Company.

1976. *Kalahari hunter-gatherers*. Cambridge, MA: Harvard University Press.

Lee, Richard B., and Mathias Guenther. 1991. Oxen or onions? The search for trade (and truth) in the Kalahari. *Current Anthropology* 32(5): 592–603.

1993. Problems in Kalahari historical ethnography and the tolerance of error. *History in Africa* 20:185–235.

Lee, Richard R., and S. Hurlich. 1982. From foragers to fighters: South Africa's militarization of the San. In *Politics and history in band societies*, edited by E. Leacock and R. B. Lee, pp. 327–45. Cambridge, UK: Cambridge University Press.

Lessels, C. M. 1991. The evolution of life histories. In *Behavioral ecology*, edited by J. R. Krebs and N. B. Davies. Oxford: Blackwell Scientific Publications.

Lévi-Strauss, Claude. 1963. *Structural anthropology*. New York: Basic Books.

Lewis-Williams, D. 1981. *Believing and seeing*. New York: Academic Press.

1982. The economic and social context of southern San rock art. *Current Anthropology* 23:429–49.

Lewis-Williams, D., and T. Dowson. 1989. *Images of Power*. Johannesburg: Southern Book Publishers.

Livingstone, David. 1857. *Missionary travels and researchers in South Africa*. London: John Murray.

1860. *Travels and researchers in South Africa*. Philadelphia: G. G. Evans.

Lovejoy, C. O. 1981. The origin of man. *Science* 211:340–50.

Mahieu, W. de. 1985. *Qui a obstrué la cascade? Analyse sémantique du rituel de la circoncision chez les komo du Zaire*. Paris: Londres.

Marks, Stuart. 1972. Khoisan resistance to the Dutch in the seventeenth and eighteenth centuries. *Journal of African History* 13:55–80.

Marshall, John, and Claire Ritchie. 1984. *Where are the Ju/Wasi of Nyae Nyae? Changes in a bushman society: 1958–1981.* Communications No. 9, Center for African Area Studies, University of Cape Town. Cape Town: University of Cape Town.

Marshall, Lorna. 1962. !Kung bushman religious beliefs. *Africa* 32(3): 221–52.

1965. The !Kung bushmen of the Kalahari desert. In *Peoples of Africa*, edited by J. Gibbs, Jr., pp. 241–78. New York: Holt, Rinehart and Winston.

1969. The medicine dance of the !Kung bushman. *Africa* 39(4): 347–81.

1976. *The !Kung of Nyae Nyae.* Cambridge, MA: Harvard University Press.

Maynard Smith, J. 1977. Parental investment: a prospective analysis. *Animal Behavior* 25:1–9.

Mazonde, I. N. 1992. *Remote Area Development Programme Baseline Studies. Diphuduhudu and Tshokwe Settlements.* Vol. I: *Social and Economic Data.* Gaborone, Botswana: National Institute of Research, Norwegian Agency for International Development, and Ministry of Local Government, Lands, and Housing.

McDowell, W. 1981. A brief history of the Mangola Hadza. Ms. prepared for the Rift Valley Project, Ministry of Information and Culture, Dar es Salaam, Tanzania.

McGinley, M. A., and E. L. Charnov. Multiple resources and the optimal balance between size and number of offspring. *Evolutionary Ecology* 2:77–84.

McLloyd, V. C. 1990. The impact of economic hardship on black families and children: psychological distress, parenting, and socioemotional development. *Child Development* 61:311–46.

Mehlman, M. 1988. Later quaternary archaeological sequences in northern Tanzania. Unpublished Ph.D. dissertation, University of Illinois, Champaign-Urbana, Department of Anthropology.

Milton, K. A. 1985. Ecological foundations for subsistence strategies among the Mbuti pygmies. *Human Ecology* 13:71–8.

Moffat, R. 1969 [1842]. *Missionary labour and scenes in southern Africa.* Introduction by C. Northcott. New York: Johnson Reprint Corp.

Mogwe, Alice. 1992. *Who was (t)here first? An assessment of the human rights situation of Basarwa in selected communities in the Gantsi district.* Occasional Paper No. 10. Gaborone, Botswana: Botswana Christian Council.

Morelli, G. A. 1987. A comparative study of Efe (pygmy) and Lese one-, two- and three-year-olds of the Ituri forest of northeastern Zaire: The influence of subsistence-related variables and children's age and gender on social-emotional development. Ph.D. dissertation, University of Massachusetts.

Morris, B. 1976. Whither the savage mind? Notes on the natural taxonomies of a hunting and gathering people. *Man* 11:542–57.

1982. *Forest traders: a socio-economic study of the Hill Pandaram.* London: Athlone Press.

Mosko, M. S. 1987. The symbols of "Forest": a structural analysis of Mbuti culture and social organisation. *American Anthropologist* 89(4): 896–913.

Motte-Florac, E. 1980. A propos des thérapeuthes pygmées Aka de la région de la Lobaye (Centrafrique). *Journal d'Agriculture Traditionnelle et de Botanique Appliquée* 27(2): 113–32.

1982. *Les plantes chez les pygmées Aka et les Monzombo de la Lobaye (RCA)*. Paris: SELAF.

1991. Thérapeutes et devins. In *Encyclopédie des pygmées Aka*, I (2), edited by S. Bahuchet and J. M. C. Thomas, pp. 215–52. Paris: SELAF.

Motte-Florac, E., S. Bahuchet, and M. C. Thomas. 1993. The role of food in the therapeutic of the Aka Pygmies of the Central African Republic. In *Tropical Forests, People and Food*, edited by C. M. Hladick *et al.*, pp. 549–51. Paris: UNESCO/Parthenon.

Motzafi-Haller, P. 1990. Comments on Solway and Lee. *Current Anthropology* 31:132–3.

Murdoch, W. 1980. *The poverty of nations. The political economy of hunger and population*. Baltimore and London: Johns Hopkins University Press.

Murray, M. L. 1976. Present wildlife utilisation in the central Kalahari game reserve, Botswana. Unpublished Department of Wildlife report, Gaborone, Botswana.

Myers, Fred R. 1986. *Pintupi country, pintupi self: sentiment, place and politics among Western Desert Aborigines*. Smithsonian Institution Press and Aust. Inst. of Abor. Studies.

1988. Critical trends in the study of hunter-gatherers. *Annual Review of Anthropology* 17:261–82.

Ndagala, D. 1986. Free or doomed? Images of the Hadzabe hunters and gatherers of Tanzania. Paper presented at the 4th International Conference on Hunting and Gathering Peoples, London School of Economics, London.

Ndii, S. D. 1968. *Problèmes pygmées dans l'arrondissement de Djoum (Cameroun). Essai de développement intégré*. Paris: Mémoire EPHE.

Ndunbo, K. 1980. *Majina ya miti katika luka ya Kirega na inafasiia kwa kila muti inafanyaka kazi gani*. Kyoto: Kyoto University (in Kingwana and Japanese).

Newson, X. and Newson, Y. 1968. *Four years old in an urban community*. London: Allen & Unwin.

Nurse, G. T., and Trefor Jenkins. 1977. *Health and the hunter-gatherer*. Basel: Karger.

Nurse, G. T., J. W. Weiner, and Trefor Jenkins. 1985. *The peoples of southern Africa and their affinities*. Research Monographs on Human Population Biology No. 3. Oxford: Clarendon Press.

O'Connell, James F., Kristen Hawkes, and Nicholas G. Blurton Jones. 1988a. Hadza scavenging: implications for plio/Pleistocene hominid subsistence. *Current Anthropology* 29:356–63.

1988b. Hadza hunting, butchering, and bone transport and their archaeological implications. *Journal of Anthropological Research* 44(2): 113–62.

1990. Reanalysis of large mammal body part transport among the Hadza. *Journal of Archaeological Science* 17:301–16.

1991. Distribution of refuse-producing activities at Hadza residential base camps. In *The interpretation of spatial patterning within Stone Age archaeological sites*, edited by T. Douglas Price and Ellen Kroll, pp. 61–76. New York: Plenum Publishing Corporation.

Obst, E. 1912. Von Mkalama ins Land der Wakindiga. *Mitteilungen der Geographischen Gesellschaft in Hamburg* 26:3–45.

Ogbu, J. 1981. Origins of human competence: a cultural-ecological perspective. *Child Development* 52:413–29.

Oko Mengue, P. 1977. *L'intégration des pygmées: cas de l'arrondissement de Lomié*. Mémoire de licence, Université de Yaoundé.

Osaki, Masakazu. 1984. The social influence of change in hunting technique among the central Kalahari San. *African Study Monographs* 5:49–62.

—— 1990. The influence of sedentism on sharing among the central Kalahari hunter-gatherers. *African Study Monographs*, Supplement 12:59–87.

Owens, Mark, and Delia Owens. 1980. The fences of death. *African Wildlife* 34(6): 25–7.

—— 1981. Preliminary final report on the central Kalahari predator research project. Report to the Department of Wildlife, National Parks, and Tourism, Gaborone, Botswana.

—— 1984. *Cry of the Kalahari*. Boston, MA: Houghton-Mifflin.

Parsons, Neil. 1973. Khama III, the Bamongmato and the British, with special reference to 1895–1923. Unpublished Ph.D. dissertation, University of Edinburgh, Edinburgh, United Kingdom.

—— 1977. The economic history of Khama's country in Botswana, 1844–1930. In *The roots of rural poverty in central and southern Africa*, edited by Robin Palmer and Neil Parsons, pp. 113–43. London: Heinemann.

—— 1982. Settlement in east-central Botswana, circa 1800–1920. In *Settlement in Botswana: the historical development of a human landscape*, edited by R. Renee Hitchcock and Mary R. Smith, pp. 115–28. Marshalltown: Heinemann Educational Books.

Passarge, Siegfried. 1907. *Due Buschmänner der Kalahari*. Berlin: Dietrich Reimer Verlag.

Peacock, N. R. 1985. Time allocation, work and fertility among Efe pygmy women of northeast Zaire. Ph.D. dissertation, Harvard University.

Pedersen, J., and E. Waehle. 1991. The complexities of residential organization among the Efe (Mbuti) and the Bamgombi (Baka): a critical view of the notion of flux in hunter-gatherer societies. In *Hunters and gatherers*, vol. I: *History, evolution, and social change*, edited by T. Ingold, D. Riches, and J. Woodburn. New York, Oxford: Berg Publishers.

Pennington, R. 1992. Did food increase fertility? Evaluation of !Kung and Herero history. *Human Biology* 64:497–522.

Pennington, R., and H. C. Harpending. 1988. Fitness and fertility among Kalahari !Kung. *American Journal of Physical Anthropology* 77:303–19.

Peterson, N., and T. Matsuyama (eds.). 1991. *Cash, commodisation and changing foragers*. Senri Ethnological Studies 30. Osaka: National Museum of Ethnology.

Peterson, Nicholas. 1993. Demand sharing reciprocity and the pressure for generosity among foragers. *American Anthropologist* 95(4): 860–74.

Potgieter, E. F. 1955. *The disappearing bushmen of Lake Chrissie: a preliminary survey*. Pretoria: J. L. van Schaik.

Price, T. Douglas, and James A. Brown (eds.). 1985. *Prehistoric hunter-gatherers: the emergence of cultural complexity*. New York: Academic Press.

Putnam, Patrick. 1948. The Pygmies of the Ituri Forest. In *A reader in general anthropology*, edited by C. Coon, pp. 322–42. New York: Holt.

Radcliffe-Brown, A. R. 1947. *A natural science of society.* Chicago: Chicago University Press.

Radford, Edwin, and Mona Radford. 1980. *Encyclopedia of superstitions,* edited and revised by Christina Hole. London: Hutchinson.

Rao, A. 1993. Zur problematik der wildbeuterkategorie. In *Handbuch der ethnologie,* edited by T. Schweizer, M. Schweizer, and N. Kokot, pp. 491–520. Berlin: Dietrich Reimer Verlag.

Rapoport, Amos. 1982. *The meaning of the built environment.* Beverly Hills: Sage Publications.

——— 1990. Systems of activities and systems of settings. In *Domestic architecture and the use of space: an interdisciplinary perspective,* edited by S. Kent, pp. 9–20. Cambridge: Cambridge University Press.

Richards, P. W. 1964. *The tropical rain forest.* Cambridge: Cambridge University Press.

Ringrose, Susan, and Wilma Matheson. 1991. A Landsat analysis of range conditions in the Botswana Kalahari drought. *International Journal of Remote Sensing* 12(5): 1023–51.

Rogers, A. R. 1990. Evolutionary economics of human reproduction. *Ethnology and Sociobiology* 11:479–96.

Rogers, A. R., and Blurton Jones, N. G. (in prep.). Allocation of parental care. Unpublished Ms.

Ross, Robert. 1983. *Cape of Torments: slavery and resistance in South Africa.* London: Routledge & Kegan Paul.

Rouget, G. 1990. *La musique et la transe.* Paris: Edn Gallimard.

Rudner, J., and I. Rudner. 1978. Bushman art. In *The bushmen,* edited by P. Tobias, pp. 57–75. Cape Town: Human and Rousseau.

Russell, Margo. 1976. Slaves or workers? Relations between bushmen, Tswana and Boers in the Kalahari. *Journal of Southern African Studies* 2(2): 178–97.

——— 1979. *Afrikaners of the Kalahari.* African Studies Series 24. Cambridge: Cambridge University Press.

Russell, Margo, and Martin Russell. 1979. *Afrikaners of the Kalahari: white minority in a black state.* Cambridge: Cambridge University Press.

Sahlins, Marshall. 1972. *Stone age economics.* Chicago: Aldine-Atherton.

Schapera, I. 1930. *The Khoisan peoples of South Africa: bushmen and Hottentots.* London: Routledge and Kegan Paul.

——— 1939. A survey of the bushman questions. *Race Relations* 6(2): 68–82.

Schmidt, S. 1989. *Catalogue of the Khoisan folktales of southern Africa.* 2 vols. Hamburg: Helmut Buske Verlag.

Schott, R. 1955. Die Buschänner in Südafrika eine studiei über schwierigkeiten der akkulturation. *Sociologus* 5:132–49.

Schrire, C. 1990. Comments on Solway and Lee. *Current Anthropology* 31:134.

Schrire, Carmel. 1980. An inquiry into the evolutionary status and apparent identity of San hunter-gatherers. *Human Ecology* 8(1): 9–32.

Schrire, Carmel (ed.). 1984. *Past and present in hunter-gatherer studies.* New York: Academic Press.

Schutz, A. 1970. *On phenomenology and social relations.* Selected writings, edited by H. R. Wagner. Chicago: University of Chicago Press.

Seiner, F. 1913. Ergebnisse einer bereisung der Omaheke in den Jahren 1910–
    1912. *Mitteilungen aus den deutschen Schutzgebieten* 26:225–316.
Serton, P. (ed.). 1954. *The narrative and journal of Gerald McKiernan in south
    west Africa 1874–79.* Cape Town: The Van Riebeck Society.
Service, Elman R. 1962. *Primitive social organization: an evolutionary perspec-
    tive.* New York: Random House.
    1979. *The hunters.* 2nd edition. Englewood Cliffs: Prentice-Hall.
Sevy, G. V. 1960. Le wama des Ngbaka de la Lobaye. *Cahier d'études africaines*
    3:103–28.
Shannon, Thomas Richard. 1989. *An introduction to the world-system perspec-
    tive.* Boulder, CO: Westview Press.
Shebesta, P. 1952. *Les pygmées du Congo Belge.* Bruxelles: Mém. Inst. Royal
    Colonial Belge, XXVI (2).
Sheller, Paul. 1977. The people of the central Kalahari game reserve: a report on
    the reconnaissance of the reserve, July–September, 1976. Report to the
    Ministry of Local Government and Lands, Gaborone, Botswana.
Sheriff, A. M. H. 1979. Tanzanian societies at the time of the partition. In
    Tanzania under colonial rule, edited by M. H. Y. Kaniki, pp. 11–50.
    London: Longman.
Shipton, P. 1991. Review of E. Wilmsen, *Land filled with flies: a political
    economy of the Kalahari* (Chicago: The University of Chicago Press, 1989).
    American Anthropologist 93:756.
Shostak, M. 1981. *Nisa: the life and works of a !Kung woman.* Cambridge, MA:
    Harvard University Press.
Shott, M. J. 1992. On recent trends in the anthropology of foragers: Kalahari
    revisionism and its archaeological implications. *Man* (N.S.) 27:843–71.
Silberbauer, George. 1965. Report to the government of Bechuanaland on the
    bushman survey. Report to the Bechuanaland government, Gaborones.
    1972. The G/wi bushmen. In *Hunters and gatherers today,* edited by M. G.
    Bicchieri, pp. 271–326. New York: Holt, Rinehart, and Winston.
    1981a. *Hunter and habitat in the central Kalahari desert.* Cambridge: Cam-
    bridge University Press.
    1981b. Hunter-gatherers of the central Kalahari. In *Omnivorous primates:
    gathering and hunting in human evolution,* edited by Robert S. O. Harding
    and Geza Taleki, pp. 455–98. New York: Columbia University Press.
    1982. Political process in G/wi bands. In *Politics and history in band societies,*
    edited by E. Leacock and R. B. Lee, pp. 23–35. Cambridge, UK: Cam-
    bridge University Press.
    1991. Morbid reflexivity and overgeneralisation in Mosarwa studies. *Current
    Anthropology* 32(1): 96–9.
Silberbauer, George, and Adam Kuper. 1966. Kgalagari masters and bushman
    serfs: some observations. *African Studies* 25(4): 171–9.
Smith, A. 1975. *Andrew Smith's journal of his expedition into the interior of South
    Africa, 1864–66,* edited by W. F. Lye. Cape Town: A. A. Balkema.
Smith, A., and J. Kinahan. 1985. The invisible whale. *World Archaeology*
    16:89–97.
Smith, C. C., and S. D. Fretwell. 1974. The optimal balance between size and
    number of offspring. *American Naturalist* 108:499–506.

Smith, E. A. 1992. Human behavioral ecology (parts I and II). *Evolutionary Anthropology* 1:20–5 and 2:50–5.

Smith, E. A., and B. Winterhalder. 1992. *Evolutionary Ecology and Human Behavior*. Chicago: Aldine de Gruyter.

Smith, P. 1979. Aspects de l'organisation des rites. In *La fonction symbolique. Essais d'anthropologie*, edited by M. Izard and P. Smith. Paris: Gallimard.

Solway, Jacqueline. 1986. Commercialization and social differentiation in a Kalahari village, Botswana. Unpublished Ph.D. dissertation, University of Toronto, Department of Anthropology.

Solway, Jacqueline S., and Richard B. Lee. 1990. Foragers, genuine or spurious? Situating the Kalahari San in history. *Current Anthropology* 31(2): 109–46.

Speth, John D. 1990. Seasonality, resource stress, and food sharing in so-called "egalitarian" foraging societies. *Journal of Anthropological Research* 9:148–88.

Stearman, Allyn. 1991. Making a living in the tropical forest: Yuqui foragers in the Bolivian Amazon. *Human Ecology* 19(2): 245–60.

Stephen, D. 1983. The San of the Kalahari. *Minority Rights Group*, Report No. 56. London.

Steward, J. H. 1936. The economic and social basis of primitive bands. In *Essays in anthropology presented to A. L. Kroeber*, edited by R. H. Lowie, pp. 331–50. Berkeley: University of California Press.

   1955. *Theory of cultural change: the methodology of multilinear evolution*. Urbana: University of California Press.

Steyn, H. P. 1971. Aspects of the economic life of some nomadic Nharo bushman groups. *Annals of the South African Museum* 56:275–322.

Stow, G. W. 1905. *The native races of South Africa*. London: Swan and Sonnenschein.

Strathern, M. 1988. *The gender of the gift*. Berkeley: University of California Press.

   1992. Parts and wholes: refiguring relationships in a post-plural world. In *Conceptualizing society*, edited by A. Kuper. London: Routledge.

Sugawara, Kazuyoshi. 1988. Visiting relations and social interactions between residential groups of the central Kalahari San: hunter-gatherer camp as a micro-territory. *African Study Monographs* 8(4): 173–211.

Sutton, J. E. G. 1986. The irrigation and manuring of the Engaruka field system. *Azania* 21:27–51.

Szalay, M. 1983. *Ethnologie und Geschichte*. Zur Grundlegung einer ethnologischen Geschichtsschreibung Mit Beispielen aus der Geschichte der Khoi-San in Südafrika. Berlin: Dietrich Reimer Verlag.

Tanaka, Jiro. 1976. Subsistence ecology of central Kalahari San. In *Kalahari hunter-gatherers*, edited by Richard Lee and Irven DeVore, pp. 98–119. Cambridge: Cambridge University Press.

   1980a. Residential pattern and livestock management among the pastoral Pokot. In *A study of ecological anthropology on pastoral and agrico-pastoral peoples in northern Kenya*, edited by J. Tanaka, pp. 78–95. Inyuama: Primate Research Institute, Kyoto University.

   1980b. *The San: hunter-gatherers of the Kalahari*. Tokyo: University of Tokyo Press.

1987. The recent changes in the life and society of the central Kalahari San. *African Study Monographs* 7:37–51.

1989. *The San, hunter-gatherers of the Kalahari. A study in human ecology.* Tokyo: University of Tokyo Press.

Tanner, A. 1979. *Bringing home animals: religious ideology and mode of production of the Mistassini Cree hunter.* London: E. Hurst and Co.

Tanno, Tadashi. 1976. The Mbuti net-hunters of the Ituri forest, eastern Zaire – their hunting activities and band composition. *Kyoto University African Studies* 10:101–35.

1981. Plant utilization of the Mbuti pygmies: with special reference to their material culture and use of wild vegetable food. *African Study Monographs* 1:1–53.

Taylor, John. 1978. Mine labor recruitment in the Bechuanaland protectorate. *Botswana Notes and Records* 10:99–112.

Terashima, H. 1983. Mota and other hunting activities of the Mbuti archers: a socioecological study of subsistence technology. *African Study Monographs,* Supplemental 3:71–85.

1985. Variation in the composition principles of the residence group (band) of the Mbuti pygmies: beyond typical/atypical dichotomy. *African Study Monographs,* Supplementary Issue 4:103–20.

1986. Economic exchange and the symbiotic relationship between the Mbuti (Efe) pygmies and the neighboring farmers. *Sprache und Geschichte in Afrika* 7(1): 391–408.

Terashima, H., M. Ichikawa, and I. Ohta. 1991. AFLORA catalog of useful plants of tropical Africa, part I: forest areas. *African Study Monographs,* Supplementary Issue 16:1–195.

Terashima, H., M. Ichikawa, and M. Sawada. 1989. Wild plant utilization of the Balese and the Efe of the Ituri forest, the Republic of Zaire. *African Study Monographs,* Supplementary Issue 8:1–78.

Testart, A. 1981. Pour une typologie des chasseur-cueilleurs. *Anthropol. Soc.* 3(1): 181–9.

Testart, Alain. 1982. The significance of food storage among hunter-gatherers residence patterns, population densities, and social inequalities. *Current Anthropology* 23:523–37.

1987. Game sharing systems and kinship systems among hunter-gatherers. *Man* (NS) 22(2): 287–304.

Tobias, Phillip V. 1956. On the survival of the bushmen, with an estimate of the problem facing anthropologists. *Africa* 26(2): 175–86.

Tobias, Phillip V. (ed.). 1978. *The bushmen.* Cape Town: Human and Rousseau.

Toerin, H. J. 1955. Transvaal bushmen: a preliminary note. *The Leech* 25:13–14.

Tomita, K. 1966. The sources of food for the Hadzapi tribe: the life of a hunting tribe in east Africa. *Kyoto University African Studies* 1:157–73.

Tooby, John, and Leda Cosmides. 1992. The psychological foundations of culture. In *The adapted mind: evolutionary psychology and the generation of culture,* edited by Jerome Barkow, Leda Cosmides, and John Tooby, pp. 19–136. Oxford: Oxford University Press.

Traill, A. 1978a. The languages of the bushmen. In *The bushmen,* edited by P. V. Tobias. Cape Town: Human and Rousseau.

1978b. Preliminary report on the linguistic situation amongst the Kua Basarwa living on the cattle posts Bae, Mosetlharobega, Metsimonate in the central district. In *Kalahari cattle posts*, edited by Robert K. Hitchcock, vol. II, pp. 252–60. Gaborone, Botswana: Government Printer.

Trenk, Oberleutnant. 1910. Die buschleute der Namib, ihre rechts- und familiienverhältnisse. *Mitteilungen aus den deutschen Schutzgebieten* 23:166–70.

Tronick, E. Z., G. A. Morelli, and S. Winn. 1987. Multiple caretaking of Efe (pygmy) infants. *American Anthropologist* 89:96–106.

Trusswell, A. S., and J. D. L. Hansen. 1976. Medical research among the !Kung. In *Kalahari hunter-gatherers*, edited by R. B. Lee and I. DeVore, pp. 166–94. Cambridge, MA: Harvard.

Turnbull, Colin M. 1955. Pygmy music and ceremonial. *Man* 57:157.

1961. *The forest people*. New York: Simon and Schuster.

1965a. The Mbuti pygmies: an ethnographic survey. *Anthropological Papers of the American Museum of Natural History* 50(3): 141–282.

1965b. *Wayward servants: the two worlds of the African pygmies*. Garden City, NY: Natural History Press.

1968. The importance of flux in two hunting societies. In *Man the hunter*, edited by Richard Lee and Irven DeVore, pp. 132–7. Chicago: Aldine.

1978. The politics of non-aggression. In *Learning non-aggression*, edited by A. Montagu. Oxford: Oxford University Press.

1983. *The Mbuti pygmies: change and adaptation*. New York: Holt, Rinehart and Winston.

1986. Survival factors among Mbuti and other hunters of the Equatorial rain forest. In *African Pygmies* edited by L. L. Cavalli-Sforza. Orlando, FL: Academic Press.

Turner, D. H. 1978a. *Dialectics in tradition: myth and social structure in two hunter-gatherer societies*. Occasional Paper 36. London: RAI.

1978b. Ideology and elementary structures. *Anthropologica* (NS) 20(1/2): 223–47.

Valiente-Noailles, Carlos. 1993. *The Kūa: life and soul of the central Kalahari Bushmen*. Rotterdam and Brookfield: Balkema.

Vallois, H. V., and P. Marquer. 1976. *Les pygmées Baka du Cameroun: anthropologie et ethnographie avec une annexe demographique. Memoires du Museum National D'Histoire Naturelle*, Tome C. Paris: Editions du Museum.

van Hoogstraten, R. C. J. 1966. *Preliminary report on field work amongst the bush people of the Okavango swamps*. Johannesburg: Witwatersrand Medical School.

Vedder, H. 1934. *Das alte Südwestafrika*. Berlin: Martin Warneck Verlag.

Vierich, Helga. 1977. Interim report on Basarwa and related poor Bakgalagadi in Kweneng District. Report to the Ministry of Local Government and Lands, Gaborone, Botswana.

1979. *Drought 1979:socioeconomic survey of drought impact in Kweneng*. Gaborone, Botswana: Ministry of Agriculture.

1981. The Kua of the southeastern Kalahari: a study in the socioecology of dependency. Unpublished Ph.D. dissertation, University of Toronto, Toronto, Ontario, Canada.

1982. Adaptive flexibility in a multi-ethnic setting: the Basarwa of the southern Kalahari. In *Politics and history in band societies*, edited by Eleanor Leacock and Richard B. Lee, pp. 213–22. Cambridge: Cambridge University Press.

Vierich, Helga I. D., and Robert K. Hitchcock. 1979. Kutse game reserve: field trip to a drought-prone environment. In *Proceedings of the symposium on drought in Botswana*, edited by Madalon T. Hinchey, pp. 21–30. Gaborone, Botswana: Botswana Society in collaboration with Clark University Press.

Wagner, R. 1981. (1975). *The intervention of culture: revised and expanded edition*. Chicago and London: University of Chicago Press.

Wallerstein, Immanuel. 1979. *The capitalist world-economy*. Cambridge: Cambridge University Press.

Watanabe, H. 1978. Systemic classification of hunter-gatherers food habits: an ecological-evolutionary perspective. In *Inzokugaku Kenkyu* 43(2): 111–37 (full text in Japanese with English summary and tables).

Weissner, P. 1982. Risk, reciprocity, and social influences on !Kung San economics. In *Politics and history in band societies*, edited by R. B. Lee and E. Leacock, pp. 61–84. Cambridge: Cambridge University Press.

West, M. M., and M. J. Konner. 1976. The role of father in anthropological perspective. In *The role of father in child development*, edited by Michael E. Lamb. New York: John Wiley and Sons.

Whitelaw, Todd. 1989. The social organisation of space in hunter-gatherer communities: some implications for social inference in archaeology. Unpublished Ph.D. dissertation, University of Cambridge, Department of Archaeology, Cambridge, UK.

Wilhelm, J. H. 1954. Die !Kung Buschleute. *Jahrbuch des Museums für Völkerkunde zu Leipzig*, 13:94–188.

Wilkie, D. S., and B. Curran. 1991. Why do Mbuti hunters use nets? Ungulate hunting efficiency of archers and net-hunters in the Ituri rain forest. *American Anthropologist* 93:680–9.

Williams, Frieda-Neta. 1991. *Precolonial communities of southwestern Africa: a history of Owambo kingdoms, 1600–1920*. Windhoek: National Archives of Namibia.

Wilmsen, Edwin N. 1976. *Summary report of research on Basarwa in western Ngamiland*. Report to the Ministry of Local Government and Lands, Republic of Botswana, Gaborone, Botswana.

   1983. The ecology of illusion: anthropological foraging in the Kalahari. *Reviews in Anthropology* 10(1): 9–20.

   1989. *Land filled with flies: a political economy of the Kalahari*. Chicago: University of Chicago Press.

   1991. Pastoro-foragers to "bushmen": transformations in Kalahari relations of property, production, and labor. In *Herders, warriors, and traders: pastoralism in Africa*, edited by John G. Galaty and Pierre Bonte, pp. 248–63. Boulder, CO: Westview Press.

   1993. On the search for truth and authority: a reply to Lee and Guenther. *Current Anthropology* 34:715–20.

Wilmsen, Edwin N., and James Denbow. 1990. Paradigmatic history of San-speaking peoples and current attempts at revision. *Current Anthropology* 31:498–524.

Wilmsen, Edwin N., and Rainer Vossen. 1990. Labour, exchange, and power in the construction of ethnicity in Botswana. *Critique of Anthropology* 10(1): 7–37.

Wilson, M., and L. Thompson. 1969. *The Oxford history of South Africa*, vol. I. Oxford: Clarendon.

Winn, S., G. A. Morelli, and E. Z. Tronick. 1989. The infant in the group: a look at Efe caretaking practices. In *The cultural context of infancy*, edited by J. K. Nugent, B. M. Lester, and T. B. Brazelton. New Jersey: Ablex.

Winterhalder, Bruce. 1990. Open field, common pot: harvest variability and risk avoidance in agricultural and foraging societies. In *Risk and uncertainty in tribal and peasant economics*, edited by Elizabeth Cashdan, pp. 67–87. Boulder, CO: Westview Press.

Winterhalder, B., and E. A. Smith (eds.). 1981. *Hunter-gatherer foraging strategies*. Chicago: University of Chicago Press.

Wolf, Eric. 1982. *Europe and the people without history*. Berkeley: University of California Press.

Woodburn, J. 1980. Hunters and gatherers today and reconstruction of the past. In *Soviet and western anthropology*, edited by E. Gellner. London: Duckworth.

1982. Social dimension of death in four African hunting and gathering societies. In *Death and the regeneration of life*, edited by M. Bloch and J. Parry. New York: Cambridge University Press.

Woodburn, James C. 1968a. An introduction to Hadza ecology. In *Man the Hunter*, edited by R. B. Lee and I. DeVore. Chicago: Aldine.

1968b. Stability and flexibility in Hadza residential groupings. In *Man the hunter*, edited by Richard Lee and Irven DeVore, pp. 103–10. Chicago: Aldine Publishing Company.

1979. Minimal politics: the political organization of the Hadza of north Tanzania. In *Politics and leadership: a comparative perspective*, edited by W. A. Shack and P. S. Cohen, pp. 244–66. Oxford: Clarendon Press.

1982. Egalitarian societies. *Man* 17(3): 431–51.

1988. African hunter-gatherer social organization: is it best understood as a product of encapsulation? In *Hunters and gatherers* I: *history, evolution, and social change*, edited by Tim Ingold, David Riches, and James Woodburn, pp. 31–64. London: Bert.

Woodburn, James C., and S. Hudson. 1982. Egalitarian societies. *Man* 17(3): 431–51.

Wrangham, R. W. and E. A. M. Ross. 1983. Individual differences in activities, family size, and food population among Lese horticulturalists of Northeast Zaire. Paper presented at the 82nd Annual Meeting of the American Anthropological Association, Chicago, IL.

Yellen, John. 1977. *Archaeological approaches to the present: models for reconstructing the past*. New York: Academic Press.

Index

Page numbers in *italics* refer to illustrations